FINDING SOLUTIONS TO SOCIAL PROBLEMS

BEHAVIORAL STRATEGIES FOR CHANGE

FINDING SOLUTIONS TO SOCIAL PROBLEMS

BEHAVIORAL STRATEGIES FOR CHANGE

**MARK A. MATTAINI, DSW, ACSW
AND BRUCE A. THYER, PHD, EDITORS**

AMERICAN PSYCHOLOGICAL ASSOCIATION
WASHINGTON, DC

Published by
American Psychological Association
750 First Street, NE
Washington, DC 20002

Copies may be ordered from
American Psychological Association Order Department
P.O. Box 92984
Washington, DC 20090-2984

In the UK and Europe, copies may be ordered from
American Psychological Association
3 Henrietta Street
Covent Garden, London
WC2E 8LU England

Typeset in Goudy by PRO-Image Corporation, Techna-Type Div., York, PA

Printer: Data Reproductions, Rochester Hills, MI
Cover and Jacket Designer: Anne Masters, Washington, DC
Technical/Production Editor: Sarah J. Trembath

Library of Congress Cataloging-in-Publication Data
Finding solutions to social problems : behavioral strategies for change / edited by Mark
A. Mattaini and Bruce A. Thyer.
     p.   cm.
    Includes bibliographical references and index.
    ISBN 1-55798-367-4 (hb : alk. paper). — ISBN 1-55798-390-9 (pbk. : alk. paper)
    1. Social problems—Psychological aspects. 2. Behaviorism
(Psychology)—Social aspects. 3. Behavioral assessment. 4. Social
psychology. I. Mattaini, Mark A. II. Thyer, Bruce A.
HN17.5.F56 1996
361.1—dc20
                                   96-9216
                                     CIP

British Library Cataloguing-in-Publication Data
A CIP record is available from the British Library.

Printed in the United States of America
First edition

This volume is dedicated to the memory of B. F. Skinner, perhaps the key scientific figure of the 20th century; and to my friend, TCF. Hope is behavior.

MAM

For Laura Myers, spouse, life-partner, and source of my most valued reinforcers.

BAT

CONTENTS

Contributors ix

Preface xi

Introduction 1

PART I: BEHAVIORAL THEORIES OF CHANGE

1. Public Issues, Human Behavior, and Cultural Design 13
   Mark A. Mattaini

2. Behavior Analysis and Social Welfare Policy 41
   Bruce A. Thyer

3. The Ethics of Helping People 61
   B. F. Skinner

PART II: CHANGE IN THE COMMUNITY

4. Youth Violence 75
   Mark A. Mattaini, Janet S. Twyman, Wendy Chin, and
   Kyung Nam Lee

5. The Education Crisis 113
   R. Douglas Greer

6. Racism 147
   Harold E. Briggs and Robert I. Paulson

7. Productivity in the Workplace 179
   Jon S. Bailey and John Austin

8. Sexism 201
   Patricia M. Daly

PART III: CHANGE IN PRIVATE RELATIONSHIPS

9. Child Maltreatment 223
   Mark A. Mattaini, Brenda G. McGowan, and Gladys Williams

10. Teenage Sexuality 267
    Steven P. Schinke, Mary Ann Forgey, and Mario Orlandi

11. Sexual Coercion 289
    Anthony Biglan

PART IV: CHANGE FOR INDIVIDUALS

12. Psychosis 319
    Stephen E. Wong

13. Loneliness, Social Isolation, and Social Anxiety 345
    Eileen Gambrill

14. Drug Abuse 373
    Carl G. Leukefeld, Thomas W. Miller, and Lon Hays

15. "Acting to Save the World": The Elements of Action ... 397
    Mark A. Mattaini

Index 415
About the Editors 427

CONTRIBUTORS

John Austin, Department of Psychology, Florida State University

Jon S. Bailey, Department of Psychology, Florida State University

Anthony Biglan, Oregon Research Institute, Eugene

Harold E. Briggs, Graduate School of Social Work, Portland State University

Wendy Chin, Children's Aid Society, New York, New York

Patricia M. Daly, Education/Physical Education Department, Ohio Dominican College

Mary Ann Forgey, School of Social Sciences, Fordham University

Eileen Gambrill, School of Social Welfare, University of California, Berkeley

R. Douglas Greer, Teacher's College, Columbia University

Lon Hays, Center on Drug and Alcohol Abuse, Department of Psychiatry, University of Kentucky, Lexington

Kyung Nam Lee, Jewish Board of Family and Children Services, New York, New York

Carl G. Leukefeld, Center on Drug and Alcohol Research, Department of Psychiatry, University of Kentucky, Lexington

Mark A. Mattaini, Columbia University School of Social Work

Brenda G. McGowan, Columbia University School of Social Work

Thomas W. Miller, VA and University of Kentucky Medical Centers, Lexington

Mario Orlandi, American Health Foundation, New York, New York

Robert I. Paulson, Graduate School of Social Work, Portland State University

Steven P. Schinke, Columbia University School of Social Work

B. F. Skinner (Deceased), Formerly of Harvard University

Bruce A. Thyer, School of Social Work, University of Georgia, Athens

Janet S. Twyman, Fred S. Keller School, Yonkers, New York

Gladys Williams, Applied Behavioral Consultant Services, New York, New York

Stephen E. Wong, School of Social Service Administration, University of Chicago, Illinois

PREFACE

This book was born of frustration and hope: frustration that human society knows so much more than it currently makes use of in addressing critical social issues, and hope that science can make a meaningful difference in creating solutions for even the most apparently intractable of such issues. We passionately believe that the science of behavior is an essential element in "saving the world." While at a conference in New York City that dealt with bridging the gaps between research and practice, we began to conceptualize what we recognized as an almost impossibly ambitious task—a single volume that might demonstrate how this gap could be bridged with regard to the full range of major contemporary social problems. It quickly became clear that achieving this goal would require the combined expertise of many leaders in the behavior analytic community, and an outline of an edited volume quickly began to form.

Behavior analysts, beginning with B. F. Skinner, have already done considerable conceptual and empirical work that could contribute to this effort, and we hoped that many would push what is already known even further for this book. Our challenge was to organize and present the material in such a way that this volume might contribute to a process that could make a substantive difference. To do so, we presented the chapter authors with a difficult task of their own: to prepare chapters that would be scientifically adequate and still be accessible to the audiences that we hope to reach. These audiences include policymakers who might come to examine policy options through behavior and cultural analytic lenses, students who might be inspired to pursue the many critical threads that could only be introduced in the book, teachers who might adopt it for classes, and our behavior analytic colleagues who have the expertise to assist in pushing these and similar analyses much further than has been done so far.

Our seemingly impossible task was inevitably scaled back during the process of preparing the book, as we determined that only a critical but limited set of issues could be included in one volume. Nevertheless, those issues that are included suggest the potential breadth of the approach. We are enormously in debt to the chapter authors, who rose to their challenging task to an extent we did not expect. These are frustrating times, both because of an apparent preference for oversimplified solutions to complex problems, and because the usefulness of science itself for helping is commonly questioned. Based on the analyses presented in this volume, however, our hope remains.

We could not have hoped for a better choice of publisher than APA Books, which offered an intensely professional editorial staff whose assistance strengthened the volume immeasurably. Particularly valuable were the contributions of development editor Beth Beisel and technical/production editor Sarah J. Trembath.

MARK A. MATTAINI
BRUCE A. THYER

INTRODUCTION

Moving into the 21st century, the major sociocultural problems we face are primarily behavioral in nature. Science and technology have provided at least partial solutions to issues of food production, reproductive rates, housing, prevention of disease and injury, communication and transportation, and many others. These solutions are applied unevenly, however, and many social problems rooted in human action or inaction remain. Violence (personal and political); child maltreatment; the breakdown of the educational system; the lack of mutual respect and caring across cultural, ethnic, and class lines; and other primarily behavioral issues could ultimately threaten the survival of the human race and other species.

Much more is known about how to address and manage these problems than is often recognized; although there is much yet to learn, humanity now knows, in an important sense, how to address the issues that confront it. Again, science (in this case, the science of behavior analysis) must lead the way. Behavioral scientists not only know a great deal about simple, basic behavioral processes, but are also coming to understand a good deal about how these processes interact on sociocultural levels, and how they apply specifically to important human issues. This volume is an attempt to capture the contemporary state of the art—which is promising despite the enormous challenges remaining. Ongoing research will certainly lead to even greater specificity—and perhaps even new principles and models—over the next few years.

This is not to suggest that solutions will be either simple or inexpensive—only that they may be possible. The problems included in this volume were selected because of their critical impact on human life, and because of the availability of an author who has done extensive work in each area. Some important issues, such as homelessness, crime and corrections, and domestic and international violence, could not be included. The behavior analytic literature includes material in these and other crucial areas, and readers are encouraged to mine these resources further. The material included here is perhaps best viewed as a series of examples. We hope such work can be replicated in other areas and perhaps published in a subsequent volume.

This is not the first time behavior analysts have explored solutions to important social issues. Malagodi and Jackson (1989) placed a radical behaviorist frame on C. Wright Mills' classic distinction between personal troubles and public issues and explored linkages between behavior analysis and empirically rooted social science. In particular, Marvin Harris's work in cultural materialism (e.g., Harris, 1979, 1989) has been used and interpreted by a number of behavior analysts, including Sigrid Glenn (1988, 1991), Richard Malott (1988), and Malagodi & Jackson (1989). These authors suggested that Harris' materialistic anthropology, which emphasized selection at the level of *cultural infrastructure* (i.e., practices related to production and reproduction), has much to offer as behaviorists increasingly expand their view to include cultural analysis.

Lamal and his contributors (Lamal, 1991) explored the underlying principles and methods of sociocultural analysis from a behavior analytic perspective. The journal *Behavior and Social Issues* focuses specifically on related questions. The present volume concentrates a portion of this work in an effort to advance the current state of knowledge regarding practical applications of the general principles; it is, therefore, heavily applied rather than theoretical in focus.

STRATEGIC SCIENCE

The approach taken in this volume suggests that the science of behavior (often called behavior analysis and sometimes behaviorology) has much more to offer for reducing human problems than is widely recognized. Science is an organized and orderly set of practices for understanding, predicting, and making changes in the natural world while controlling for bias (to the extent possible) that may distort those processes. If human behavior is organic to the natural world, then scientific practices should help us to understand and influence that behavior. Our major social issues are rooted in behavior; therefore, applying the principles of science to patterns of such behavior should offer valuable insights into how to ameliorate human misery and reduce social problems.

In other words, we believe that science can help. Although a tremendous amount of scientific investigation that is helpful in understanding and preventing social problems has been done, only a limited amount of this work has been *strategic* in the sense that we mean it in this volume. Strategic science attempts to go beyond low- or mid-level experimentation that may be useful in understanding or affecting discrete events. Instead, strategic science focuses on identifying approaches that can have meaningful effects at a community, organizational, or society-wide level. It is, for example, one thing to find ways to treat one violent youth, but quite another to identify approaches for reducing the incidence of violent acts perpetrated by youth in a neighborhood. Strategic science also emphasizes the use of general principles (e.g., increasing the use of positive reinforcement or reducing the level of coercion) that have been shown to be powerful across a wide range of human issues and that most likely can be applied to new and emerging problems as they arise as well.

Strategic science as it relates to human behavior emphasizes the need to understand the behavioral and cultural processes that shape and maintain practices that perpetuate problems as well as those required to resolve them. For example, drug-related crime accounts for more than 50% of the homicides in some urban areas (Reiss & Roth, 1993). Knowing this statistic, however, is not the same as being able to identify the related manipulable variables that may be accessible to intervention. Strategic science offers the tools needed to disentangle and disaggregate the elementary processes at work in such situations. It also provides the means to understand cultural phenomena at their own level of organization. Although rooted in the science of behavior, strategic science also encompasses the science of *cultural design* (Biglan, 1995; Mattaini, 1996). Cultural design captures and organizes the active variables within the culture of a family, a community, an organization, or other such groups.

BEHAVIOR ANALYSIS

Behavior analysis is, at root, the science of "things done" (Lee, 1994). In other words, behavior analysis does not study bodily movements, but rather how the action of an organism "operates on," or changes, the environment. Behavior analysis also looks at how these changes affect the future rate, form, and strength of the behavior. The science of behavior focuses particularly on the *consequences* of human action and their effect on future actions. Although this may seem counterintuitive at first glance, behavior analysts believe that consequences are the central factor in understanding how and why behavior is shaped or maintained; behavior is selected by consequences through a process analogous to natural selection (Skinner, 1981). Events and conditions that precede actions (*antecedents*) also affect behavior due to their association with behavior and consequences. The actions of interest include complex human (Skinner, 1953) and social (Biglan, 1995; Lamal, 1991; Skinner, 1948) behaviors. Both private (covert) and public (overt) behaviors can be analyzed using the tools of behavior analysis (Hayes, 1989; Skinner, 1953).

Although behavior analysis as a distinct stream of scientific activity began with basic laboratory research with rats and pigeons, the contemporary science includes several interconnected but discrete clusters of activity, including basic research with humans and other animals (the *experimental analysis of behavior*), applied research and intervention in socially important areas (*applied behavior analysis*), theoretical and historical explorations (the *conceptual analysis of behavior*), and *cultural analysis and design*. The latter seeks to understand and influence social systems. These streams have produced and will continue to produce substantial cross-fertilization, particularly from basic science to the more applied subdisciplines, and many chapters in this volume draw from each of them.

Behavior analysis as a science began inductively through examination of experimental data; theoretical principles, such as how the process of reinforcement operates, were extracted from those data. The approach is deeply empirical, avoids the use of unobservable constructs that cannot somehow be tested, and continuously searches for broadly applicable principles rather than collections of low-level findings. As a result, the science of behavior has what has been called an "austere elegance" that may be unmatched by any alternative system. This parsimonious and data-based science has particular power for understanding the complex events that constitute human culture because it permits us to extract the basic processes involved, regardless of the level of noise present.

No introduction to the science of behavior would be adequate without reference to Burrhus Frederick Skinner, who was among the towering intellectual figures of the 20th century and in the history of science. Not only did Skinner define the basic terms and experimental practices on which the science has been based, he also had an unwavering vision of its potential power for changing human life in ways that could both enhance its quality and extend its survival. Much of his work was controversial and often misunderstood, but he maintained his intellectual integrity and humanism throughout. From his first book, *The Behavior of Organisms* (1938) through work completed only days before his death in 1990, his research and writing inspired and guided the field. Nearly all authors whose works are included in this volume can trace their intellectual provenance to Skinner with few degrees of separation. Many psychologists and other behaviorists have extended (and even corrected) Skinner's work in many areas, but his seminal contributions must be acknowledged.

THIS VOLUME

In this volume, the editors and authors hope to show that the science of behavior has much to offer to contemporary society, beyond its usefulness in narrow niches like special education and developmental disabilities. In a period when "anti-science" has become fashionable in many circles, we believe it is essential to demonstrate the importance and value of science—and the science of behavior in particular—for resolving major social issues. The approach taken is to trace a wide range of existing and potential applications of the science, applying it to representative social issues as they play out at the community, interpersonal, and individual levels. In addition to sketching existing knowledge and applications, chapters identify important areas for further research. Recognizing that humanity is far from final answers to many social problems, it is crucial to recognize the extent to which behavioral theory can guide us to ask the questions in ways most likely to produce effective answers.

The Organization of the Book

This volume is organized into five major sections. The three chapters in Part 1 present the basics of behavioral theory and its applications to larger sociocultural issues. Chapter 1 defines and provides examples of the basic elements of behavior analysis as well as cultural analysis and design. The material includes recent advances in the field including, for example, current work in rule-governed behavior and equivalence relations at the level of individual behavior. It also discusses contingency interlocks in cultural analysis. (Readers who are well-versed in these areas may wish to skim or skip this chapter.) Chapter 2 sketches out how the science of behavior can guide macrolevel efforts to develop social policy with the best chance of success. In Chapter 3, we have had the privilege of reprinting an important paper by B. F. Skinner, in which he considered at a theoretical level how to most effectively help people, from the perspective of the experimental approach to ethics that he consistently espoused.

The second major section of the book examines issues that need to be addressed primarily at community and larger sociocultural levels. There are chapters on youth violence, racism, sexism, the breakdown of contemporary schools, and productivity in the workplace. Although individual-level interventions may be of some use in each of these areas, the establishment and support of interlocking community practices are required in each case to make a meaningful difference at a community level.

In the third section, the authors address problems that require intervention in private relationships in addition to larger community levels. The issues included are child maltreatment, teenage sexuality, and sexual coercion, each of which is critically important in itself. In addition, the approaches taken may be of value as exemplars for similar issues, such as domestic violence or the breakdown of family relationships.

The fourth part of the book turns to problems that are commonly thought of as requiring individual treatment, and includes chapters on psychosis, loneliness and social isolation, and drug abuse. Each of these private problems also constitutes a public issue, however; the connections among psychosis or drug abuse and homelessness, for example, are well known. In addition, substantial public funding goes toward responding to these problems, and ensuring that these funds are efficiently and effectively spent, in a time of contracting resources, is clearly important. Intractable loneliness and isolation are commonly the result of many of the issues discussed in the earlier chapters of this volume. However, the need to connect people in ways that lead to an enhanced sense of community also exists. This need is now widely recognized.

The final chapter of the volume moves back from the specific to the general. In this chapter, Mattaini provides a summary sketch of how the principles and strategies outlined throughout the volume could guide social change in many areas; he suggests that applications drawn from the science of behavior can enhance human life and social justice.

Chapter Organization

Each chapter generally follows a similar outline, although the nature of the subject matter and the depth of available knowledge result in some variations. Each chapter begins with a description of the nature and scope of the problem, including its personal and social costs. This is followed by a review of current approaches to the issue. The authors examine the extent to which current approaches are grounded in empirical data. The heart of each contribution is a detailed behavioral analysis of the issue that often clarifies the reasons why traditional approaches have had limited success. The reasons for the success of a particular approach are also reviewed. The authors then sketch the contours of behavioral approaches to intervention and prevention at both personal and community levels, offering data on efficacy when these are available. Because the research is quite advanced in some areas and quite preliminary in others, the depth of discussions of interventive options varies substantially. In some cases, clear guidelines are available. For others, only conceptually promising hypotheses can be presented. Because the current state of knowledge is less than adequate for any of the issues presented, lines of research are suggested throughout.

The overall approach taken in this volume, of which each chapter is only an exemplar, is that the science of behavior and cultural analysis provides a framework for understanding social issues and developing comprehensive approaches for addressing them. In other words, this is a book not so much about a few specific problems, but rather about an approach for integrating evidence from many fields in a coherent way that is likely to lead to effective solutions for a broad range of issues. Each chapter makes a specific contribution, but also offers a slightly different cut on a general approach to human issues.

THE AUDIENCE FOR THIS VOLUME

Authors were asked to prepare their chapters to be of value to multiple audiences. We hope that practitioners working in each area will find here specific guidance for their work as well as a framework for thinking about the problem in ways that may lead to programmatic innovations. Researchers will discover no shortage of critical questions awaiting answers and many crucial hypotheses to test. In many chapters, the most pressing research questions emerge clearly. Behavior analysis emphasizes single-case designs, and practitioners–researchers can contribute a great deal to the field by pursuing these.

Perhaps students are the most important audience for this book. They are the ones who will construct a future that may work better than the past. Students will find a good deal of information here, and, perhaps, some inspiration to dedicate their professional careers to making the world a more reinforcing and just habitat for humanity—an ideal that we believe to be a genuine possibility.

Policymakers and informed citizens may also find the material here useful, in part because of the practical and applied focus taken by the chapter authors, and in part because until now, most of this material was not available in one place. This volume emphasizes clarifying and presenting the current state of the art. It also provides specific and prescriptive recommendations wherever possible. It therefore may be useful for informed decision making and for suggesting the questions that need to be asked before decisions are taken. Although we are not suggesting that there are easy answers to complex issues, we do believe that the specificity and applied nature of the analyses and evidence presented here implies that substantive and positive change is realistic.

A FINAL WORD

The approach advocated in this volume is, of course, a more difficult process than simply exhorting people to change (e.g., "Just Say No!" or "Squash It!"—antecedents with few ties to consequences) and doing so "louder, longer and meaner" (Daniels, 1994, p. 17) if the desired results don't appear. The more complete approach is likely to be essential, however, to producing lasting social change responsive to important public issues. What is required are new practices, stabilized by new networks of interlocking contingencies, in some cases within new cultural entities. This strategy would allow the application of the tremendous power of behavior analytic methods to the root causes of major sociocultural problems. The differences between this framework and more traditional ones are paradigmatic, and resistance to any new paradigm is only to be expected (see the final chapter). Nevertheless, we believe it is an ethical imperative to consider—and test—approaches that might profoundly affect the quality of life for large numbers of people. The following chapters provide many examples of beginning efforts to do so.

REFERENCES

Biglan, A. (1995). *Changing cultural practices: A contextualist framework for intervention research*. Reno: Context Press.

Daniels, A. C. (1994). *Bringing out the best in people*. New York: McGraw-Hill.

Glenn, S. S. (1988). Contingencies and metacontingencies: Toward a synthesis of behavior analysis and cultural materialism. *The Behavior Analyst, 11*, 161–179.

Glenn, S. S. (1991). Contingencies and metacontingencies: Relations among behavioral, cultural, and biological evolution. In P. A. Lamal (Ed.), *Behavioral analysis of societies and cultural practices* (pp. 39–73). New York: Hemisphere.

Harris, M. (1979). *Cultural materialism: The struggle for a science of culture*. New York: Vintage.

Harris, M. (1989). *Our kind*. New York: HarperCollins.

Hayes, S. C. (1989). *Rule-governed behavior: Cognition, contingencies, and instructional control*. New York: Plenum.

Lamal, P. A. (1991). *Behavioral analysis of societies and cultural practices*. New York: Hemisphere.

Lee, V. L. (1994). Organisms, things done, and the fragmentation of psychology. *Behavior and Philosophy, 22*, 7–48.

Malagodi, E. F., & Jackson, K. (1989). Behavior analysts and cultural analysis: Troubles and issues. *The Behavior Analyst, 12*, 17–33.

Malott, R. W. (1988). Rule-governed behavior and behavioral anthropology. *The Behavior Analyst, 11* 181–203.

Mattaini, M. A. (1996). The new frontier [Review of the book *Changing cultural practices: A contextualist framework for intervention research*]. *The Behavior Analyst, 19*, 135–141.

Reiss, A. J., Jr., & Roth, J. A. (1993). *Understanding and preventing violence* (Vol. 1). Washington, DC: National Academy Press.

Skinner, B. F. (1938). *The behavior of organisms: An experimental analysis*. Acton, MA: Copley Publishing.

Skinner, B. F. (1948). *Walden two*. New York: MacMillan.

Skinner, B. F. (1953). *Science and human behavior*. New York: Free Press.

Skinner, B. F. (1981). Selection by consequences. *Science, 213*, 501–504.

I

BEHAVIORAL THEORIES OF CHANGE

1

PUBLIC ISSUES, HUMAN BEHAVIOR, AND CULTURAL DESIGN

MARK A. MATTAINI

This chapter presents an overview of the current state of psychological knowledge about how behavior and cultural practices are acquired, maintained, increased, or reduced. It also introduces the terms and concepts used throughout the remainder of the book. Recent advances enable us to capture and conceptualize complex verbal, social, and cultural phenomena more coherently than we could even a few years ago. This chapter is organized as follows: First, the critical and often neglected importance of *consequences* (events that follow an action) for shaping and maintaining human behavior is discussed. Then a description of the connections among *antecedents* (events and conditions that precede actions), consequences, and behavior is presented. These are the basics of the science of behavior. The chapter also presents the fundamentals of *cultural design*, a recent expansion of behavior analysis to higher-level sociocultural phenomena. This is followed by a small example of the application of the principles of cultural design, a description of the Community Reinforcement Approach for the treatment of substance abuse. Other larger-scale examples are provided in subsequent chapters.

SELECTION BY CONSEQUENCES

Skinner (1981), writing in *Science*, identified the three levels at which behavior, including human behavior, is shaped, as well as the connections and similarities among them. The core notion is that behavior is *selected* at the genetic, the operant, and the cultural levels by conditions and events that follow it. In other words, behavior is selected by its consequences. This relatively simple statement implies enormous potential for addressing issues of social importance; therefore, the concept will be briefly summarized here, with particular emphasis on cultural selection. Cultural selection is the active principle in which this book is rooted.

Genetic Selection

In natural selection, those genetic variations that produce organisms better adapted to environmental conditions are more likely to survive. Adaptive variations are thereby selected by their environmental consequences. Sociobiologists occasionally exaggerate the extent to which human behavior is shaped in this way (Harris, 1979), but there are biological substrates for much human behavior. Some aggressive behavior may be hard-wired, for example, and it makes biological sense that aggressive action toward any nearby organism when one is exposed to pain would result in improved survival (Sidman, 1989).

As is often true in science, an elegant principle like that of natural selection, while basically valid, oversimplifies to some extent. Gould (1994) argued that random processes are also important in tracing why some variations survive and others don't; some things just don't matter much for survival and may vary a fair amount or drift over time without apparent adaptive advantage. Sudden major environmental changes also sometimes select certain traits serendipitously. Similar random processes also probably are operative at the other levels of selection. For example, some behaviors may occur, be followed by a positive outcome, and be maintained, whereas other potentially adaptive variations may never occur. Random events (precipitation, for example) may also occur after some cultural practices are performed, thus shaping superstitious behavior.

Operant Selection

Through natural selection, living organisms developed, at some point, the capacity to respond flexibly to environmental events and conditions, to learn from experience through operant and respondent behavior. *Operant* behavior—action that actively "operates" on the environment—is the primary focus of the material presented in this volume. Such action shows enormous variability in humans and is the most substantial contributor to, and resource for, most social problems. Another variety of learning involves *respondent* behavior—visceral activity that comes under the control of novel stimuli through conditioning, as in the development of some phobias. In respondent conditioning, a stimulus (food) that naturally produces a response (salivating) is paired with the novel stimulus (e.g., McDonald's golden arches). Eventually, the novel stimulus produces the response on its own. Although respondent behavior is involved in a few issues discussed here, its role is generally peripheral in this book.

Once the capacity to adapt behaviorally had evolved, organisms began to learn from their transactions with the environment. Roughly, those behaviors that worked tended to be performed more often, whereas those that didn't work or had negative outcomes tended to drop out. Although a thorough understanding of operant behavior would require a much more complex discussion, generally speaking, this is what operant behavior is about. The organism's environment selects behavior by differential outcomes (consequences). For example, children learn to walk by experience; motor behavior that leads to falling drops out, while that leading to stability and movement is gradually refined.

The Selection of Cultural Practices

Sociocultural phenomena constitute the most crucial level of selection for addressing public issues. *Cultural practices* are a special case of operants—behaviors that are transmitted among individuals and across generations—and are maintained by established and relatively stable networks of reinforcement (often but not always social in nature). Skinner defined a *culture* as, "The contingencies of social reinforcement maintained by a group" (Skinner, 1986, p. 74). *Contingencies* are the relationships and dependencies among behaviors and their consequences and antecedents. A group that shares a culture in this sense is a *cultural entity*. Note that this definition encompasses groups of many different sizes, some with relatively simple repertoires of practices, and others maintaining exceedingly complex social patterns. Families, communities, and organizations fit this definition, as do nations. There are crucial similarities and differences among these, an issue to which we will return later in the chapter.

As special cases of operant behavior, cultural practices are also rooted in biological selection and may also involve specific genetic variations. The evolution of physiological adaptations that make language possible, for example, were essential for this most important set of cultural practices to emerge, although social reinforcement from the group is also required for language to develop.

Natural selection, in a sense, operates at two levels: the evolution of particular characteristics, and the emergence of new—and extinction of existing—species. Cultural evolution involves both the shaping of particular practices that produce better outcomes for members of the group and, in some cases, the survival or demise of entire cultural entities (Skinner, in Catania & Harnad, 1988, p. 36). Although cultures like those of nation-states or the Aztec empire only occasionally are formed or disappear, smaller entities (businesses, families) do form and disappear relatively frequently.

Sigrid Glenn (1988, 1991) introduced the term *metacontingency* to describe the dependencies between a cultural practice and its aggregate outcomes for the group. The processes by which these aggregate outcomes emerge depend on basic operant principles. A cultural practice consists of behavior emitted by individuals, but the level of organization is different here. Roughly, individuals perform the practice because doing so is reinforced, but the reinforcement is often provided by other people. Why? Because they, in turn, are reinforced for doing so.

Such a system of interlocking social reinforcement is often required to stabilize a cultural practice. The way interlocking practices and the cultures that support them result in an aggregate outcome is depicted in Figure 1. Various classes of actors (e.g., students, teachers, administrators, parents, media, and voters) maintain practices that interlock in multiple ways, with the result that only 45% of students complete high school in a particular community. There is no single cause of this unsatisfactory outcome. If the outcome leads to changes in the interlocking practices, which in turn lead to a different outcome over time, a metacontingency has been established. Lacking such a feedback loop, the outcome can be viewed as a relatively random result of the practices. The discussion of cultural design later in this chapter is an effort to specify in finer detail the interlocking practices and contingencies represented on the left side of Glenn's image, as well as to provide a technology for moving toward more desirable aggregate outcomes.

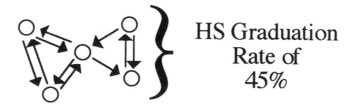

Figure 1. A depiction of the way interlocking practices and the cultures that support them result in an aggregate outcome. Adapted with permission from "Contingencies and metacontingencies: Toward a synthesis of behavior analysis and cultural materialism," by S. S. Glenn, 1988, *The Behavior Analyst, 11*, p. 170. Copyright 1988 by The Association for Behavior Analysis.

Note that such interlocks may not be required if the practice results in immediate natural reinforcement for the behavior; if a person sees someone else eat a novel food, imitates that person, and finds the food delicious, social reinforcement is not required to maintain the behavior. However, in cases in which consequences are delayed or cumulative, or in which the behavior results in improved outcomes for others rather than the person (e.g., altruism), interlocking contingencies are generally required.

Basic behavioral terms and principles used throughout this volume are summarized in the sections that follow, with examples. For further technical detail, readers may want to consult Malott, Whaley, and Malott (1993), Michael (1993), or other standard works.

BEHAVIORAL CONSEQUENCES

Consequences, that is, events and conditions that follow an action, are of central importance in the science of behavior. The basic forms of consequences include positive and negative reinforcement and punishment. *Extinction*, the result of a lack of contingent consequences, is also an important process. The material that follows provides an introduction to each of these possibilities.

Reinforcement

The basic process of reinforcement is straightforward. Behavior is followed by an event or condition (a *postcedent* or *consequence*) that is somehow "better" than the situation existing before the behavior occurred. As a result, the rate of that behavior tends to increase in the future. When the behavior is followed by presentation of a reinforcer, the process is called *positive reinforcement*; when it results in escape from or avoidance of a negative condition, the process is called *negative reinforcement*. Operationally the two are different, but both lead to increases in behavior, and to a situation after the behavior that is in some way improved over the situation before. They can, therefore, be viewed as subtypes of the same process.

Negative reinforcement often seems confusing, because the term is commonly misused in everyday language. By definition, all reinforcement increases behavior. If a parent spanks a child to stop a behavior, that is *punishment*, not reinforcement, because the rate of the behavior of interest *decreases* rather than increases. By contrast, when your alarm clock goes off, it *produces* behavior to *escape* from the irritating tone, so the process is negative reinforcement. When people wake up before the alarm goes off, they may be acting to prevent it from doing so. This is an example of *avoidance*, the other form of negative reinforcement.

Why does an event or condition reinforce behavior? It is not adequate to say that it is reinforcing because presenting it leads to an increase in behavior, because that is how we defined it as a reinforcer in the first place. Ultimately, reinforcement must be seen as rooted in biology. Food, water, sex, and, probably, affection produce effects that were adaptive for survival. Some anamolous and accidental reinforcers—like cocaine—also have immediate biological effects, including stimulating the pleasure centers of the brain. Other reinforcers are learned through temporal association with primary reinforcers. Money, for example, is a powerful learned generalized reinforcer that can lead to high levels of behavior (and substantial physiological arousal) for adults, but is not reinforcing to an infant. The capacity to respond to conditioned reinforcers is an important biological root of behavior.

There are many complexities involved in these concepts. The schedules on which reinforcement is provided have a good deal to do with exactly how behavior changes. Intermittent schedules of reinforcement can lead to stable behavior that is difficult to eliminate. For example, many people regularly check their paper or electronic mail, even though they only occasionally find something of real value to them. Many behaviors also have multiple effects. Some acts of street violence provide a good example. Although the robbery of a jacket by a member of a street gang may appear to be reinforced by the jacket itself, the kind of jacket that reinforces theft behavior has often been shaped socially, and the reinforcers (e.g., respect) provided by other members of the group—both for the act of robbery and for wearing the jacket—are usually the more crucial consequences. Avoiding punishment (disrespect) from others for failing to take such action may also be relevant.

These simple processes can explain rather complex patterns of social behavior if the elements are assembled in the right ways. Further, much of human behavior is verbally mediated, responding to "rules" that may be extracted by observation, learned accidentally from or explicitly taught by others, and may or may not be accurate. "If I study hard, I'll get a good grade," or, "It doesn't matter how hard I try, I can't do this," are examples. Rules, and their connections with reinforcement, are considered in a later section of this chapter.

Extinction

Although positive and negative reinforcement increase rates of behavior, our biological makeup also provides avenues for reducing behavior. When a behavior has previously been reinforced (positively or negatively), but that reinforcement at some point stops occurring, the behavior tends to drop out. The adaptive advantages of susceptibility to such extinction seem clear; when a behavior no longer works, it is best if it fades. In many cases, the rate and intensity of the behavior tends first to increase (an *extinction burst*) when reinforcement is no longer forthcoming, which also makes sense—"trying harder" often does result in reinforcement. The behavior will often reappear at intervals over a period of time, also probably an adaptive pattern.

Many children, sadly, obtain few reinforcers in school settings, particularly those children whose initial repertoires are the weakest. It is therefore only to be expected that paying attention, studying, and attending school then tend to extinguish, especially if there is little attention from home for these generalized response classes. With little or no reinforcement forthcoming from home or school, reinforcers available elsewhere, in particular on the street, are potentiated, often leading to increased antisocial behavior. If the child also has a long history of severe punishment, the effects will be compounded; punitive processes often have many problematic side effects.

Punishment

Punishment is the application of an *aversive* (i.e., something the individual tends to escape) or the removal of a reinforcer following the occurrence of a behavior. Under some conditions, punishment may lead to a decrease in the behavior. Punishment is generally experienced as unpleasant and may result in behavioral and emotional side effects. Skinner (1989) suggested that excessive punishment is responsible for many clinical problems. Sidman (1989) further argued that the many personal and social side effects of coercive strategies (in which he included both punishment and negative reinforcement), including depression, counteraggression, and some forms of emotional disturbance, are so problematic that such strategies should be avoided except in emergencies.

Mild punishment (like water-mist spray or small fines), on the other hand, can sometimes have dramatic effects, reducing life-threatening behavior or helping people achieve important and difficult health-related self-management goals (Malott et al., 1993). The issue, therefore, is not straightforward. To be effective, punishment must be relatively certain and usually immediate. Because the punished behavior is being reinforced by something else, the behavior is likely to occur again so long as the reinforcer remains available. If the punishment is withdrawn, the problem will then usually resurface.

There are two other possible issues with punishment that should be taken into account. First, punishment may reduce inappropriate behaviors, but it does not teach more effective ones; for this reason, if used at all it should always be combined with the teaching of, and reinforcement for, better alternatives. Second, punishment can be seductive; historically, it has been abused primarily, although not exclusively, under nonprofessional auspices (e.g., by families and governments). Punishment sometimes works quickly, thereby reinforcing further use of punishment in the future. There is a danger that the punisher may then turn increasingly to punitive strategies, without thoughtful consideration of possible long-term costs or side effects. For these reasons, an emphasis on and preference for positive reinforcement procedures, and extinction where necessary, seems generally indicated.

Consider, for example, the case of antisocial actions committed by young people (e.g., vandalism or violence). If such behaviors are being maintained in part by the respect of others (social reinforcement), connecting the youths with alternative sources of reinforcement for more socially acceptable behavior (which in the long run will also pay off better for them) is a good place to begin. When possible, working with the peer group to reduce the reinforcement for antisocial behavior would also seem to be an effective (though admittedly challenging) strategy. A culture in which positive behavior provides access to valued items and privileges might be established (Cohen & Filipczak, 1971/1989; Stuart, 1971; Stuart & Lott, 1972). In some cases, it may prove necessary to add, say, small-point fines to achieve optimum results, but this decision should be made based on the data.

There is an immense body of literature regarding the effective use of consequences. The material just discussed provides only an introduction to the basic principles and terms used in later chapters in this volume. Because behavior is ultimately selected by consequences over time, antecedents also have powerful effects, as a result of their connections with consequences.

ANTECEDENTS

Circumstances prior to an act, *antecedents*, affect its occurrence, rate, frequency, and intensity. Five subtypes of antecedents are discussed here, some of which have been thoroughly explored over decades of research, and some of which have only recently been clearly articulated.

Occasions

Occasions are the circumstances under which a particular consequence is likely to follow a particular behavior. (The technical term for an occasion is a *discriminative stimulus*). Under some circumstances, a behavior is likely to be reinforced (or punished); under others, it is not. Children often learn that if they ask for a cookie from, say, a grandparent, they are likely to receive it, whereas if they ask their parent, they probably will not. The act of asking then becomes more likely on occasions when the grandparent is present, and less likely when the parent is present. The grandparent is a discriminative stimulus signaling the availability of cookie reinforcement; the presence of the parent signals lack of availability (i.e., is a *stimulus delta*).

A more complex example would be the making of sexist remarks. If such remarks are maintained by peer attention, such behaviors may occur primarily when peers are present (although verbal behavior complicates the situation, because a later report may also be reinforced). Threatening with a gun is only likely if a victim is present (or in front of a mirror, but this is a different behavior, with different functions, although it looks identical). Victims and peers, under some circumstances then, become associated with reinforcement of violent threats and actions. Note that unless the connection among the presence of peers, a violent act, and social reinforcement has been established, the presence of peers would not prompt violence. The consequence is the crucial determinant, whereas the occasion serves as a signal or cue for the availability of the consequence.

Structural Antecedents

The term *structural antecedents* is used in this instance to describe aspects of a person or situation that are relatively invariant, and that may provide the means, or tools, for the behavior to occur. For example, vocal language can only occur when the necessary physiological structures are in place. And although running 50 miles per hour would probably be highly reinforced, it is apparently not structurally possible for humans. Structural antecedents, then, include the availability of the behavior. They may also involve the availability of other antecedents and consequences; this is particularly true for aspects of environmental structure, which can limit the available behaviors. If no gun is available, a person will not shoot someone in the course of a robbery; if there are no dark corners available, muggings in dark corners will not occur.

In some cases, working with structural antecedents can be among the most effective intervention strategies. Some forms of violence can be reduced by redesigning streets and buildings or by limiting the availability of handguns. Physiological structure is a trickier prospect. The National Research Council has called for increased research into biological determinants of violence (Reiss & Roth, 1993). Although such research, sensitively conducted, is valuable, the potential use of medications or genetic interventions for a problem that seems to be largely shaped and maintained by social forces raises important ethical issues.

Establishing Operations

Establishing operations are events or conditions that in some way affect sensitivity to a consequence and tend to evoke the behaviors associated with that consequence (Michael, 1993). Establishing operations affect motivation. Food deprivation, for example, is an establishing operation that potentiates the reinforcement value of food and often leads to an increase in food-seeking and consuming behaviors. By extension, generalized deprivation potentiates the value of what reinforcers, of whatever type, are available. The matching law, which has been well established among humans and with other species, indicates that the relative rates of multiple behaviors are determined by the relative levels of reinforcement available for each (McDowell, 1988). If one has many behaviors available that are likely to lead to reinforcement, he or she is less likely to perform any particular one of them, particularly those that may also be costly.

Satiation, on the other hand, tends to decrease the valence of that form of reinforcement. Too much reinforcement too easily obtained leads to a drop in behavior (and in some cases the emotional–physiological condition called boredom). Technically, satiation is an *abolishing operation*, but the term *establishing operation* often is used generically to refer to both those that decrease sensitivity to a reinforcer as well as those that increase it.

There are other establishing operations beyond deprivation and satiation, including certain schedules of reinforcement, some forms of verbal behavior, and those that have been conditioned by association with others. These will be discussed as they come up in subsequent chapters, but two additional examples may be useful. Many children at high risk for antisocial behavior have never been exposed to a wide range of alternative types of reinforcers (e.g., those associated with sports, libraries, arts, activities, and organizations) that may be available in their neighborhoods and are often accessible by public transportation. One useful strategy may well be to give them opportunities to sample such alternative reinforcers, which is simply termed *reinforcer sampling*.

Obtaining available reinforcers, like some of those already discussed, sometimes requires preexisting repertoires that may need to be constructed first. For example, libraries may be accessible, but reading is not reinforcing in itself for most people until a certain level of fluency is achieved. Other reinforcers (attention, approval, gold stars, points) may be required to help individuals reach the level of proficiency that potentiates intrinsic reinforcement for reading.

Imitating Models

Another repertoire with genetic roots is that of *imitation*. There were, and continue to be, many adaptive advantages for imitating what others do, both to obtain reinforcers and escape or avoid aversives. Children learn early on that if they do what others do, they may achieve similar consequences. There is an extensive literature on imitation and modeling that suggests that this response class is crucial among human beings. An entire stream of contemporary psychological thought—*social learning*—draws heavily on this repertoire.

Some differences exist, however, in the way that social learning theorists and behavior analysts construe the process. The former tend to rely more on hypothesized unobservable constructs like self-efficacy than do the latter. Social learning theorists also tend to attribute behavior to internal, autonomous causes while behavior analysts view environmental factors as central (Poppen, 1989). Behavior analysts also may emphasize somewhat more than social learning theorists that people can learn to imitate those who are not similar to themselves and that contingencies can override the effects of modeling.

Imitation is crucial to the development of many sophisticated cultural practices, and research on the processes involved informs much contemporary behavior analytic work in those areas. Clearly, imitation is an important consideration in reducing violence. Although growing up with violence does not automatically result in becoming a perpetrator, it seems apparent that observation and imitation of violence at home, on the street, and in the media is associated with increased violent behavior (Widom, 1989), perhaps particularly for those with limited alternative repertoires for obtaining reinforcement and avoiding aversives. Note, however, that violence may be tolerated and reinforced in many of those settings, so separating the effects of imitation from other contingencies is not simple.

Rules and Rule-Governance

An important area of contemporary behavior analytic research and theoretical development involves the understanding of *rule-governed* behavior. This refers to behavior that is not shaped by immediate contingencies, but rather by verbal descriptions of such contingencies (see Hayes, 1989, for a review of this work). For example, imagine that someone you trust (a person whose advice has become a discriminative stimulus for reinforcement) told you that if you drop everything and read a particular article, she would give you $1,000. Chances are good you would read the article. You have probably never read the article before, and most likely never have been paid $1,000 for reading any article. Therefore, if you read it, you did so because you were responding to the verbal rule provided by your friend.

Rule-governance is crucial in the learning of complex behaviors and cultural practices, identifying the potential consequences of the act. It can also guide the topography of the behavior (how it looks). Rules, once learned, are sometimes relatively insensitive to the actual contingencies in effect. Excessive or inaccurate rule-governance can be of clinical significance; much of what occurs in cognitive therapy involves work to change those patterns.

Weak repertoires involving rules can also be problematic. Youths with underdeveloped rule-following repertoires are unlikely to do well in school, for example. Although antisocial and aggressive behaviors usually involve direct-acting contingencies, many alternative ways to obtain reinforcement (say, participating in sports) or to escape aversives (say, using negotiation skills) require at least moderately developed rule-identifying and rule-following repertoires. Rules help to bridge the gap between behavior and delayed consequences and thus are critical to deferring gratification and completing the long chains of behavior required to achieve distant, difficult goals. Malott and his colleagues (Malott & Garcia, 1991; Malott et al., 1993) argued that rules actually bridge delays by providing covert, direct-acting contingencies. They view stating the rule as an establishing operation that increases the aversive effects of not following the rule. These elegant, if controversial, discussions cannot be adequately captured here, but are likely to lead to significant advances in the field.

CONCURRENT CONTINGENCIES

Human beings are immersed in a "sea of concurrent contingencies" (Malott et al., 1993, p. 378). Many acts are concurrently possible, and each may have multiple reinforcing—and aversive—consequences. Look, for example, at Figure 2, which identifies some of the multiple contingencies that may simultaneously be involved in a violent attack on the street in which a leather jacket is taken. Multiple and conflicting biological, simple operant, and cultural-level outcomes are involved, as are rules, establishing operations, discriminative stimuli, structural antecedents, and imitation. These contingencies are only those related to one possible class of acts; but there are an almost infinite variety of others that might occur instead. And many of the relevant antecedents and consequences are themselves behaviors, often performed by other people, each of which has been selected by its own often inconsistent network of consequences over time.

This image may help to portray how the rather simple elements of behavior combine and permute, resulting in complex repertoires. The basic principles are relatively straightforward, but recognizing multiple concurrent contingencies is essential to the analysis of the kinds of behavior involved in most problems of social importance. And because of the interlocking nature of these contingencies, intervention focused on single points in the system may fail if other powerful elements tend to return the system to its previous homeostasis. Adding an unlikely jail term almost at random (see Figure 2), for example, will not change the other elements of the picture and, therefore, is unlikely to result in a stable decrease in viol-

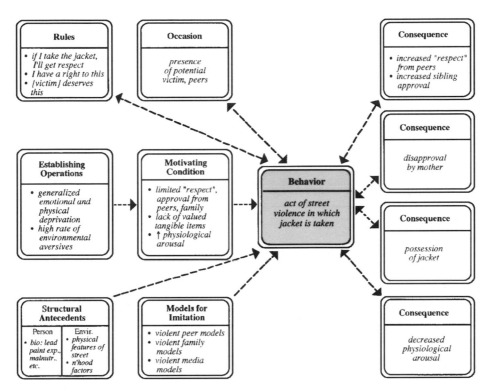

Figure 2. Contingencies associated with an act of street violence.

ence. The interlocking networks of (primarily social) consequences need to be modified—and this is the concern of cultural design.

CULTURAL DESIGN

Cultural design refers to the explicit planning, establishment, and stabilization of cultural practices, cultural entities, and cultures, as previously defined in this chapter. Existing cultural practices may once have been relatively functional, but their aggregate outcomes may be quite costly now. An example is aggression against members of other groups; although such behavior patterns were certainly protective for bands of early hominids, tribalism and racism continuing into the present have become critical sociocultural problems. The associated practices have largely negative aggregate outcomes at this point, but the networks of interlocking contingencies that shape and maintain these behaviors remain in place.

Other practices may have emerged superstitiously and are also maintained by cultures (of whatever size), although their actual outcomes may be largely neutral. In these cases, more effective variations may not have occurred, or if they have, they may not have been supported by existing social contingencies and may drop out before their utility can be established (i.e., being "ahead of one's time").

Cultural design is by its nature planned and rooted in either hypothesized or established rules—descriptions of contingencies and of probable aggregate outcomes. Design involves the explicit arrangement of not only new contingencies, but also new interlocking and therefore self-stabilizing *networks*, or systems of contingencies. It begins with what is often called *cultural analysis*, but note that cultural design goes beyond analysis (which primarily seeks understanding) to establishing new systems. These new systems are developed not for purposes of inquiry, but rather to achieve improved practical outcomes. Cultural design, therefore, is a highly applied science.

Malott (1988) argued that cultural innovation has often been largely rule-governed throughout human history. Malott theorized that at least the innovators themselves often understood rules in terms of cultural outcomes, although sometimes they couched their proposals in other (often supernatural) terms. At any rate, proposals for social change in the modern world generally are explicitly couched in terms of their aggregate outcomes—for the persons affected as well as for the cultural entities involved. For instance, the advertisements shown on television during the health care debate of 1994–95 emphasized negative and positive outcomes of particular policy choices. These outcomes were, generally speaking, untested, so what emerged were primarily samples of generalized classes of rules maintained by the cultures of political entities. The current proposals to redesign welfare are proceeding along similar lines—most decisions have been made based on existing repertoires of rules, not on empirical data.

The cultural design alternative is to apply the methods of science to cultural issues. This involves extracting the rules empirically rather than emotionally or superstitiously, and applying them to design. Such a process would introduce and stabilize cultural practices while leading to improved outcomes. Although understanding and establishing interlocking networks of contingencies is more complex with large cultural entities like nation-states than with small ones like families, once their commonalities as cultural entities are recognized, strategic similarities also emerge.

Natural History as Method

Families, schools, or nations cannot ordinarily be brought into the laboratory for fully controlled study. Even if they could be, by amputating these entities from the environmental networks within which they and their members are embedded, the phenomena observed would no longer be those in which behavioral scientists are interested. But this need not mean that the questions cannot be approached scientifically (consider how meteorological or astronomical phenomena are studied). Behaviorists do need to turn to different tools, however, for such investigations. There are many methods of inquiry available that can be useful here, ranging from research with animals to statistical analyses (Pierce, 1991). In particular, the methods of natural history (including some drawn from ethology, ecology, astronomy, and other disciplines) may be valuable for cultural analysis and design, because they allow rigorous examination of phenomena that remain rooted in their natural ecological situations.

Marston Bates (1950/1990), a founder of ecological science, identified the intertwining of (a) *organized observations*, (b) *controlled* (to the extent possible) *experiments* in the natural environment guided by those observations, and (c) the *development and evolution of conceptual frameworks* rooted in these observations and experiments as the essential method of natural history. My colleagues and I are currently working on the design of new cultural practices that we hope to embed and stabilize in both existing and new cultural entities. These practices will produce, as an aggregate outcome, a reduction in youth violence. The first step in our developmental research program was to specify a preliminary conceptual model of violence (including subtypes) that relies on an integration of behavior analytic theory with existing data from multiple sources. What we expected—and, indeed, what we are finding—is that some of the crucial contingencies have not been clearly established; we are therefore now turning to *theoretically guided* observations in natural settings to gather more information. Note that at this point, two of Bates' three processes have been applied in our investigations, leaving the third, experimentation.

Experimentation in the natural environment is different from that conducted in the laboratory. Different forms of control are usually required because, for example, random assignment is often not possible. An important behavior analytic tool for work with individuals also can be of service: the single-case, or *single-system* experimental design. A full discussion of applications of this methodology to cultural analysis and design is beyond the present purposes, but it is important to note that this technology is well-adapted to work in natural settings (Biglan, 1995). Reversal, multiple baseline, changing criteria, and alternating treatment designs are all possible in work with cultural practices and entities, as well as the less powerful, but easier to apply, AB designs with replications.

Ecologists also provide strategic guidance for the design of realistic experiments in natural cultural environments. Rigorous observation and conceptual analyses—the two other legs of the natural history tripod—often suggest questions that can be studied with quite modest experiments. Wilson wrote:

> [T]heory, even if airtight and plausible, is not enough to put the seal on . . . complex . . . processes. . . . There must be experiments to con-

firm the predictions of theory and, in the case of ecology particularly, to expose them to the exhilarating intrusions of natural history. But how can experiments be performed on archipelagoes and entire faunas and floras? *The answer is to miniaturize.* [italics added] (Wilson, 1992, p. 223)

He goes on to describe experiments that test the rate of species recolonization on tiny islands averaging 15 meters across. Physicists do much the same thing, addressing literally universal questions at the level of subatomic particles. Similarly, behavioral scientists may often need to begin with very small cultural entities, such as single families, small groups of peers, a city block—a process that will not be foreign. There may later prove to be differences of scale, but this will be a start.

In the case of our work in reducing youth violence, data from our naturalistic observations will be integrated with the conceptual model, producing modifications and enrichment. Based on that model, we will design a first approximation to an interventive package, including plans to establish the necessary contingencies to obtain and stabilize support from existing cultural entities. We will then test the package on a very small scale and use the results to further refine the conceptual model. This will lead to a next iteration of design and testing. The process we will use is likely to involve multiple iterations of each of Bates' three strategies. It will result not only in potentially substantial new scientific information, but also in a replicable package that can be tested and, with designed variations, used to establish similar practices elsewhere.

Varieties of Cultural Entities

Substantial evidence exists that new practices and new cultures can be established with entities of many different sizes and levels of complexity. Each of these new practices could constitute a chapter in itself; however, a few comments here will set the stage for the following discussion about practical details of cultural design.

Much of the existing behavior analytic research at first glance involves changing the behavior of individuals, rather than changing cultural practices or networks of contingencies maintained by groups. Note, however, that individual behavior is changed by changing the environment. A major issue in the literature relates to how to maintain change once it has been obtained (Sulzer-Azaroff & Mayer, 1991). The problem is not that new behavior somehow breaks free of the contingencies and disappears, but rather that contingencies required to maintain the behavior are often not designed with adequate attention to maintaining the behavior of those in the environment that provide those contingencies. The individual remains responsive to the contingencies, but as soon as the environment reverts to its original state, so does the behavior of the individual.

Preventing this requires the design of self-maintaining networks of interlocking contingencies. In clinical work with individuals, for example, unless the actions of either the client or the clinician result in exposure to stable networks of new consequences, change is unlikely to be maintained.

Families, in all of their multiple forms, are social entities that produce substantial stability of culture over time. Family therapists often refer to what we are defining here as cultural practices maintained by interlocking contingencies as the *structure* of the family, a term emphasizing the stability of family culture. Minuchin (1974; Minuchen & Nichols, 1993), for example, emphasized two primary treatment processes: *joining*, which involves becoming a significant part of the consequating system, and *restructuring*, which refers in our terms to the establishment of new, stable systems of interlocking contingencies. The principles of cultural design, therefore, should apply to families. (The same is true for formed and natural groups, although the details will not be elaborated in this chapter.)

Those working with formal organizations such as businesses and schools were among the first to recognize the importance of introducing not so much isolated new practices as redesigned behavioral systems to achieve lasting change. The subdiscipline of *organizational behavior management* has developed an extensive technology (e.g., Daniels, 1994), much of which can be adapted for work with other types of cultural entities.

The potential for systems redesign in education has also been clearly demonstrated (e.g., Mayer, Butterworth, Nafpaktitis, & Sulzer-Azaroff, 1983). The CABAS (Comprehensive Application of Behavior Analysis to Schooling; Greer, 1991, and chapter 5, this volume) schools are perhaps the most thorough-going example, in which all participants (students, teachers, parents, administrators) are involved in explicitly designed interlocking contingencies. Increased teacher compensation in the CABAS system, for example, depends on documented student learning—the behavior of the student controls the functions of all components of the school system.

Larger systems (e.g., communities, political entities) also are cultural entities, and the design of new practices and new networks of interlocking contingencies to support them is crucial to improved aggregate outcomes at those levels as well. A fair amount is known about work with neighborhoods and communities (Mattaini, 1993), but the level of complexity involved in transactional patterns within such larger systems becomes geometrically more challenging. Think for a moment about the changing health care system in American society. As this is written, the extent of possible health care reforms that may occur in the future is not known, but it is clear that the momentum toward managed care and cost containment will continue. How is this happening? Generally speaking, these changes are not based on explicit attention to health outcomes; on the contrary, the incentives built into managed care in fact support underserving (Strom, 1992). Rather, the trajectory toward managed care is the result of (rule-governed) decisions by various interest groups concerned about reducing costs and increasing or maintaining profit in the business sector, and freeing limited resources for other priorities in the nonprofit sector.

For work with such cultural entities, the scientific challenge is not so much to discover entirely new technologies to shape and maintain cultural practices (remember that cultural practices are special cases of operant behavior). Rather, the challenge is to find ways to organize what is known about behavior analysis and change in ways that take into account contingency interlocks.

Practical Steps Toward Cultural Design

Cultural design is by nature an iterative process that occurs as part of an ongoing steam of events. Therefore, the choice of where to begin is somewhat arbitrary. But a first step often is to determine those practices society would like to see established or increased, based on what existing data, observation, and theory suggest will lead to desired aggregate outcomes. The choice of such targets should be tested by experimentation as soon as possible, often by miniaturizing. For example, Newman (1992) suggested that legalization of drug use and sales may produce the best cultural outcomes. There is room to disagree here; my own analysis suggests the opposite (Mattaini, 1991). If Newman's proposal were viewed by a political entity as potentially valuable—if high-risk—it certainly would be best to try it first on a small and reversible scale.

Designing Contingencies to Support a New Practice

If we are interested in what at least appears to be a discrete class of behavior, say, rate of school attendance by young mothers on welfare, cultural designers ought first to look at the current consequences, both those supporting other incompatible behavior and those discouraging attendance. (I am leaving aside for simplicity the often crucial antecedents, which would need to be examined as well for a comprehensive analysis.) These are roughly sketched in Figure 3. Some improvement might, as data from Ohio suggest, occur by simply adding a small financial incentive to the existing network. (In the Ohio experiment, a reduction in welfare benefits is also made for nonattendance. Because this results in increased poverty for most of the families involved, including their children, it is doubtful that this can be justified; Opulente & Mattaini, 1993). To achieve more powerful results, however, it may be important to think about ways to change at least the more powerful of the other consequences involved. As

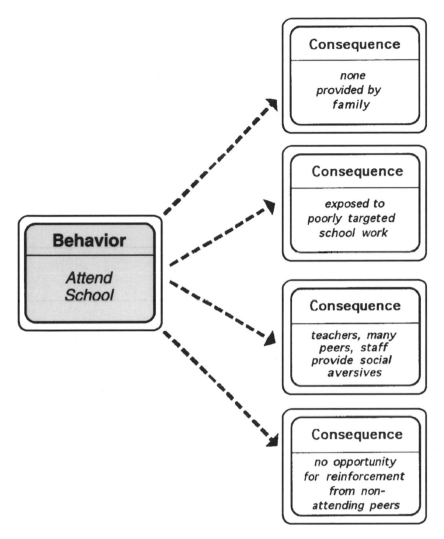

Figure 3. Consequences associated with school attendance for some young welfare mothers. Adapted with permission from Mattaini (1995).

behavioral scientists begin to think about changing these contingencies, they are actually dealing with changing the behavior of other people that interlinks with that of the student. For example, a scientific analysis may suggest that changing teacher behavior, parent behavior, and peer behavior is important. In each case, cultural designers must not only specify how that behavior should change, however, but also determine what consequences will maintain such changes. Preparing contingency diagrams for each may be a useful first step here.

In many cases, behavioral scientists are interested in more than increasing or decreasing a single practice; they are interested in designing supports for a desirable sequence of interaction known as a *scene*—a concept borrowed from the anthropologist Marvin Harris (1964). To do so, it is necessary to specify:

1. Who the participants are (classes of actors taking on particular roles, because individual participants are often interchangeable in cultural practices; it is not clear that the behaviors emitted should be viewed as cultural practices if each participant in the exchange always acted in individually distinct ways);
2. What the behaviors are that each participant displays;
3. What the sequences of actions are (if that is important); and
4. What the relevant antecedents and consequences are for each behavior identified.

Figure 4 illustrates how this might be done. In this example, the interest is in increasing positive exchanges between a couple, a crucial aspect of relationship enhancement (Bornstein & Bornstein, 1986; Stuart, 1980). In this very simple culture, prompts to begin the exchange may result in a self-perpetuating process. Note that the desired behavior classes are spe-

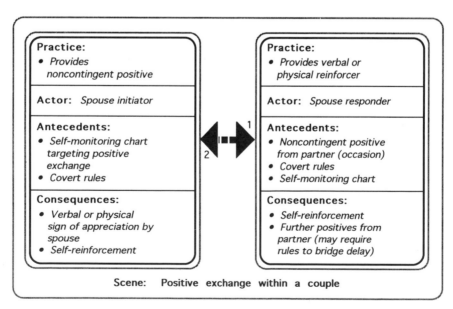

Scene: Positive exchange within a couple

Figure 4. A basic set of interlocking contingencies in a very simple culture.

cified, as are the classes of actors, critical antecedents of each behavior class, and consequences. To establish this sequence of practices, it is generally not adequate to simply identify the preferred behavior, which, in this case, would be to give advice to act nicely to one another. The antecedents and consequences must also be specified, with plans to introduce and stabilize them.

The scene is also a useful way of framing interactions in far more complicated systems. It is known from previous research that increasing the level of positive reinforcement used by teachers results in improved student behavior and learning, even with highly disadvantaged groups of students (e.g., Cohen & Filipczak, 1989; Mayer et al., 1983). We also know, from centuries of experience, that this is not a practice that is spontaneously emitted and maintained. Although it may seem that a simple explanation would result in increased reinforcement as shown within the boundary of the scene in Figure 5, it often does not. There are other classes of actors outside the immediate scene that may be able to provide crucial antecedents and consequences to the teacher (note the administrators and

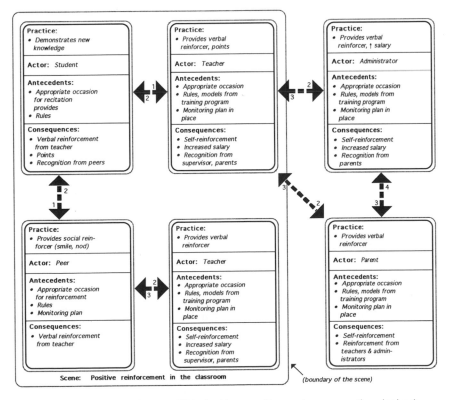

Figure 5. A relatively stable set of interlocking contingencies supporting desired cultural practices.

parents of actors outside the right boundary). However, there is also no reason to suppose that those administrators and parents will spontaneously emit the desired actions. Contingencies for their behavior must also be designed. Only in this way will stable patterns of interlocking contingencies emerge. Otherwise, the existing contingencies may damp down the new variations. This is the beauty of systems like the CABAS schools, in which contingencies for all relevant actors are explicitly designed. The final test, of course, comes in examining changes in aggregate outcomes, in this case documentation of student learning.

AN EXAMPLE: CULTURAL DESIGN AND ALCOHOL ABUSE

At first glance, alcohol abuse would appear to be quintessentially an individual issue—a physical addiction that requires only that the person and the substance to be present. In fact, available data suggest that alcohol addiction and problem drinking can be dramatically affected via cultural design. The prevalence of alcohol-related problems is substantial. Although specific numbers vary depending on the diagnostic criteria used, the estimate that 5% to 7% of the adult U.S. population suffered from alcohol dependence during the past year, and perhaps twice that over a lifetime, is consistent with the data (American Psychiatric Association, 1994). Problem drinkers—persons who experience significant problems as a result of drinking, but do not show signs of dependence—are substantially more common, perhaps by a ratio of 4:1 (Institute of Medicine, 1990). Social costs (financial, family, and otherwise) associated with alcohol abuse may exceed those of any other problem discussed in this volume.

The first barrier with which those interested in effectively responding to these problems need to grapple is a set of beliefs (rules) that are widely supported in the broader, and to a substantial extent the professional, cultures. These include the following:

1. Nothing works very well, and the results of all approaches tested are roughly the same (only slightly better than the rate of "spontaneous remission," which may be around 20%; Miller & Hester, 1980).
2. The primary issue in initiating treatment is breaking through denial through confrontation.
3. A person must "hit bottom" (lose those things most important to him or her) before he or she will be ready for treatment.
4. Abstinence is the only appropriate goal for everyone who experiences alcohol-related problems.

None of these statements is consistent with available data. Something works. In fact, several things work, depending on the client's situation. For problem drinkers who are not physically dependent, guided self-change treatment (Sobell & Sobell, 1993), a very brief behavioral treatment focused on identifying and modifying relevant contingencies associated with problem drinking, appears to be adequate in about 50% of cases. Guided self-change treatment apparently enhances motivation for further treatment for most of the remaining 50% as well. For those with more severe problems, the Community Reinforcement Approach (CRA), developed more than two decades ago by Nathan Azrin and his colleagues (Hunt & Azrin, 1973), and iteratively enhanced and extended since (Azrin, 1976; Azrin, Sisson, Meyers, & Godley, 1982; Budney, Higgins, Bickel, & Kent, 1993; Budney, Higgins, Delaney, Kent, & Bickel, 1991; Meyers & Smith, 1995; Sisson & Azrin, 1989), is an outstanding example of the power of cultural design, and also a clear example of how interlocking contingencies among cultural entities can stand in the way of effective responses to social problems.

Components of the Community Reinforcement Approach

Although not especially staff intensive as treatments for addictions go, the Community Reinforcement Approach is a multicomponent model that assists clients in building a rich network of connections with non-drinking cultures. Included are procedures to

1. Improve marital functioning (where relevant);
2. Assist clients in finding jobs—not just any jobs, however, but those that encourage social contact and stability;
3. Build connections with nondrinking social networks and recreational opportunities, including a buddy system, involvement with a specialized social club, reconnection with family and friends, and even pets (and plants!);
4. Implement Antabuse[1] assurance (this is not simply a prescription, but rather a set of interlocking practices structured into family culture, an approach we will discuss later in this chapter);
5. Provide drink-refusal training; and
6. Train in controlling urges to drink.

Results

In four controlled studies with both inpatients and outpatients, the CRA has proven substantially more effective than standard treatment. For

---

[1]Antabuse is a medication that will make a person ill if combined with alcohol.

example, at 6-month follow-up, patients originally treated with the CRA on an inpatient basis drank on fewer than 1% of days, compared with 55% in the standard treatment group; 20% of the CRA clients were unemployed, compared with 56% of the control participants (Azrin, 1976). At 6-month follow-up in a study with outpatients (Azrin, et al., 1982), the standard treatment group reported more than 50% drinking days, whereas the CRA treatment group experienced almost total sobriety. For patients who were married or living together (who also tended to have richer social networks), only the Antabuse assurance procedure was required; for single patients, the entire CRA package was important. Variations of the CRA have recently been tested with drug abusers as well. Results have been very encouraging in work with persons with cocaine and marijuana problems (Budney, Higgins, Bickel, et al., 1993; Budney, Higgins, Delaney, et al., 1991). Pilot data for work with inner-city crack cocaine users and heroin addicts suggests that the CRA may have promise for work with that population as well (Meyers & Smith, 1995; Ojeda & Mattaini, 1995).

The Community Reinforcement Approach as Cultural Design

One way to think about the CRA is simply as a multicomponent intervention package that appears to reliably produce excellent outcomes, and this is clearly true. At the same time, the work of Azrin and his colleagues and those who are replicating that work can be more precisely viewed as being deeply rooted in the concepts of cultural design on several levels. A central target of the approach is to establish new practices in the microculture of the family. For example, establishing a ritual for the person in treatment around the daily taking of Antabuse in the presence of a significant other involves reciprocal interlocking behaviors and consequences for both parties (note how different this is from a simple commitment to take Antabuse on one's own). In addition, the CRA was among the pioneering approaches that emphasized the need to establish a culture (set of social contingencies) of positive exchange in the marital relationship (Reciprocity Marriage Counseling), a concept that has been extended by a number of behavioral innovators (Holtzworth-Munroe & Jacobson, 1991; Stuart, 1980).

Establishing new practices in the family is only the beginning, however. The CRA in its full implementation also involves the design of new cultural entities (e.g., the Job Club and the United [social] Club), each of which is established specifically to reinforce positive alternative behavior patterns among members and is explicitly designed to ensure that important contingency interlocks are present. These are not simply new arrangements of contingencies that are set up to support an individual, but rather they are networks of practices that involve interlocking contingencies for classes of participants that are transmitted to new members of the group over time—new cultural entities with their own cultures.

At yet another level, the CRA strongly encourages clients to participate in existing cultures (particular types of jobs and recreational activities) in which contingency arrangements support sobriety for the individual who joins those cultures. Just how different the CRA is from other approaches that primarily emphasize exhortation, confrontation, individual commitment, and encouraging the client to take particular steps without explicit attention to the network of consequences that will support and maintain the new behavior, may not be immediately apparent. If, however, one steps back and examines the respective contingencies for each, the distinctions are crucial. Exposing the client to new systems of consequences (some of which he or she is involved in creating, and all of which he or she is involved with maintaining) is the key difference. Often, the traditional approach simply provides new rules with the hope that the client will follow them (and perhaps be exposed to alternative sets of contingencies). It does not address this issue directly, however. By emphasizing a kind of conversion experience, the traditional model places the causes of drinking as well as the responsibility for recovery firmly with the individual (despite the concept of powerlessness). Although new rules can often help for a time, some clients may follow the new rules for varying periods without experiencing adequate reinforcement for alternative behavior soon enough to maintain sobriety. The differences between the CRA and traditional approaches may appear subtle when taking a crosssectional look at the events occurring in treatment; however, the CRA's emphasis on explicitly rooting the client in new contingency interlocks is, in fact, profound. Note that for those for whom they work, self-help groups such as Alcoholics Anonymous and therapeutic communities also involve exposing the client to a new culture, and those who do best in such programs appear to be those who become deeply immersed in them. I argue that explicit attention to the operative interlocking contingencies in such settings may be valuable in enhancing and extending their effectiveness. Why is a demonstrably effective model like the CRA not better known and in widespread use? This question is also a matter of cultural practices that probably needs to be analyzed with the tools discussed in this chapter; the cultures of the treatment community and funding sources are important places to start.

Although not yet well known, programs rooted in cultural design already exist in the alcohol treatment field and, in retrospect, may appear to be obviously sensible. But with regard to many of the other problems discussed in this volume, a cultural design perspective has not commonly been taken. Responses (even behavioral responses) to violence and sexual coercion, to school failure, and to many other problems, have typically emphasized the problem behavior of the individual. These responses have looked at finding ways to change the individual (biologically, psychologically, cognitively, etc.), but have not focused on the interlocking behavioral systems needed to maintain new individual behaviors over time, much less on the need to establish behavioral cultures that prevent problems—and respond effectively to them when they do occur—for entire classes of persons.

REFERENCES

American Psychiatric Association. (1994). *Diagnostic and statistical manual of mental disorders* (4th ed.). Washington, DC: Author.

Azrin, N. H. (1976). Improvements in the community-reinforcement approach to alcoholism. *Behaviour Research and Therapy, 14,* 339–348.

Azrin, N. H., Sisson, R. W., Meyers, R., & Godley, M. (1982). Alcoholism treatment by disulfiram and community reinforcement therapy. *Journal of Behavior Therapy and Experimental Psychiatry, 13,* 105–112.

Bates, M. (1990). *The nature of natural history.* Princeton, NJ: Princeton University Press. (Original work published 1950)

Biglan, A. (1995). *Changing cultural practices.* Reno, NV: Context Press.

Bornstein, P. H., & Bornstein, M. T. (1986). *Marital therapy: A behavioral-communications approach.* New York: Pergamon.

Budney, A. J., Higgins, S. T., Bickel, W., & Kent, L. (1993). Relationship between intravenous use and achieving initial cocaine abstinence. *Drug and Alcohol Dependence, 32,* 133–142.

Budney, A. J., Higgins, S. T., Delaney, D. D., Kent, L., & Bickel, W. K. (1991). Contingent reinforcement of abstinence with individuals abusing cocaine and marijuana. *Journal of Applied Behavior Analysis, 24,* 657–665.

Catania, A. C., & Harnad, S. (Eds.) (1988). *The selection of behavior: The operant behaviorism of B. F. Skinner: Comments and Consequences.* Cambridge, England: Cambridge University Press.

Cohen, H. L., & Filipczak, J. (1989). *A new learning environment.* Boston: Authors Cooperative. (Original work published 1971)

Daniels, A. C. (1994). *Bringing out the best in people.* New York: McGraw-Hill.

Glenn, S. S. (1988). Contingencies and metacontingencies: Toward a synthesis of behavior analysis and cultural materialism. *The Behavior Analyst, 11,* 161–179.

Glenn, S. S. (1991). Relations among behavioral, cultural and biological evolution. In P. A. Lamal (Ed.), *The behavioral analysis of societies and cultural practices* (pp. 39–73). New York: Hemisphere.

Gould, S. J. (1994). The evolution of life on the earth. *Scientific American, 271*(4), 85–91.

Greer, R. D. (1991). The teacher as strategic scientist: A solution to our educational crisis? *Behavior and Social Issues, 1*(2), 25–41.

Harris, M. (1964). *The nature of cultural things*. New York: Random House.

Harris, M. (1979). *Cultural materialism: The struggle for a science of culture*. New York: Vintage.

Hayes, S. C. (Ed.). (1989). *Rule-governed behavior: Cognition, contingencies, and instructional control*. New York: Plenum.

Holtzworth-Munroe, A., & Jacobsen, N. S. (1991). Behavioral marital therapy. In A. S. Gurman & D. P. Kniskern (Eds.), *Handbook of family therapy* (pp. 96–133). New York: Brunner/Maxel.

Hunt, G. M., & Azrin, N. H. (1973). A community-reinforcement approach to alcoholism. *Behaviour Research & Therapy, 11*, 91–104.

Institute of Medicine (1990). *Broadening the base of treatment for alcohol problems*. Washington, DC: National Academy Press.

Malott, R. W. (1988). Rule-governed behavior and behavioral anthropology. *The Behavior Analyst, 11*, 181–203.

Malott, R. W., & Garcia, M. E. (1991). Role of private events in rule-governed behavior. In L. J. Hayes & P. N. Chase (Eds.), *Dialogues on Verbal Behavior* (pp. 237–257). Reno: Context Press.

Malott, R. W., Whaley, D. L., & Malott, M. E. (1993). *Elementary principles of behavior* (2nd ed.). Englewood Cliffs, NJ: Prentice-Hall.

Mattaini, M. A. (1991). Choosing weapons for the war on "crack": An operant analysis. *Research on Social Work Practice, 1*, 188–213.

Mattaini, M. A. (1993). Behavior analysis in community practice. *Research on Social Work Practice, 3*, 420–447.

Mattaini, M. A. (1995). Contingency diagrams as teaching tools. *The Behavior Analyst, 18*, 93–98.

Mayer, G. R., Butterworth, T., Nafpaktitis, M., & Sulzer-Azaroff, B. (1983). Preventing school vandalism and improving discipline: A three-year study. *Journal of Applied Behavior Analysis, 16*, 355–369.

McDowell, J. J. (1988). Matching theory in natural human environments. *The Behavior Analyst, 11*, 95–109.

Meyers, R. J., & Smith, J. E. (1995). *Clinical guide to alcohol treatment: The community reinforcement approach*. NY: Guilford.

Michael, J. L. (1993). *Concepts and principles of behavior analysis*. Kalamazoo, MI: Society for the Advancement of Behavior Analysis.

Minuchen, S. (1994). *Families and family therapy*. Cambridge, MA: Harvard.

Minuchen, S., & Nichols, M. P. (1993). *Family Healing*. New York: Free Press.

Newman, B. (1992). *The reluctant alliance: Behaviorism and humanism*. Buffalo: Prometheus.

Ojeda, M., & Mattaini, M. A. (1995, May). Services for homeless drug abusing persons: Contingency management and community reinforcement. In M. A.

Mattaini (Chair), *Teaching behavior analysis: Learning by doing.* Symposium conducted at the 21st Annual Convention of the Association for Behavior Analysis, Washington, DC.

Opulente, M., & Mattaini, M. A. (1993). Toward welfare that works. *Behavior and Social Issues, 3,* 17–34.

Pierce, W. D. (1991). Culture and society: The role of behavioral analysis. In P. A. Lamal (Ed.), *Behavioral analysis of societies and cultural practices* (pp. 13–37). New York: Hemisphere.

Poppen, R. L. (1989). Some clinical implications of rule-governed behavior. In S. C. Hayes (Ed.), *Rule-governed behavior: Cognition, contingencies, and instructional control* (pp. 325–357). New York: Plenum.

Reiss, A. J., Jr., & Roth, J. A. (Eds.). (1993). *Understanding and preventing violence.* Washington, DC: National Academy Press.

Sidman, M. (1989). *Coercion and its fallout.* Boston: Authors Cooperative.

Sisson, R., & Azrin, N. (1989). The community reinforcement approach. In R. K. Hester & W. R. Miller (Eds.), *Handbook of alcoholism treatment approaches* (pp. 242–258). New York: Pergamon.

Skinner, B. F. (1981). Selection by Consequences. *Science, 213,* 501–504.

Skinner, B. F. (1986). The evolution of verbal behavior. *Journal of the Experimental Analysis of Behavior, 45,* 115–22.

Skinner, B. F. (1989). The operant side of behavior therapy. *Recent issues in the analysis of behavior.* Columbus, OH: Merrill.

Sobell, M. B., & Sobell, L. C. (1993). *Problem drinkers: Guided self-change treatment.* New York: Guilford.

Strom, K. (1992). Reimbursement demands and treatment decisions: A growing dilemma for social workers. *Social Work, 37,* 398–403.

Stuart, R. B. (1971). Behavioral contracting within the families of delinquents. *Journal of Behavior Therapy and Experimental Psychiatry, 2,* 1–11.

Stuart, R. B. (1980). *Helping couples change: A social learning approach to marital therapy.* New York: Guilford.

Stuart, R. B., & Lott, L. A., Jr. (1972). Behavioral contracting with delinquents: A cautionary note. *Journal of Behavior Therapy and Experimental Psychiatry, 3,* 161–169.

Sulzer-Azaroff, B., & Mayer, G. R. (1991). *Behavior analysis for lasting change.* Fort Worth: Holt, Rinehart and Winston.

Widom, C. S. (1989). Child abuse, neglect, and adult behavior: Research design and findings on criminality, violence, and child abuse. *American Journal of Orthopsychiatry, 59,* 355–367.

Wilson, E. O. (1992). *The diversity of life.* Cambridge, MA: Belknap/Harvard.

2

BEHAVIOR ANALYSIS AND SOCIAL WELFARE POLICY

BRUCE A. THYER

This chapter provides a review of the application of elementary principles of operant behavior (more accurately, rule-governed behavior), toward the conceptualization, design, and evaluation of social welfare policy. All social policy is intended to influence human behavior, and it does this most often through the contrived manipulation of contingencies of punishment and, sometimes, reinforcement. Policy examples that use contingency management are provided in this chapter to support this thesis.

The interdisciplinary field of behavior analysis takes as its purview the empirical investigation of how environmental events affect the actions of organisms. No activity in the realm of human comportment is excluded from this definition. Within our field, behavior has been defined for the past 50 years as the actions of a person—whether externally observable or private. (Private actions occur within the skin and are not obviously detectable to a second party.) The silent movements of one's lips, the spoken word, and the thoughts that occur prior to speech are all grist for the

Portions of this manuscript were delivered in B. A. Thyer (Chair). *Science and social welfare: Selection by consequences.* A symposium presented at the annual convention of the American Psychological Association, August, 1992, in Washington, DC; and at the annual meeting of the Southeastern Association for Behavior Analysis, 14–16 October, 1993, in Chapel Hill, NC.

analytic mill of the behaviorist. Contrary to the common view, behavior analysts have long been concerned with the scientific investigation of thinking, feeling, insight, motivation, and attitudes in addition to overt actions. In fact, the entire domain of what may be called psychology, sociology, economics, anthropology, political science, and all those academic fields relevant to understanding the human condition are of interest to the behavior analyst.

Simply speaking, the dependent variables of the behavior analyst are all of what human beings do and experience. The independent variables consist of environmental events and how they affect us. Through the use of such a broad brush, it is easy to see how the field of social welfare policy could be contended to be a part of the purview of behavior analysis. Take, for instance, several convenient definitions of social policy:

> Established social policy is *a settled course of action* [italics added] with respect to selected social phenomena that govern social relationships and the distribution of resources in a society. (Baumheier & Schorr, 1977, p. 1453)

> Policy is (1) an idea that is embodied in (2) a written document, which is (3) ratified by legitimate authority and serves as (4) *a guide to action* [italics added] and is (5) the result of the policy process. (Tropman, 1984, p. 5)

> [G]overnment and private social agencies respond . . . to social welfare problems and that those responses result in . . . *regulation* of behavior of persons and groups. (Heffernan, 1992, p. 17)

There is no doubt that a wider variety of definitions of social welfare policy could be cited. It is also equally certain that virtually all such conceptions contain the common element that policy is intended to influence behavior. Because social welfare policies form a part of the environment in which we live, the segue into the domain of behavior analysis seems quite natural. Indeed, it is reflected in the writings of many behaviorists. B. F. Skinner authored books, articles, and chapters devoted to topics such as *Reflections on Behaviorism and Society* (1978), *The Design of Experimental Communities*, *The Design of Cultures*, *Freedom and the Control of Men* (in Skinner, 1972) and *Utopia as an Experimental Culture* (in Skinner, 1969). Dinsmoor (1992) prepared an excellent overview of the progressive nature of Skinner's social views, and other behavior analysts have prepared conceptual works relating their field to social policy, including public welfare and other areas (e.g., Fawcett et al., 1988; Kunkel, 1983; Lamal, 1984; Task Force on Public Policy, 1988). With the evolution of the journal *Behavior Analysis and Social Action* into *Behavior and Social Issues* (now published by the Cambridge Center for Behavioral Studies), the association of these two fields seems assured for the foreseeable future.

WHAT IS THE PURPOSE OF SOCIAL WELFARE POLICY?

The common view seems to be that a major function of social welfare policy is to influence attitudes or knowledge, or both, of the citizenry. It is believed that changes in behavior will follow the exposure to appropriate information or the experience of an attitudinal change. This logic follows the current zeitgeist that a person's thoughts, knowledge, and attitudes cause behavior. Behavior analysts dispute this notion on both empirical and philosophical grounds. From our perspective, attitudes, beliefs, thoughts, feelings, and private events are themselves a function of environmental experiences undergone by an individual, and all are worthy of scientific inquiry. Simply put, a person behaves *and* thinks in a particular manner because of his or her prior learning experiences. The thoughts (feelings, attitudes, etc.) are correlates of one's prior learning, but are not held to be the source of new behavior itself. In fact, the view that the function of welfare policy is to alter attitudes could be destructive to the design of more effective policies that ignore these mental waystations and focus primarily on altering the environmental contingencies in which people spend their lives.

For the behavior analyst, the purpose of social welfare policy is not primarily to influence attitudes, change minds, or inculcate a certain point of view per se, but rather to predict and control the behavior of the citizenry. For example, the purpose of social welfare legislation related to birth control is not only to promote favorable attitudes toward the use of condoms or oral contraceptives but also to get men and women to engage in responsible birth control practices. The purpose of legislation intended to reduce the incidence of domestic violence is not necessarily to induce more respectful attitudes of men toward women but primarily to prevent men from beating women. Rather than establish commissions to promote self-esteem (as the state of California recently did), government should promote policies and practices that establish appropriately reinforcing environments that give rise to both self-esteem and effective behavior. For the behavior analyst, the focus is not on the feeling. Rather, the focus is on what is felt by the individual that gives rise to the feeling (and to comportment). What is felt are the effects of environments. We know a great deal about altering environments—changing the circumstances in which people live. The prospect for an effective welfare policy is considerably enhanced when the focus is on establishing appropriately reinforcing environments in which people work, live and love, rather than on amorphous efforts to alter feeling states directly, about which we know very little.

The perspective that the actions of men and women are of overriding importance was laid out nicely by political scientist John Wahlke in his

1979 presidential address to the annual meeting of the American Political Science Association. In this speech, Wahlke advocated that researchers devote more attention to the analysis of the behavior of *individuals*, as opposed to the aggregated actions of large numbers of people. He noted that reified concepts such as roles, groups, cultures, institutions, and other purported entities are *theoretical constructs* and that their very existence is only derived from the aggregated data obtained from individual persons. He also criticized political scientists' overreliance on citizens' self-reports of past actions or of future intended behavior as dependent variables, claiming that "inadvertently, political behavior research has become steadily more preoccupied with explaining the variance in attitudinal dependent variables and has progressively lost sight of the more genuinely behavioral variations which constitute the material essence of politics and government." (Wahlke, 1979, p. 24). Even more forcefully, Wahlke suggested that political scientists "should abandon the notion that verbal self-reports about attitudes are isomorphic surrogates for supportive or nonsupportive attitudes, and should stop using verbal self-reports as dependent variables. To understand obedience or rebellion against political authority requires taking a more realistic look at such *behavior*" (p. 29). Wahlke's reference list contains numerous citations to articles that exemplify the type of behaviorally oriented research in political science that he advocates (see also the earlier article by Kariel, 1967).

Similar perspectives about the value of a truly behaviorally oriented approach to understanding large-scale social behavior can be found in the disciplines of sociology (Burgess & Bushnell, 1969), anthropology (Malott, 1988), public administration (Presthus, 1965), and economics (Hursh, 1984; Kagel & Winkler, 1972). The following paraphrase of a statement usually attributed to Dr. Martin Luther King, Jr., illustrates this pragmatic approach: "I don't care if the government cannot eliminate racist attitudes among White men, as long as it can pass laws to prevent them from beating us up." I believe that a clear case can be made in support of the behavior analysts' position that the function of social welfare policy is to alter the behavior of citizens. In a nutshell, the dependent variables of research into social problems and of the effects of social welfare policy involve what people actually *do*.

HOW DOES SOCIAL WELFARE POLICY REALLY WORK?

From the viewpoint of a behavior analyst, the purpose of social policy is the establishment of contingencies of reinforcement or punishment, or both, toward the furtherance of some social end, presumably related to the survival of the culture. These ends are decided upon by the community's lawmakers, not by experts in behavior analysis. This is not without its problems. As Skinner (1979, p. 51) pointed out, "Today the average congressman and senator is controlled mainly by *political* contingencies . . . If the contingencies which govern political behavior are more powerful than the contingencies that govern statesman-like behavior, then it is difficult to see how congressmen and senators can effectively deliberate on matters of state". Skinner went on to say:

> In each case, a group of people is given the power to control the behavior of others. But the behavior of the controlling group itself is controlled by other contingencies. And because none of these contingencies are carefully and explicitly designed to induce people to behave for the good of the whole group, it is difficult to prevent the reinforcement of selfish partisan behaviors . . . . Those who get into power are no better than those they have thrown out. The reason is that both behave under the same contingencies of reinforcement. (Skinner, 1979, p. 48)

INEFFECTIVE CONTINGENCY MANAGEMENT

Sometimes social welfare policies seemingly ignore the science of behavior analysis and contingencies of reinforcement. The following quote from *The New York Times* provides an example:

> The court official who supervises child support in Grand Rapids, Mich., described a 26-year-old local man who had fathered eight children with five mothers. "Before you condemn him for moral laxity," said the official, William D. Camden, "look what he did for these women . . . He gave each one of them a safety net." Mr. Camden said, referring to the welfare the women and children can receive, "They will have a steady income and full medical coverage until their kids are 18 . . . The system seems designed to encourage this kind of dependency." (Eckholm, 1992, p. 1)

Martha Ozawa's (1988) multistate analysis of the effects of the contingencies associated with Aid to Families with Dependent Children (AFDC) payments found that illegitimacy was inadvertently encouraged by the policies in force. It was not that the numbers of out-of-wedlock births were increased by the prospect of welfare payments, but rather that single mothers were effectively deterred from getting married to the fathers of their children because of the threatened loss of benefits (Ozawa, 1988).

Mulick and Meinhold have examined at an institutional level the deleterious effects of the contingencies of reimbursement established by Medicaid and other insurance programs and by various regulatory agencies that certify mental retardation service programs (Meinhold & Mulick, 1992; Mulick & Meinhold, 1990). Here are some examples, cited in Meinhold & Mulick (1992):

More money was provided for residents who were more dependent than for residents who were independent. Partial independency, which would be the case during teaching of a skill, resulted in decreased reimbursement rates. This created an administrative disincentive for documenting adaptive-skill acquisition and the strong possibility of a disincentive for teaching those skills at all. (p. 158)

Time pressures, competing staff responsibilities, and the difficulty of maintaining adaptive skills of residents with profound mental retardation and physical handicaps sometimes resulted in the loss of functional independence. Areas often affected including feeding, mobility, and toileting. In some cases, these outcomes resulted in levels of dependency that produced higher reimbursement rates. (p. 158)

[T]ime-consuming and important interventions could not be described in the written format required for reimbursement. The agency received no money for doing them. Consequently, staffing was sometimes unavailable for real-time behavior modification and incidental teaching programs" (p. 158)

Closer to home, in my community of Athens, Georgia, the executive director of our local public housing authority has noted that the rules legislate against socially responsible behavior. "In effect, the rules make the good things people do less rewarding than the bad things, which do not draw penalties and may even result in a benefit to the offender" (Whidden, 1991, p. 1). "There's a reward now for being homeless . . . some people now purposely put themselves in that situation to enhance opportunities to admission into public housing, so we reward the very behavior that we don't want, which is what is wrong with most social welfare policy in this country . . . For example, if there are two working members in a family, the rent is going to be higher (30% of household income, regardless of income level) than if one person works, so it is to the person's benefit to conceal the number of persons working so that only one income is reported" (Parker, cf. Whidden, 1991, pp. 1, 10).

Programs known as *workfare* are currently receiving favorable publicity. Under the rules described for such programs, welfare recipients would be required to participate in some form of employment-related training, or actual employment, to obtain or retain benefits. The exception would be single mothers with children *under the age of three*. Now, what do you think will be the likely consequences of saying to someone, in effect, "Unless you get pregnant and have another child soon, you will have to participate in workfare?" One need not be a skilled behavior analyst to predict that such a program will likely result in greater numbers of, and more frequent, pregnancies.

THE NONEMPIRICAL NATURE OF
WELFARE POLICY DEVELOPMENT

Among the many problems involved in the design and evaluation of social welfare policy is the nonempirical approach that is often taken. This avoidance of empiricism may begin in (a) the identification and selection of problems for which policy is designed; (b) a lack of attention to empirically supported policies and practices; and (c) too little attention being paid to the empirical evaluation of social welfare policies once they have been implemented.

Those involved in the design of policy know that the problems that receive the most attention and resources may not be those that are the most pressing or urgent, but rather those that have the strongest advocates. For example, smoking-related illnesses, cancer, heart disease, and homicides account for far more fatalities in the United States than AIDS. Yet AIDS receives far more attention proportionately from the mass media, professional journals, and funding sources than other public health problems. This is in spite of the fact that the other problems cause greater and continuing numbers of fatalities. This situation is attributable to the laudable zeal of those advocating for increased resources devoted to the prevention and treatment of HIV disease; however, it is not necessarily the rational allocation of funding based on societal benefits.

When a social welfare goal has been established—such as developing low-cost housing for the poor or reducing child abuse—all too often, little attention is given to interventive practices that have some degree of empirical support. Rather, interventions are selected for other reasons. For example, large sums of state and federal monies are spent each year for the treatment of parents who abuse their children. Among the more empirically supported interventions for working with abusive parents are those derived from a behavior analytic model (e.g., Gambrill, 1989; Greene, Norman, Searle, Daniels, & Lubeck, 1995; Isaacs, 1982). However, the vast majority of funds dedicated to ameliorating child abuse continue to be expended upon nonbehavioral programs that the research evidence shows are largely ineffective (cf. Howing, Wodarski, Gaudin, & Kurtz, 1989). Similarly, despite the well-documented effectiveness of a behavioral intervention to help the chronically unemployed obtain well-paying and lasting jobs (e.g., Azrin, Flores, & Kaplan, 1975; Jones & Azrin, 1973), this "Job-Finding Club" approach remains poorly used.

Apart from the negative outcomes associated with a number of massive social welfare programs, the public is rightly concerned about the infrequency with which such programs are systematically evaluated as a whole. For example, the Aid to Families with Dependent Children (AFDC) program, the U.S. Food Stamp program and the Women, Infants, and Children's Program (WIC) are all intended to improve the health and well-being of the poor by providing access to an adequate diet. Immense sums are spent on these programs—more than $25 billion annually for AFDC alone (cf. Eckholm, 1992). The goal is a laudable one with which few members of the general public and even fewer social workers or psychologists would argue. However, the public is frequently made aware of fraud and abuse in the system, both by the recipients of such nutritional services and occasionally by welfare workers. The occurrence of such fraud and abuse, if maintained at sufficiently low levels, may be tolerated by the Republic if it is clear that the services provided to the majority of honest recipients are truly meeting their needs. Unfortunately, this is not the case. I am not aware of any study, for example, which has demonstrated that the recipients of food stamps enjoy an improved nutritional status relative to similarly qualified poor citizens who do not receive such services. Yet such an improved nutritional status and its consequent effects on intelligence, health, and general resistance to disease is the explicit goal of these welfare programs. Behavior analysts, along with many other empirically oriented human service professionals, would contend that such outcome studies are long overdue and, in fact, should be an integral component of all welfare programs.

A few examples of social welfare program evaluations do exist that could be construed as roughly behavior analytic in methodology. That is, these evaluations employed time-series analysis (TSA) to investigate changes over time in some dependent variable, as opposed to using between-groups designs (e.g., Marsh, 1981). DiNitto (1983) provides an excellent description of the integration of the fields of TSA and the evaluation of social welfare policy that is worth consulting.

By positing the need for certain social welfare policies and programs to be derived from empirically based data and advocating that the services provided be selected from those interventions that have an adequate research base, the behavior analyst is responding not only to the moral imperative of providing necessary welfare services to those in need but also to the charge that public monies be expended in a responsible manner as effectively and efficiently as possible. That is also why behavior analysts suggest that rigorous and ongoing program evaluation be an inherent component of such programs. To suggest that existing and proposed services need to be critically scrutinized by the empiricist is not to condemn the goals of such programs. Rather, such scrutiny is the means of avoiding the all too frequent failure of such programs and achieving the goals that are so nobly conceived. Clearly, whether construed in the language of behavior analysis or not, the essence of social welfare policy consists of establishing contingencies of reinforcement and punishment to promote or deter various actions of the citizenry. That being the case, it would seem that knowledge of behavior analysis in general, and of the principles of contingency management in particular, should inform the design, implementation and evaluation of social welfare policy. A brief sketch of these principles is presented next.

BASIC PRINCIPLES OF CONTINGENCY MANAGEMENT

The field of behavior analysis addresses the role by which various learning processes affect our actions. The three major learning mechanisms studied include those of respondent conditioning, operant conditioning, and observational learning or imitation. Debate continues about the distinctions among respondent, operant and observational learning, and these processes may eventually be subsumed under a grand unified theory of behavior change, but they will likely be considered differing processes for the foreseeable future. Other mechanisms have their behavioral effects (genetics, physiology, drugs, deprivation states, etc.) but these are usually the subject matter of other disciplines.

For the purposes of this chapter, the most salient learning processes relevant to the design of social welfare policy would seem to be those of operant learning, a category which itself can be subdivided into two distinct mechanisms of behavior change—contingency-shaping and rule governance. Contingency-shaped behavior occurs when a person directly, relatively immediately, and personally experiences the consequences of his or her actions. Rule-governed behavior involves the provision of *descriptions* of contingencies that are in effect, rather than direct contact with such contingencies. Laws, social policies, regulations, instructions, and so forth are examples of such rules. As Skinner pointed out:

1. Rules can be learned much more quickly than the behavior shaped by the contingencies that the rules describe.
2. Rules make it easier to profit from similarities between contingencies.
3. Rules are particularly valuable when contingencies are complex or unclear. (1974, p. 125)

The following of rules (or policies) is itself shaped by prior contingencies associated with adherence or disobedience to rules. Most adults have a repertoire of generalized rule-following, akin to our abilities in generalized imitation. Much of the literature on rule-governed behavior has focused on the establishment of self-rules and of rule-following on an individual scale (e.g., Hayes, 1989; Riegler & Baer, 1989). I believe that extending these principles to social policy holds promise for developing a more complete understanding of policy and law as instances of rule-governance, not direct contingency-shaping.

Positive Reinforcement

If a stimulus is presented after a particular behavior and that behavior is observed to be strengthened or to increase in the future, the operation is called positive reinforcement. Loosely speaking, positive reinforcement could be called the use of rewards. Many (but too few) social welfare policies rely on positively reinforcing contingencies in the furtherance of some social end. When I was a child growing up in Canada in the 1950s, for example, my parents received a so-called "baby-bonus" each month—a check for $15 to $20—from the Canadian government. The more children Canadian citizens had, the more money they received each month! At the time, the Canadian government was interested in promoting population growth, hence this policy. Because of the time lag between the act of conception and receipt of the money, it is technically incorrect to call this type of policy an instance of positive reinforcement. It does, however, represent the contrived manipulation of contingencies, removed from behavior, to promote socially desired behavior. To the extent that citizens engaged in more frequent or stronger acts of unprotected connubial relations, the baby bonus can be legitimately construed as making use of the principles of rule-governed behavior and contingencies of reinforcement.

A more contemporary example is the proposal considered by the state legislature of Kansas to offer a payment of $500 to any mother on welfare who uses the Norplant contraceptive, a subcutaneous birth control drug that prevents pregnancy for up to 5 years. The proposal called for the state to pay for the insertion of the drug and for annual health checkups. The women would also have received an additional $50 for every year the medication remained in place (see Lewin, 1991). Recently, the state of Rhode Island began a program of providing full scholarships at state colleges for low-income students who remain in school, pass all their courses, remain drug free and do not become pregnant or get in trouble with the law. Called the Rhode Island Children's Crusade, this program begins in the third grade. Tutors and mentors are provided and the state monitors report cards in later school years ("Full Scholarships," 1989). Charles Catania, director of the Chicago Bureau of Community Health, enrolls parents in lotteries wherein they can win automobiles or bicycles in return for bringing their children in for immunizations ("Gimmicks Used," 1988).

Private health care providers are also joining the positive reinforcement bandwagon. One program, called the Prudential Health Care Plan, provides health care to more than 45,000 Medicaid recipients living in Baltimore. Low-income pregnant women are given an incentive to attend prenatal education and care classes—they receive $10 every time they show up for a scheduled appointment. The program, which costs about

$6,000 a month, has resulted in missed appointments dropping from about 60% to less than 20% (Kolata, 1994). One consequence attributed to the Prudential program is a considerable reduction in average lengths of stays in newborn intensive care units. The widespread use of state-sponsored lotteries is another example of using positive reinforcers and contingency-management techniques with great efficacy to raise funds for social programs.

Negative Reinforcement

If a stimulus is removed following the occurrence of some behavior, and the future probability of that behavior is strengthened, the operation is labeled negative reinforcement, or in lay language, as "relief." An example of a social welfare policy that uses principles of negative reinforcement would be one that exempts a portion of a wage earner's income from taxation in return for that wage earner engaging in certain desired behaviors. For example, legislation has been considered by the U. S. Congress that would allow a $3,000 tax deduction for the expenses incurred by potential parents adopting a handicapped or older child. A related bill would reimburse federal employees an additional $2,000 for adoption-related expenses, above and beyond the tax deduction (Devroy, 1989). As this chapter was going to press, the U.S. Congress passed legislation authorizing a tax credit of $5,000 to couples who adopt a chid. This tax credit can be seen as negatively reinforcing adoptions by providing some relief from aversive taxation. This assumes, of course that adoptions actually do increase as a result of this new social policy.

An article in *Time* magazine provided several other illustrations, such as: "For years corporations have helped meet blood shortages by rewarding employees who roll up their sleeves with extra time off" (Gorman, 1994, p. 51). Allowing time off from work (assuming work is mildly aversive) is consistent with the principle of strengthening behavior by the contingent removal of aversive states or stimuli. The use of enterprise zones—areas that attract companies to locate within inner cities by granting considerable tax concessions—or the sale of tax-free municipal bonds to raise revenue for public works are other examples of using negative reinforcement principles in the design of policy.

Positive Punishment

Punishment contingencies are employed far more often in the development of social welfare policy than are reinforcing ones, especially in the field of criminal justice. If a behavior is followed by a consequence that is presented, and the behavior declines in strength, this operation is called positive punishment. If a person who is released from jail or completes some community service sentence is deterred from recommitting crimes, then criminal behavior may be said to have been positively punished. It is positive in the sense that something unpleasant—jail or imposed labor—is presented and punishment in that behavior is weakened. Punitive consequences are effective to the extent that they can be continuously enforced. But if the chances are that committing a crime has a high probability of a short-term gain (e.g., money) and a low probability of a long-term aversive outcome (e.g., prison), punishment contingencies are not likely to be extremely effective.

Negative Punishment

If a stimulus is removed following the occurrence of a behavior, and the future likelihood of that behavior decreases, the operation is called negative punishment. This concept is loosely equated with the use of the term *fines*. This operation seems to be a favored option for policymakers designing contingencies to promote some social goal. If a particular behavior is deemed undesirable, fines are imposed on those whom engage in that behavior. For example, in an effort to reduce the number of high school dropouts in Wisconsin, the state instituted the policy of cutting welfare payments to the parents of truants. This so-called "Learnfare" program directly links welfare benefits with high school attendance records (Moses, 1991). Similar policies involving what looks like negative punishment contingencies are associated with "no pass, no play" and "no pass, no drive" programs, where in the former case the failing student is not permitted to engage in extracurricular activities (e.g., football), and in the latter case high school dropouts must relinquish their driver's license.

Before its recent political dissolution, Yugoslavia attempted to lower the birthrate of its ethnic minority Albanians by eliminating state living allowances to families with more than two children ("Population," 1989). Yet, another example would be the mother on welfare who stands to lose her benefits if her boyfriend moves in with her. If, as a result of this policy, the woman does not allow her boyfriend to move in, principles of negative punishment have exerted their influence. Again, it is important to recognize that some people may not come into contact with the contingencies at all (the mother on welfare never allows a boyfriend to move in; thus, her benefits are never at risk). It is clear, then, that the operations at work here, are more those of rule-governed behavior than those of contingency-shaped behavior.

Extinction

In the use of extinction procedures, it is important to determine what consequences are maintaining a target behavior and then arrange for such contingencies to be halted. If the consequences have been completely and correctly identified, the behavior will decline over time and, perhaps, cease entirely. For example, an individual playing a slot machine typically is reinforced to pull the lever after putting in coins, because the machine "returns" the coins on an irregular basis. If a given machine stopped providing *any* returns, the individual would eventually stop playing (at least at that machine). If it could be arranged that the gambler would never again win at slot machines—ever, anywhere—it is likely that he or she would give up on slot machines entirely.

The discontinuance of subsidies that results in a reduction in certain behaviors is an example of social welfare policy via extinction. If Canada stopped its baby bonus, and the birthrate declined, then extinction would have occurred. If the tax deduction currently permitted on mortgage interest was prohibited, and the purchase of homes declined, or if the federal government stopped subsidizing tobacco farmers, and the planting of tobacco declined, again extinction procedures could be said to have been in operation. The principle is simple: Determine what governmental reinforcers are maintaining a behavior that is targeted for reduction (recognizing that these policies exert their influence via rule-goverance rather than direct contingency-shaping) and discontinue those reinforcers (typically subsidies or tax exemptions).

Summary

There are a number of lessons to be learned from the behavioral examination of social welfare programs. They include:

1. Social welfare policy (like all public policy) is a crude form of contingency management.
2. Effective contingency management makes optimal use of the principles of rule-governed behavior. There are similarities and differences between rule-governed behavior and behavior shaped by immediate consequences.
3. Whenever possible, effective welfare policies should use reinforcing contingencies rather than punishing ones. This is both a pragmatic and a value-based recommendation.
4. Too often, welfare policies inadvertently establish incentives for long-term dysfunctional or dependent behavior.
5. Welfare policies should be empirically evaluated in demonstration projects before being widely implemented. The design and implementation of welfare policies should be empirically based; they should not be approached solely from rational or political perspectives.

THE ETHICS OF SOCIAL WELFARE POLICY:
ENTITLEMENTS VERSUS CONTINGENCIES

The field of ethics may seem far removed from that of behavior analysis, yet discussions of social welfare policy often turn on what is deemed fair or ethical. In fact, behaviorism (itself a philosophy of science) has long been concerned with broader philosophical issues such as values and ethics (as well as epistemology, ontology, free will, verbal behavior, private events, etc.; see Thyer, in press). More than 20 years ago, B. F. Skinner published an essay titled "The Ethics of Helping People" (see chapter 3, this volume). The concepts of values and ethics have themselves received considerable attention in this regard (e.g., Graham, 1977; Vargas, 1975; Waller, 1982; Wottschaefer, 1980), so Skinner's treatment of the topic should not come as a surprise. Indeed, the entire field of behavior analysis is premised on the notion that it is a good thing to promote the good life for individuals in society (witness this book). Behaviorism, as a philosophical field, is constructed by living, breathing people—individuals with families and practical concerns—and the treatment of what constitutes ethical comportment can be seen as an essential element in the behavioral enterprise.

What Skinner chided society for is confusing the provision of goods to others on the basis of their needs or expressed wants, with the provision of actual assistance. In part, what we see is a clash between the *entitlement* perspective versus the *contingency* perspective. The *Social Work Dictionary* defines entitlements as "government-sponsored benefits of cash, goods, or services that are due to all people who belong to a specified class" (Barker, 1995, p. 121). By definition, the benefits of an entitlement program are allocated on a noncontingent basis. One need not engage in constructive behavior to receive such benefits. Skinner suggested that this is ill-advised. If no reinforcer for productive behavior is included in a policy or program, it is not surprising that such a policy would result in low rates of productivity. In this sense, productivity would refer to obtaining employment, earning money, or otherwise making reasonable efforts to provide for one's self and one's family to receive benefits.

Skinner cautioned that human service agencies providing *noncontingent* benefits (money, goods, and services) could also be producing two unintended consequences: passivity and dependence. My office dictionary defines *help* as "to make things easier or better for [a person]." The noncontingent provision of entitlements may in fact *not* constitute true help unless things do become easier or better for the recipient. Much of this is obvious. Although few would advocate that money should be given to destitute persons who actively use drugs, most would agree that small children should be entitled in principle to noncontingent food and other conditions of a minimally acceptable life. Shouldn't free health care for the indigent (i.e., Medicaid) be given noncontingently? What should society expect from the impoverished in return for free health insurance? These are knotty issues, and the delineation of what would constitute functional contingency arrangements between benefits and recipients' efforts should not be an armchair exercise, no matter how rational. In keeping with the overall theme of this book, what is likely to prove most useful are actual behavior analytic investigations. Pilot studies and demonstration projects (local or state) that are carefully evaluated in terms of short- and long-term effects are needed, and programs or policies should only be implemented on a larger scale (e.g., nationwide) after convincing evidence has accrued of their merits.

I highly recommend a recent book by Theodore Caplow (1994) titled *Perverse Incentives: The Neglect of Social Technology in the Public Sector* as one example of a contingency analysis of social and public policies. In that book, Caplow wrote:

> Most of them [legislators] did not have accurate pictures of the behavior they were trying to change or the context in which that behavior occurred. Consequently, they had no clear idea of how a given change in the rules of the game might influence the actions of the players . . . . [W]hen they infused new federal or state money into an existing system, they seldom stopped to consider how it might effect [*sic*] the existing price structure, or the relative power of professionals and clients, or whether it might offer irresistable opportunities for cheating and stealing . . . . Above all, they never really tried to see the system from the standpoint of the people in the system—welfare mothers, high school teachers, drug dealers, physicians, lawyers. Flying blind as they did, they inadvertently created perverse incentives. The welfare mothers were given good reasons to bear more children, the drug dealers to recruit new customers, the physicians to double their fees, the lawyers to sue and sue . . . . It was, and is, the custom of this country to evaluate social programs by the goodness of their intentions not the goodness of their results. Because there is so little concern with results, it is not customary for legislators and reformers to set specific goals. (Caplow, 1994, pp. 2–3)

A somewhat earlier and more authoritative book contained many of the same conclusions: "They rewarded me evil for good to the spoiling of my soul" (Psalms, 35:12), and "that which should have been for their welfare, let it become a trap" (Psalms, 69:22). In Skinner's analysis,

> the question is not who should have how much of what but, rather, how they are to get what they have . . . . What they are suffering from is a world in which their behavior is not positively reinforced . . . . The "good life" is not a world in which people *have* what they need; it is one in which the things they need figure as reinforcers in effective contingencies. (pp. 65 & 69, this volume)

It is difficult to reconcile the behavior analytic approach and the entitlement perspective when it comes to providing for basic human needs. The former is predicated upon an individualized assessment of a person's behavioral repertoire (what they are capable of) and the delineation of reinforcers specific to that person, all arranged in a contingency management system that shapes successive approximations of productive behavior. This is directed to help take an individual from his or her present capabilities to some socially desirable goal (e.g., obtaining a quality job, developing effective parenting skills, ceasing to abuse drugs, to complete an educational program, etc.). In constrast, the entitlement approach does not provide much in the way of identifying individually effective reinforcers or specificity in one's current behavioral skills. It is difficult to envision a welfare system that would employ the skilled personnel necessary to develop individualized behavioral plans for the millions of citizens currently receiving entitlements. The fact that there are individuals with severe disabilities (intellectual, physical, behavioral) who may not be able to engage in "productive" behavior complicates the issue even further. As a civilized society, we have decided that noncontingent entitlements should be provided to such persons, and the imposition of behavioral requirements to earn benefits could be seen as cruel. A third issue is the simple availability of the necessities of life. For someone to obtain gainful employment, reinforcing jobs must be available. A single mother with young children may also need low-cost day care before she can even consider the possibility of looking for work, much less accept a position. When the social infrastructure necessary for success in finding and keeping a job, buying low-cost food, or obtaining health care is not in place, it is a cruel burden to make entitlements contingent on performing certain behaviors that have little chance of success.

Skinner was correct—the noncontingent provision of benefits to many persons may not help them in the long run. Integrating behavior analytic solutions may conflict with the philosophy of entitlement. Reconciling these two perspectives will require the best from psychologists and other human service professionals concerned with finding effective responses to serious social problems.

CONCLUSION

To the extent that social welfare policy consists of the design, implementation, and evaluation of contingencies of reinforcement and punishment to promote practices that ensure the survivability of the culture, behavior analysis has much to contribute. Conceptually, psychologists can assist in designing effective policies based on the empirical knowledge base of contingency management and rule-governed behavior. Methodologically, we can conduct rigorous evaluations of welfare policies. Henningfield and Higgins (1989) provided a fine example; they described the profound influence behavior analysis had in the Surgeon General's report on the health consequences of smoking. The conclusions reached were based on behavior analytic research and consistent with a behavioral conception of drug dependence and addiction. The majority of the discussion on the nonpharmacological treatments for smoking are behavioral, and the report recommended that use of nicotine gum is supplemented by behaviorally based smoking reduction programs. It would be marvelous to see similar behavioral influences in the realm of public welfare policy. There are a number of political philosophies (e.g., liberalism, conservatism, socialism) that influence the policy development process, but social welfare policy generally seems to lack a comprehensive theory of behavior change. Behavior analysis would seem to be a viable candidate to fill this conceptual lacunae.

I'll close with prescient quote from a book published in 1928 by Robert Kelso called *The Science of Public Welfare*:

> The new sciences afford us a better understanding of *causes and consequences* [italics added] in human affairs. It remains only to continue our research and to apply sensibly the knowledge we already have. (p. 421)

REFERENCES

Azrin, N., Flores, T., & Kaplan, S. J. (1975). Job-finding club: A group-assisted program for obtaining employment. *Behaviour Research and Therapy, 13*, 17–27.

Barker, R. (Ed.). (1995). *The social work dictionary* (3rd ed.). Washington, DC: National Association of Social Workers.

Baumheier, E., & Schorr, A. (1977). Social policy. In R. Morris, (Ed.). *Encyclopedia of social work* (pp. 1453–1462). Washington, DC: National Association of Social Workers.

Burgess, R., & Bushnell, D. (Eds.). (1969). *Behavioral sociology: Towards the experimental analysis of social process*. New York: Columbia University Press.

Caplow, T. (1994). *Perverse incentives: The neglect of social technology in the public sector*. Westport, CT: Praeger.

Devroy, A. (1989, September 14). Bush fulfills promise on adoption legislation. *The Washington Post*, p. A7.

DiNitto, D. (1983). Time series analysis: An application to social welfare policy. *Journal of Applied Behavioral Science, 19*, 507–518.

Dinsmoor, J. (1992). Setting the record straight: The social views of B. F. Skinner. *American Psychologist, 47*, 1454–1463.

Eckholm, E. (1992, July 26). Solutions on welfare: They all cost money. *The New York Times*, pp. 1, 12.

Fawcett, S. B., Bernstein, G. S., Czyzewski, M. J., Greene, B. F., Hannah, G. T., Iwata, B. A., Jason, L. A., Mathews, R. M., Morris, E. K., Otis-Wilborn, A., Seekins, T., & Winett, R. A. (1988). Behavior analysis and public policy. *The Behavior Analyst, 11*, 11–25.

Full scholarships proposed for poor. (1989, September 3). *The New York Times*, p. 12.

Gambrill, E. (1989). Behavioral family therapy with child abuse and neglect. In B. A. Thyer (Ed.). *Behavioral family therapy* (pp. 79–101). Springfield, IL: Charles C. Thomas.

Gimmicks used to lure youths to vaccinations. (1988, March 20). *The New York Times*, p. 27.

Gorman, C. (1994, May 16). Dollars for deeds: How do you keep students from getting pregnant or motivate students to make the grade? Offer them cash. *Time*, p. 51.

Graham, G. (1977). On what is good: A study of B. F. Skinner's operant behaviorist viewpoint. *Behaviorism, 5*, 97–112.

Greene, B. F., Norman, K. R., Searle, M., Daniels, M., & Lubeck, R. C. (1995). Child abuse and neglect by parents with disabilities: A tale of two families. *Journal of Applied Behavior Analysis, 28*, 417–434.

Hayes, S. C. (Ed.). (1989). *Rule-governed behavior*. New York: Plenum.

Heffernan, W. J. (1992). *Social welfare policy*. New York: Longman.

Henningfield, J. E., & Higgins, S. T. (1989). The influence of behavior analysis on the Surgeon General's report, "The health consequences of smoking: Nicotine addiction" *The Behavior Analyst, 12*, 99–101.

Howing, P. T., Wodarski, J. S., Gaudin, J. M., & Kurtz, P. D. (1989). Effective interventions to ameliorate the incidence of child maltreatment: The empirical base. *Social Work, 34*, 330–338.

Hursh, S. R. (1984). Behavioral economics. *Journal of the Experimental Analysis of Behavior, 42*, 435–452.

Isaacs, C. D. (1982). Treatment of child abuse: A review of the behavioral interventions. *Journal of Applied Behavior Analysis, 15*, 273–294.

Jones, R. J., & Azrin, N. H. (1973). An experimental application of a social reinforcement approach to the problem of job-finding. *Journal of Applied Behavior Analysis, 6*, 345–353.

Kagel, J. H., & Winkler, R. C. (1972). Behavior economics: Areas of cooperative research between economics and applied behavioral analysis. *Journal of Applied Behavior Analysis, 5*, 335–342.

Kariel, H. S. (1967). The political relevance of behavioral and existential psychology. *American Political Science Review, 61*, 334–342.

Kelso, R. W. (1928). *The science of public welfare*. New York: Henry Holt.

Kolata, G. (1994, May 4). Clinic entices patients by paying them $10 a visit. *The New York Times*, p. B8.

Kunkel, J. H. (1983). The behavioral-societal approach to social problems. *Behaviorists for Social Action Journal*, 4(1), 8–11.

Lamal, P. A. (1984). Contingency management in the People's Republic of China. *The Behavior Analyst*, 7, 121–130.

Lewin, T. (1991, February 9). A plan to pay welfare mothers for birth control. *The New York Times*, p. A8.

Malott, R. W. (1988). Rule-governed behavior and behavioral anthropology. *The Behavior Analyst*, 11, 181–203.

Marsh, J. C. (1981). Combining time series with interviews: Evaluating the effectiveness of a sexual assault law. In R. F. Conner (Ed.). *Methodological advances in evaluation research* (pp. 93–108). Beverly Hills, CA: Sage.

Meinhold, P. M., & Mulick, J. A. (1990). Counter-habilitative contingencies in institutions for people with mental retardation: Ecological and regulatory influences. *Mental Retardation*, 28, 67–75.

Moses, S. (1991, February). Incentive programs earn mixed grades. *The APA Monitor*, pp. 42–43.

Mulick, J. A., & Meinhold, P. M. (1992). Analyzing the impact of regulations on residential ecology. *Mental Retardation*, 30, 151–161.

Ozawa, M. N. (1988). Welfare policies and illegitimate birth rates among adolescents: Analysis of state by state data. *Social Work Research and Abstracts*, 25(1), 5–11.

Population. (December, 1989). *World Press Review*, p. 4.

Presthus, R. (1965). *Behavioral approaches to public administration*. University, AL: University of Alabama Press.

Riegler, H. C., & Baer, D. M. (1989). A developmental analysis of rule-following. *Advances in child development and behavior*, 21, 191–219.

Skinner, B. F. (1969). *Contingencies of reinforcement: A theoretical analysis*. New York: Appleton-Century-Crofts.

Skinner, B. F. (1972). *Cumulative record: A selection of papers* (3rd ed.). New York: Appleton-Century-Crofts.

Skinner, B. F. (1974). *About behaviorism*. New York: Knopf.

Skinner, B. F. (1978). *Reflections on behaviorism and society*. New York: Appleton-Century-Crofts.

Skinner, B. F. (1979). Interview with B. F. Skinner. *Behaviorists for Social Action Journal*, 2(1), 47–52.

Task Force on Public Policy, Association for Behavior Analysis. (1988). Recommendations of the Task Force on Public Policy. *The Behavior Analyst*, 11, 27–32.

Thyer, B. A. (in press). *The philosophical foundations of behaviorism*. Dordrecht, The Netherlands: Kluwer Academic Publishers.

Tropman, J. (1984). *Policy management in the human services*. New York: Columbia University Press.

Vargas, E. A. (1975). Rights: A behavioristic analysis. *Behaviorism, 3,* 178–191.

Wahlke, J. C. (1979). Pre-behavioralism in political science. *American Political Science Review, 73,* 9–31.

Waller, B. (1982). Value conflict in a Skinnerian analysis. *Behaviorism, 7,* 25–34.

Whidden, B. (1991, March 4). Fed rules promote slide into poverty, AHA director says. *Athens Banner Herald,* pp. 1, 10.

Wottschaefer, W. A. (1980). Skinner's science of values. *Behaviorism, 8,* 99–112.

3

THE ETHICS OF HELPING PEOPLE

B. F. SKINNER

We sometimes act for the good of others. We feed the hungry, clothe the naked, and heal the sick. We say that we care for them, provide for their needs, do good to them, help them. Our behavior often has unforeseen consequences which need to be taken into account.

We presumably help people in part for reasons that concern the survival of the species. Maternal behavior is a kind of help which is either part of an organism's genetic equipment or which is quickly acquired because of a genetic susceptibility to reinforcement; it is obviously important for survival. The human species is, presumably, more likely to survive if people generally help each other or are naturally reinforced by signs that they have done so. Something of the sort may contribute to the behavioral disposition which is part of what we call love or compassion.

It is more obvious that we learn to help or do good and that we learn because of the consequences which follow. We sometimes help because we find the helplessness of others aversive. We help those who help us in return, and we stop doing so when they stop—when, as we say, they are ungrateful. We often fail to help those who are too weak to reciprocate, or to protest effectively when we fail to help. The very young, the aged,

From B. F. Skinner (1975). The ethics of helping people. *Criminal Law Bulletin, 11*, 623–636.

the infirm, the retarded, and the psychotic are classic examples of people who often have been not only not helped but positively mistreated.

We may also help others because in doing so we further the survival of the group to which we belong. A social environment (a "culture") may induce us to give help even though we gain nothing directly from the advantage for the group. Thus, we may be a Good Samaritan at some personal sacrifice, and the group supplies overriding reasons for doing so with practices which have been selected simply because they have contributed to its survival. The group plays such a role when it steps in to guarantee adequate care for the very young, the aged, the infirm, the retarded, and the psychotic. There are few, if any, behavioral processes which provide for such care in the absence of a disposing social environment, with the possible exception of such genetic consideration as the care of the very young.

The sanctions arranged by a group are often treated in a different way. They are "justified" as defending individual *rights*, as guaranteeing that people shall get what they deserve or what is fair or just. It was perhaps easiest to justify helping those who were most in need of help, but, in many cultures, people are now said to have the right not only to life, liberty, and the pursuit of happiness, but to a share in the common wealth. "To each according to his [or her] need" was St. Augustine's program before it was Karl Marx's, and it is still a program, rather than an achievement. But it suggests the extent to which groups are now engaged in the business of making sure their members help each other. The program is not without problems of an ethical nature. In solving them, all the consequences of an act of help must be considered. The following discussion deals with certain possibly relevant behavioral processes.

To begin with a very simple example, we may not really help others by doing things for them. This is often the case when they are learning to do things for themselves. We watch a child tying a shoelace, grow jittery, and to escape from our jitteriness, we "help" the child tie the lace. In doing so, we destroy one chance to learn to tie shoelaces. Comenius made the point nearly 400 years ago when he said that "the more the teacher teaches, the less the student learns." The metaphor of "communication," or the transmission and receipt of information, is defective at just this point. We ask students to read a text and assume that they then know what they have read. Effective communication, however, must provide for the so-called acquisition of knowledge, meaning, or information. A traditional method has been to repeat what is said, as in a verbose text. However, new methods in which textual help is progressively withdrawn have emerged in the field of programmed instruction. The aim is to give as little help as possible when readers are saying things for themselves.

By giving too much help, we postpone the acquisition of effective behavior and perpetuate the need for help. The effect is crucial in the very profession of helping—in counseling and psychotherapy. Therapists, like teachers, must plan their withdrawal from the lives of their clients. One has most effectively helped others when one can stop helping them altogether.

More serious unanticipated effects of the good we do to others often arise because "goods" function as "reinforcers." It has long been known that behavior is affected by certain kinds of consequences. That is why rewards and punishments are such well-established social measures. The Utilitarians proposed to quantify consequences in terms of pleasure and pain, for social purposes. For example, the pleasure enjoyed as the reward of unethical or illegal behavior was to be offset by a corresponding amount of pain administered as punishment. Both rewards and punishments were regarded as compensation; and when they were fairly balanced, the ethical account was closed.

The formulation neglected certain contingent relations between behavior and its consequences which were recognized by the American psychologist Edward I. Thorndike in his *Law of Effect*. By "effects" he also meant feelings, but they were more than compensation; they strengthened the connection between behavior and the situation in which it occurred. The strengthening effect of reinforcement has been an important consideration in the experimental analysis of operant behavior. Extremely complex environments are constructed in which reinforcing consequences are contingent upon both behavior and the setting in which it occurs; and the effect upon the probability that a given instance of behavior will occur upon a given occasion is analyzed.

The fact that strength in the sense of probability of occurrence is an important property of behavior has come to be understood only very slowly. With respect to the present issue, an important point is that strength is not related in any simple way to quantity of reinforcers and, therefore, not in any simple way to the help we give or the good we do to others, as these are traditionally evaluated. We need to consider the possibility that strength of behavior is more important than the receipt or possession of goods.

Those who are in a position to help others by giving them things can use the things as contingent reinforcers. This is, of course, the point of behavior modification. The right to change the behavior of others in this way has been challenged on ethical grounds, as we shall see, and Carl Rogers has suggested that the help given by the therapist (and one could also say teacher or friend) should be made carefully *non*contingent on the behavior of the recipient. Unfortunately, reinforcers are always temporally contingent on some behavior, and they are effective, even though there is no causal connection. Adventitious reinforcements build superstitions. For example, whatever people are doing just before rain falls at the end of a drought, they are more likely to do again in another drought. And since the more conspicuous their behavior, the more effective the adventitious contingencies, a ritual such as a rain dance may emerge, and in turn a myth to explain it—for example, as the propitiation of a giver of rain. The grace of God was defined by St. Paul as noncontingent upon works—"for if by works, then grace is no longer grace," and Rogers is proposing essentially that therapeutic help should have this divine quality. But there are behavioral processes which cannot be denied, and offerings and sacrifices to the Giver of Help are an important problem for the therapist.

Unanticipated consequences which follow when we are said to give people help can be much more serious. In an environment in which such things as food, shelter, and safety are guaranteed as rights, these things are less likely to serve as reinforcers. The recipients of bountiful help are rather in the position of those who live in a benign climate or possess great wealth. They are not strongly deprived or aversively stimulated and, hence, not subject to certain kinds of reinforcement. Some important forms of behavior are never acquired or, if they have been acquired, are no longer exhibited. But such people do not simply do nothing; instead, they come under the control of lesser reinforcers. No objection is likely to be raised to the classic examples found in art, music, literature, and scientific exploration. Individuals are encouraged to devote themselves to these fields through the kind of help called patronage or grants-in-aid. But these reinforcing consequences are, unfortunately, seldom as immediate or as personally effective as others, which have long given the leisure classes a special character. Sweets remain reinforcing to the nonhungry; alcohol and drugs have anomalous reinforcing effects; sexual reinforcement survives because we do not leave satiation to others; certain special schedules of reinforcement (such as those basic to all gambling devices) make weak reinforcers effective; and just the spectacle of other people living seriously or dangerously is often reinforcing, as in films or television.

These are the reinforcers, rather than those of art, music, literature, and science, which are more likely to be given free play by any help which preempts the serious business of life, and there is little to be said for them. Some are stultifying, and none leads to the full development of the human genetic potential. One's behavior may be reinforced for a lifetime in these ways and yet undergo almost no important change, and when these alternative reinforcers lose their power or are suppressed by societal rules, behavior falls to a very low ebb. We call the child who has been given excessive help "spoiled," and the term applies as well to the adult.

Organisms are at least as strongly disposed to take goods away from others as to supply them in the form of help, particularly when unmerited, and the disposition may serve as a natural corrective to excessive help. (We are inclined to speak of the feeling of compassion that accompanies helping others and the feeling of resentment that accompanies taking goods away from those who have not worked for them, but it is the tendencies to act which are involved here.) Aggressive behavior offsets or corrects compassionate help and may have survival value, for either species or group, if it leads to a more equitable distribution of goods, but *the question is not who should have how much of what but, rather, how they are to get what they have.*

The plight of those whose behavior is not often reinforced—because others do things for them, or because they have not learned to do things for themselves, or because they are given the things their behavior would otherwise be reinforced by—is familiar enough. Traditionally, their behavior is attributed to feelings and states of mind. Such people are said to lack initiative, to show little strength of character, to have weak wills, to lack spiritual strength, or to have egos that are not well developed. They are said to suffer from abulia (lack of will), acedia (spiritual torpor), apathy (lack of feeling), or boredom. *What they are suffering from is a world in which their behavior is not positively reinforced.*

It is easy to dismiss that statement as the idée fixe of a behavioral analyst, but strength of behavior, in the sense of the probability that behavior will occur, is a basic aspect of human nature. It is to be attributed to external contingencies of reinforcement, rather than internal deficiencies. Hence, it is an aspect about which something can be done. Something *is* being done by those who understand the important of contingencies of reinforcement.

A good example of the neglect of relevant aspects of the environment is to be found in analyses of incentive conditions in modern industry (Heilbroner, 1975). The "degradation of labor" is said to have begun with the systematic destruction of craft skills. Workers move from craft to industrial conditions for many reasons. Work is usually easier and, because a task is divided among many workers, each share is simpler and can be learned during a briefer apprenticeship. Workers produce more in less time and can be paid more. Yet something has been lost. Many interpretations have appealed to feelings and states of mind: The worker has come to think of himself as a cog in a machine; he is no longer the possessor of the "accumulated knowledge of the materials and processes by which production is accomplished"; work has been reduced to "a series of bodily movements entirely devoid of meaning"; the worker is separated ("alienated") from the product of his labor; and so on. But why is this degrading? It is true that work on a production line is probably faster than the work of a craftsman without a deadline. Because it has been reduced in scope, it is also necessarily more repetitious and, hence, likely to yield the "fatigue of repeatedly doing the same thing" (not to be confused with physical exhaustion). Yet the gambler "works" fast and repetitiously and calls his life exciting; and the craftsman uses machines to save labor when he can and often works with a time-and-motion efficiency that an industrial engineer would give much to duplicate.

The important difference lies in the contingencies of reinforcement. It is often supposed that industrial workers work to get a reward, rather than avoid punishment. But as Marx and others have noted, they work because to do anything else would be to lose a standard of living maintained by their wages. They work under the eye of a supervisor upon whose report their continued employment depends. They differ from slaves only in the nature of the "punishment" they receive for not working. They are subject to *negative* reinforcement, a condition obscured by the uncritical use of the term reward.

The craftsman's behavior, in contrast, is reinforced at every stage by those conditioned reinforcers called signs of progress. A particular task may take a day, a week, a month, or a year, but almost every act produces something which will form part of the whole and is, therefore, *positively* reinforcing. It is this condition of "nondegrading" work which has been destroyed by industrialization, and some of those concerned with incentive conditions have used the principles of behavior modification to restore it.

A similar correction needs to be made to offset the unwanted by-products of helping others by supplying goods. Unfortunately it is difficult to see this and to act accordingly just because our behavior in helping others is determined to such a large extent by reciprocal reinforcement. Given a choice between receiving something gratis and the opportunity to work to get it, those whom we help are likely to choose the former, and they will therefore more abundantly reinforce our behavior when we give them things rather than the opportunity to work for things. It is in the long run that the advantage of getting, rather than possessing, makes itself felt, both by them and by us, and what happens in the long run does not often have much of an effect. What a person is said to deserve as a right is subject to a similar bias.

It is just at this point that behavior modification plays a unique role. The term needs careful definition. Behavior has been modified ever since it was modifiable—which is to say, from the beginning. Behavior is modified by the threat of the bully or of the nation with a nuclear stockpile, by incentive tax allowances, by advertising, by religious rituals, by state lotteries and other gambling enterprises, and, recently, by certain physiological measures and explicit Pavlovian conditioning. The term was introduced, however, to refer to certain applications of the experimental analysis of behavior, particularly through the arrangement of contingencies of positive reinforcement. Behavior modification in that sense helps people by arranging conditions under which they *get* things rather than by *giving* them things. That is its essential feature. And for that very reason, it was inevitable that there would be some conflict with traditional views of helping others—especially with principles of what was just or fair to be defended as the rights of the individual.

The issue first arose when behavior modification was used in institutional care. In many cultures, food, shelter, clothing, security, and possibly privacy have been made available to those who for any reason cannot otherwise obtain them. Homes for the very young, the aged, the infirm, and the retarded; hospitals for psychotics; and prisons are far from a benign world, but those who live in them, characteristically, have little reason to work for the basic reinforcers because the reinforcers have been guaranteed as rights. Most of the alternatives, such as gambling, sex, alcohol, and drugs, are not available (except surreptitiously in prisons). As a result, such people suffer all the ills of having nothing to do. Troublemaking may be unintentionally reinforced, and if possible they escape, but otherwise we say that their behavior tends to be marked by boredom, abulia, acedia, and apathy.

Behavior modification, properly defined as "the applied analysis of behavior," is precisely what is needed to correct this shortcoming of institutional life *because it is concerned with establishing effective contingencies of reinforcement*. Actual practices need not be described here, but the behavior modifier usually begins with a search for available reinforcers and then arranges especially clearcut contingencies—as with the use of tokens. Contingencies can be programmed to shape complex topographies and to bring behavior under the control of complex stimuli. For those who will eventually leave the institution, such a program is called educational, therapeutic, or rehabilitative. For those, who must remain, the goal is simply a "prosthetic" environment—an environment in which people behave in reasonably effective ways in spite of deficiencies, in which they take an active interest in life and begin to do for themselves what the institution previously did for them.

Whether we are concerned with education, therapy, and rehabilitation, or with the construction of a prosthetic environment, we need those reinforcers which have acquired special power in the evolution of the species. Yet they are the very things supplied in the act of helping or caring for people—the things guaranteed as rights. In order to make them contingent on behavior in an institutional setting, we must withhold them until the behavior occurs. The individual must, therefore, be deprived to some extent and, consequently, will appear to remain unhelped or to be denied certain rights. We cannot avoid this conflict so long as we continue to view help as providing goods rather than as arranging contingencies of reinforcement.

The conflict first came into the open in an attack upon operant reinforcement programs in mental hospitals. One set of proposed regulations contained the following:

> Deprivation is never to be used. No patient is to be deprived of expected goods and services and ordinary rights, including the free movement of his limbs, that he had before the program started. In addition [sic] deficit rewarding must be avoided; that is, rewards must not consist of the restoration of objects or privileges that were taken away from the patient or that he should have had to begin with. The ban against deficit rewarding includes the use of tokens to gain or regain such objects or privileges. (Lucero, Vail, Scherber, 1968 pp. 53–54)

The authors insist that they are concerned with the legitimacy of the rationale for using operant conditioning, but it is the rationale of rights which is at issue. Why have these things been guaranteed to the patient? What "should" patients have had to begin with? The mistake is to generalize from those who cannot help themselves to those who can. For the latter, a much more fundamental right—the right to live in a reinforcing environment—must be considered. If the function of an institution is education, therapy, or rehabilitation, all available resources should be used to speed the process, and the strong reinforcers are undoubtedly to be classified as such. For those who will never return to the world at large, a strongly reinforcing environment is equally important.

Under proper contingencies, many institutional people can engage in productive work, such as caring for themselves, keeping their quarters clean, and working in laundry, kitchen, or truck garden. But when these things have previously been done by paid personnel, suspicion falls on the motives of management. Should residents not be paid the same wages? One answer is that they should unless the contingencies are "therapeutic," but that raises the question of help in only a slightly different form. Residents are receiving help when their behavior is being reinforced in a prosthetic environment, though they are not necessarily being "cured." Especially when we consider the economics of institutional care, can there be any objection to the residents themselves producing all the goods and services it was once supposed to be necessary for others to give them?

At least one state has recognized the issue. A bill was recently passed in Iowa with the provision that:

> The administrator may require of any resident of the County Care Facility with the approval of a physician reasonable and moderate labor suited to the resident's age and bodily strength. Any income realized through the labor of a resident together with the receipts from oper-

ation of the County Farm if one is maintained shall be appropriate for use by the County Care Facility in such manner as the Board of Supervisors may direct (Behavioral Voice, undated).

The constitutionality of the bill is being questioned.

The so-called rehabilitation of the prisoner raises a special problem. Prisoners usually undergo very little useful change. They have been separated from society for the latter's protection or as punishment and are unable to help themselves only because they have been cut off from the usual means. The destructive changes which follow are well known. Some promising results have been obtained from the application of an experimental analysis of behavior—for example, in a project at the National Training School for Boys in Washington, DC (Cohen & Filipczak, 1971). Unfortunately, experiments of this sort have been confused with efforts to change prisoners with drugs or the more violent forms of aversive conditioning, and protests against the latter—for example, by the American Civil Liberties Union—have been extended without warrant to efforts to construct more sustaining prison environments.

Like everything else, operant conditioning can be misused. Management may solve some of its problems by arranging contingencies which suppress disruptive behavior and under which a child, a prisoner, or a psychotic may simply sit quietly and do little or nothing all day long. Even so, this may be better than achieving the same result through punishment, but both solutions may be challenged if nothing further is done. Much more can be done through the applied analysis of behavior when the problem is understood.

Some of the same issues arise in the world at large, where helping people takes on a much broader meaning. Very little has ever been achieved simply by supplying goods and services. Governments do not help their citizens by *giving* them order and security—that is the claim only of the police state; they help them by arranging environments in which they behave in orderly and mutually supportive ways. They do not defend the rights to life, liberty, and the pursuit of happiness as things which their citizens *possess*; they maintain environments in which people do not threaten the lives and political freedoms of one another. Schools and colleges do not *give* their students information, knowledge, or skills; they are environments in which students acquire informed and skillful behavior. The "good life" is not a world in which people *have* what they need; it is one in which the things they need figure as reinforcers in effective contingencies.

A case history will show how easily the basic issue is missed. After the Second World War, Denmark entered upon a program of "modern reformatory guidance" to raise the standard of living of the Eskimos of Greenland (Jensen, 1973). Thousands of construction workers were sent in to build modern houses and facilities. But the local industry, fishing, could not support these material standards, and an annual subsidy of many millions of dollars will now be needed—indefinitely—for the 50,000 inhabitants. The goods supplied are not contingent on productive behavior, and it is not surprising that a long-established, cooperative culture has broken down. Under the surface, there is said to be "an alarming chaos of human frustration." An antagonistic class society is developing. Good dyadic social relations have yielded to drunken brawls.

It means little to say that a high standard of living was "an artificial creation," that it can be made natural by giving each person a more direct influence in government, or that a "strategy of wholeness" is needed. The trouble is that certain basic contingencies of reinforcement have been destroyed. And it is difficult to see how they can ever be restored except by greatly increasing the behavioral repertories of the Eskimos or by sharply reducing their so-called standard of living. It will not be enough that the teams of construction workers are now to be followed by teams of social workers. The United States is repeating the experiment on a small scale on the island of Bikini, and it will be interesting to see whether the result is the same.

Even in the restricted sense of the applied analysis of behavior, behavior modification has grown with astonishing speed and much of that growth has been uncharted and chaotic. Practitioners have ranged from scientists highly skilled in the basic analysis to laymen applying a few cookbook rules. But the accomplishments are too substantial to be dismissed—among them, programmed instruction and contingency management in the classroom, the design of prosthetic environments for the retarded and psychotic, personal and family counseling in ethical self-management, educational environments for juvenile delinquents, and new incentive systems in industry. In retrospect, much of this often seems to be simply a matter of common sense, but people have had common sense for thousands of years, and it has not helped them solve the basic problem. It has been too easy to put possession ahead of acquisition, and to miss the importance of strength of behavior and its relation to contingencies of reinforcement. In the classroom, hospital, factor, prison, home, and the world at large, the obvious fact is that some of the good things in life are in short supply. We are just beginning to see that a mere shortage is not what is causing trouble and that people will not necessarily be helped by increasing the supply. Behavior modification through the management of contingencies of reinforcement is a special way of helping people just because it is concerned with changing the probability that they will behave in given ways.

For just that reason, it is now under attack. A recent example is the report of the Ervin Committee, *Individual Rights and the Federal Role in*

Behavior Modification, based on a three-year investigation of federal support of a variety of programs. According to Senator Ervin, "The most serious threat posed by the technology of behavior modification is the power this technology gives one man to impose his views and values on another. . . . If our society is to remain free, one man must not be empowered to change another man's personality" ("Individual Rights and the Federal Role in Behavior Modification," No. 5270–026201). But individuals have always had the power to impose their views on others; the relevant behavioral processes were not recently invented. One of the greatest and certainly the most convenient of all reinforcers is money, and we have recently seen some extraordinary examples of its misuse. Why does the Ervin Committee not consider constitutional safeguards against the power which a person can amass by accumulating money? We have minimum wage laws and other laws restricting some uses of money, but we have no maximum wage laws restricting the extent to which money can be acquired for use. And money is only one of the more conspicuous instruments of control. Possibly, the experimental analysis of behavior will play its greatest role in forcing an examination of *all* the ways in which "one man can change another man's personality."

Like any other means of control—say, physical force—behavior modification should be supervised and restrained. The concept of the rights of the individual is concerned with that problem. Some traditional principles have emphasized freedom from coercive or punitive control, and they are as badly needed today as they have ever been. Other traditional principles have emphasized the possession of goods and services, and here a sweeping revision is needed. Neither a capitalist defense of private property nor a socialist program of state ownership as a means of equitable distribution takes into account the full scope of relevant behavioral processes.

It has been suggested that Gross National Product should be subordinated to Gross National Happiness in evaluating a culture, but nothing much would be gained if happiness were identified as a static condition of satisfaction derived from the possession of goods. Indeed, in that case, there would scarcely be a distinction. The greatest good of the greatest number may be the greatest bore, and the Utilitarians lost their case just because they neglected the reinforcing contingencies which build the condition we describe by saying that we are happy.

The intense current interest in ethical, moral, legal, and religious matters is no doubt largely a response to worsening world conditions. A burgeoning population forces us to take another look at birth control, abortion, and selective breeding. Increasing violence, as in bombings, hijacking, and political kidnappings, forces us to look again at legal sanctions, possibly reversing a humane trend against capital punishment. In addition, however, a surprising number of critical issues have to do with what is called helping people. "Aid" is a synonym of "help," and foreign aid raises many ethical, moral, and legal problems. In the name of aid, the United States has become one of the Zaharoffs of the last half of the twentieth century—one of the great munitions makers who were once held in utter contempt. In the name of aid, we rescue some of the starving peoples of the world while allowing others to die, and refuse to admit that we are practicing triage. With both military and nonmilitary "help," we have nearly destroyed Indochina. And so we begin again to ask to what extent the rich nations of the world are to help the poor, or, in domestic affairs, how far a government should go in increasing the help which its rich citizens must give to its poor?

But it is a mistake to turn again to certain earlier principles. For reasons which in themselves illustrate a powerful behavioral principle, we have grossly overemphasized the importance of simple possession. Neither happiness nor the survival of the group depends on the satisfaction derived from having things. And the most generous help may fail as ignominiously as the most aggressive despoliation. Something else is needed to achieve conditions under which human beings will show the productivity, the creativity, and the strength inherent in their genetic endowment and which are essentially to the survival of the species.

REFERENCES

Behavioral Voice. (n.d.). Center for Human Development, Drake University, Des Moines, Iowa. (The bill is called "The Redesignation of County Homes as County Care Facilities," HF6$_{59}$).

Cohen, H. L., & Filipczak, J. (1971). *A new learning environment*. San Francisco, CA: Jossey-Bass.

Heilbroner, R. (1975, January 23). [Review of the book *Labor and Monopoly Capital: The Degradation of Work in the Twentieth Century*]. *New York Review of Books*.

Jensen, B. (1973). Human reciprocity: An Arctic exemplification. *American Journal of Orthopsychiatry*, *43*, 477–458.

Lucero, R. J., Vail, D. J., & Scherber, J. (1968). Regulating operant-conditioning programs. *Hospital and Community Psychiatry*, *19*(2), 53–54.

Nozick, R. (1974). *Anarchy, state, and utopia*. New York: Basic Books.

Rawls, J. (1971). *A theory of justice*. Boston, MA: Harvard University Press.

II

CHANGE IN THE COMMUNITY

4

YOUTH VIOLENCE

MARK A. MATTAINI, JANET S. TWYMAN, WENDY CHIN, and
KYUNG NAM LEE

Many Americans literally fear for their lives on the streets, at home, at work, and at school. This fear is rooted in fact: 24,526 persons were victims of homicide in 1993 (Bureau of Justice Statistics, 1995); the National Crime Survey found that an estimated 6.5 million violent crimes occurred in 1992, not including homicide (Bureau of Justice Statistics, 1994). The United States experiences more violence than any other industrialized nation; homicide rates are far higher in this country than in any other industrialized nation (8.3 per 100,000 versus rates of about 1 to 2 in most European countries, as surveyed by the World Health Organization in the 1980s). Rates of other violent crimes are also substantially higher (more so the more serious the offense; Reiss & Roth, 1993a). There is a common perception that the rate of violent crime is steadily increasing; however, nationally this is not the case—the incidence of homicide was actually higher in the 1930s and 1970s. But in the largest U.S. cities, total violent crime has almost doubled since 1973 (Reiss & Roth, 1993a).

Violence perpetrated by and against youth is a particularly urgent social concern. The risk of victimization by violent crime peaks for both men and women between the ages 16 and 19 (Reiss & Roth, 1993a). Homicide is the leading cause of death for African American youth both male and female (American Psychological Association [APA], 1993). APA also reported that, in a study of first and second grade students in Wash-

75

ington, DC, 31% of the participants had witnessed shootings, and 39% had seen dead bodies. In another study, more than 90% of elementary-age children in New Orleans reported witnessing violent incidents; 70% of these crimes involved weapons (Groves, Zuckerman, Marans, & Cohen, 1993). The severity of youth violence has increased in recent years, in part because of the increased availability of firearms, with associated increases in lethality (Reiss & Roth, 1993a). In many urban areas in the United States, children routinely hear gunshots outside their homes at night. This chapter focuses in particular on acts of violence among inner-city youths, because of the high risk of injury, death, incarceration, and other sequelae of violent acts among this population. Note that the theoretical analyses are universal, however. All acts of youth violence among all cultural groups fit into the classes of violence to be discussed here, but there are often differences in terms of consequences and establishing operations that need to be explored to develop adequate responses.

Approximately 10% of the reported incidents of nonfatal violence against persons 12 and over occurred in school buildings or on school property (Bureau of Justice Statistics, 1992). Because students and school personnel constitute a relatively small proportion of persons 12 and over, and given the high likelihood of nonreporting among adolescents, school violence appears to be a particularly serious problem. Available data regarding school violence are limited and of uneven quality. A national survey commissioned by the Metropolitan Life Insurance Company, however, gives strong indication of how significant the problem is: Many children are afraid they will be victims of violence at school. Nearly a quarter of 3rd- to 12th-grade students nationally are worried about being hurt at or near school (Louis Harris and Associates, 1993). There is reason to believe that in some areas, the rate of school violence is much higher. New York City schools, for example, reported 1,981 serious incidents during the 1993–94 school year—an increase of 41% from the year before (a result due in part to improved reporting)—many of which involved violence (Division of School Safety, 1994). Because school success is crucial to life success, both incidents of actual violent behavior and the fear of violence may interfere with learning; thus, they are pressing issues.

Patterns of aggression and violence in youth often persist into adulthood (Dishion, Patterson, Stoolmiller, & Skinner, 1991; Farrington, 1989; Patterson, DeBaryshe, & Ramsey, 1989). Although most aggressive youth are not convicted of violent crimes in adulthood, both the risks associated with violent acts during adolescence and the possibility of continuing aggression (including battering and child abuse regardless of whether such acts result in criminal charges) are reasons for concern.

As is true for violence of other types, violence among youth is a heterogeneous problem. In this chapter, we focus primarily on violent acts committed by, and usually perpetrated on, youth. Occasionally, however, extensions to adult violence that emerge from the discussion will be briefly made. The material that follows begins with a brief examination of the increasingly popular biological explanations for violent acts and an alternative explanation based on the science of behavior analysis. This discussion will set the stage for a review of several representative violence prevention programs that are currently being implemented, followed by an elaboration of a research program we believe is called for to better understand violence as behavior. The core of this chapter then follows: a data-based conceptual behavior analysis of major functional classes of violent acts among youth and a discussion of the implications of these analyses for prevention and intervention efforts.

BIOBEHAVIORAL EXPLANATIONS OF VIOLENCE

Because violence is physical behavior, its physical processes could, and perhaps eventually will, be specified in biological terms. Biobehavioral theorists and researchers hope to find, at a minimum, genetic and physiological markers of violence, and perhaps even biological causes of violence. Many argue that a medical model comprising prevention, diagnosis, and treatment is the preferred approach (Gibbs, 1995). Violence, within this perspective, is viewed as being "maladaptive" and emitted by "abnormal (presumably) human subjects" (Mirsky & Siegel, 1994, p. 9). Mirsky & Siegel further stated that "it seems reasonable to hypothesize that humans who are engaging in maladaptive, violent behavior have some brain abnormality" (p. 79). Near the end of their review, however, they note that the links between human aggression and disordered brain mechanisms clearly have not yet been established.

Space limitations preclude full consideration of biobehavioral hypotheses; however, some comments are in order. First, there appears to be no possibility that genetic factors account for the rapid changes found in the societal incidence of violent behaviors, behaviors that vary far too quickly to be accounted for by allelic changes (Wilson & Herrnstein, 1985). Similarly, genetic and other biological variations among groups and nations cannot account for the tremendous differences across time and place in levels of violence. It also seems unlikely that brain disorders are distributed unequally enough to account for differential and rapidly changing incidence data. Although some persons apparently are biologically more or less prone to aggressive and violent acts, this must be a relatively universal phenomenon that some groups and cultures clearly manage better than others. Biobehavioral explanations for violent acts have an additional limitation: Existing data consistently suggest that biology can account for at best a very small, highly inconsistent proportion of the variance (Miczek, Mirsky, Carey, DeBold, & Raine, 1994).

The assumptions that most persons who commit acts of violence are abnormal and that violence cannot be understood in the same ways as other behaviors are also problematic. The most parsimonious approach to explaining violent actions is to try to understand them in the same way we do other behavior (except in cases of clear brain injury). Violent behavior is not primarily organized at a biological level, any more than, say, driving a car or writing a symphony is (although all rely on biological activity). Attempts to understand any of these repertoires through biological reductionism, therefore, are unlikely to capture the active causal factors adequately. Even biobehaviorists like Miczek et al. (1994) agree that violence is not a simple response to biological factors. For example, they state:

> In animals, testosterone (or its metabolites) has effects on the probability of aggressive responses to conspecifics or other environmental events. This is frequently referred to as an activational effect although, mechanistically, androgens are not stimulating aggressive behavior *in vacuo*; more accurately, they appear to be altering the response to aggression-provoking stimuli. (p. 6)

This kind of influence is an example of what behavior analysts call an *establishing operation*, a condition or event that establishes sensitivity to consequences and evokes behavior that produces those consequences. Note that these same authors go on to state that the effects in humans are more often the reverse; winning in an aggressive encounter appears to result in increases in testosterone. In other words, the biological/physiological effects occur as the result of environmental events.

On the other hand, there are biological factors that appear to be associated with increased risk, particularly exposure to environmental toxins (e.g., lead, in utero alcohol and cocaine). Such exposure may play a part in academic and peer-relations failures, two factors which appear to be part of a developmental trajectory toward aggression (Patterson, De-Baryshe, & Ramsey, 1989). There are also other areas where a biological analysis can contribute to our understanding of violence. There is, for example, strong evidence of different subclasses of aggressive behavior in other animals, for which there may be human analogues (supporting the underlying argument of this chapter that it is crucial to understand the multiple response classes that constitute violent topographies). Among cats, the most extensively researched group, there are two clear classes:

> Affective defense behavior may be classified as having aversive properties (such as those associated with fear), whereas predatory attack is associated with more positively reinforcing objectives such as the acquisition of food. (Mirsky & Siegel, 1994, p. 62)

The first is associated with a high level of physiological arousal, the second is not. Behaviorists would identify slight confusion in this last quote, as we do not view behavior as "having aversive properties"; rather, we would view the behavior as a response to an aversive situation. Nevertheless, Mirsky and Siegel appear to be differentiating here between aggressive behavior associated with negative reinforcement and that shaped by positive reinforcement, a distinction we see as basic and essential for the development of interventive strategies.

VIOLENCE IS BEHAVIOR

Violence is behavior. This apparently simple statement suggests the importance of applying what we know about behavior, especially about complex human behavior, to finding a solution to the problem of violence. As stated by the National Research Council, "the principal scientific goal is to understand violent behavior in terms of the same concepts that attempt to explain other human behavior" (Reiss & Roth, 1993a, p. 3). Although there is, of course, no single or simple cause of a multidetermined issue like violence, the science of behavior offers the potential for a theoretically consistent and coherent understanding of the available data and suggests testable strategies for preventive action.

The Need for Theory

The American Psychological Association (APA; 1993) and the National Research Council (Reiss & Roth, 1993a; 1993b) have reviewed the literature regarding what is known about violence. Both organizations noted the lack of a coherent theoretical framework for understanding violence and called for testing approaches derived from theories with strong empirical bases of support. The APA noted:

> Effective intervention programs share two primary characteristics: (a) they draw on the understanding of developmental and sociocultural risk factors leading to antisocial behavior; and (b) they use theory-based intervention strategies with known efficacy in changing behavior, tested program designs, and validated, objective measurement techniques to assess outcomes. (APA, 1993, pp. 53–54)

Violent behavior does not constitute a single response class. The topography of violent acts varies tremendously (e.g., threats, physical attack, the use of weapons, state-sponsored terrorism). The functions of violent behavior also vary widely, from obtaining desirable tangible items, to gaining social approval, to obtaining relief from unpleasant conditions. A search for universal causes or universally effective interventions is therefore likely to be futile. As an example, some violence prevention curricula used widely in school systems focus exclusively on teaching conflict resolution or anger management. As will be illustrated later in this chapter, however, some classes of violent acts involve conflict in the classic sense (a demand for immediate change followed by noncompliance; Patterson, 1975), but many others do not. Similarly, the emotional arousal we call anger accompanies some violent acts but not others, and its centrality in those which it is present also varies. The following analyses seek to clarify major classes of violent acts and offer guidance for developing responsive interventive strategies.

CURRENT APPROACHES AND PROGRAMS

A variety of youth violence prevention programs have been implemented, sometimes on a national scale, and generally with little or no evaluation (a common but deeply troubling pattern for educational innovations). Peer mediation, conflict resolution, and anger management programs are among the most common of these. Many are school-based because of the large captive audience available in schools. One problem with this approach is that it misses those who have dropped out as well as those who attend erratically; the evaluation done of the *Violence Prevention Curriculum for Adolescents*, for example, found that those most likely to be at risk for involvement in violent incidents were also likely to be absent for the posttest (DeJong, Spiro, Wilson-Brewer, Vince-Whitman, & Prothrow-Stith, n.d.).

A range of violence prevention programs have been proposed or initiated. The material that follows discusses several examples of clearly conceptualized programs that have been established.

Violence Prevention Curriculum for Adolescents

This curriculum was developed by Deborah Prothrow-Stith (1987), a psychiatrist whose interest in violence prevention emanated from her work to prevent suicide and homicide among 10th graders. The curriculum package includes a teacher's guide, student handouts, and a teacher-training video. In its most recent version, the package also includes a community awareness component developed to accompany the school-based program. The curriculum, conducted over 10 sessions, focuses almost exclusively on violence among peers. It aims to provide secondary school students with the skills, knowledge, and understanding that will enable them to act on behalf of themselves and others in nonviolent ways. The objective is to offer positive ways to deal with anger and arguments, viewed as the leading precipitants of homicide among adolescents. The curriculum views anger as a normal and potentially constructive emotion to which students need to learn to respond in healthy and nonviolent ways.

One unpublished evaluation of the *Violence Prevention Curriculum* has been conducted (DeJong et al., n.d.). The results suggested limited behavior change, with self-report data suggesting some change on one of seven measures. The National Research Council report viewed these results as disappointing, stating that "the results of this evaluation are not persuasive that this approach is helpful in reducing aggressive behavior by high school students" (Reiss & Roth, 1993a, p. 19). Nevertheless, the curriculum may have some value, particularly the currently untested version that ties more broadly into the larger community. In the meantime, the *Violence Prevention Curriculum* has been purchased by many schools and used with thousands of students nationwide.

Straight Talk About Risks (STAR)

The STAR curriculum (Center to Prevent Handgun Violence, 1992) was developed by the Center to Prevent Handgun Violence, a national, nonprofit educational organization. The prekindergarten to 12th-grade curriculum focuses primarily on handgun violence education. The program is unique in that it includes Spanish-language versions of the materials so students whose first language is Spanish can be full participants. The curriculum educates students about gun risks and gun violence through activity plans (implemented by the teacher), that target increased awareness of the extent, prevalence, and nature of gun violence. STAR also teaches students to understand the nature of anger and to build skills needed to manage conflict peacefully. Controlled evaluation data have not yet been published.

Howard University Violence Prevention Project

The Howard University project, under the direction of Hope Hill, is a research effort to develop an appropriate conceptual framework from which to understand the effect of violence on the development of African American children and youths (Isaac, 1992). Hill and her colleagues have developed a research-based, afterschool, group intervention for children who have witnessed incidents of urban violence. The children were selected because they were considered to be at high risk for later psychological distress and for possible involvement in violence. The group program is designed to provide support and reduce psychological risk factors. Program objectives include promoting an understanding of culture while fostering a positive sense of cultural identity, and providing opportunities for children and families to receive debriefing and supportive treatment after situations of community violence. The project also attempts to build spiritual values. The support network developed among parents and teachers is seen as a key component of the program. This network is viewed as empowering parents to be more effective buffers for their children and to work toward transforming the community to reduce violence. Given its research focus, evaluation data should eventually be available for this project.

It seems clear that collaboration with families, schools, and the broader community will be crucial to effective preventive efforts. Each of the programs discussed now recognizes this to some extent, although only in the Howard University project is the centrality of working with multiple cultural entities in this way identified. The *Violence Prevention Curriculum for Adolescents* and the STAR curriculum are more narrowly focused, potentially missing some of the classes of violent acts, although each has areas of strength. None of the projects comprehensively involve all of the relevant cultural systems that may be important to reducing youth violence (e.g., churches, formal institutions and services such as the mental health and justice systems, and street culture). None has so far been rigorously evaluated, with results submitted for peer review. And, probably most crucially, all place heavy emphasis on the antecedents of violent acts (teaching new rules, offering models for imitation) and often on rehearsing new repertoires, but to a greater or lesser extent miss the crucial role of designing new systems of *consequation* that could stabilize new practices learned. The science of behavior suggests that developing cultures of nonviolence in families, schools, neighborhoods, and other networks that not only prompt alternatives to violence, *but also consistently reinforce such actions*, will be crucial to lasting success.

A PROGRAM OF RESEARCH

Given the conceptual and empirical limitations of the existing interventive approaches and the severity of violence in society, the development of coherent alternatives is a public priority. As already noted, the National Research Council and APA have specifically called for theory-driven approaches. Developing a coherent and comprehensive program of research firmly rooted in the science of behavior may be especially valuable. Much of the existing work on violence has identified a variety of weak but significant correlations among violent acts of one kind or another and a large range of individual, situational, and community risk factors (Reiss & Roth, 1993a; Sampson & Lauritsen, 1993). Much of the preventive and analytic work that has been done focuses heavily on antecedents of violent behavior (i.e., triggers and high-risk situations) rather than on consequences.

Behavior analysts recognize the power and importance of antecedents (setting events, rules, models for imitation, and discriminative stimuli), but we also theorize that, at its core, behavior is selected by its consequences; most antecedents are relevant precisely because of their connections with consequences. Just "Say[ing] No" or "Squash it!" is unlikely unless following these (or similar) rules has an immediate benefit or has been relatively consistently reinforced in the past. For these reasons, antecedent-based strategies will be considered in the analyses that follow, but strategies emphasizing postcedents (consequences) will be stressed.

Natural History as Method

Laboratory experimentation, with its potential for exercising extensive control over multiple variables, has proven extraordinarily useful in science. This research strategy is extremely limited for studying violence, however, because violent acts are deeply embedded in complex interlocking environmental matrices. These conditions cannot be adequately duplicated in the laboratory. This does not mean, however, that we cannot study violence in a rigorous way. To do so, investigators need to turn to alternative strategic methodologies, similar to those that are used to study other phenomena that are heavily context-dependent, like those studied by ecological science, meteorology, or cosmology.

Marston Bates (1950/1990), a founder of ecological science, described the method of natural history as the intertwining of (a) *organized observations*, (b) *controlled* (to the extent possible) *experiments* in the natural environment guided by those observations, and (c) the inductive *development and evolution of conceptual frameworks* based on these observations and experiments. This tripartite approach, which has broad applicability for cultural design (see Chapter 1) is the organizing strategy in the program that we are pursuing.

The Research Program

What is needed is an integrated, multistage program of developmental research that applies each of the three methodological components identified by Bates in an iterative and integrated manner. This chapter constitutes a report of the results of the first phase of our investigations, a conceptual behavior analysis of classes of youth violence based on the extensive literature in this field and informal observations. Subsequent phases, described later, will modify and further specify these results. We hope they lead ultimately to a demonstrably effective interventive package ready for wide dissemination. The phases of the overall research program are presented next.

Phase 1: Conceptual Analysis of Violent Behaviors

During this phase, we have examined the existing research base, available intervention packages, and other material in the literature to develop an initial conceptual model of the varieties of youth violence. This conceptual model is based on an analysis of violence *as behavior*. Because behavior analytic theory suggests that violent acts, like other behaviors, are selected by consequences at the biological, behavioral, and cultural levels, we searched the literature to identify the most relevant consequences at each level. Antecedents (also important because of their relationships to consequences) were also traced. This chapter reports the results of this first step.

Phase 2: Observational Studies

Existing information can only take us so far; because the existing studies are not rooted in the theoretical paradigm we are applying, they have not always asked the right questions to provide the answers we seek or examined the variables suggested by this paradigm. The next step, therefore, is to engage in several types of observational studies, structured in response to the prior conceptual analysis. We are actively engaged in this process, and we expect to complete at least three types of related studies:

1. A study in which the professional staff in youth facilities describe violent incidents that have occurred, with their responses classified according to our theoretical model;
2. An interview study, in which we will interview teens about specific violent incidents to allow us to better understand their verbal descriptions of violence and its controlling variables; and
3. An observational study, in which we will directly observe preteens in natural settings; the focus will be on extracting relevant antecedents and consequences for coercive incidents that may escalate into violence.

The first study has begun; the second and third are in planning stages at this time. Reports on each study will be prepared and disseminated as they are completed.

Phase 3: Revision of Conceptual Analysis Based on Findings From Observational Studies (Concurrent With Phase 2)

As in any scientific analysis of empirical data, we expect that our conceptual model will be progressively adjusted and modified based on findings from the observational studies. This information will gradually enhance the model in a cumulative shaping process, which will continue over the subsequent phases.

Phase 4: Develop and Empirically Test Intervention Package

During this phase, we will develop what we hope to be a model interventive package, one based on the revised conceptual model and findings from our observational studies. Existing packages are being examined to isolate components consistent with our theoretical model, some of which may be adapted for inclusion in our package. A relatively small-scale test, emphasizing single-subject designs, will be conducted using the package developed; the results will then inform subsequent phases. A beginning outline of such a package, based on the material reported here, is found in the concluding section of this chapter.

Phase 5: Revision of Interventive Package Based on Outcome Data

One or more iterations testing successive modifications of the initial interventive package will be conducted until the results are substantial enough for a larger scale test. Once the results of the intervention package are shown to be effective under a variety of conditions and to have adequate social validity, we will be ready to begin dissemination.

Phase 6: Dissemination

The interventive package will be distributed as widely as possible, both through scholarly publication and through production of a curriculum with accompanying practitioner's guide. Meanwhile, further refinement of the package will continue.

The material that follows is the result of Phase 1 activities. It identifies major classes of youth violence that we have extracted from the literature and unstructured observation. In it, we begin to unpack the contingency networks within which violent behaviors appear to be embedded. Other classes and subclasses will probably be identified in later studies as a part of this iterative research strategy. Our understanding of the contingencies will also evolve and deepen, but this material provides beginning guidance for subsequent observations and interviews.

CLASSES OF YOUTH VIOLENCE

Our examination of the violence literature within a behavioral frame resulted in the identification of two core classes of violent acts (one supported by negative reinforcement, the other by positive) and several special cases—particular examples of one or both of the basic classes, in some cases with significant biological and cultural overlays.

In applied situations, the distinctions between positive and negative reinforcement are not always absolute (Iwata, 1987), and in many cases multiple concurrent consequences are associated with single acts. Sometimes one consequence may be the primary determinant of a violent act, and others may be present but not active. In other circumstances, it seems likely that multiple consequences are active, and the behavior is overdetermined. Much finer grained data will be required to strip such cases down to the essential controlling features. Nevertheless, it seems at least heuristically useful to separate positive and negative reinforcement situations here.

Before describing these classes, a few other points should be discussed. First, what is the definition of a violent act? Violent acts, as defined by the National Research Council, are: "behaviors by individuals that intentionally threaten, attempt, or inflict physical harm on others" (Reiss & Roth, 1993a, p. 2). Behavior analysts have some trouble with the word *intentionally*. We, for example, doubt that every violent act is rule-governed or that any are "freely" chosen. We therefore prefer the definition: "nonaccidental behaviors by individuals that threaten, attempt, or inflict physical harm on others." By accident, we mean a behavior under the control of unrelated contingencies; the question of negligence is not central to our purposes, and we leave that aside.

Malott indicated (1994) that it is important to look at why those who do *not* commit violent acts do not and suggested that the reasons are heavily rooted in aversive control. If antisocial acts are punished in highly probable and predictable ways (especially early in life), they become less likely. In other words, reinforcement may maintain and lead to an escalation of violent behaviors, but a history of punishment may, under some circumstances, decrease the rate of those behaviors. In the abstract, this is probably true; the details matter immensely here, however, and will therefore be considered in the discussion of each class of violent acts. We have some concerns about strategies that rely heavily on aversive control.

The science of behavior emphasizes that behavior (including violent acts) is ultimately under the control of environmental contingencies and is not a matter of unconstrained volition. The goal, from this perspective, should not be simply to persuade youths to choose to control their violent tendencies, but rather to establish a network of environmental conditions and events that have significant effects on the rate of violent behavior. Self-control is achieved by exposing one's self to new contingencies, some of which may be internal, but all of which are ultimately shaped by or inherent in environmental conditions and events. The contingencies, the relationships among violent acts and relevant events and conditions that precede them (antecedents) and follow them (postcedents), therefore, are what must be understood.

Most youth violence seems to be under relatively direct-acting contingencies (those that are immediate and not rule-governed), but some is not. For example, the behaviors associated with planning a robbery involve quite delayed reinforcement and must, therefore, be under the control of rules or other verbal mediation (Malott, Whaley, & Malott, 1993). It may, in fact, be easier in some ways to intervene with persons who have such rule-governed repertoires available, because teaching new rules does sometimes result in changes in behavior. Many young persons lack such repertoires, have not learned to delay gratification, or do not recognize that their actions now will reliably produce predictable consequences in the future. In such cases, it is essential to teach such skills, for example: *tracking* (acting in accordance with descriptions of consequences) following rules established by self or others (*pliance*), and selecting better quality reinforcers even when this involves a delay in delivery of the reinforcer. Such repertoires often need to be explicitly taught and carefully shaped, sometimes with the addition of more immediate contrived reinforcers on an interim basis until rule-governance can be established.

Given these conceptual clarifications, we turn to the specifics of a conceptual behavior analysis of violence. The material that follows describes the major classes of violent acts by youths that our analysis has extracted. Some also have relevance to other forms of violence (e.g. battering and robberies by adults).

Class One: Violent Acts Producing Negative Reinforcement

The animal literature makes quite clear that organisms will aggress to escape from aversive conditions (Mirsky & Siegel, 1994); the same appears to be true for humans (Sidman, 1989). It is common in the violence literature to attempt to identify potential triggers for violence—aversive antecedents that somehow lead to a violent act. Behavior analysts believe this way of framing the issue can preclude adequate answers. Consequences are not included in an analysis of triggers that lead to violence, yet history of consequation is what ultimately shapes behavior (Skinner, 1981). Furthermore, most antecedents matter primarily because of their connections with consequences. The simple contingency diagram shown in Figure 1 provides an example. In this case of domestic violence, an aversive condition exists, that is, one partner making noise in the kitchen. This noise might be viewed by some as a trigger that leads to the violent act. This description, however, does not adequately capture the causal chain. To understand the events, we need to look at what happens after the violent act—the noise stops. (This analysis is consistent, incidentally, with the power and control model feminists have explicated for understanding domestic violence; Pence & Paymar, 1993).

There are often many other active contingencies present in acts of youth violence. In Figure 2, we trace some contingencies that are consis-

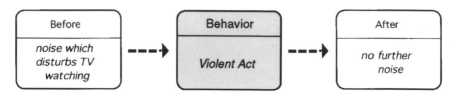

Figure 1. A simple contingency diagram portraying an act of battering.

tent with the literature, by depicting a violent episode in which one young person "disrespects" another verbally. The youth who has been disrespected then responds violently. (Elijah Anderson's ethnographic work suggests that for many youth on the street, respect is a more potent reinforcer than safety and, perhaps, even survival [Anderson, 1994]. Escape from the conditioned aversive of disrespect may be a more important factor here than obtaining respect.) Experiencing disrespect is a motivating condition for the behavior. (Presence of peers may often be an important discriminative stimulus, signaling availability of reinforcement in many such cases; these circumstances are discussed as a subclass below.)

There are almost certainly other factors that increase sensitivity to the consequences of the violence, other establishing operations (see chapter 1). Extensive literature reviews conducted by the National Research Council (Reiss & Roth, 1993a, 1993b) suggested that high overall levels of deprivation and environmental aversives may potentiate violence. The matching law clarifies that if there are few available reinforcers, the valence of those that are available is increased (McDowell, 1988). In addition, aggression toward any available target when exposed to high levels

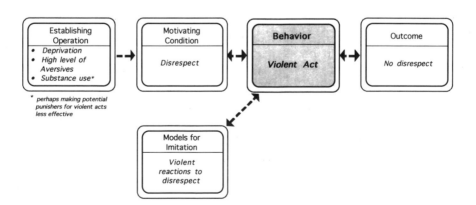

Figure 2. An analysis of a Class 1 violent actions resulting from negative reinforcement.

of aversives has been extensively documented and analyzed by behavior analysts (e.g., Sidman, 1989, 1993). Some forms of substance use also increase the likelihood of violent acts such as those being described here (Miczek et al., 1993), and in this role are probably best viewed as establishing operations.

The apparently simple act of hitting or shooting someone who disrespects you is clearly much more complex than it may appear at first glance. There are other potentially relevant dimensions. The impact of imitation, of seeing how others on the street respond to such provocation (as well as the way that street culture reinforces such acts and punishes their omission; Anderson, 1994) is viewed as crucial by most observers, and it is certainly consistent with a behavioral analysis. In some cases, the behavior is verbally mediated to some extent, but the rules involved refer to immediate rather than longer-term consequences. In fact, we suggest that deficits in rule-governed repertoires relevant to sensitivity to distant and uncertain consequences are important areas to address in preventive efforts. One exception is behavior that occurs when an individual acts to avoid drug withdrawal, a situation in which he may take actions, including violence, that eventually result in relief. Given the delays between behavior and eventual reinforcement, some such behaviors are probably to some extent rule-governed (Malott, 1989).

Implications for Prevention

Behavior supported by reinforcement (positive or negative) often can be eliminated using extinction (withdrawing reinforcement). Because the natural environment provides a variety of opportunities for the reinforcement of violent acts, however, extinction is usually not a realistic strategy here. Adding additional aversives (punishment) is the most common approach used, but there are many problems with punishment, including possible emotional and aggressive side effects, the difficulty of ensuring consistency, and the fact that the individual may not have a functional alternative repertoire available. In many urban environments, traditional face-to-face contingencies have eroded to such an extent that social disapproval from parents, peers, and neighbors is no longer the powerful factor it may have been in the past. Such contingencies are most effective in situations in which everyone knows each other and where a powerful and consistent culture of mutual approval is in place. Arrest and criminal penalties are inconsistent and often delayed; rule-governance must, therefore, be well established before these are likely to be of any significant utility.

Some strategies based on changes in antecedents may be somewhat useful. There has been a dramatic rise in increasingly realistic models of violent responses to unpleasant situations in movies, television, and video games. Although these responses may not significantly affect behavior among those who have learned strongly rule-governed repertoires, a strong association seems to exist between media violence and aggressive behavior for many youths (APA, 1993; Reiss & Roth, 1993a). For those who do not have strong rule-governed repertoires, imitation is likely to be a more salient factor. Persuasive models of alternative approaches for dealing with aversive events may be valuable. New self-talk (self-emitted verbal rules) and instructions from others (e.g., "Squash it!") may be of some use if, but only if, rule-governance is well established, and following these instructions has resulted, at least sometimes, in better consequences (e.g., a reduction in the aversive condition, or social reinforcement from significant persons for walking away).

Action directed toward decreasing material and social deprivation and reducing often high levels of noncontingent aversive events experienced by many youths at risk for violence is essential. It is clear that such problems as school failure, family dysfunction, and racism will require application of substantial societal resources for resolution. No one should be misled that a simple, time-limited curriculum provided in school can adequately compensate for these powerful establishing operations.

Consequence-based strategies other than extinction or punishment are perhaps the most important. The matching law, a statistical statement describing how choice among alternative behaviors occurs (McDowell, 1988) suggests that one way to reduce any specific behavior is to increase reinforcement for other behavior, either by reinforcing particular alternative behaviors (the preferred strategy for reasons still to be discussed) or by providing noncontingent ("free") reinforcement. In theory, then, enriching a young person's life should lead to a reduction in violence. This approach may sometimes not be sufficient, because, in some situations (e.g., rage or peer-mediated circumstances), other consequences may become powerfully salient. It is also difficult to reduce the rate of a behavior to near zero using matching exclusively. Still, unless rich alternative sources of reinforcement for productive behavior are made available, well-established science suggests that intervention will probably fail. Therefore, enrichment, especially contingent enrichment that emphasizes shaping new repertoires, should probably be pursued as a primary strategic direction. (See discussion of Class Two violent acts later in this chapter for further detail regarding the matching law.)

Finally, and perhaps most importantly, the function of the behavior must be taken seriously. Alternative ways to escape or avoid the aversive condition (e.g., being disrespected) need to be learned. Teaching alternatives and ensuring that their performance is reinforced is the core of effective approaches to reducing Class One violent acts. It may also be helpful to find ways to decrease the aversiveness of the stimulus. When the stimulus is verbal, its power is the result of social learning. Changes in how the words are treated by family and peers could, therefore, attenuate the valence of such stimuli. Identifying how some youths successfully escape or avoid these situations has been examined at preliminary level (Stumphauzer, Veloz, & Aiken, 1981) and is part of our current research; decreasing the aversiveness of disrespectful words, however, is clearly a question of cultural design.

Class Two: Violence Producing Positive Reinforcement

The second major class of violent behavior appears to be shaped largely by the process of positive reinforcement. We have known for more than 35 years that physical aggression can be shaped by reinforcement in laboratory animals (Reynolds, Catania, & Skinner, 1963; Skinner, 1959). Military trainers have known this for thousands of years (military training typically consists of a mix of positive and negative reinforcement strategies). A careful reading of the animal literature suggests that positive reinforcement can induce a laboratory subject to take the first steps in an aggressive chain and that natural contingencies may then take over. This is roughly similar to placing an infantryman in harm's way, at which point he will typically take the next steps, especially if they are well-learned parts of his repertoire (Sun Tzu, 1991).

Reynolds et al.'s (1963) work also crucially demonstrates that physical aggression can be brought under relatively tight stimulus control; a pigeon can be taught to attack under one color of light and not under another, although some generalization across conditions may occur. This sort of phenomenon may be occurring in the occasional case reported of violent acts by college students whose behavior was shaped in other, more violent settings (and whose behavior may change dramatically from one setting to another); those who know such a student while at college may find it inconceivable that the person they know could engage in violence anywhere. But, in fact, the contingencies may simply be different.

The class of violent acts shaped by positive reinforcement (e.g., an attack to obtain money or a leather jacket) is depicted in Figure 3. Prior to the attack, the perpetrator does not have money, the jacket, attention from members of the opposite sex, or whatever the salient reinforcer may be. The attack results in access to the reinforcer(s); that is, the violent act "pays off." Under such circumstances, it is not surprising that the next time similar circumstances arise, similar behavior may occur, because the offender has learned that it worked. Note also the other relevant factors shown or implied in Figure 3. First of course, is the occasion. The victim in possession of the potential reinforcer must be present and wearing the jacket; otherwise, an attack motivated by possession of the jacket would not occur. There may be other circumstances (e.g., the presence or absence of certain individuals who may provide social reinforcement) that increase or decrease the probability of reinforcement. (See Figure 2, chapter 1, for

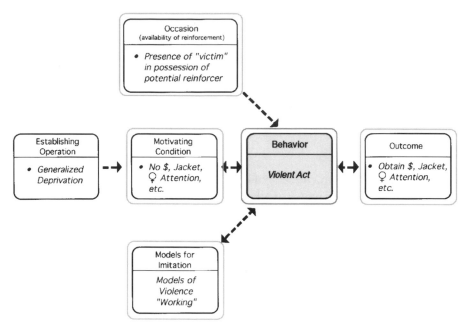

Figure 3. Analysis of a Class 2 violent act supported by positive reinforcement.

a more comprehensive diagram of multiple concurrent contingencies that may shape such behavior).

This last point raises another. Unlike the pigeon whose violence is shaped by tangible, primary reinforcement (food), much Class Two violence involves social reinforcement. This is a crucial point. The jacket is usually taken not primarily because the perpetrator is cold (if so, this would be an example of negative reinforcement), but rather because the particular type of jacket taken is socially valued or because immediate social reinforcement results from the violent act of taking it. Money, a powerful generalized reinforcer, is a special case. A great deal of criminal activity occurs to obtain it, and regular perpetrators often report that they view crimes such as robbery as their "work"; when violence is required to complete this work, the victim is commonly blamed for refusing to cooperate.

Simple violence of the type under consideration here appears to be primarily under the control of direct-acting contingencies, rather than rules (some subclasses, to be noted later, are exceptions). We believe that weak rule-governance repertoires (tracking, pliance, etc.) are common among perpetrators of such violence, who have often not learned how to work toward more distant and uncertain reinforcers resulting from cumulative efforts. Models of violent acts resulting in reinforcement are usually present in the lives of perpetrators as well, and imitation no doubt plays a part in the learning of Class Two violent acts, as it does in Class One violent acts.

Generalized deprivation increases the value of whatever reinforcement is available. The form of the matching law (a statistical statement of choice behavior) that accounts for the rate of a particular behavior is:

$$B = \frac{kr}{r + r_e}$$

B is the rate of behavior, k is the (asymptotic) maximum rate of behavior, r is the rate of reinforcement available for the behavior, and r_e is the rate of extraneous reinforcement available in the contextual situation (whether contingent on specific other behaviors or free; McDowell, 1988). This last term (r_e) is the crucial one here. In an impoverished, sparse environment, the sensitivity to reinforcement for violent action is substantially higher than would be the case in a richer setting. This is why deprivation is often a crucial factor.

A significant proportion of violent acts committed by youths and adults are committed in the course of other crimes, such as robbery. Although a detailed analysis of this behavior goes beyond the purposes of this chapter, the basic outlines would closely trace the discussion here. The violence that occurs as a part of such crimes is generally modeled by others, often mediated by rules, and ultimately results in reinforcement that may include the money or items obtained in the course of the robbery, as well as status on the street (see the following discussion of Class Five violent acts). Preventive strategies required to have a significant effect on this form of violence would need to address these motivating factors. It is clear that making alternatives available—preferably before an entrenched pattern is established—would necessarily be an important dimension of such strategies, for all the reasons elaborated previously regarding any form of violence supported by positive reinforcement.

Implications for Prevention

Once again, the preceding analysis provides rich strategic guidance for preventive efforts (at all levels, from primary to tertiary). Some of the implications are similar to those listed under the negative reinforcement paradigm, whereas some are different. Because consequences are ultimately the crucial factor in changing behavior, we begin with them. Youths at risk for perpetrating violence must have rich alternate sources of reinforcers available, including those reinforcers that often are accessed through violent acts (e.g., social acceptance, attention from those who are sexually intriguing, money, recognition, and respect). A single approach will not work either for all youths or for any individual youth at all times. Midnight basketball, for example, is a potentially valuable strategy for some young persons, but should only be one item on a rich menu of possibilities. Even for those for whom it is effective, satiation is to be expected unless it is only one of multiple varieties of reinforcing activities available. Reinforcement of various kinds by peers and by those whom the youths view as sexually attractive is particularly powerful in adolescence. The establishment of peer cultures of nonviolence and of respect and valuing of accomplishments of many kinds is therefore crucial with this population. Interlocking contingencies supporting such practices in other cultural entities of which youth are part (families, schools, neighborhoods, street culture, the cultures portrayed in the media) are also critical. Given the presence of a rich menu of available reinforcers like these, mild penalties such as social disapproval for coercive or violent actions may have some utility. However, when an infrastructure of alternative reinforcers is lacking, punishment is unlikely to effective.

Turning to antecedents, structural supports providing easy access to the kinds of reinforcers already described must be in place. Other structural factors of some potential value may include changes in the physical environment to make monitoring of behavior easier and reduce risk at multiple levels. Examples include placing automatic teller machines in well-lit, high-visibility areas, and placing physical barriers in streets to limit easy access by strangers and make targets less accessible (see Reiss & Roth, 1993a, for a review of environmental management and public health risk-reduction strategies). Current evidence indicates that such changes in the physical environment are most effective when linked to changes in cultural practices. They tend to have limited effects when implemented alone.

Different models to be imitated—those supporting nonviolence—are clearly crucial, both on personal and broader media levels. A good deal is known about this, thus coordinated campaigns may have real power. At the same time, it is crucial that when youth imitate these models, the imitation is reinforced in the natural environment. Ensuring that this happens requires (a) that models of nonviolent actions as well as models of *reinforcing* nonviolent actions be provided, and (b) that cultures of such reinforcement be established at a primary group level. Immediate intervention after highly visible violent episodes have occurred (for example, in schools) may also be important to reducing the negative effects of such modeling. Immediate intervention may also reduce fear associated with situations similar to the one that has been publicized. Teaching new rules (and rule-governed repertoires like tracking and pliance) may also be quite valuable, but again, only if following the new rules is reinforced, a situation which requires that appropriate cultures be in place.

In summary, the science of behavior suggests that the processes of positive and negative reinforcement can account for much of the violence that troubles society. If basic behavioral principles can account for violent acts, they can also account for and guide the development of alternatives. Although the two basic classes of violent behavior discussed here have broad applicability, there are several specific classes of violent acts that may be particularly instructive to examine. Each is a subclass of one, or both, of the basic classes, but the contingencies are distinctive enough that analyzing them in more detail offers specific guidance for interventive and preventive efforts.

SPECIAL CASES

Class Three: Acts Resulting From Rage

One of the primary classes of aggressive behavior among infrahuman species occurs under conditions of high physiological arousal. In other words, the animal responds to environmental events with apparent rage (Mirsky & Siegel, 1994). The sites and anatomical pathways at and through which such arousal occurs have been reasonably well established, and some knowledge of the physiological processes involved (perhaps including a role for the opioid peptide system) is gradually emerging (Mirsky & Siegel, 1994). Common experience and some data suggest that a similar phenomenon occurs among humans, although the controlled research required to examine this closely would often be highly intrusive and difficult to pursue with humans for ethical and practical reasons.

Class Three violent acts are, from a behavior analytic perspective, a subclass of violence supported by negative reinforcement, as shown in Figure 4. Roughly, in such episodes, an aversive event occurs (an establishing operation), that leads to the motivating condition experienced as rage, which is relieved by the violent act. Although this is the central thread,

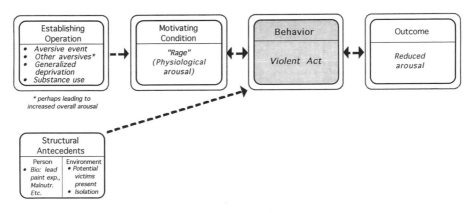

Figure 4. Violence (Class 3) that relieves "rage."

other relevant antecedents are often present (and possibly other concurrent postcedents, although these are not traced here). There must be a target (animate or inanimate) present; the same reinforcement may not result from striking out at the air (in fact, some suggest that the actual reinforcers in such circumstances include the physical contact; this may have phylogenic roots [Skinner, 1953; Ulrich & Azrin, 1962]). To some extent, for some persons, violent responses to rage may be under some level of stimulus control; they may be more likely with the spouse, and less likely with the boss, for example.

The concurrent presence of other aversive conditions or events may potentiate the consequences of rage-related violence as well; perhaps arousal is to some extent additive. (Substance use may also increase or decrease the effectiveness of the consequence.) Structural antecedents, including biological factors resulting from exposure to environmental toxins, and environmental factors such as isolation may also be relevant.

Implications for Intervention

It is instances of this class of violent behaviors for which packages focused on anger management are most relevant. Reducing the incidence of triggering aversive events should help, as should reducing the overall levels of aversive stimuli present. Reducing the level of physiological reactivity, as well as teaching alternative, less-costly ways to escape it, is central. Other strategies, including reducing the availability of safe targets, changing the physical and social environment to reduce isolation and increase accessibility to face-to-face contingencies from others, and introducing different models, may have significant cumulative value as well. Many of the basic strategies relevant to the class of violent behaviors supported by negative reinforcement may be of help here. These include decreasing deprivation, teaching rule-governance, increasing overall reinforcement for other behavior, and others already discussed.

Anger management programs, to be most effective, should include components designed to:

- Reduce physiological reactivity. It is important to note that how this is objective pursued matters a great deal. We are skeptical of the use of medications that simply depress the activity of the central nervous system (e.g., benzodiazepines), because learning to respond differently under natural conditions is crucial. (Maintaining the person on tranquilizers for any long-term period would also involve substantial risk.) We also have ethical concerns about genetic manipulation that may become possible in the future. With some persons, relaxation, meditation, or physical exercise may well help; experience suggests that maintaining these activities often requires that a strong self-management program including regular external monitoring be present. Given such supports, natural methods of reducing overall arousal may be valuable components of a program.

- Recognize potential high risk situations for anger and implement tactics to prepare for such situations. This includes the use of relaxation and cognitive techniques, which behavior analysts view as a subset of rule-governance (see Poppen, 1989). In some cases, avoidance tactics might also prove useful.
- Recognize arousal and use such recognition as a prompt for taking well-rehearsed alternative steps to reduce arousal.
- Learn (and rehearse to mastery and fluency) alternative behaviors that can be used when aroused (assertiveness, relaxation, walking away).
- Establish networks of social reinforcement for using these skills in natural settings. The previous components listed, in one form or another, have been emphasized in anger management programs for some time (cf. Novaco, 1975; Prothrow-Stith, 1987). What is often underemphasized in these programs, however, is the crucial need to establish and maintain networks of interlocking contingencies to support use of new repertoires.

Although not all violent behavior among youth involves uncontrolled anger, some clearly does. Some interactions that begin as examples of other classes of violence (e.g., robbery) may degenerate into rage as well. This is, therefore, an important functional class of violent acts that should be included in planning preventive programming.

Class Four: Violence to Resolve Conflict

Violence is often described as the result of conflict, and violence prevention programs often emphasize some form of conflict resolution. Conflict can be defined broadly, either as any condition of interpersonal unpleasantness or more narrowly as disagreement about an issue in which two or more parties each have interests (valued reinforcers or significant aversives are at stake). We prefer the latter for precision; other forms of aversive interpersonal events fit into one or another of the other classes discussed in this chapter. The most common topography of conflict, as described by Patterson (1975), is that one party makes a demand for immediate change, and the other fails to comply. The stage is then set for escalation of aversive exchanges that, at some point, may involve strong emotion (see the discussion of Class Three regarding rage).

As can be seen in Figure 5, the chain of events in conflict is more complex than in the other examples given. The sequence is initiated by an unsatisfactory condition: Young woman (B) is talking to another young women's (A) boyfriend. In some cases, this scenario may result in immediate violence, in which case it is a relative pure example of violent behavior Class 1 (or Class 3). But in conflict situations as we are using the term, the first behavior on A's part is to demand that the other girl leave

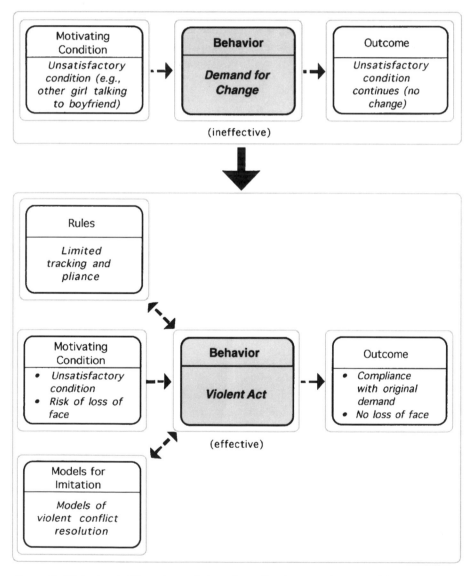

Figure 5. Violent act, Class 4: resolution of conflict that escalates to violence.

(and never do this again). Demands like this (for which many models may exist) sometimes result in change, and the incident ends for the moment. Because both young women have an interest in the young man—a source of highly valued reinforcers—the conflict may be replayed at later times however, and may escalate. If the demand works, demanding behavior is reinforced and is more likely to occur again in the future.

Conflict situations may end in violence, however, if the demand is ineffective, and the situation after the demand (the outcome) is similar to the situation before (the motivating condition). The situation may now be even more unsatisfactory because noncompliance on the part of others can be aversive in its own right. If the young woman has previously resolved such conditions with violence, she may attack the other; if this is effective, the aversive condition is relieved. If she has a weapon (use of which is more effective than unarmed combat), she may use it. Additional complexities commonly occur in conflict situations, including reciprocal and escalating demands. The less the person's behavior is under the control of rules supporting nonviolence, the more likely the direct-acting contingencies supporting violence will control the situation. Saving face in front of peers can also be a powerful motivating factor.

Implications for Intervention

A good deal is known about the skills of conflict resolution and mediation; they have been recognized for many years as important in families, organizations, and other settings in which people's interests may conflict (e.g., Carnegie, 1936/1981; Fisher & Ury, 1991; Gordon, 1970; Patterson, 1975). The present analysis provides an explanation of why, when, and how such skills may be effective, as well as some guidance for program design.

Beginning at the beginning, reducing the incidence of aversive interpersonal situations may be helpful. This would require helping youths identify the kinds of situations likely to lead to trouble and teaching them ways to avoid them. Note that this approach requires a measure of rule-governance to be effective. In fact, discussions about high-risk situations can provide a first step in teaching those skills. Such disclosures, for example, would include identifying the likely consequences of particular courses of action and following the rules once they are identified (tracking). One challenge for the program developer is to establish and support genuinely effective reinforcers for such behaviors, as simple verbal praise from an adult may not be powerful enough.

Many of the aversive events to which people respond are conditioned aversives. Attenuating their aversiveness is important. As cognitive therapists have suggested, there are very few genuine disasters, and the way people describe events and the probable consequences of those events to themselves and others can act as important establishing (or abolishing) operations, increasing or decreasing sensitivity to those situations as aversive or reinforcing. Of course, a program would not use these terms. It would instead, perhaps, talk about "warped thinking," "awfulizing" and so forth.

Young people also need to learn other possible responses to aversive situations, alternatives to demanding and alternatives to physical violence. These repertoires are emphasized in the conflict resolution and mediation literature (e.g., use of "I-statements", active listening, and identification of "win/win" options) and need not be described in detail here. What the science of behavior does clarify, however, is that teaching these skills through modeling, imitation, and new rules can provide important antecedents for alternative reactions but is not, by itself, adequate. What is missing is establishment of interlocking contingencies to prompt but especially to reinforce use of those new skills in the natural environment. Failing this, new skills are unlikely to generalize. If the young person tries these skills in his or her life space and they don't work—either they are punished or no positive consequence results—the new repertoires are likely to fade.

Conflict resolution training is not sufficient to eliminate all violence among youths; however, it does appear to be one of the important areas on which preventive efforts can focus. Some of the associated skills are specific, for example, making "I-statements"; other skills required for effective action in potentially conflictual situations overlap with those required to ameliorate other classes of violent acts (e.g., strengthening rule-governed repertoires as a class). What is common across all classes of violence so far discussed is the need to focus efforts not only on what the young person should do, but on *why* he or she should do it: to establish effective networks of reinforcement for positive practices. This will continue to be true for the other classes of violence still be discussed in this chapter.

Class Five: Street Violence to Gain Respect

Up to this point, the primary actors in the violent incidents we have discussed are those directly involved: the victim and the perpetrator. We now turn to somewhat more complex situations—those in which a wider network of antecedents and consequences constitute the most salient contingencies. As an example, some violent acts committed by gang members are driven primarily by the reinforcing effects of so-called respect. (Actually, in some settings, a young person can expect significant aversives, even threats to his own life, if he fails to act as directed by the street culture. So this class is far from a pure example of positive reinforcement, although that will be emphasized in this discussion. It is also worth noting that, overall, gang members engage in more violent acts *within* the gang than outside it, often in a transactional process of establishing and maintaining respect and status; Reiss & Roth, 1993a.)

In the simplest terms, Class Five could be diagrammed as follows: limited respect → violent act → more respect (motivating condition → behavior → outcome). In reality, of course, the situation is far more complex, involving multiple sets of actors, some of whom are present as the scene unfolds, others who are not. Rather than the simple contingency diagrams used so far, we turn here to a cultural practice diagram that allows examination of the multiple interlocking antecedents and consequences present in the scene (see Figure 6).

There are members of four classes of actors present in the scene illustrated in Figure 6: a victim, a perpetrator, peers of the perpetrator, and bystanders. No effort was made to include every possibly relevant antecedent and postcedent in this graphic; only certain apparent ones are depicted. Each class of actor emits, or fails to emit a particular cultural practice. Generally speaking, a cultural practice can be defined as a behavior transmitted and supported by a cultural entity (see Chapter 1 for details). In this figure, the sequence of events is shown with numbers. The sequence starts (1) when the victim walks down the street going home from school (his motivations for doing so are unrelated to other actors in the scene). The perpetrator confronts and attacks him (2). One of the most powerful motivating factors for the attack is the respect (social reinforcement) provided by peers who are present (3). This reinforcement may be reciprocated by the perpetrator himself (4). Bystanders take no action, perhaps because they have had previous experiences with violent groups of young persons on the street or because of self-talk (rules). Specific chains of events that occur in such incidents, depicted here in a generic manner, have been extensively described in the professional and popular literature (e.g., Anderson, 1994; Kotlowitz, 1991; Reiss & Roth, 1993a). It is important to note that in some cases, later verbal reports by the attacker may also be reinforced; in some cases, this may indicate a measure of rule-governance. In other cases, the effective contingencies may be those present in the scene, and later social exchanges may simply reinforce reporting.

Notice that behaviors emitted by others, even those not present in the scene, are among the relevant contingencies supporting the practices emitted by each class of actors that is present. (Each of the practices shown, within and outside the scene, could be expanded into a contingency diagram in its own right, and some are also components of other, interlocking scenes.)

Implications for Intervention

The first crucial point that is clarified by the diagram is the complexity of the situation. Any simple intervention, such as teaching

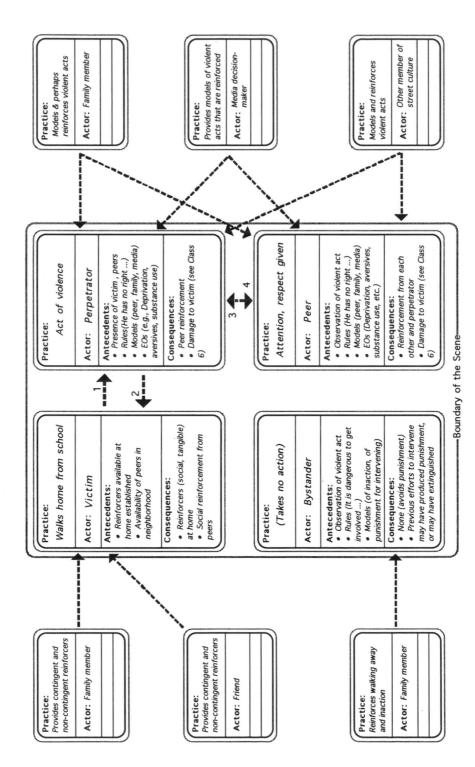

Figure 6. Analysis of an act of street violence to gain respect.

potential perpetrators conflict resolution skills, may fail due to the lack of change in other parts of the contingency network, the behavioral system. Although all of the strategies described so far may be important and relevant to this class of violent acts as well, an additional layer of conditions and events needs to be addressed here—new *cultures* need to be established that support changes in the multiple practices that mutually support each other in the diagram. This will require concurrent changes in antecedents and consequences within at least several classes of practices shown.

Note that the practices outside the scene have been collapsed on the diagram for simplicity, but also commonly need to be expanded and addressed; for example, antecedents (e.g., models) and consequences (e.g., respect from their own peers, money) associated with parents' reinforcement of gang-related activity may need to be changed to make it more likely that parents will reinforce alternative practices by their children. Analysis may need to go yet further out. For example, motivating conditions for parents' friends to respect them if their child is a gang leader may need to be addressed. To be effective, such analyses need to extend far enough that changes in the multiple microcultures involved (family, peer group, street culture) achieve a new, interlocking steady state. This is complicated, but behavior, particularly when maintained by interlocking cultural entities, is complex. This is a good example of why there are no easy answers to many serious social issues.

Class Six: Violence Directed Toward a Culturally Defined "Enemy"

One final class of violent acts exemplifies another form of complexity. Members of a local microculture (e.g., a youth gang) commonly define members of other groups as enemies. (Something similar happens at the level of nation-states and in interethnic violence, of course.) Attacking such an enemy results in consequences at several levels, from multiple sources. Some of the relevant factors are depicted in Figure 7.

This is clearly a complex situation. Looking first at consequences, recall Skinner's (1981) explanation that behavior is selected at three levels: the phylogenic, the operant, and the cultural (see Chapter 1 for further discussion). All three levels may be active in this scenario. Skinner (1984) indicated that seeing damage to an enemy is reinforcing and that sensitivity to this reinforcer may have a genetic component. Malott et al. (1993) suggested that the physical sensations involved in attack can themselves be reinforcing. Personal learning history also is relevant; the aversive condition generated by the enemy no longer being present and succeeding (and sometimes the reduction in personal risk that the presence of the enemy may engender) may be relieved by the attack. In addition, groups of which the individual is a member (family, gang, peer group) often support such attacks as a cultural practice.

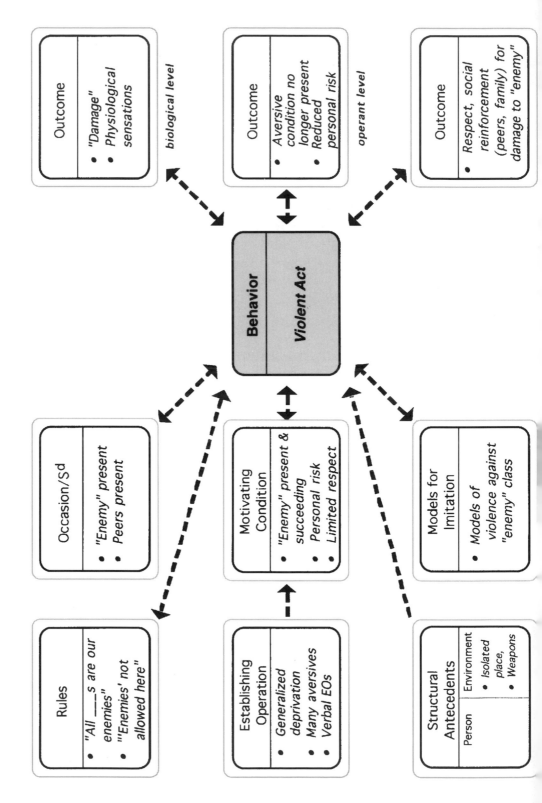

Antecedents are also important here. The occasion for the attack is the presence of the member of the enemy group; presence of peers may also increase the likelihood of some types of reinforcement (and punishment, should the attack not occur). Rules are also extremely relevant, including descriptions of any member of some other group as an enemy (whose success leads to aversives for members of one's own group) and verbal rules emitted when a member of the enemy group appears ("this is disgusting," etc.). Self-talk of this kind, the presence of the enemy, high levels of overall aversives and low levels of reinforcement for other behavior all establish sensitivity to the consequences of the attack. In other words, they are establishing operations. Many young persons in such situations have a long history of observing models who attack members of the enemy group and are reinforced for those attacks. Structural factors, including the availability of weapons that facilitate effective attack and reduce risk of personal injury (so long as the enemy does not have similar weapons), are also relevant.

Implications for Intervention

Cultural-level interventions are clearly fundamental here. Simply teaching a new rule, like "Squash it!", without support from the tight networks within which the young person acts is unlikely to have much effect; the emphasis must be on providing different consequences. There are two—and probably only two—ways to do this. The first is to change the cultural practices maintained by relevant groups such as families and peers. This requires precisely the sort of analysis introduced with regard to Class 5. The second is to embed the youths in different webs of contingencies. The second strategy is very effective, so long as the new contingencies remain in place; if they are withdrawn, and the young person finds him or herself exposed to the original antecedents and consequences that previously supported violent acts, the original behavior is likely to reemerge (Cohen & Filipczak, 1971/1989). For this reason, Wolf and his colleagues have suggested that serious delinquent behavior be regarded as a "significantly handicapping condition" requiring long-term supportive intervention (Wolf, Braukmann, & Ramp, 1987, p. 347).

Unless we plan to place millions of young people in specially designed environments, however, it seems clear that an emphasis on the first alternative—changing interlocking contingencies supporting cultural practices within the natural environment—is the most reasonable, if challenging choice. Determining how to do this effectively is the goal of our overall program of research, but a few principles seem clear immediately:

- It will be important to first trace the networks of contingencies supporting current practices to the extent possible, to determine the functions of current practices.

- It will be important to determine which new practices might work better. This will be an inductive process requiring iterative testing of "best guesses" based on observational studies of less violent groups and conceptual analyses.
- It will be important that once desired practices have been identified, the antecedents and consequences supporting them are specified. Because many of the antecedents and consequences will also be cultural practices maintained by groups, the antecedents and consequences of those second-order (and third- and subsequent-order practices as necessary) will need to be examined.

In general, to prevent Class 6 forms of violence, building youths' respect and appreciation for those different from themselves will be critical. There are other reasons why building such practices is important to societal survival and even to that of the human species; refer to chapter 6 and the conclusion of this volume for further discussion.

OVERALL IMPLICATIONS OF THIS ANALYSIS

The analysis of the two major classes and several subclasses of violent acts by young persons identifies a number of critical points at which preventive action might be directed. This does not mean the solutions are simple, only that they are possible. It is also a certainty that first efforts will not be optimal, and that refinement and even reconceptualization of interventive strategies will be necessary to develop an approach that is genuinely effective.

It is crucial to note that the aim is not to develop discrete interventions to prevent single violent acts, but rather to produce a package that results in the creation and stabilization of mutually supporting networks of new practices, maintained by interlocking contingencies within cultural entities. This is a different emphasis than has commonly been described. For example, Goldstein and Keller (1987), in a useful guidebook for work with aggressive individuals, conceptualized the work as clinical treatment—they devoted only about half a page to programming reinforcement for new behaviors into the natural environment. Our suggestion is that the latter needs to be the central focus and that the development of interlocking cultures of nonviolence should be our goal as a society.

Such a model will require a multisystemic approach like that recently proposed by Biglan and his colleagues to produce "successful children" on a community level (Biglan, Metzler, & Ary, 1994). Such an approach includes interventions at the peer, family, school, neighborhood, political, and media levels. Greenwood, Hart, Walker, and Risley (1994) have also proposed a similar, broad approach for preventing and remediating developmental retardation (including multisystemic, intergenerational programs within the home, day care center, preschool, school, and community). To achieve the level of effects required to have a major impact on youth violence, the focus should not be on developing single interventions, but on ways to develop and strengthen cultures of nonviolence at multiple levels.

Until we have completed the second and third phases of our research program, it would be premature to state definitively what should be included in an effective preventive package. The goal of the package is to reduce acts of violence among a target group of young people through the establishment of interlocking cultures of nonviolence at multiple system levels. Based on the analyses presented here, the first iteration of the package is likely to include components that facilitate:

- Exposure to and opportunities for success in obtaining significant reinforcement in alternative ways (rooted in the matching law; McDowell, 1988), including the development of alternative peer networks in which alternative behaviors are reinforced;
- Teaching and academic assistance to ensure school success and reinforcement for such success;
- Development of a network of older community members to support nonviolence, including family members and representatives of community organizations;
- Parent training in noncoercive discipline and communication, and establishment of a network of parents and families to support these new practices;
- Environmental interventions that reduce occasions for violence;
- Training in rule-governance;
- Training in ways to avoid potentially violent situations, and support for using those approaches;
- Anger management and nonprovocability training, and establishment of peer supports for use of skills learned; and
- Training in nonviolent approaches to conflict resolution and self-defense, and development of networks of mutual reinforcement for such actions.

Note that there is a heavy emphasis placed on consequences rather than simply on exhortation and other antecedents in this listing. In the beginning, a package including multiple components will be developed; once effectiveness is established, isolated components can be manipulated to determine which are most critical. Every effort will be made to develop approaches that are sustainable with local resources that are simple, flexible, and consistent with community values (Fawcett, Mathews, & Fletcher, 1980); and that avoid colonial relationships (Fawcett, 1991).

Finally, there is both reason for hope and reason for deep concern. If we were unable to account for violence—to identify its roots—it would be nearly impossible to act to prevent it. That, luckily, does not appear to be the case. Although there is much we do not know, the science of behavior tells us where to look and, to a considerable extent, what to look for. It also provides us with strategic direction for action. The research program proposed here should ultimately provide answers to some of our questions about the specific causes of and specific possible responses to violence. At the same time, it is likely to take a great deal of time and considerable focused effort to have a significant effect on a problem that is so immense and so deeply rooted in cultural networks. Some of the critical contingencies (e.g., poverty, deprivation, media portrayals glorifying violent solutions to problems) are unlikely to change quickly, no matter how clearly they are shown to be important facets of the problem. Many more people, many of our children, will die or be damaged for life as a result of violence before we can prevent it. But it is time to begin.

REFERENCES

American Psychological Association. (1993). *Violence and youth: Psychology's response*. Washington, DC.

Anderson, E. (1994, May). The code of the streets. *Atlantic Monthly*, pp. 81–94.

Bates, M. (1990). *The nature of natural history*. Princeton, NJ: Princeton University Press. (Original work published 1950).

Biglan, A., Metzler, C. W., & Ary, D. V. (1994). Increasing the prevalence of successful children: The case for community intervention research. *The Behavior Analyst, 17*, 335–351.

Bureau of Justice Statistics. (1992). *Criminal victimization in United States, 1990*. Washington, DC: Author.

Bureau of Justice Statistics. (1994). *Criminal victimization in the United States, 1973–92 Trends*. Washington, DC: Author.

Bureau of Justice Statistics. (1995). *Bureau of Justice Statistics Clearinghouse*. Washington, DC: Author.

Carnegie, D. (1981). *How to win friends and influence people*. New York: Pocket Books. (Original work published 1936).

Center to Prevent Handgun Violence. (1992). *Straight talk about risks*. Washington, DC: Author.

Cohen, H. L., & Filipczak, J. (1989). *A new learning environment*. Boston: Authors Cooperative. (Original work published 1971).

DeJong, W., Spiro, A. III, Wilson-Brewer, R., Vince-Whitman, C., & Prothrow-Stith, D. (n.d.). *Evaluation Summary: Violence Prevention Curriculum for Adolescents*. Newton, MA: Educational Development Center.

Dishion, T. J., Patterson, G. R., Stoolmiller, M., & Skinner, M. L. (1991). Family, school, and behavioral antecedents to early adolescent involvement with antisocial peers. *Developmental Psychology, 27,* 172–180.

Division of School Safety. (1994). *Reported incidents—Comparison report*. New York: New York City Board of Education.

Farrington, D. P. (1989). Early predictors of adolescent aggression and adult violence. *Violence and Victims, 4,* 79–100.

Fawcett, S. B. (1991). Some values guiding community research and action. *Journal of Applied Behavior Analysis, 24,* 621–636.

Fawcett, S. B., Mathews, R. M., & Fletcher, R. K. (1980). Some promising dimensions of behavioral community technology. *Journal of Applied Behavior Analysis, 13,* 505–518.

Fisher, R., & Ury, W. (1991). *Getting to yes* (2nd ed.). New York: Houghton Mifflin.

Gibbs, W. W. (1995). Seeking the criminal element. *Scientific American, 272,* 100–107.

Goldstein, A. P., & Keller, H. (1987). *Aggressive behavior: Assessment and intervention*. New York: Pergamon.

Gordon, T. (1970). *Parent effectiveness training*. New York: Wyden.

Greenwood, C. R., Hart, B., Walker, D., & Risley, T. (1994). The opportunity to respond and academic performance revisited: A behavioral theory of developmental retardation and its prevention. In R. Gardner, III, D. M. Sainato, J. O. Cooper, T. E. Heron, W. L. Heward, J. W. Eshleman, & T. A. Grossi (Eds.), *Behavior analysis in education: Focus on measurably superior instruction* (pp. 213–223). Pacific Grove, CA: Brooks/Cole.

Groves, B. M., Zuckerman, B., Marans, S., & Cohen, D. J. (1993). Silent victims: Children who witness violence. *JAMA, 269,* 262–264.

Isaac, M. R. (1992). *Violence: The impact of community violence on African American children and families*. Arlington, VA: National Center for Education in Maternal and Child Health.

Iwata, B. A. (1987). Negative reinforcement in applied behavior analysis: An emerging technology. *Journal of Applied Behavior Analysis, 20,* 361–378.

Kotlowitz, A. (1991). *There are no children here*. New York: Doubleday.

Louis Harris and Associates, Inc. (1993). *The Metropolitan Life survey of the American teacher 1993*. New York: Author.

Malott, R. W. (1989). The achievement of evasive goals: Control by rules describing contingencies that are not direct acting. In S. C. Hayes (Ed.), *Rule-governed behavior: Cognition, contingencies, and instructional control* (pp. 269–322). New York: Plenum.

Malott, R. W. (1994). From the tabula rasa to murder, massacre and genocide. *The ABA: International Newsletter, 17*(4), 10.

Malott, R. W., Whaley, D. L., & Malott, M. E. (1993). *Elementary principles of behavior* (2nd ed.). Englewood Cliffs, NJ: Prentice-Hall.

McDowell, J. J. (1988). Matching theory in natural human environments. *The Behavior Analyst, 11*, 95–109.

Miczek, K. A., DeBold, J. F., Haney, M., Tidey, J., Vivian, J., & Weerts, E. M. (1993). Alcohol, drugs of abuse, aggression, and violence. In A. J. Reiss, Jr. & J. A. Roth (Eds.), *Understanding and preventing violence: Vol. 3. Social Influences* (pp. 377–570). Washington, DC: National Academy Press.

Miczek, K. A., Mirsky, A. F., Carey, R., Debold, J., & Raine, A. (1994). An overview of biological influences on violent behavior. In A. J. Reiss, Jr., K. A. Miczek, & J. A. Roth (Eds.), *Understanding and preventing violence: Vol. 2. Biobehavioral influences* (pp. 1–20). Washington, DC: National Academy Press.

Mirsky, A. F., & Siegel, A. (1994). The neurobiology of violence and aggression. In A. J. Reiss, Jr., K. A. Miczek, & J. A. Roth (Eds.), *Understanding and preventing violence: Vol. 2. Biobehavioral influences* (pp. 59–172). Washington, DC: National Acadamy Press.

Novaco, R. (1975). *Anger Control.* Lexington, MA: Lexington Books.

Patterson, G. R. (1975). *Families: Applications of social learning to family life.* Champaign, IL: Research Press.

Patterson, G. R., DeBaryshe, B. D., & Ramsey, E. (1989). A developmental perspective on antisocial behavior. *American Psychologist, 44*, 329–335.

Pence, E., & Paymar, M. (1993). *Education groups for men who batter: The Duluth model.* New York: Springer.

Poppen, R. L. (1989). Some clinical implications of rule-governed behavior. In S. C. Hayes (Ed.), *Rule-governed behavior: Cognition, contingencies, and instructional control* (pp. 325–357). New York: Plenum.

Prothrow-Stith, D. (1987). *Violence prevention curriculum for adolescents.* Newton, MA: Educational Development Center.

Reiss, A. J., Jr., & Roth, J. A. (Eds.). (1993a). *Understanding and preventing violence.* Washington, DC: National Academy Press.

Reiss, A. J., Jr., & Roth, J. A. (Eds.). (1993b). *Understanding and preventing violence: Vol. 3. Social Influences.* Washington, DC: National Academy Press.

Reynolds, G. S., Catania, A. C., & Skinner, B. F. (1963). Conditioned and unconditioned aggression in pigeons. *Journal of the Experimental Analysis of Behavior, 6*, 73–74.

Sampson, R. J., & Lauritsen, J. L. (1993). Violent victimization and offending: Individual-, situational-, and community-level risk factors. In A. J. Reiss, Jr. & J. A. Roth (Eds.), *Understanding and preventing violence: Vol. 3. Social influences* (pp. 1–114). Washington, DC: National Academy Press.

Sidman, M. (1989). *Coercion and its fallout.* Boston: Authors Cooperative.

Sidman, M. (1993). Reflections on behavior analysis and coercion. *Behavior and social issues, 3*, 75–85.

Skinner, B. F. (1953). *Science and Human Behavior*. New York: Free Press.

Skinner, B. F. (1959). An experimental analysis of certain emotions. *Journal of the Experimental Analysis of Behavior, 2*, 264.

Skinner, B. F. (1981). Selection by Consequences. *Science, 213*, 501–504.

Skinner, B. F. (1984). The evolution of behavior. *Journal of the Experimental Analysis of Behavior, 41*, 217–21.

Stumphauzer, J. S., Veloz, E. V., & Aiken, T. W. (1981). Violence by street gangs: East Side story? In R. B. Stuart (Ed.), *Violent behavior: Social learning approaches to prediction, management, and treatment* (pp. 68–101). New York: Brunner/Mazel.

Sun Tzu. (1991). *The art of war* (T. Cleary, Trans.). Boston: Shambhala. (Original work written approximately 500 BCE)

Ulrich, R. E., & Azrin, N. H. (1962). Reflexive fighting in response to aversive stimulation. *Journal of the Experimental Analysis of Behavior, 5*, 511–520.

Wilson, J. Q., & Herrnstein, R. J. (1985). *Crime and human nature*. New York: Simon & Schuster.

Wolf, M. M., Braukmann, C. J., & Ramp, K. A. (1987). Serious delinquent behavior as part of a significantly handicapping condition: Cures and supportive environments. *Journal of Applied Behavior Analysis, 20*, 347–359.

5

THE EDUCATION CRISIS

R. DOUGLAS GREER

There is no lack of literature about our educational crisis. The litany of problems that are attributed to education range from crime, to unemployment, to an inadequately trained work force. It has been said that our schools are unable to teach students to write effectively or to perform simple calculations (Hamburg, 1992). Too many of our graduates lack knowledge about current affairs; they do not know the Bill of Rights or the scientific method and its role and utility in contemporary life (National Center for Education Statistics, 1990; National Commission on Excellence in Education, 1983; Secretary's Commission on Achieving Necessary Skills, 1991). An unacceptable number of adults are illiterate (National Center for Research on Evaluation and Student Testing, 1992). Our nation ranks behind other economically comparable countries in mathematics and science (National Center for Education Statistics, 1992).

The public schools in our large cities are besieged by crime and violence, and they have become increasingly segregated by race and economic status (Hamburg, 1992). The flight of the middle class to the suburbs is comparable only with their flight to private schools in the cities—a phenomenon now on the increase in our suburbs, too (Herrnstein & Murray, 1994). The problems are said to be symptomatic of the problems of society at large (Cremin, 1970). Nevertheless, it is to schools that we turn for solutions to societies' ills. After all, if we cannot solve the problems of our schools, what hope have we for the community at large? In this chapter, I outline the existing problems with schools as well as the reasons why efforts to reform schools so often fail. A new model of schooling that is based on the science of behavior is presented; this is followed by an analysis of the advantages of this model over current schooling practices. A cost analysis of the new system concludes the chapter.

EXISTING REFORM EFFORTS

Many excellent suggestions and procedures have been proposed by various reform efforts to improve school outcomes. These suggestions include: (a) increasing standards, (b) increasing funding, (c) empowering teachers, (d) requiring teachers to have undergraduate majors in the arts or sciences, (e) decentralizing administration, (f) decreasing classroom and school size, (g) increasing the influence of parents, (h) providing a core-cultural curricula together with an appreciation of diverse cultural groups, (i) developing professional partnerships between schools and colleges of education, (j) teaching the use of language in its multiple functions, and (k) developing and using measures of short-term and long-term outcomes of instruction (National Commission on Excellence in Education, 1983; Wilson & Daviss, 1994).

All of these suggestions for improving education are important elements in the development of better schools. However, none of these changes will help unless schools can teach students—who have increasingly diverse backgrounds—more effectively than ever before. If we raise standards without raising the performance of more students to meet those standards, we will simply widen the gap between the economic classes. Likewise, none of the suggestions cited will result in significantly better teaching operations. Better pedagogy is a component that is usually omitted in most efforts to improve educational outcomes; yet, without an improved pedagogy all of the other efforts at reform will be to little avail.

The major obstacle to improved educational outcomes is the continued reliance of our schools on prescientific pedagogy (Keller, 1978; Skinner, 1984). Realizing the benefits of the range of important suggestions for educational reform requires a sophisticated pedagogy (Greer, 1989). My definition of a sophisticated pedagogy includes not only the presentation of material, but also the teaching operations provided by a teacher or teaching device that results in new student repertoires.

There are consistent findings from the behavior analytic, educational, and psychological research literatures that, if combined in a coordinated fashion, would constitute a science of teaching and pedagogy (Greer, 1991;

Keller, 1978). Such a pedagogy is needed to realize significant improvements in the effects of schooling for the individual and society (Greer, 1991). Several centers of research, research literatures, and educational demonstration models have contributed to a pedagogy including: Precision Teaching, the consulting behavior analyst model; Programmed Teaching; Direct Instruction; Ecobehavioral Analysis; the Personalized System of Instruction (PSI); the Morningside Generative Model; and the Comprehensive Application of Behavior Analysis to Schooling (CABAS[sm]; Becker & Carnine, 1981; Buskist, Cush & de Grandpre, 1991; Gardner et al., 1994; Greenwood, Hart, Walker, & Risely, 1994; Greer, 1994a; Greer, McCorkle, & Williams, 1989; Johnson, & Layng, 1992; Keller, 1968; Lindsley, 1991; Sulzer-Azaroff et al., 1988; Vargas & Vargas, 1991).

The problems in our schools occur despite the continuing expansion of scientific teaching interventions and related behavioral models of schooling for disseminating those interventions (Gardner et al., 1994). Moreover, the findings from researchers studying the behavior of groups and problem solving are consistent with those findings from the behavior analytic literature (Berliner, 1984; Heward, 1994).

I argue that part of this dissemination problem stems from the lack of a systems approach to schooling that itself is based on research (Greer, 1994a). It is one thing to know the organic chemistry of the pieces of an ecological system (e.g., specific scientific interventions as the repertoire of pedagogical strategies and tactics to draw on as needed) and quite another to have the science to produce and maintain that ecological system (e.g., a science of schooling systems that ensures the delivery of the strategies). One cannot simply insert a solution to part of the system without monitoring and analyzing the entire system in which that solution is to be inserted. A solution that is not systemic will not be supported.

How can the diverse findings from research be put in place in a practical manner in a system that supports them in terms of student benefits? And if they are systemically implemented, will the system work? In this chapter, I attempt to provide some answers to these questions.

Over the last few years, my colleagues and I have arrived, through a behavior analytically inductive scientific process, at just such a systems analysis of schooling on a small scale. We call our particular model the Comprehensive Application of Behavior Analysis to Schooling, or CABAS.

The research base for the model is briefly outlined in Table 1 (see also Greer, 1991, 1992a, 1992b, for a summary of that work). The data base for the efficacy of the model has grown in recent years, ranging from studies about the components of the system (Albers & Greer, 1991; Babbit, 1986; Ingham & Greer, 1992) to multiyear analyses of the entire package

(Greer et al., 1989; Lamm & Greer, 1991; Selinske, Greer, & Lodhi, 1991). Similarly, the number of schools adopting the model has increased from one to seven (Greer, 1992a).

In addition to its own research base, CABAS draws on the entire corpus of behavior analytic research, including the behavioral models of education that I have listed here (see Greer, 1991, for a description of how this is done). It is a system for introducing all the findings of educational research that can be tied to the individual learner.

Finally, CABAS uses the scientific method itself to continuously test the effectiveness of each research finding that is inserted into the system as it is used with each student (Bushel & Baer, 1994). Although our particular research-based system is a long way from providing a solution to the overall crisis in education, it has been effective in small schools for children with behavioral anomalies as well as for children with normal learning repertoires, major developmental handicaps, or minor learning disabilities (Greer, 1991, 1992a). Moreover, the model resulted in the implementation of most of the suggestions for improved educational outcomes cited earlier (e.g., higher standards, teacher empowerment, parent involvement, partnerships between universities and schools, teaching the multiple functions of language). It does so by using the findings and methods of the science of behavior analysis to provide the means for implementation of these global suggestions. I will first describe the CABAS system before moving on to a discussion of why current educational systems fail students and how the CABAS system sidesteps these problems.

THE CABAS APPROACH

In a well-designed system, all of the components of the system work together in a self-correcting fashion for a common goal, such that all benefit. In the CABAS system, the students and the parents are the customers and they drive the system. This system includes the roles of the individual students and their parents, as well as teachers, psychologists, counselors, social workers, supervisors, administrators, the school board, the university where the professionals are trained, and the community at large. All of these roles are a part of the analysis and the design of schooling practices. Pervasive, continuing, and absolute-unit measurements are used to coordinate the system and to provide the basis for contingency analyses of learning problems as they arise (e.g., problem-solving strategies). The measurement operations ensure that the system works and that it is constantly revised consistent with the objective of the system—learner benefits. The interrelationships among the components of the system are shown in Figure 1.

TABLE 1
A Synopsis of the Research Base for CABAS[sm]

Study	Summary
Albers & Greer (1991)	Two experiments replicating the function of the learn unit as a predictor of correct responses with seventh-grade students in a remedial math class.
Diamond (1992)	Two experiments testing learn unit presentations versus opportunity to respond. These studies demonstrated that learn unit presentations were more effective than opportunity to respond (7th-grade remedial math).
Dorow, McCorkle, Williams, & Greer (1989)	An experiment with several replications showing that setting learn unit targets for teachers resulted in higher numbers of learn units taught and also resulted in higher numbers of correct answers and fewer incorrect rates.
Greer (1994b)	A conceptual paper that included data on the comparative costs and outcomes of a CABAS school and a comparable school not using the CABAS model.
Greer, McCorkle, & Williams (1989)	A yearlong week-by-week analysis of the measures of schooling in a CABAS school demonstrating significant correlations among supervisors' tasks, teaching behaviors, and students' learning.
Greer, Phelan, & Sales (1993)	An analysis of learn units and objective criteria achieved in a graduate class and the costs per learn unit and objectives.
Hogin (1994)	Data on a CABAS classroom for students with early self-editing skills.
Hogin (1995)	A functional analysis of the role of the antecedent in the learn unit. Omitting the antecedent in the review of the learn unit with the student results in significantly lower performance.
Lamm & Greer (1991)	A yearlong experiment done in classrooms in Italy demonstrating 4 to 7 times more learning after CABAS was implemented than during baseline conditions. This was a systematic replication of Selinski, Greer, & Lodhi (1991)
Selinski, Greer, & Lodhi (1991)	A three-year experimental analysis of the effect of the introduction of the complete CABAS package on student learning (e.g., correct responses and objectives achieved). Students learned 4 to 7 times more under the CABAS conditions.

Williams & Greer (1993)	An experimental analysis comparing the verbal behavior or functional approach to curriculum used in CABAS schools with a linguistic or structuralist approach to teaching communication. We held behavioral pedagogy constant. Significantly better maintenance occurred under the verbal behavior curriculum.
Greer (1991)	A statement of the philosophy of the CABAS system as learner-driven and data-driven systemwide application of the science of the behavior of the individual to schooling.
Babbitt (1986)	An experiment demonstrating measures of supervisor behaviors that predict student learning and effective teaching.
Ingham & Greer (1992)	A series of experiments demonstrating that the use of the teacher observation procedure used in CABAS schools (compared with typically untechnical observations) changed teacher behaviors and, in turn, student learning. This may be the first experiment to demonstrate a functional relationship between the activities of a supervisor in schools and improvements in student learning.

Student Curricula

The existing *repertoires* are identified for each student as outlined in Figure 1. Repertoires include the range of behaviors within the context of their target-setting events and their target antecedent and consequent controlling variables. Students do not simply learn behaviors or antecedents (e.g., concepts); rather, effective instruction teaches the student antecedents, behaviors, and consequences and the setting in which these result in effective outcomes (e.g., reinforcements). An example of one such repertoire for a preschooler might be the student's listener repertoire. That is, does the student respond immediately to verbal instructions by parents and teachers in a context in which he or she should to achieve effective outcomes? A more advanced repertoire, such as effective writing, might include the student writing in such a way that a reader could follow the written instructions, given a context in which effective written instruction is needed. This outcome for the writer would benefit the writer, too. In short, the setting events, relevant antecedents, range of behaviors having a common effect, and the resulting reinforcement is learned.

Teachers, parents, and various members of the community set priorities for the immediate and long-term instructional objectives or repertoires to be taught to the student. Programmed, scripted, existing curricular ma-

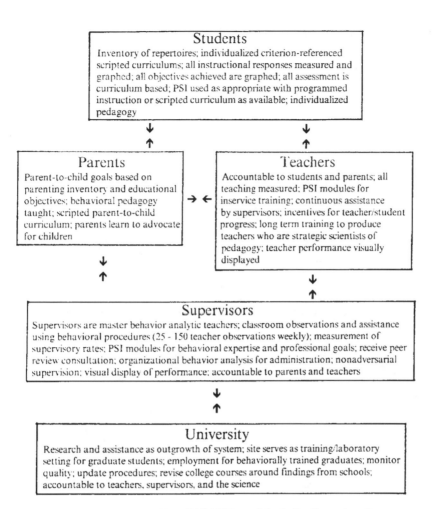

Students
Inventory of repertoires; individualized criterion-referenced scripted curriculums; all instructional responses measured and graphed; all objectives achieved are graphed; all assessment is curriculum based; PSI used as appropriate with programmed instruction or scripted curriculum as available; individualized pedagogy

Parents
Parent-to-child goals based on parenting inventory and educational objectives; behavioral pedagogy taught; scripted parent-to-child curriculum; parents learn to advocate for children

Teachers
Accountable to students and parents; all teaching measured; PSI modules for inservice training; continuous assistance by supervisors; incentives for teacher/student progress; long term training to produce teachers who are strategic scientists of pedagogy; teacher performance visually displayed

Supervisors
Supervisors are master behavior analytic teachers; classroom observations and assistance using behavioral procedures (25 - 150 teacher observations weekly); measurement of supervisory rates; PSI modules for behavioral expertise and professional goals; receive peer review consultation; organizational behavior analysis for administration; nonadversarial supervision; visual display of performance; accountable to parents and teachers

University
Research and assistance as outgrowth of system; site serves as training/laboratory setting for graduate students; employment for behaviorally trained graduates; monitor quality; update procedures; revise college courses around findings from schools; accountable to teachers, supervisors, and the science

Figure 1. The systemic, interlocking CABAS^{sm} model of effective education.

terial or teacher-designed curricula are located for the student and applied using individualized curricular and teaching tactics from the science of pedagogy (Sulzer-Azaroff et al., 1987). This means that carefully sequenced instruction is wedded to research-based pedagogy and used by teachers, who are taught and supported by supervisors who themselves are expert in the science (Babbit, 1986).

Repertoires are taught for the four major divisions of instruction. These are repertoires associated with (a) academic literacy, (b) self-management, (c) problem solving (Mithaug, 1993), and (d) an enlarged community of interests (Greer, 1980). These categories are present throughout the students' education, regardless of the particular status of the student in the progression of the curriculum.

Student–Teacher Ratios Driven by Student's Verbal Repertoires

According to the theory of the CABAS system, the ratio of teachers to students ought to be governed by the students' current and immediate target repertoires of verbal behavior rather than chronological ages or constructs of "handicappedness" (see Table 2; see also Greer, 1994a, for a description of how this is done). For example, the student who does not yet have a firm repertoire of listener behavior will require more direct teacher-controlled individualized instruction until the listener repertoire is mastered and fluent.

However, a more advanced student, who is in the process of acquiring effective written repertoires, can benefit from written instruction and self-instruction because he or she has mastered the prerequisite repertoires shown in Table 2. Such students can learn effectively in a setting with a larger student–teacher repertoire.

Measurement: Learn Units, Objectives, and Curricula Categories

The continuous measurement of student outcomes and teacher efforts drive the individualization of instruction. The type of individualization is guided by the existing repertoires of the students as just described (see Table 2). Teachers in schools that use the CABAS system, record the correct and incorrect responses of each student to all instruction. Students who are at more advanced stages participate in the measurement of their own progress, both as a process of instruction and as an outcome of instruction (e.g., they learn to monitor their progress, set realistic goals, and reinforce themselves or be reinforced by behavior outcomes). Also, because all instruction follows certain research-based formats (i.e., learn units and criterion-referenced objectives), the presentation of instruction by the teacher or other instructional delivery devices can also measured. Thus, measurement includes the performance of teachers as well as students (Greer, 1994b).

The basic measure of instruction that includes the teacher and the student's performance is called the *learn unit* (Greer, 1992a, 1994b). The learn unit includes the teacher's presentation of the antecedent stimulus to the student (e.g., "What is the term for the process that produces chlorophyll?"), the student's correct or incorrect response (e.g., "photosynthesis"), and the teacher's response to the student's answer or idea (e.g., reinforcement of correct responses or teaching operations to correct incorrect student responses). The learn unit is also considered in light of the number of learn units required for the student to acquire a criterion-based and standardized learning objective. Thus, learn units tell us the moment-to-moment results of instruction and the criterion-referenced objectives tell us about more long-term outcomes. They are adaptable to any level of

TABLE 2
Relations Among the Learning of Verbal-Behavior Repertoires, Student Independence, and Teacher–Student Ratios

Status	Description
1) Pre-Listener	The student requires intensive one-to-one instruction by teachers and teacher assistants, total dependence, small student–teacher ratio
2) Listener	The acquisition of instructional control increases the student–teacher ratio slightly, instructional control, minimal independence
3) Speaker	Students increase their independence, which allows a proportionate increase in the number of students possible per teacher
4) Speaker-as-Own Listener	Early forms of rule-governed behavior possible, larger student–teacher ratio
5) Reader	Students can follow written instructions, thereby increasing the possibility of using textual and delayed learn units. The class size can increase accordingly
6) Writer	Even more dramatic increase in the class size is possible given the potential for textual learn units between the teacher and the students, large student–teacher ratios
7) Writer as Own Reader (Repertoires of Self-Editing)	Problem-solving repertoires are made observable, thereby allowing a leap in the number of learn units that can be taught by even fewer teachers relative to class size, large student–teacher ratios, and learn units involving many self-edited responses
8) Verbal Mediation for Solving Problems: An Expansion of the Self-Editing Repertoire	Students increasingly function independently, consistent with their increase in self-management, large classes, learner responsibility for educational outcomes, learner independence

learning. A criterion-referenced objective specifies what degree of correct responding constitutes mastery (e.g., 100% correct responding on two successive instructional sessions). Note that measurement is not something done independently of instruction; rather, it is an integral part of each learn unit. Finally, the attainment of a collection of criterion-referenced objectives related to a domain of learning constitutes a repertoire and is recorded on the student's inventory of repertoires to provide an even longer term assessment of the outcomes of instruction.

Teachers and their supervisors, as well as consultants from a university, work to incorporate different research tactics for different levels of performance or difficulties experienced by individual students. All instruction is individualized, and different research-based tactics may be necessary to teach different students the same repertoire or the same student different repertoires. Much of the teacher's expertise is tied to how effective he or she is at deriving appropriate research-based tactics for solutions to learning problems.

The correct responses of the student to each piece of instruction (e.g., learn unit) and the achievement of criterion-referenced objectives are measured and graphed daily (see the section of this chapter devoted to measurement). Each student has objectives related to the major components of the curriculum (e.g., academic literacy, self-management, problem solving, and an expanded community of interests or reinforcers).

The Teachers' Curricula: Teachers as Strategic Scientists

The teachers are assisted and monitored according to their performance with individual students relative to the practices of the science and the needs of the student. All teachers also have their own individualized professional development curricula based on: (a) their mastered and deficient skills in the classroom vis-à-vis their students' performance (e.g., classroom-practice repertoires from the science), (b) their knowledge of the science (e.g., the vocabulary of the science) and their ability to characterize student learning and instructional operations using this vocabulary, and (c) their expertise at finding and solving learning problems using contingency analyses (e.g., rule-governed problem-solving strategies from the science and its related epistemology). These different categories of teacher expertise are described at length in Greer (1989) and Greer (1991). The levels of expertise are extensive and continue throughout each teacher's career.

In some CABAS schools, teacher advancement in rank and salary is determined by each teacher's progress in acquiring expertise in all of the components of the science of pedagogy vis-à-vis the progress of his or her particular students. The teacher is assisted and supported by supervisors who have demonstrated excellence in the pedagogy and curricular design based on the epistemology of the science (Babbit, 1986; Greer et al., 1989; Ingham & Greer, 1992). Work environments are arranged to ensure that the teacher's work and study is positively reinforced, and that supervision is nonadversarial (Selinske et al., 1991).

The teacher assistants and the paraprofessionals are trained, monitored, and reinforced in the same manner as the teachers. They, too, learn about the science and acquire expertise as reliable transducers of incidences of instruction (Greer et al., 1989; Selinske et al., 1991). Some acquire expertise that is comparable with that of the novice teachers. They are trained and supervised by both the teachers and the supervisors.

Other support professionals, such as school psychologists, social workers, and speech therapists, also participate in the continuous measurement of student performance. They participate in individualized training just as the teachers do. However, their training is geared to the support roles that they play in the system (i.e., educating parents, programming generalization from home to school or from classroom to classroom, and maintaining portfolios or inventories of students' repertoires).

Supervisor Curriculum: The Supervisor as Strategic Scientist

The supervisors function as coaches, mentors, and consultants for the teachers (Greer, 1992a; Ingham & Greer, 1992). To become supervisors, they must have previously completed all of the ranks of teaching. Their supervisory and administrative performance is measured, reinforced, and evaluated in terms of their assigned teachers' performance with students and their teachers' achievement of expertise (via the teachers' own individualized curricular modules). Supervisor performance is graphed and displayed along with that of the teachers and students. Supervisors also have their own set of professional development modules. Like the teachers, supervisors progress through a series of modules, and their advancement in rank and salary is based on their progress.

The Parent Curriculum: Parents as Knowlegeable Advocates

Parents are offered the opportunity to receive individualized instruction in the basic tactics of the science, including how to advocate for and tutor their children. The progress of parents is measured and reinforced in a manner similar to that of the teachers (Greer, 1992b). In the CABAS models, parents are treated, as are their children, as customers. They, in turn, have been the principle advocates for the system and have been responsible for its spread to other schools and grade levels. The parent education program uses the Personalized System of Instruction to individualize the parents' education.

The University Role

Professors from the Columbia University who have CABAS expertise serve as continuing consultants to the professionals in the school. The effectiveness of the model within the school determines the continued presence of the university consultants. The schools also serve as the internship and residency sites for graduate students, many of whom have stayed on as employees and leaders. For example, CABAS schools currently employ 10 to 15 master's-level students in paid teacher-assistant internships, and more than 10 doctoral students are in key leadership roles or internships annually. Thus, the graduate students' schooling is funded by the needs of the system for their expertise. The schools serve as the research sites for the professionals, graduate students, and the university consultant. The data gathered from both research and the school applications of CABAS are used to modify the curriculum at the university (Greer, Phelan, & Sales, 1993). The same pedagogical expertise that is applied in the schools is applied to teacher training at the university (Greer et al., 1993). The expertise of the teachers and their mentors and colleagues is critical to this university training. Indeed, the school becomes the center of inquiry for everyone involved in raising the child.

Community Accountability

The data from all the members involved with the system are presented in summary form to the school board as accounts of the learning and the costs. As a result, the community at large becomes incorporated into the CABAS system. A costs-benefits analysis allows the school board to make decisions based on the program's effects on all components of the system (Greer, 1994a). That is, each year, the school board and the community are informed about the costs per learn unit and the costs per objective of the model, as well as what happens to graduates. Other opportunities for the community to more directly affect the process are possible (Greer, 1994b). The Appendix to this chapter summarizes the components of the system in more detail. Obviously, this degree of accountability allows the local governing bodies of the school the possibility of making decisions about education on an informed basis that has not been possible in the past. Currently, state and local governments can only monitor education in terms of a gross measure of whether or not services are delivered. With the kind of accountability made possible by a costs-benefits analysis, however, it is possible to make decisions based on the effectiveness of services provided.

Continuous Systemwide Modifications

Problems at the level of the student drive changes throughout the system. No single component is treated in isolation either from the system as a whole or from its individual components. Each school requires data-driven modifications; therefore, the system is constantly in revision. When properly run, the system is self-correcting in a true cybernetic fashion. Raising and teaching a child becomes the task of all in the system—as is the case in small and culturally cohesive communities. The CABAS system generates this sense of community through systemic application of the data from the roles of all involved.

REDESIGN OF SCHOOLING DERIVED BY THE BEHAVIOR ANALYTIC SYSTEMS APPROACH

The CABAS approach is an example of just one behavior analytic systems approach. It provides one of many possible models for how we might go about redesigning education through thematic and inductive research and demonstration efforts on a systemwide basis. The development of a learner-driven science of schooling led to several major changes in schooling. The changes might even be characterized as paradigm shifts. These changes grew out of the existing research and the CABAS systems redesign of schooling (Greer, 1991; 1994b).

To date, I have identified seven major characteristics of the CABAS system in its current evolution. They are (a) comprehensive individualized instruction, (b) new conceptions of curriculum and pedagogy based on the epistemology of behavior selection, (c) a systemwide perspective that is learner driven, (d) schools that prime a sense of community, (e) total redesign of schools based on the individual—and what science tells us works—rather than piecemeal approaches to educational reform, (f) a system that works because there is continuous measurement of the important behaviors of each member of the system, and that measurement drives the system, and (g) teachers who function as strategic scientists of instruction.

In Table 3, I have summarized how our approach differs from existing approaches. The changes in practices that accrued as a result of the CABAS system do not provide prepackaged solutions that can be used by teachers who are not scientifically sophisticated; rather, the CABAS system provides a new set of analytic strategies for solving new and learner-relevant questions by teachers who function as strategic scientists of individualized instruction.

The traditional approaches listed in Table 3 are, I believe, the major problems facing schools today. They are not the problems identified by the major reform commissions (National Commission on Excellence in Education, 1984). Why do each of these identified areas constitute problems, from the perspective of the CABAS system, and why were these problems overlooked by others? In the next section I address each of these issues, in turn.

Group Versus Individualized Instruction

Before the advent of public schooling, only children from the aristocracy and the ruling classes were educated. These children were tutored individually. The few children who were not from the ruling classes and who received formal schooling obtained it from religious institutions for specific religious reasons (e.g., the Schola Cantorum trained boys' choirs

TABLE 3
Changes in Schooling Occasioned by CABAS Research

Traditional Approaches	CABAS Innovations
1) Limited view of schooling within society that has lost sight of the learner	Comprehensive systems view that is learner driven
2) Group teaching methodology	Comprehensive individualization
3) Structuralist conception of curriculum	Functionalist conception provided by the epistemology of behavior selection
4) Add-on educational reform efforts (e.g., changes are made to fit existing structures)	Research-driven redesign of schools (e.g., structures determined by what works for the individual learner)
5) Poor and infrequent measurement	New and comprehensive measurement
6) Lack of a sense of community that allows parents and the community to have a voice	Schools that prime a sense of community and a voice for parents; cost-benefits analysis
7) Prescientific and simplified approaches to teaching and the role of the teacher	Sophisticated scientific approach to instruction; the teacher as strategic scientist of instruction.

for the church; Cremin, 1970). The education of this latter group was also done in an individualized fashion through apprenticeships. Group methods of instruction became the predominant method *only* with the advent of free public schooling (Cremin, 1970). Currently, procedures that do not seem amenable to group methods are discounted out-of-hand (Brophy, 1983). The group approach is not the only choice, however.

A particular science of behavior, developed through B. F. Skinner's experimental analysis of behavior, led to a science that was about *the behavior of the individual* (Greer, 1994a; Skinner, 1938). In fact, Skinner's own early attempts to apply the science to education came in the form of programmed instruction as a means of individualizing instruction (Skinner, 1968). His approach was far more sophisticated than the attempts used in many of today's educational software programs, and it probably would have flourished if the personal computer had been available at the time (Vargas & Vargas, 1991). A science of instruction that is based on the science of the behavior of the individual must be one that builds on the differences among individuals, such that each individual achieves mastery and fluency (e.g., mastery with a speed of responding criterion) consistent with his or her phylogenetic and ontogenetic history. It would also include the efficient use of the culture's resources.

The purpose of schools in society is to teach those repertoires that society needs to function, not to eliminate or track students. This does not mean teaching only part of the repertoire; mastery is required. The process of teaching to mastery calls for instruction that is individualized relative to the presenting repertoires of each student. Moreover, the necessity for teaching mastery that incorporates fluency may be critical (Johnson & Layng, 1992; Kelly, 1995).

Although there have been attempts to incorporate the science into educational practice, these efforts have fallen short of the mark. Adapting behavioral objectives in education requires that instruction be individualized so that these objectives are properly applied. Behavioral objectives—and a host of other influences—are derived from the science of the behavior of the individual. However, most of these have been applied in a piecemeal fashion or inadequately done, mostly because teachers have not been taught or supported in the use of the necessary expertise needed to individualize instruction in a comprehensive fashion.

Many good educational research efforts that were devoted to improvements in schooling have used those sciences that are concerned with the behavior of groups as their methodological model (Brophy, 1983; Johnston & Pennypacker, 1980). No science of group instruction has evolved beyond the use of group contingencies (Axelrod & Greer, 1994). Increasingly, nonbehavioral educators, at least those who are concerned directly with pedagogy, have expressed disappointment with their inability to measure results as well as the lack of findings from research practices associated with the study of group behavior (Perone, 1991). Standardized tests have a limited instructional function because they are designed for the study of groups; they frequently are tied to psychological constructs that are only peripherally related to direct instruction. They are useful for actuarial purposes (e.g., group comparisons) but not at the level of individual pedagogy.

Some educators now advocate portfolio assessment. This approach requires that the accomplishments of each individual be documented and preserved as the major form of assessment of students (Perone, 1991). However, portfolios that are not grounded in objectivity and standards of science cannot provide the level of accountability that both learners and communities desire. Also, if procedures are not put in place to teach until the student has mastered the material, portfolios will consist of lists of deficits that will be attributed to the presumed inadequacies of the student.

At first blush, group instruction would appear to be the only economically viable method of instruction for public schools; after all, public schools must educate the masses in classrooms housing large numbers of students. However, the research from several applications of behavior analysis to schooling has identified numerous ways to individualize instruction in classrooms housing large numbers of students. This literature has been largely ignored by educators. One conspicuous example of this oversight is the evidence associated with the personalized system of instruction (PSI) model. An extensive number of studies exist that show how instruction can be individualized—even in large lecture classes with 200 to 500 college students—through the use of PSI. However, the lessons learned from these studies have not been applied to the educational mainstream (Keller, 1968; Buskist, et al., 1991). PSI provides procedures for individualization and mastery-learning when used in conjunction with programmed instruction, precision teaching, direct instruction, and systemwide behavior analysis.

The traditional group method assumes that instruction consists of the presentation of material by the teacher, with the responsibility of learning placed on the student. There is a time when the responsibility for learning should be shifted to the student, of course, but this should be an instructional objective. When the responsibility for learning is prematurely shifted to the students, problems arise. Students who are not ready for that responsibility (i.e., they don't have the component skills) fall out of the educational system. The result is often unemployment or other social problems that, in the long run, are more expensive to deal with than ensuring mastery in the schooling process. First, we must teach the repertoires that lead to individual responsibility—then we can look at costs. The lack of appropriate measurement opportunities in the current educational system means that there is no way to ascertain the costs of education relative to learning—until long after the damage has been done. Simply speaking, there are no adequate accountability measures relative to educational outcomes, given the lack of hard individual measures of learning.

There are numerous and solid findings from the basic and applied science of behavior that provide effective tactics for most instructional purposes (Cooper, Heron, & Heward, 1987; Greer, 1980, 1992a; Sulzer-Azaroff & Mayer, 1986). They apply to individual students and are adaptable to wide variances in individual student repertoires. In fact, they are inherently suited to the variable genetic and instructional differences and even capacities among individual students. These strategies and tactics call for individualized instruction, as does precision teaching, programmed instruction, and the personalized system of instruction.

In summary, group methods of instruction are based on the sciences of the behavior of groups (e.g., sociology, educational psychology, and other sciences that are concerned with the distribution of behaviors or traits across populations). That is not to say that the sciences of group behavior have not made many contributions to education. Group methods have identified factors that correlate with more successful schools regardless of socioeconomic status (Berliner, 1984), and they provided the tools to compare educational policy among schools and between countries. But, these methods are not fitted to identifying fine-grained instructional tactics and strategies for teaching a wide range of students in a manner consistent with their individual strengths and deficits (Keller, 1978). In fact, to expect such methods to solve problems of individualized pedagogy is a misapplication of the methodology. These methods show even less promise for locating teacher tactics as the diversity of students continues to increase.

Individualized forms of pedagogy must become the method of choice. To date, however, only a science of the behavior of the individual can form the basis of an effective pedagogy for individualized instruction. There is an existing set of strategies and tactics that can be put in place, if the predominant methodology shifts from the group to the individual. Mastery and even fluency can be the norm rather than the exception, once instruction is individualized on a systemwide basis, and once that system is tied to the educational and economic outcomes and interests of all of those involved in the community.

Structuralist Versus Selectionist Curriculum

The philosophy of the science of the behavior of the individual has been characterized as *behavioral selection*. It is this nomenclature that I shall use because of its logical and scientific continuity with its most related philosophy of science (e.g., natural selection; Palmer & Donahoe, 1992). Like natural selection, and like instrumental pragmatism to a lesser extent (Dewey, 1910), behavioral selection looks to the environmental effects of behavior or repertoires of behavior as the means of selecting and, therefore, defining the *functions* of behavior. The identification of such functions of behavioral repertoires is critical to curricular design because it is the function and the setting variables that must be taught in addition to the behaviors.

I suggest that there is an interesting and long overdue rapprochement between behavioral selection and educational tenets, even though this may be considered antithetical to contemporary behaviorism. These tenets include the effective use of language, instrumental pragmaticism, independent thinking, self-determinism, and the fostering and nurturing of creativity. However, the structuralists' views on these tenets of current educational theory, on which these theories have traditionally been based, cannot provide the functions or controlling variables for teaching such repertoires. For example, it is not enough to advocate for creativity; if it is not operationally defined, it is unteachable. If the variables that provide the motivation and effects of the repertoire cannot be manipulated by expert instruction, then it is unteachable (Skinner, 1968).

Although Skinner suggested applications to these critical repertoires from the tactics and the epistemology of the science of the behavior of the individual, only a portion of their implications has been understood (Skinner, 1957, 1968, 1984). Behavior analysts in education have concentrated on applications of the science and epistemology in developing a set of teaching or pedagogical practices, and to obvious good ends (Sulzer-Azaroff et al., 1988); but there are some equal, if not more important, applications needed for the identification and design of curriculum. I shall describe a few of them as they apply to the solution of the educational crisis, which, I argue, is a problem of curricular conception as well as pedagogical innovation.

Students need several types of repertoires to be competent and to flourish in a global economy; these repertoires are also needed for students to have a desirable quality of life. The major ones that schools need to provide include (a) academic literacy, (b) self-management, (c) problem solving, and (d) an enlarged community of interests (i.e., an enlarged community of reinforcers that are part of the learned repertoires) (Greer, 1980; Mithaug, Martin, Agran, & Rusch, 1988).

Students need to master and be fluent with the basics of composition, mathematics, social studies, and the findings and methods of science. Academic fluency and mastery entails not only producing calculations with zero latency (e.g., immediate recall of multiplication or addition facts), but also performing the more complex operations associated with these forms of academic literacy when needed. Structuralists would characterize these latter skills as cognitions. Such a characterization does not necessarily tell us how the student is to acquire these skills, however. We have a pedagogy that can do this—provided an adequate curricular conception is in place. The new questions are there; they need only be tested through research and development. The evidence and operations necessary to implement them are described elsewhere (Cooper et al., 1987; Gardner et al., 1994; Greer, 1994a, 1994b; Sulzer-Azaroff et al., 1988).

There are also an extensive set of strategies and tactics for teaching students to manage their own behavior by teaching them to control and analyze the contingencies of reinforcement and punishment in their own environment. Mithaug et al. (1988) have broken these down into repertoires associated with (a) setting goals, (b) monitoring progress, and (c) providing reinforcers for the attainment of goals or successive approximations of those goals. It is also likely that rule-governed verbal behavior (e.g., verbally mediated behavior), in the form of the person functioning as "his or her own listener," is a necessary component if the student is to be taught how to manage the contingencies that affect his or her behavior. This listener acts as a reinforcer or punisher for responses that function to manage the contingencies in the person's environment (Hayes, 1989; Lodhi & Greer, 1989; Malott & Garcia, 1991; Skinner, 1957). There are two repertoires involved: The *repertoires to be changed* and the *repertoires of changing behavior* (Catania, Matthews, & Shimoff, 1982; Hayes, 1989; Skinner, 1953). Selectionist conceptions of self-management (e.g., contingency analysis and contingency management) make such repertoires amenable to curricular design and implementation in a spiral fashion such that the hierarchy of repertoires can be taught simultaneously with the teaching of academic literacy and problem-solving repertoires (Greer, 1994a; also see Table 2).

Problem-solving repertoires constitute the third major category. When problem solving is conceptualized as a form of verbal behavior based on Skinner's (1957) conception of communicative behavior, the repertoire becomes amenable to curricular design and pedagogical treatment by a properly taught teacher. It is no longer nonobservable, but rather it is a functional form of written or spoken behavior that can be directly observed in the behavior and environmental contingencies of the classroom. In effect, it can be observed, measured, and taught using measurably effective pedagogical procedures. The specifics of the process is beyond the scope of this chapter, but it has been treated in-depth elsewhere (Greer, 1992a, 1994b). Students can be taught to select verbal repertoires (or, more appropriately, the verbal behavior will select the solution responses) associated with types of problems and apply those verbal repertoires—characterized as the methods of history, logic, or science—to verbally mediate between the problem and the solution.

Finally, it is not enough to have effective academic literacy, self-management, and problem-solving repertoires. The repertoires themselves must be learned as tools for problem solving. Additionally, they must be taught in such a way that new reinforcers are learned along with the behaviors. In fact, that is what is implied by the term *repertoire* as it relates to CABAS and to behavioral selection. The repertoire comprises the setting events, including the motivational variables, the group of behaviors, and the consequences (the reinforcement of effective behaving). Fortunately, when state-of-the science pedagogical procedures are used in the instructional process, the reinforcers accrue as a matter of course (Greer, 1980). Literature, science, music, mathematics, writing, speaking, and art will acquire reinforcing properties relative to the antecedents and consequences common to such activities (Greer, 1980). That is, the stimuli associated with these will evoke attending responses and subsequent engagement relative to other motivational variables in existence at the moment. The active conditioning of new reinforcers will take care of many of the problems associated with generalized stimulus control (e.g., generalization of learning).

Thus, a behavioral selectionistic conception incorporates the goals of instrumental pragmatism (e.g., learning to predict the outcomes of behaving), the multiple functions of communication (e.g., writing and reading to affect the behavior of another or to verbally mediate one's own behavior), independent thinking as verbal behavior, and proficient mathematical, writing, and speaking repertoires that are tied to real-world problems in a systematic way. It is not possible to precisely characterize these goals or design instruction for them, much less teach them, without the tools of the science and their related epistemological perspective.

Add-On and Piecemeal Educational Reform Versus Redesign

An overwhelming number of responses to the educational crisis have taken the form of additions to, or modifications of, existing practices based on traditional assumptions that are themselves problematic (Wilson & Daviss, 1994). Moreover, such efforts have not taken into account the existence of a science of individualized instruction. The use of empirically determined objectives, the primacy of the student and the parent, and the needs of the community (in terms of the outcome needed by employers and a democracy) have also been left out of these reform efforts. Valid costs and benefits analyses have not been possible, and the lack of concern for the ecology of the system has been the result of a perspective that was narrowly focused rather than systemic. The short-term interests of each component of the ecology of the school has controlled efforts at reform.

The current and prescientific approach to schooling predates what we have learned about the controlling variables of the behavior of the individual. The existing approaches listed in Table 3 characterize the problems. Because the system itself is faulty, add-on attempts to reform or drastically improve educational outcomes or the processes leading to those outcomes are limited in their effects. This occurs because the natural laws underlying the maximization of learning or the controlling variables for system-cohesiveness are thwarted.

It is a fact, for example, that students learn at their own rate; thus, group methodologies that present curricula at a rate that appears right for the average learner is inconsistent with what we know about learning. Measurement that doesn't help the instruction of the individual student is irrelevant to learning. Similarly, curricula that are unrelated to the niches of a given culture that a student will need to occupy result in inert knowledge (Whitehead, 1929).

The initial premise of CABAS was to design schooling from the ground up, based on the following criteria: (a) what does the student need to know for his or her own benefit and for society's benefit, (b) what do we know about learning, (c) what is the nature of the ecological system in which the student learns, and (d) what are the resources available in terms of the long-term effects of adequate rather than inadequate instruction. Other than the small-scale attempts of the CABAS efforts, comprehensive and data-based school design has never been tried.

Society's current approaches to education evolved without the benefits of the findings of a science of the behavior of the individual. Redesign cannot be done via national proclamation, nor can it be done only in such a top-down approach. The role that the government can play is to supply adequate incentives and contingencies that support learner-driven forms of accountability or, at least, avoid punishing comprehensive design strategies that depart from common epistemological assumptions. Given that political climate, environmental redesign can be done on an individual school and individual school-district basis using the strategic science each step of the way. More effective schooling practices can evolve inductively from good science directed toward the objectives of schooling. Given the current problems that plague schools, little will be lost by such experimentation, and much may be gained. In short, we can design schools from the ground up, rather than try to patch a faulty system.

New Forms and Uses of Measurement

The basis of science and any well designed system is measurement. Measurement is an essential ingredient for any goal-directed effort that holds promise for achieving its goals. Not just any type of measurement will do. The measurement must be tied to natural processes if it is to identify and use the natural fractures of learning and teaching and the ecology of the community. Natural fractures encompass the behaviors, as well as their outcomes, antecedents, and settings, otherwise known as *contextual events*. The discovery of natural fractures has been the job of the science of the behavior of the individual.

The most basic units of teaching and learning that are used in the CABAS model are learn units and criterion-referenced learning objectives (Greer, 1994b; Greer et al., 1993). Other measures are used for other components in the system, but the learn unit, in conjunction with the criterion-referenced objective, is the most important. All of the other units of measurement (e.g., supervisor measures and parent measures) must be found to be related to learn units or they are discarded as critical components.

Learn units are identified and defended as the most basic measure of teaching because they are both the smallest units and natural fractures that incorporate both the teacher and the student component of pedagogy. The learn unit includes the student's response to an instructional presentation and the antecedent and postcedent behaviors of the teacher. We know that (a) the number of learn units received and (b) learn units that are complete and accurately done predict student learning and teacher success with students (Albers & Greer 1991; Greer et al., 1989; Ingham & Greer, 1992; Lamm & Greer, 1991; Selinske et al., 1991). Moreover, reliable measures of learn units and learning objectives can be converted into costs; therefore, learning-based measures of both educational effects and their related costs can be calculated (Greer, 1994b). Such measures allow us, for the first time, to plan and modify schooling practices based on the relative costs and benefits of both instructional practices and specific curricular objectives. In a relatively short period of time, we can ask whether the practices are effective and economical and whether the goals are relevant to needs. They are referred to as natural fractures because the research has identified them as strong predictors of learning (Greer, 1994b; Heward, 1994).

For example, in the CABAS schools, we can summarize the cost of each learn unit and each objective, and we can evaluate the relative benefits. Furthermore, we can compare costs between various school models using both the methodology and the practices of the science of the behavior of groups, depending on the question (Greer, 1994b).

The learn-unit component for the student includes the number and rate of that student's correct responses. Measuring of responses provides accurate and direct assessment of the student's progress, because these measures are standardized and are collected by instructional personnel who are trained and monitored relative to a common standard. Such measures provide students, parents, teachers, supervisors, and interested others with useful accounts of progress and achievement. These are used in conjunction with counts of the number and character of the learning objectives achieved by the student.

The student's achievement is not measured with a rating (e.g., letter grades, such as A, B, C, D, and F, or word labels, such as Pass, Fail, and Excellent), but, rather, the student's mastery and fluency for a particular repertoire is provided for instructional or portfolio purposes (e.g., the student reads 2nd-grade material aloud at a rate of 60 correct words per min and 0 words per min incorrect; the student answers why, where, when, and how questions from the readings with 100% accuracy using complete sentences).

Measures of learn units and objectives are provided for instruction in each of the major curricular areas already described (i.e., academic literacy, self-management, problem solving, and interests), as well as for the traditional categories of math, language arts, and social studies. Also, measures are taken according to certain repertoires of verbal behavior (e.g., writer, reader, writer/reader, speaker, or listener repertoires). Portfolios, or inventories, of what the student has learned and produced also include the context (e.g., setting events, antecedent stimuli, the behaviors in the response class, and whether the reinforcers are prosthetic or natural). The portfolios provide the information that parents, students, teachers, employers, and other schooling professionals need, and they do not call for between–student comparisons. In effect, what is made available to the consumers is a reliable and scientifically sophisticated curriculum vita.

Measures of teachers' performance include the number (total and correct) of learn units taught by curricular areas, the objectives achieved by curricular area, the number of inservice modules achieved (see Greer, 1992, for a description) in the teacher's individual curricular program by the teaching categories described above, and teacher rate and accuracy measures collected several times weekly by teacher supervisors. These measures are *not* used to compare teachers with one another. The measures are not allowed to be adversarial; rather, they serve instructional and portfolio purposes. They are used to determine rank and salary advancement in some of our schools, but the specific goals are set by the teacher and teacher-coach jointly, relative to each individual teacher and his or her group of students.

Different subject areas, the different verbal behavior repertoires of the teacher's students, the expertise of the teacher in the science of teaching, and the ratio of instructional staff to students naturally and properly affect learn unit productivity and effectiveness. Students who do not have reliable listener repertoires (e.g., they do not respond to the verbal behavior of a speaker) require teacher-intensive learn units, whereas students who have advanced writer-as-own-reader repertoires require less immediate teacher responding, particularly if those students have advanced self-management skills. The number of learn units possible in the two cases are vastly different. A well-trained teacher in the class composed of students with few listener skills will produce significantly fewer learn units than the well-trained teacher with a class of students who have independent writer repertoires. The mix of students and the relative teacher expertise will vary (see Table 2).

Supervisor performance measures include all of the measures of their particular group of teachers (e.g., modules mastered, learn units taught, teacher rate and accuracy measures, student objectives achieved) as well as increases or decreases in teacher performance relative to each teacher's prior performance and the repertoires of their students. In addition, the supervisors have their own measures consisting of counts of particular tasks shown to predict effective teacher performance (Greer et al., 1989; Ingham & Greer 1992).

Similarly, measures of the other school professionals involve a mix of teacher and supervisor measures. Those professionals involved in the parent education program—social workers, school psychologists, teacher coaches—incorporate the measures of parent progress, such as quizzes passed at criterion levels, objectives achieved by parents with their children, or in some cases objectives achieved by students. Summaries of the performance of all of the professionals provide measures of the supervisors and the school as a whole, allowing within- and between-year comparisons (Kelly & Greer, 1992).

Summaries of the individual and composite data serve as measures of the consultant's effectiveness and as a continuing means for adjusting the system consistent with the goals. Based on our research, we have come to expect from 4 to 7 times more learning after CABAS is implemented than in pre-CABAS baselines (Lamm & Greer, 1991; Selinske et al., 1991). We also expect significant increases from year to year consistent with the increased sophistication of the professional staff (Kelly & Greer, 1992).

When the learning, instructional, and management data are converted to costs per unit, we can provide costs and benefits analyses that can be used by the school board and the community, data they can use to make decisions about budgets and staff deployment as well as curricular changes. If used consistent with the systems approach, these data drive the system such that the long- and short-term effects serve to reinforce system-wide cooperation and cohesiveness.

A Sense of Community

How do we attempt to replicate the benefits of raising children in a small and culturally cohesive community (i.e., communities in which individuals are naturally part of a community)? That is, how can we create a sense of community that will compensate for the plurality of cultures and the displacement of families from original communities that so often exists within schools? A sense of community is critical to the successful function of schools for students, parents, school professionals, and the members of the school board as representatives of the community that requires competent graduates.

What do I mean by a sense of community? A sense of community is evident when the members of the community have a voice in the operation of agencies of the community, as in the case of villages and extended families in which everyone participates in the education of all children as well as their own children. In the CABAS system, the student's voice is constantly present in the data. The parents have a role in generalizing instruction, advocating for future placement of their children. They have membership in a parental group that knows what their children should receive in the way of instruction. The parents are taught these skills in parent education courses and in their role as major voices in setting the curricula for their children.

The measurement of the teachers' and supervisors' performance is graphically displayed in public areas of the school; thus, parents can monitor the performance of the staff at all times as well as the performance of their children. Taken together, these operations ensure that each member of the community is heard—which, in turn—helps to create a sense of community.

A sense of community is not always present in neighborhood schools for several reasons. Because the nature and origins of the student body have changed—due to the international mobility of society's members—a sense of community or cultural cohesiveness is often lacking. An effective systems approach to schooling must often prime a sense of community. In the CABAS approach, we do this by involving parents through our parenting education program and by providing continuous progress reports on

each student to the parents along with the public posting of the performance evaluations of all professionals.

When a parent–teacher conference occurs, the graphs depicting the
child's actual performance, day in and day out, serve as the basis for joint
parent–teacher decisions about the child. Those parents who have participated in the parent education program are knowledgeable consumers.
They are prepared to assess teachers even in school sites that do not use
the science. They know what to look for in a teacher and how to advocate
for particular teachers and programs in schools. Parents meet in groups as
part of their training; the training groups provide continuing support for
the parents' efforts to improve their children's educational options in a
non-CABAS school. In fact, this advocacy by parents is the reason
CABAS has spread to several school systems.

In this manner, we prime a sense of community and we learn more
about how we can do so more effectively. Such an effort is critical. As the
natural communities are changed on a wholesale basis by mobility and
diversity of cultures in modern society, we must find effective ways to create
a new sense of community in schools relevant to the objectives of education broadly conceived. We all have one common objective—to provide
the best for our children.

Professional and System Sophistication

Admittedly, the professional and systems expertise described here is
vastly more sophisticated than that required of professionals in current
approaches to schooling. However, the mini-system known as CABAS has
worked, and it has been developed in schools with teachers who acquired
their expertise as a result of the implementation of the approach. However,
at least two professionals who have the necessary expertise are needed to
get the system started. The expertise that is required includes not only
expertise in the science of the behavior of the individual, but also sophistication in what can only be described as pedagogy and systemic schooling.
What does this increased sophistication mean for teachers? What are the
ramifications from the perspective of the teachers' and administrative
unions? What are the ramifications for the university that will facilitate
the CABAS system in a particular school?

The university must train teachers such that they, too, master and are
fluent in the repertoires already described. The actual classroom setting in
which they are taught must be one that exemplifies the model. Moreover,
the university itself must apply the same instructional sophistication to its
education of teachers. The same costs-benefits analyses are possible here
also, as we have demonstrated (Greer, Phelan, & Sales, 1993).

It is in the best long-term interests of teachers and their bargaining
agents to support efforts that are likely to increase the long-term economic

value of teachers to the community. With measures and nonadversarial systems similar to or better than the ones described, the value of teachers will be readily apparent; the natural selection inherent in an economy that demands expertise will select out the competent and justly reward their expertise. In a system that truly supports the development and monitoring of that expertise, many teachers will acquire the needed sophistication, and the economic rewards will select out more promising candidates for the teaching profession—a profession with a valid discipline that is commensurate with the growing expectations that society places on the schooling process. In the current system, everyone is losing on a long-term basis. Short-term gains for vested interests work to the long-term detriment of all.

The current teacher incentive systems are not tied to valid, learner-driven, and nonadversarial practices; thus, they are prone to abuses. A profession in which the reliable identification of teacher expertise drives the system will select out expert teaching. The identification of the repertoires that constitute a science of pedagogy makes a real career ladder possible—one that is truly tied to the economic viability of the community. This means that different levels of expertise can be rewarded in a differential fashion. Savings for the community will be possible, and at the same time, the more expert teacher will be financially rewarded at the highest levels. The possibility of high levels of remuneration will pull along increased expertise. Some will choose less expertise and their remuneration will be commensurate.

COST-EFFECTIVENESS

At present, it is difficult to determine whether building schools this way is more or less costly than using traditional methods. The existing model has been developed and used, for the most part, in small schools for students with disabilities or in classrooms for students with behavioral disorders or learning disabilities in a medium-sized school district. Special education classes are significantly more costly than are classrooms for non-categorized students (Barbanel, 1994). Because the schoolwide applications have been done with students who are categorized as "handicapped", the costs have been higher than they are for classrooms for students without disabilities. However, much of the increased costs are tied to administration rather than pedagogy or curriculum changes in the classroom, according to Barbanel.

In the few comparisons done with comparable students, CABAS tuition costs have been either less than or equivalent to those of the non-CABAS programs. When the costs per learn unit and the costs per instructional objective (e.g., a costs-benefits analysis of educational outcomes) were compared between CABAS and non-CABAS schools, the CABAS programs were significantly more cost-effective; for examples, CABAS learn units costs 65 cents in one of our schools and in excess of $10 per learn unit in one comparison school (Greer, 1994b).

The natural fracture that should govern student–teacher ratios, according to what our data currently suggest, are the particular sets of verbal behavior that are in the students' repertoires (Greer, 1994a). That is, students with little or no listener behavior require intense one-to-one learn unit presentations by teachers and other instructional staff, regardless of the age or the presence or lack of a disability (see Table 2). Once the student masters and is fluent with new verbal and self-management repertoires—that is, the student acquires reader and writer repertoires and related self-management skills—the number of students per teacher increases dramatically.

Our current estimates suggest that prelistener to early-reader repertoires, with or without developmental disabilities, would have small student–teacher ratios, whereas students of middle school age (provided they had the prerequisite verbal repertoires) could have student–teacher ratios significantly larger than those in our current schools. Students would graduate to more learner independence and learning responsibility only as they master the prerequisites. Also, as the learn unit increasingly appears in written form to students who have mastered the necessary prerequisites, with corresponding increases in the number of responses or products that constitutes learn units by both the student and the teacher, the manner in which the teaching occurs allows a different and potentially a more cost-effective delivery system (e.g., a form of classroom E-mail). A brief summary of the verbal and self-management repertoires relative to student–teacher ratios is given in Table 2, and an in-depth description is provided elsewhere (Greer, 1994a). However, true cost analyses of larger systems await large-scale applications that are now possible with CABAS-type measurement. There are, however, two probable economic outcomes of the application of the system. First, CABAS-type programs would be significantly less wasteful, because they result in 4 to 7 times more learning for the same costs (Greer et al., 1989; Lamm & Greer, 1991; Selinske et al., 1991). The latter result should tell us whether the costs are worth it. Finally, like any large experimental program, after the desired effects are possible, subsequent research and marketing will lead to more cost-effective methods.

CONCLUSION

The obstacles to effective schooling that have been identified from a systems perspective are solvable with the appropriate strategies, tactics, and sophisticated epistemological perspective. An effective system has been done on a small scale, and it may be possible on a large scale. Such an approach does not result in a quick fix, and there are more questions than answers; but one behavior analytic systems approach has raised better questions and provided some new tools. If we use good science, maintain a learner-driven system, introduce a selectionist perspective to curricular design, and provide expertise for teachers and supervisors that is tied to pedagogy, all may not be lost.

REFERENCES

Albers, A., & Greer, R. D. (1991). Is the three-term contingency trial a predictor of effective instruction? *Journal of Behavioral Education*, 1, 337–354.

Axelrod, S., & Greer, R. D. (1994). A commentary on cooperative learning. *Journal of Behavioral Education*, 4, 41–48.

Babbit, R. (1986). Computerized data management and the time-distribution of tasks performed by supervisors in a data-based educational organization. (Doctoral Dissertation, Columbia University, 1986). *Dissertation Abstracts International*, 47, 3737a.

Barbanel, J. (1994, January 23). $7,512 per pupil: Where does it go? *New York Times*, section 13, pp. 1, 12, 13.

Becker, W. (1992). Direct instruction: A twenty year review. In R. West & L. Hammerlynck (Eds.), *Design for educational excellence: The legacy of B. F. Skinner*. Longmont, CO: Sopris West.

Becker, W. C., & Carnine, D. W. (1981). Direct Instruction: A behavior theory model for comprehensive educational intervention with the disadvantaged. In J. Leblanc, W. B. Etzel, & R. Ruiz (Eds.), *Behavior modification: Contributions to education* (pp. 145–207). Hillsdale, NJ: Erlbaum.

Berliner, D. C. (1984). The half-full glass: A review of research on teaching. In P. L. Hosford (Ed.), *Using what we know about research* (pp. 51–77). Alexandra, VA: Association for Supervision and Instruction.

Brophy, J. E. (January, 1983). If only it were true: A response to Greer. *Educational Researcher*, 12(1), 10–12.

Bushel, D., Jr., & Baer, D. M. (1994). Measurably superior instruction means close continual contact with the relevant outcome data. Revolutionary! In R. Gardner, III, D. M. Sainata, J. O. Cooper, J. E. Heron, W. L. Heward, J. Eschelman, and T. A. Grossi (Eds.). *Behavior analysis in education: Focus on measurably superior instruction* (pp. 33–64). Pacific Groves, CA: Brooks Cole.

Buskist, W., Cush, D., & de Grandpre, R. J. (1991). The life and times of PSI. *Journal of Behavioral Education*, 1, 215–234.

Catania, A. C., Matthews, B. A., & Shimoff, E. (1982). Instructed versus shaped human verbal behavior: Interactions with nonverbal responding. *Journal of the Experimental Analysis of Behavior*, 38, 233–248.

Cooper, J. O., Heron, T. E., Heward, W. L. (1987). *Applied behavior analysis*. Columbus, OH: Merrill.

Cremin, L. A. (1970). *American education: The colonial experience 1607–1783*. New York: Harper & Row.

Dewey, J. (1910). *How we think*. Boston: Heath.

Diamond, D. (1992). *Beyond time on task: Comparing opportunities to respond to learn units to determine an accurate means of measuring educational gains*. Unpublished paper, Teacher's College, Columbia University.

Dorow, L. G., McCorkle, N. P., Williams, G., & Greer, R. D. (1989, May). *Effects of setting performance criteria on the productivity and effectiveness of teachers*. Paper presented at the international convention of the Association for Behavior Analysis, Nashville, TN.

Gardner, R., III, Sainata, D. M., Cooper, J. O., Heron, T. E., Heward, W. L., Eschelman, J., & Grossi, T. A. (Eds.). (1994). *Behavior analysis in education: Focus on measurably superior instruction*. Pacific Groves, CA: Brooks Cole.

Greenwood, C. R., Hart, B., Walker, D. I., & Risley, T. (1994). The opportunity to respond and academic performance revisited: A behavioral theory of developmental retardation. In R. Gardner, III, D. M. Sainata, J. O. Cooper, T. E. Heron, W. L. Henward, J. Eschelman, & T. A. Grossi (Eds.), *Behavior analysis in education: Focus on measurably superior instruction* (pp. 213–244). Pacific Groves, CA: Brooks Cole.

Greer, R. D. (1980). *Design for music learning*. New York: Teachers College Press.

Greer, R. D. (1989). A pedagogy for survival. In A. Brownstein (Ed.), *Progress in behavioral studies* (pp. 7–44). Hillsdale, NJ: Erlbaum.

Greer, R. D. (1991). The teacher as strategic scientist: A solution to our educational crisis? *Behavior and Social Issues, 1*, 25–41.

Greer, R. D. (1992a). *L'enfant terrible* meets the educational crisis. *Journal of Applied Behavior Analysis, 23*, 65–69.

Greer, R. D. (1992b). Teaching practices to save America's children: The legacy of B. F. Skinner. *Journal of Behavioral Education. 1*, 159–164.

Greer, R. D. (1994a). A systems analysis of the behaviors of schooling. *Journal of Behavioral Education, 4*, 255–264.

Greer, R. D. (1994b). The measure of a teacher. In R. Gardner, III, D. M. Sainata, J. O. Cooper, T. E. Heron, W. L. Heward, J. Eschelman, & T. A. Grossi, (Eds.), *Behavior analysis in education: Focus on measurably superior instruction* (pp. 325–335). Pacific Groves, CA: Brooks Cole.

Greer, R. D., McCorkle, N. P., & Williams, G. (1989). A sustained analysis of the behaviors of schooling. *Behavioral Residential Treatment, 4*, 113–141.

Greer, R. D., Phelan, C. S., & Sales, C. (1993, May). *A costs-benefits analysis of a graduate course*. Paper presented at the International Conference of the Association for Behavior Analysis, Chicago, IL.

Hamburg, D. A. (1992). *Today's children: Creating a future for a generation in crisis*. New York: Times Books.

Hayes, S. C. (1989). *Rule governed behavior: Cognition, contingencies, and instructional control.* New York: Plenum.

Herrnstein, R. J., & Murray, C. M. (1994). *The bell curve: Intelligence and class structure in American life.* New York: Free Press.

Heward, W. L. (1994). Three low tech strategies for increasing the frequency of active student responses during instruction. In R. Gardner, III, D. M. Sainata, J. O. Cooper, T. E. Heron, J. Eschelman, & T. A. Grossi (Eds.), *Behavior analysis in education: Focus on measurably superior instruction* (pp. 283–320). Pacific Groves, CA: Brooks Cole.

Hogin, S. (1994, March). *CABAS for students with early self-editing repertoires.* Paper presented at the annual convention of The International Behaviorology Association, Guanajuato, Mexico.

Hogin, S. E. (1996) *A functional relationship between the student's antecedent in the learn-unit and correct responding.* Unpublished doctoral dissertion, Columbia University, New York.

Ingham, P., & Greer, R. D. (1992). Changes in student and teacher responses in observed and generalized settings as a function of supervisor observations. *Journal of Applied Behavior Analysis, 25,* 153–164.

Johnson, K. R., & Layng, T. V. J. (1992). Breaking the structuralists barrier: Literacy and numeracy with fluency. *American Psychologist, 47,* 1475–1490.

Johnston, J., & Pennypacker, H. (1980). *Strategies and tactics of human behavioral research.* Hillsdale, NJ: Erlbaum.

Keller, F. S. (1968). Goodbye teacher. *Journal of Applied Behavior Analysis, 1,* 79–90.

Keller, F. S. (1978). Instructional technology and educational reform: 1977. *The Behavior Analyst, 1,* 48–53.

Kelly, R. L. (1995). *Functional relations between mastery with a rate criterion and long term maintenance of learning.* Unpublished doctoral dissertation, Columbia University, New York.

Kelly, T. M., & Greer, R. D. (1992, May). *Functional relationships between learn units and maladaptive behavior.* Paper presented at the International Conference of the Association for Behavior Analysis, San Francisco, CA.

Lamm, N., & Greer, R. D. (1991). A systematic replication of CABAS in Italy. *Journal of Behavioral Education, 1,* 427–444.

Lindsley, O. R. (1991). Precision teaching's unique legacy from B. F. Skinner. *Journal of Behavioral Education, 1,* 253–266.

Lodhi, S., & Greer, R. D. (1989). The speaker as listener. *Journal of the Experimental Analysis of Behavior, 51,* 353–359.

Malott, R., W., & Garcia, M. E. (1991). Role of private events in rule-governed behavior. In L. J Hayes, & P. N. Chase (Eds.), *Dialogues on verbal behavior.* Reno, NV: Context Press.

Mithaug, D. E. (1993). *Self-regulation theory: How optimal adjustment maximizes gain.* Wesport, CT: Praeger.

Mithaug, D. E., Martin, J. E., Agran, M., & Rusch, F. R. (1988). *Why special education graduates fail: How to teach them to succeed.* Colorado Springs, CO: Ascend.

National Center for Education Statistics. (1990). *The state of mathematics education.* Washington, DC: U. S. Government Printing Office.

National Center for Research on Evaluation and Student Testing. (1992). *Measurement of workplace readiness competencies.* Washington, DC: U. S. Department of Education.

National Commission on Excellence in Education (1983). A nation at risk: The imperative for educational reform. Washington, DC: Government Printing Office.

Palmer, D. C., & Donahoe, J. W. (1992). Essentialism and selectionism in cognitive science and behavior analysis. *American Psychologist, 47,* 1344–1358.

Perone, V. (1991). *Expanding student assessment.* Washington, DC: ASCD.

Selinske, J., Greer, R. D., & Lodhi, S. (1991). A functional analysis of the comprehensive application of behavior analysis to schooling. *Journal of Applied Behavior Analysis, 13,* 645–654.

Secretary's Commission on Achieving Necessary Skills (1991). *What work requires of schools.* Washington, DC: U. S. Department of Labor.

Skinner, B. F. (1938). *The behavior of organisms.* New York: B. F. Skinner Foundation. Appleton-Century-Crofts.

Skinner, B. F. (1957). *Verbal behavior.* New York: Appleton-Century-Crofts.

Skinner, B. F. (1968). *The technology of teaching.* New York: Appleton-Century-Crofts.

Skinner, B. F. (1984). The shame of American education. *The American Psychologist, 39,* 947–954.

Skinner, B. F. (1953). *Science and human behavior.* New York: Macmillan.

Society for the Experimental Analysis of Behavior. (1992). *Journal of Applied Behavior Analysis Monograph* No. 7. The education crisis: Issues, perspectives, solutions. (1992).

Sulzer-Azaroff, B., Drabman, R. M., Greer, R. D., Hall, R. V., Iwata, B. A., & O'Leary, S. G. (1988). *Behavior analysis in education from the Journal of Applied Behavior Analysis: Reprint series vol. 3.* Lawrence, KS: Society for the Experimental Analysis of Behavior.

Sulzer-Azaroff, B., & Mayer, R. G. (1986). *Achieving educational excellence.* Columbus, OH: Merrill.

Vargas, E. A., & Vargas, J. (1991). Programmed instruction: What it is and how to do it. *Journal of Behavioral Education, 1,* 235–252.

Whitehead, A. E. (1929). *The aims of education.* New York: Mentor Philosophy Library.

Williams, G., & Greer, R. D. (1993). A comparison of verbal and linguistic curricula. *Behaviorology, 1,* 31–46.

Wilson, K. G., & Daviss, B. (1994). *Redesigning education.* New York: Henry Holt.

APPENDIX

SUMMARY OUTLINE OF CABAS COMPONENTS

1) *Student Components*
   A) Inventory of existing repertoires that becomes the portfolio of re-
      pertoires
      1) Range of inventories: Pre-listener to advanced "Writer as Own
         Reader"
   B) Curricula
      1) Types
         a) Teacher "scripted curricula" for students
         b) Automated instruction (e.g., "programmed instuction")
         c) Modifications of nonprogrammed material (e.g., identifying
            and creating learn units and criterion-referenced objectives
            using the existing nonprogramed materials)
   C) Components of curricula from a behavioral selection perspective
      1) Academic literacy (mastery & fluency, intraverbals or "fact learn-
         ing," operations, concepts)
      2) Self-management (coordinated according to levels of verbal be-
         havior repertoires as summarized in Table 2)
      3) Problem solving (rule-governed repertoires associated with meth-
         ods of history, logic, and science, for example)
      4) Enlarged community of conditioned reinforcers or interests (e.g.,
         appreciation of the arts, science, literature, diverse cultural prac-
         tices, and core cultural practices)
   D) Continuous measures of all curricula (all measures are always avail-
      able as visual displays)
      1) Learn units (e.g., pre-listener to self-editing repertoires)
      2) Criterion-referenced objectives in subject matter hierarchy
      3) Record in inventory or portfolio specifying antecedent, postce-
         dent, motivational conditions (e.g., settings)
2) *Teacher Components* Including a curriculum for a continuous inservice
   education conducted via Keller's (1968) Personalized System of Instruction (promotion and salary performance based in an individualized manner above cost-of-living increments in the private schools). These components are applied to school psychologists and social workers equally,
   but with adaptation to their roles in the system
   A) Contingency-shaped repertoires in the classroom (designed in situ
      training)
      1) Supervisor demonstration, shaping via teacher rate/accuracy ob-
         servations, visual displays

144   R. DOUGLAS GREER

2) Graduated levels of expertise

B) Verbal behavior about the science (vocabulary of the science)

   1) Written or vocal responses to written or vocal antecedents (teachers respond intraverbally)

   2) Characterization of student or teacher or target-antecedent interactions using the vocabulary of the science precisely (scientifically identify the contingencies or motivational variables)

   3) Accurate operational reponses to the components of the verbal community (emit the operations that the term[s] identify[ies])

C) Verbally mediated repertoires (scientific problem solving)

   1) Characterize the settings and contingencies scientifically and ask the relevant strategic questions (is the problem located in the three-term contingency for the student, the teacher component of the learn unit, the program, the "motivative" variables, the student's instructional history?)

   2) Apply the existing tactics from the literature or, alternatively, conduct a relevant analysis to locate the likely source(s) of the problem(s)

   3) Carry out or direct the relevant instructional tactics prescribed by the community of verbal behavior (e.g, one uses general case strategies without prior experience under the control of descriptions described in the research)

   4) Evaluate using rules that govern the behavior of teachers who are strategic scientists of pedagogy and schooling

D) In-class training, monitoring, and consultation from supervisor and university consultant

   1) Teacher performance rate/accuracy observations (Ingham & Greer, 1991)

   2) Summary graphs of combined performance of all students and individual student's performance

   3) All components individualized and progressively sequenced

   4) Public posting of measures of performance outcomes

3) *Supervisor Components* (Performance-based promotion and salary increases above cost-of-living increments)

A) Master teacher background and senior behavior scientist (two of them, doctorates or advanced doctoral student status); supervisor spends majority of school time in classrooms with teachers, meets with teachers individually, functions as tutor/coach/mentor, non-adversarial leadership

B) Inservice modules for supervisors

C) Task rate measures (data-based, organizational behavior analysis)

D) Public posting

4) *Parent Component* (accomplished by behaviorally trained social worker, school psychologist, teacher, or CABAS supervisor)

A) An individualized parent education system using the Personalized System of Intruction (PSI). Parent education in basic behavior analytic strategies and tactics with parenting inventory as source of objectives; measured in parent learn units or objectives, or both

B) Advocacy instruction also as part of the curriculum (e.g., how, where, and what to advocate for your child in the school system)

C) Daily and weekly feedback about their child's performance

D) Critical role in setting objectives for their child

E) Maintenance of followup communication after the child leaves the CABAS School

5) *University and University Consultant Components*

A) Schools serve as practica site for training MA students as teachers or researchers and Ph.D. students as supervisors or researchers

B) Consultant on site one to three days per month; responsibility for maintaining reliability of the CABAS model and introducing changes with the supervisors; summary data of schools posted at the university

C) Subject matter of courses at the university driven by research and practice at the schools

   1) Relevant courses in behavior analysis and pedagogy, the epistemology of behavior selection related to pedagogy and curriculum

D) Research publications tied to school efforts (see Table 1)

6) *Community* (board of education, parents, employers)

A) Provide summary of learn units, criterion-referenced objectives for all students combined

B) Provide yearly summary of teacher and supervisor portfolios including learn units taught, objectives taught, and inservice modules achieved by teachers and supervisors

C) Summarize costs per learn units and objectives for students (Greer, 1994b)

D) In the future, provide ongoing assessments of the relationship between objectives achieved and postschool effects.

6

RACISM

HAROLD E. BRIGGS and ROBERT I. PAULSON

INTRODUCTION

Most White Americans are aware that our democracy is less than perfect. Historically, White citizens have discriminated against minority groups and attempted to exclude them from the mainstream of American life. Today, however, many Whites tend to see the problem of racial discrimination as either having been perpetrated in the past, or in terms of prejudices held by a minority of bigots (whom they assume to be either Southerners or blue-collar workers). Few White Americans appreciate the fact that well into the 20th century the bulk of scientific, psychological, and social theories supported racist arguments (see Gould, 1981). Nor do they realize that liberals tended to use these arguments, too. At all levels of society, many people—including writers, scientists, presidents, statesmen, and educators—subscribed to beliefs of White superiority in one form or another. Furthermore, many of today's so-called enlightened explanations for social problems, which are accepted by much of White society, are little more than subtle forms of the same line of reasoning. In fact, these explanations have a strong historical continuity with ideas expressed earlier in our history by people we would now call racist (Fredrickson, 1971; Gosset, 1965).

In this chapter, we will use a behavioral analysis perspective to explore the problem of institutional racism. Prejudice is an individual phenomenon; therefore, we will discuss it in passing. We believe that such individual phenomena are shaped by societal processes (Gaines & Reed, 1995), particularly reinforcing and punitive consequences, and until this macrolevel is addressed, little change can be expected at the individual level. Furthermore, considerably more attention has been paid to the subject of prejudice than to institutional racism (Duckitt, 1992), and this chapter represents one attempt to rectify this relative inattention.

In the first part of the chapter, we will briefly discuss the prevalence of racism in this country. We will then focus on the weaknesses associated with the traditional explanations of racism. Current theories of racism will be augmented with behavioral analysis, so that a new learning theory framework for looking at the problem of institutional racism can be established. Affirmative action will be used as an extended case example of this approach. We will conclude with a discussion of the implications for policy and practice to address this problem.

INCIDENCE AND PREVALENCE

One of the results of the civil rights movement of the 1960s was the extensive documentation of racism in all aspects of American life (Blauner, 1972; Knowles & Prewitt, 1969; Schwartz & Disch, 1970; Tabb, 1970). This research culminated in the National Advisory Commission on Civil Disorders (Kerner, 1968). The Kerner Commission, as it came to be called, declared that the United States was moving toward becoming two divided nations. In every area, African Americans fared less well than Whites. Although there can be no argument that individual African Americans have made substantial progress—that there have been improvements for the Black middle class since the 1960s—as a group African Americans, in particular the poor, have fallen further behind. During the 1980s, federal assistance to the inner cities was cut substantially. Staples (1988) saw this change in federal funding as an opportunity for the government to redistribute resources to Whites:

> While insisting on governmental aid to private schools and increases in the so-called entitlement programs such as social security, veteran benefits unemployment insurance that benefit the white middle class, they [whites] call for reductions in welfare, food stamps and public housing that minorities heavily rely on. (p. 2)

The result of such White insistence, according to Staples, has been that

> While every statistic available shows Blacks to be underrepresented in every positive area of American life, and to be losing what gains were

achieved in the 1960s and 1970s, the eighties bear witness to the fiction that reverse discrimination is a more serious social problems than white racism. (Staples, 1988, p. 3)

Whether one is talking about housing, education, income, health status, or occupational status, African Americans still fare significantly worse than their White counterparts (Hacker, 1995). Within the social service sectors such as foster care, mental health, juvenile justice, and general assistance, people of color receive more restrictive modes of treatment even if they have the same diagnosis as Whites. When age is held constant, women, children, and the elderly are the poorest in this country; when race is added, African American children and senior citizens are at the bottom of the income structure (Baun, 1991). Social services in many instances have perpetuated these differences. Steno (1982) emphasized that the differential experiences of African American children are a consequence of inadequate service delivery systems and the racism inherent in these systems (Billingsley & Giovannoni, 1972). Similarly, the differential treatment effects of African American men and boys have been explored by Gibbs (1988) and Wulczyn (1991) as producing limitations on the life chances and experiences in service delivery systems. In other words, the color line continues to be a major determinant of placement in the social hierarchy. This even seems to be true within the Black community as well (Hall, 1992). In the next section we look at theories of racism that seek to explain these different outcomes for African Americans.

Conceptual Models of Racism

As noted in the introduction, many theories of racism focused on individual prejudice and discrimination rather than on organizations or society. *Individual racism* refers to attitudes, beliefs, or behaviors of individuals that result in unequal treatment or opportunities for minorities (we will provide examples later in this chapter). In contrast, *institutional racism* focuses on organizational policies and practices that have unequal consequences for minorities, regardless of whether these policies are accompanied or undergirded by racist beliefs. With the advent of the civil rights movement, it was no longer socially acceptable in most situations to talk openly in a prejudiced manner or to practice overt discrimination. In its stead there arose a new kind of individual racism and racist theories. We will examine this new breed of racism first, before turning to a discussion of institutional racism. The new racism, instead of classifying social problems in terms of biological inferiority, shifts the explanation to one of cultural inferiority. The effect of this cultural determinism is the same (Briggs, in press). Minority group members are still blamed for their condition, whereas White social institutions that maintain White privilege escape condemnation. These explanations are part of the process described by Wellman (1977) whereby White middle-class people are able to explain structurally generated contradictions in terms that are not in conflict with their egalitarian ideals. These explanations of social problems, which invoke cultural determinism, are widely used by White Americans, especially liberals who practice a new form of racism.

Robert Blauner was right in saying that "prejudiced attitudes are not the essence of racism" (Blauner, 1972, p. 9), but he underestimated the closeness of the relationship between extremist prejudiced ideas and the beliefs held by the rest of "reasonable" White society. As Blauner pointed out, it is reasonable White society that helps to maintain racism in America despite its "favorable" opinion of minority groups. Prager's (1973) analysis of the beliefs of White people established that a common ideology of whiteness does in fact exist despite apparent differences in beliefs of different social groups. This result provides further evidence that there are links among prejudice and the other social explanations of the same phenomena.

Throughout American history, even the most extreme racist groups have seen themselves as acting within a moral framework; their beliefs and resultant actions were not based on unchristian hatred. Rather, these groups used many "respectable" and scientific ideas widely accepted in their time to bolster and justify their actions. In actuality, the real problem is that conflicting interests generally do exist, and the defense of the White majority's interests or privilege has the same result as actions inspired by prejudice. For example, opposition to school busing for integration purposes may be explained by a concern for quality education rather than racism. This conflict of interest is best illustrated by the recent controversy over affirmative action. Affirmative action has generally been defined in terms of reverse discrimination—that is, the conflict between minority and majority rights. In addition to conflicts over particular privileges, minorities, if nothing else, often represent a real threat to bureaucratic security, that is, operating organizations in a way comfortable to the White male majority, as minority group members are now challenging many of the assumptions upon which organizations operate.

In contrast to the organizational racism perspective, we argue that within organizations, the rewards and punishments are usually distributed in such a way that minority-group concerns are at best secondary commitments, if not contrary to, the best interests of the individual's organizational success. In other words, individuals are not likely to get rewarded and may be punished for championing minority group issues. Under these circumstances a person is much less likely to act in way favorable to minority groups, irrespective of their personal attitudes toward them, because of the organizational consequences to such behavior. If racism is to be eliminated, therefore, many of these seemingly neutral bureaucratic imperatives will have to change.

The Web of Urban Racism

Harold Baron (1969) was not concerned with analyzing racism in the general society but rather in the interorganizational network that characterizes the urban setting where most minority groups are now located. He argued that direct discrimination and the application of racist, oppressive policies are no longer necessary because the effect of the total system working together is the same as is if each institution was acting alone. This is not so much a result of the process by which the Black middle class has changed its role in the community, although this could certainly be a complementary process, but rather it is a consequence of institutional arrangements and procedures. In any city, there are five major sectors operating: the housing system (including planning), the labor market, the educational system, the political structure, and the welfare sector. This last sector is controlled by the political sector. In any given sector, there is often a division between a dominant White and a subordinate minority subsector that is, of course, subject to the control and the priorities of the dominant system (Baron, 1969). These dual systems developed historically and were initially maintained through the direct application of force that is no longer necessary.

A critical aspect of the dual systems is the way they interlock and reinforce each other in their subordinate status. They are the major means through which racial distinctions are reflected in institutional arrangements. According to Baron (1969), "The second-class outcomes for blacks from any one institutional sector are so strong and enduring because the subordinated subsectors provide concrete organizational forms and procedures which can be bolstered" (p. 144).

Because of this mutual reinforcement, institutions no longer have to actively discriminate to maintain majority prerogatives. In fact, intentional racist actions may not be necessary at all because the procedures effectively do the job themselves. There is no longer a necessity for totally excluding minority group members from these institutions, which, in fact, are actively recruiting at least token representation from minorities. Baron's model indicates that the indirect control and reduction of direct overt oppression that characterize neocolonialism would probably occur in any event because of the structure of interorganizational relationships in the cities. Baron stated the problem well:

> The effectiveness of urban racism is dependent upon the manner in which the racial controls and differentiation in one institutional sector fit together to reinforce the distinctions in other sectors. As the specific barriers become less distinctive and less absolute, their meshing together into an overriding network compensates, so that the combined effect of the whole is greater than the sum of the individual institutions. The minute operations of these institutions are so interrelated

and bolster one another so efficiently they form a coherent system of control without the sanction of a legal framework.

Maintenance of the basic racial controls is now less dependent upon specific discriminatory decisions. Such behavior has become so well institutionalized that the individual generally does not have to exercise a choice to operate in a racist manner. The rules and procedures of the large organizations have already prestructured the choice. The individual only has to conform to the operating norms of the organization and the institution will do the discriminating for him. . . [Furthermore] the actual racial discrimination in a particular institution need not be as great as the differential in its racial outcome, for the other institutional sectors have previously performed much of the discrimination for it (Baron, 1969, pp. 142-143; 160).

Here is a concrete example: A suburban school system does not need to have its school board pass a discriminatory policy to prevent minorities from being in its school system. African Americans are less likely to have the education needed to get well-paying jobs. If a minority group member were successful in getting the necessary education, he or she would still have less chance of getting the same job, and he or she would get paid less then a White person with similar education (Hacker, 1995). Assuming the non-White person was successful in obtaining the job and had the income to buy a house in the suburbs, "steering" occurs among many real estate firms, so that a non-White person is less likely to be shown housing in a predominantly White suburb (Baron, 1969; Williams, 1984). The real estate agents might actually believe that they are following their customer's wishes and that their customers would be more comfortable living in neighborhood with others in the same ethnic group. A Black client, for instance, might be more likely to seek out a Black real estate agent or company that is more likely to have listings and expertise in African American neighborhoods. If, for the sake of argument, the Black person locates a house in a White suburb, he or she is more likely to have problems getting financing for that home. It has also been shown that "red-lining"[1] occurs, particularly in minority group or mixed-ethnicity neighborhoods, which are considered to be less stable. Mixed neighborhoods are frequently on the fringe of a White suburb, and the loan officers involved in the financing process could honestly proclaim the reason for denying the loan was not race but rather the greater risk inherent in the mixed, less stable neighborhood. As can be seen at each step in this example, individuals may be following organizational rules that in and of themselves do not discriminate. The combined effect of these rules, however, results in discrimination based on race. The system as a whole assures that fewer African Americans end up in the

---

[1]The term *red-lining* refers to the loan-institution practice of drawing a red line around a neighborhood in which they refuse to invest or lend money.

White school districts without the school board taking any direct, deliberate discriminatory action.

A better understanding of the way privilege and procedures are interrelated can be appreciated by concentrating on a particular institution.

Individual Institutions

In this section, we explore how the normal operations of organizations may lead to racist results. Organizations do not operate in a neutral manner but instead reflect the values (and hence, biases) of their decision makers. Organizational procedures develop historically, usually through extending tradition. They are often modified informally in response to organizational needs. Once established, these procedures frequently have an inertia all their own, even when they no longer serve any useful purpose and do in fact discriminate.

These procedures serve important functions for the organization. First they act as a means of control because they standardize the way employees look at the environment (i.e. categorize it). Second, they control the organization's response to inputs. Third they structure rewards and punishment. Once these procedures are mastered by employees through learning the organizational norms and reward structure, they offer security to a worker, who eventually identifies them as the one and only way of doing things.

Another important organizational concern that is affected by these procedures is the reduction of uncertainty (Cyert & March, 1963; Thompson, 1967). It can do this in two ways: (a) by trying to make sure rules are adhered to within the organization; and (b) by creating negotiated interlocks with important elements in its external environment (the "web" to which Baron referred).

There are a number of important implications to be drawn from this process. People learn to pay attention to those things the organization favors and to use the points of view or "filters" (with their inherent biases) reinforced by the organizational leadership. The very act of categorizing through a set procedure frequently leads to stereotypic action. In relation to minorities, these are most often negative images. In addition, most workers are concerned with fulfilling those criteria used for judging their performance, criteria that will eventually lead to promotions. If these criteria involve procedures that conflict with equal benefits to minorities, the latter will be of secondary importance. Individual commitments to minorities will be at best secondary to those of their profession and their career; they are commitments that will only be met if there is any energy left over after these primary tasks are finished. Furthermore, as Molotch and Wolf (1971) noted in their analysis of the University of California at Santa Barbara, there usually are no institutional rewards for activities such as either recruiting minorities or providing service to the community, so that even if resources do exist, motivation will be low.

Perhaps most important, because organizational procedures serve to reduce uncertainty and are a form of security for both the organization and the individuals within it, any changes will be resisted. Once a worker learns the ropes and knows how to get the most reward for the least effort, he or she will not welcome any changes of the rules. This is what Blauner (1972) referred to as "bureaucratic security." It is an important privilege of Whites (who usually create these procedures for their own convenience and who thus have a stake in maintaining the status quo). As a result, Molotch and Wolf (1971) observed, "racism is fundamentally the result of past practices being applied to ongoing situations" (p. 38). That is, changes to accommodate different life styles or circumstances will be resisted.

There is an even more important privilege implicit in this discussion of procedures, however. The dominant decision makers in White society have the power to define the codes and premises, the rules and procedures, and the criteria for rewards and punishments in relation to them. These are inevitably designed to make life as convenient as possible and to conform with White middle-class values and standards of behavior such that each person has an interest in upholding and defending these procedures. The power of definition has been considered to be an important mechanism in perpetuating racism by many theorists (e.g., Blauner, 1972).

White institutional resistance to organized minority demands, therefore, may stem as much—or more—from these organizational facts (i.e., the behavioral incentives rewarding and punishing them in the organization) than from prejudice or racist intent per se. Organizational decision makers can, of course, justify their defensive actions in nonracial terms regardless of their ultimate effect. Because, in fact, accepting the minority demands would create a great deal of uncertainty and result in sweeping changes in procedures, they will be strongly resisted.

Molotch and Wolf (1971) showed how the procedures of the University of California do, in fact, result in the unequal distribution of benefits between minorities and Whites, even though they do so inadvertently. For example, extension programs are usually self-financing, meaning that expensive fees must be charged and only courses likely to attract people who can pay the fee will be offered. Such programs cut out courses of interest to minority communities, whose ability to pay is usually less than that of Whites.

The university provides another good example of how racism and racial conflict are reinforced. Procedures for accepting both students and faculty ensure the kind of students and colleagues desired by the White controlling interests. These procedures are, to a great extent, however, neither relevant nor a fair measure of minority abilities or needs, although the procedures themselves are nonracial in character.

Farrell and Jones (1988), in their content analysis of racial incidents in higher education, concluded that this is a problem that is growing in size, nature, and complexity in all regions of the country. The scope of racial incidents cited by Farrell and Jones (1988) included situations such as racial discrimination, racists remarks, racist behaviors, racist literature, cross burnings, and physical attacks. They described the antecedents of these incidents as risk factors that need to be assessed and modified on university campuses.

After listing recent racial incidents at California State University in Sacramento, Platt (1990) summed them up:

> When we see these separate incidents in their totality and understand their accumulated impact, then we know that racism is much more than a problem of rotten apples or bad attitudes, much more than a matter of personal ignorance or malice. Then it becomes an institutional and structural problem—deeply embedded, persistent, experienced, and skilled in its resistance to change. (p. 33)

The conclusion to be drawn, therefore, is that White racial attitudes are not the most important component of racism in America. Rather, it is the way the society justifies and structures its institutions' operations that ends up subjugating minorities and protecting White privileges built into the system. This is a universal phenomenon and is not isolated to a particular segment of White society. The system operates in such a way that direct controls are not necessary, nor are direct racist acts. In order for changes to be made under these circumstances the concept of zero sum power (i.e., gains for minorities mean losses for Whites) must be changed. In certain cases—such as absorbing all minority unemployed people through an expanding economy and public employment without directly challenging White jobs—this would be extremely difficult.

Traditional theories of racism, however, have tended to structure the inquiry and analysis of the problem at the individual level rather than at the societal level. Personality variables have been sought to explain individual acts of prejudice and discrimination. Similarly, these conceptual frameworks have resulted in solutions that focus on how to overcome racist attitudes or how to change individual personalities. The new approaches, in contrast, suggest that programs, policies, and procedures can be changed in such a way that their discriminatory effect is eliminated. This can be done if supported by an appropriate reward structure so that benefits are distributed for aiding minorities; prejudice then would have little effect. Clearly there is a congruence between these newer approaches and applied behavioral analysis. To better understand these issues, we will next explore in greater detail a behavioral analysis of racism.

TOWARD A BEHAVIORAL ANALYSIS OF RACISM

Racism can be understood as arising, at least to some extent, from the interaction of three forms of learning: respondent (i.e., Pavlovian or classical) conditioning, operant (i.e., Skinnerian or instrumental) conditioning, and learning via observation (i.e., modeling or imitation). This latter one is likely a special instance of operant learning. Other factors may be salient, such as sociobiological ones (e.g., Chapman, 1993; Reynolds, Falger & Vine, 1986), but these are the subjects of study of other disciplines apart from behavior analysis. The major explanatory principles of behavior analysis are outlined in the following sections.

Classical Conditioning

The principles of classical conditioning are familiar to most educated persons who have heard about Pavlov's work with dogs. Certain events that humans can be exposed to are naturally unpleasant or pleasurable, producing correspondingly natural or unlearned reactions. A puff of air in the eye produces an eyeblink, a jab with a sharp object evokes both pain and a flinch, a loud noise produces a startle reaction, and so on. These events are labeled unconditioned stimuli (UCS), and they produce unconditioned responses (UCR). Sometimes neutral stimuli become paired with unconditioned stimuli. If this is done in a particular manner, the neutral stimuli can come to evoke reactions similar to the unconditioned reactions produced by unconditioned responses. For example, if a raised paternal hand is followed by a slap (UCS), which produces pain and a crying and flinching response (UCR), after one or more such occasions, the raised paternal hand itself can produce a flinch. In such cases, the formerly neutral stimulus—the raised hand—has become a conditioned stimulus (CS); the flinch at the sight of the raised hand—a learned reaction based upon experience—has become a conditioned response (CR).

Respondent learning occurs in virtually every animal species ever tested, ranging from one-celled organisms to humans. The capacity for this form of learning is unlearned and apparently present at birth and earlier (Bernard & Sontag, 1947; Kisilevsky & Muir, 1991; Kisilevsky, Muir & Low, 1992). Its adaptive significance in terms of survivability of a species is obvious. Take for example taste aversion. If someone consumes a food or drink (UCS) that subsequently makes him or her sick (UCR), often the subsequent sight or smell of that food or drink (CS) evokes nausea and avoidance (CR) of the product. Rapidly learning to avoid spoiled or toxic foods may help species survive. Many times respondent learning is functional for an individual; however, sometimes it is problematic, as in the case of cancer chemotherapy. Sometimes patients receiving cancer chemotherapy treatments (UCS) experience nausea (UCR) as a side effect of the medication. It is a serious problem if, after a number of such episodes, patients become nauseated (CR) when entering the clinic (CS), prior to receiving the medication. They become nauseated when exposed to the previously neutral stimuli (the sights, sounds, and smells of the clinic) associated with past episodes of medication-induced illness.

Respondent learning does not just apply to simple activities, but also to very complex ones. For example, if certain words are followed by painful stimuli, the words themselves can subsequently come to evoke fear and avoidance (Gale & Jacobson, 1970). Moreover, affective responses to words seem particularly resistant to extinction (Baeyens, Crombez, Van den Bergh, & Eelen, 1988). Once we acquire aversive or pleasant reactions to words, it takes an extremely long time for those conditioned reactions to diminish.

It appears that attributes such as prestige can be induced via respondent conditioning (Blanford & Sampson, 1964), as can the very "meaning" of words (Doyo, 1971; Miller, 1966, Staats & Staats, 1957) and various attitudes (Staats & Staats, 1958). This is not to say that *everything* about attributes, meaning, and attitudes is causally explained through respondent conditioning, only that such learning processes are involved to some, unknown extent. However, to the extent they are involved (and they most assuredly are), an understanding of their role is important in developing ways to potentially prevent or eliminate racism.

The respondent learning of affective or attitudinal reactions need not be acquired through direct, personal experience. Few of us have ever been bitten by a vampire, yet if late one evening Bela Lugosi made an appearance in our bedroom, fangs all aglitter, we would be very frightened, a CR acquired solely through exposure to vampires in the media (movies, television, and books).

Conditioned responses may *generalize*. For example, a person attacked by a bee may come to fear all insects, not just bees. Someone who has been trapped and severely frightened in a small elevator may develop an aversion to being in all small and enclosed spaces, such as closets, not just to elevators.

What are the implications of respondent conditioning for the development of racism? For one thing, we could expect that a person who has an unpleasant experience with someone of a different race may generalize fear and avoidance to all persons of that race (gender, ethnic group, and so forth). Many Black persons encounter abusive Whites, and the anger and resentment engendered by such encounters may spread to a pervasive aversive response to all White people. Similarly, Whites threatened or intimidated by a Black person may come to fear not just that particular person but all Blacks. Consider the media's portrayal of racial stereotypes, particularly those concerning Blacks. Society is subjected to a constant barrage of stories about Black burglars, rapists, muggers, drug dealers, and so forth—stories whose cumulative effect can only yield a harvest of conditioned emotional reactions characterized by fear and avoidance, the primary features of racism. Typically, media reports mention a perpetrater's race if he or she is Black; no mention of the criminal's race is made if the person is White. This is anecdotal but significant: Jessie Jackson commented not long ago that he was walking the streets of Washington, DC one evening when he heard footsteps behind him. He said that he was relieved when he glanced back to find out that it was a White person!

Operant Conditioning

The primary processes of operant conditioning involve reinforcement (positive and negative) and punishment (positive and negative). If one receives social acceptance and approval from peers after expressing racist views, then the likelihood that such views will be expressed again is strengthened. Similarly, if the expression of temperate racial viewpoints or tolerance and acceptance of others of a different race is met with derision, condemnation, or other forms of abuse, then the willingness to express such tolerant views will likely weaken. If bullying or mugging or lynching someone of a different race is reinforced by one's peers, then such activities can be expected to increase. If the affirmative action efforts of a personnel manager are met with disdain, it can be predicted that strong efforts at affirmative actions will weaken.

Parents, of course, are also major sources of contingencies provided to children and youths, and parental reinforcement and punishment practices are especially salient in establishing racial attitudes. If a White child places a poster of a Black movie star or singer in his or her room, and that action is followed by parental ridicule or other punishment, it is possible that the Black star will become less favored by the child (of course the opposite is possible if parental nagging is reinforcing!).

Such early childhood experiences are critical in determining how Whites respond to minorities. Greenberg and Pyszczynski (1985) found in their research that Whites who were socialized early to discriminate on the basis of race tended to recall these stereotypes and to negatively evaluate African Americans either when they overheard ethnic slurs or subsequently observed an African American behaving in a manner consistent with the stereotype. In follow-up research, Kirkland and Pyszcynski (1987) found that persons who overheard ethnic slurs also negatively evaluated people who were in association with the person of color.

The antecedents of modern racist behavior (Howitt & Owusu-Bempah, 1990) are early socialization, predisposed racial attitudes, and belief systems. These antecedents are supported by unclear, ineffective, or nonexistent punitive contingencies for the display of racist behavior (Dovidio & Gaertner, 1983). Environmental cues, however, are important in signaling whether racist behavior will be reinforced or punished based on prior experiences in those settings. This is why it is important for organizations to have clear policies and incentives that reinforce nondiscriminatory behavior and punish racist behavior. If racist behaviors are not punished, or if the organizational culture reinforces racism informally, than nondiscriminatory behavior will be extinguished.

Observational Learning

If a child is exposed to a consistent stream of racist remarks from parents, we should not be surprised to find the child expressing similar sentiments. If these are then reinforced and modeled by one's peer group outside the home, then the stage may be set for a strong racist repertoire that can be lifelong. People become racists, in part, by watching others engage in discriminatory behaviors without suffering punitive consequences for such behaviors, or even being reinforced for them. The lack of consequences is a cue, signaling that there is no cost or penalty for displaying racist behaviors.

Just as racism can be learned by watching others, nonracist behaviors can be learned through cooperative arrangements, collaboration, participation in shared decision making, and though other positive contact experiences. Weigel and Howes (1985) indicated that positive interracial interactions are possible; however, the way in which people of color are depicted in the media and their interaction with Whites reinforces preexisting stereotypes. For many people, media influence is the most frequent exposure and the most powerful influence. In some areas of the United States, Whites never meet people of color except through television. Although it occurs much less often now, historically television advertising reinforced negative stereotypes of minorities. Similarly, news coverage of racist activities can be a double-edged sword. While it focuses attention on these issues, it also presents persons who would not normally get exposure an opportunity to present their views to a much wider audience. The extent to which such people are in positions of authority (e.g., Governor George Wallace standing in the schoolhouse door to block black students from entering) can further provide modeling to persons who have been reinforced—or not punished—for such behavior in the past. At best, it presents a mixed message as to what is acceptable.

On the institutional level, Weigel and Howes (1985) recommended the need for strong leadership, egalitarian norms and practices, and enforcement of egalitarian standards. Those in subordinate positions will observe what racial behaviors are practiced by their supervisors—and what the consequences are—and model their behavior based on these experiences. Weigel and Howes (1985) concluded that:

> since racial prejudice is embedded in a network of beliefs and values
> that reflect deference to established authority and preoccupation with

. . . conventionally acceptable standards of conduct, the contemporary
racist may be particularly responsive to the forceful invocation of normative standards by persons in authoritative roles. (p. 135)

A more complex model of behavioral analysis is necessary when discussing
racism on an organizational level. Thus, in the next section, we present a
more complex, multiple-contingency model that allows one to look at the
parallel reinforcement systems simultaneously operating within organizations and society. We will use the implementation of affirmative action
programs as an extended case example of how such an organizational behavioral analysis of racism can be conducted using this more complex model.

WHY AFFIRMATIVE ACTION HAS NOT WORKED:
A CASE EXAMPLE

Recent studies have shown that affirmative action programs have not
significantly reduced discrimination in public agencies. (For reviews see
Katz & Proshanksy, 1987; Zwerling & Silver, 1992.) One reason for this
result is the special implementation problems of affirmation action programs. Social service agencies frequently lack appropriate contingencies to
implement affirmative action and are thus reluctant to commit resources
to it. When implementing affirmative action, administrators have not managed the official incentive system to reflect changes in behavioral expectations and to minimize worker resistance. The uncertainty caused by the
changes accompanying affirmative action can further reinforce resistance.
Implementation problems also arise if including minorities in the decision-
making process changes the balance of power in an organization. Government pressure is needed to generate the necessary task-environment support for affirmative action. In addition, financial incentives are needed to
offset the costs incurred by agencies implementing affirmative action programs if real success is to be achieved.

The Bakke case originally focused the nation's attention on affirmative action programs and on how past racial discrimination can be com-
bated without negatively affecting White employees. In this case, Bakke,
a White man, contended that he was unfairly rejected from admission to
the University of California because minorities who scored lower than he
did on certain admission criteria were admitted. Recently, these concerns
have been revived by the Republican "Contract With America." The con-
troversies generated by the "Contract With America" and the recent affirmative action/reverse discrimination debate have obscured the fact that
affirmative action programs have usually not worked. A number of studies
of public organizations and a recent investigation of private companies

(Greenhaus & Parasuraman, 1993) have shown that minorities and women have made little, if any, progress, particularly in reaching key leadership positions in public organizations (Alstyne & Elliot, 1977; Harver, 1977; Lepper, 1976; Stewart, 1976). It is frequently assumed that much of the reason for the failing of affirmative action plans has been the lack of support from top administrators or the generalized resistance of the staff. Although this has undoubtedly been a factor in many cases, the difficulties in implementing affirmative action plans when such support exists have not been fully recognized. A 1977 study of a public welfare agency in which affirmative action plans were never implemented—despite widespread support from all staff levels—, suggests that there is much in the organizational context and normal operational procedures of public agencies that militates against the successful implementation of affirmative action plans (Paulson, 1977). An analysis of recent organization literature shows why this is so.

Multiple-Contingency Framework

After years of comparative neglect, there has been a growing interest in implementation analysis (Williams & Elmore, 1967). Yet most of the literature has either borrowed analytic models inappropriate to the context of complex organizations in urban society or has been restricted to describing the generalized obstacles to implementation in the specific case being studied (Gross, Giacquinta, & Bernstein, 1971). An understanding of organizational dynamics is also necessary, however, if corrective and preventive actions are to be taken and if realistic implementation is to take place. Such an understanding is provided by a multiple-system framework based on learning theory and contingency-management practices. A contingency system is defined as the rewards and punishments dispensed, the mechanisms by which they are distributed, and the assessment criteria used for evaluating performance to determine what the appropriate consequences of the performance should be.

The theoretical basis of incentive and contingency analysis is that behavior is determined by its consequences. Some approaches have recognized the need to analyze the interrelationships among individuals, groups, and subunits in an organization because the behavior of individuals in a given unit is, in part, a response to consequences resulting from the other units in its environment (Brethower, 1972; Kunkel, 1970; Luthans & Kreitner, 1974; Mager & Pipe, 1970; Tossi & Hammer, 1974). Nonetheless, none have fully integrated these interrelationships into a single framework. Regardless of the interrelationships, the underlying behavioral principles are the same.

The conceptual underpinning of the behavioral analysis framework is that there are four major sources of reinforcement and punishment (i.e. contingency systems) in a organization. They are the (a) external, (b) official, (c) unofficial, and (d) intrinsic task characteristics. It is the structure and interaction of these various contingencies that shape and maintain organizational behavior; they must be taken into account when analyzing implementation problems. These four sources are described next and are briefly accompanied by an example relating to affirmative action.

The external contingency system is made of the external task environment elements that regulate an organization or that control important resources (reinforcers). These external elements structure the contingencies (rewards and punishments) for the organization. The assessment criteria used by key task environment elements to measure the organization's performance to determine whether it will be rewarded is crucial in determining the nature of the internal (official) contingencies established by the organization. For instance, the county commission that funds a public agency might insist that the agency adopt an affirmative action program or risk losing its funding.

The official contingency system consists of the important incentives (e.g., promotions, assignments, job discretion, and training opportunities) distributed by an agency through its official mechanism according to agency-set criteria. To illustrate, agency administrators might reward a personnel manager for actively recruiting minorities into the organization and developing a career ladder for them. Similarly, the system might punish workers whose style of service delivery was inappropriate to the needs of the minority clientele being served.

Informal groups that form around work units, common jobs (e.g., secretarial or supervisory), union shops, and professional affiliations can be considered as alternative unofficial contingency systems operating in the organization over which agency administrators have little control. These groups can play an important socialization function and can also become an informal base of power in the organization (Blau, 1963; Crozier, 1964). Such groups can either encourage or discourage active participation in an affirmative action plan.

Finally, there are aspects of a particular job that a worker finds to be either intrinsically rewarding or aversive. These make up the intrinsic reinforcement characteristics of the task. For example, a personnel manager might find filling out affirmative action forms (to show that discrimination did not occur in hiring) to be an unpleasant, added burden to his or her normal responsibilities.

For implementation of a program to be successful, these various contingency systems must interact in such a way that the desired implementation behavior of the workers occurs. The interaction among the systems thus varies with each unique situation. In the examples given, some of the contingencies favored affirmative action, whereas others discouraged it. The outcome would depend on which systems had a greater effect on the worker at a given point in time. In each of these four sources of reinforcement, however, there are special problems for the implementation of affirmative action programs. In each contingency system, implementation problems existed, all of which were observed in the second author's study of a public welfare agency.

Implementation Problems of Affirmative Action Programs

Affirmative action programs are especially susceptible to implementation problems because they are peripheral to the primary mission of most organizations; they do not vitally affect the agency's survival and well-being. The extent and type of implementation problems will, in part, depend on what is included in such programs.

Operational definitions of affirmative action programs have eluded most public administrators (Nigro, 1974). Most definitions of affirmative action have usually been restricted to employment and promotional practices as they affect employment opportunities for minorities. Such programs concern themselves only with the effects of agency policies and practices on the employees within the organization. Some affirmative action programs, however, consider the effect of the agency's policies and practices on the clientele being served by the agency. This broader conception of affirmative action considers such questions as: (a) the population being served in contrast to those eligible for services, (b) the style and method of service delivery and its applicability to the life-style of the population being served, (c) the location of offices in relation to minority population concentrations, and (d) inequities in the quality and quantity of service delivered. This broader conception of affirmative action, which addresses the effect of policies both internally and externally, has been used by regional offices of the federal Department of Health and Human Services in its guidelines for the evaluation of public welfare programs, and it will also be used in this discussion.

External Contingencies

There are a number of characteristics of the relations between public social service agencies and their task environments that make affirmative action implementation problematic. First, social service agencies are highly dependent on local governments. Even if federal funding is their principle source of monies, financial resources and budget approval usually must go through the local government structure, and personnel resources must go through a civil service system. In many cases, even relatively minor expenditures and personnel changes must be approved by the local government officials. In addition, publicly provided social services are usually not a high priority item when compared with other services such as fire, police, waste disposal, or health services; thus, they are placed in a relatively weak position against these key task-environment elements.

This position has several consequences. First, a social service agency could only take limited independent action in implementing an affirmative action program without getting the active consent, if not support, of the local governmental bodies that control these resources. This would, therefore, increase the agency's dependence on these organizations. Increased dependency is usually aversive to organizations in and of itself (Thompson, 1967). Administrators would avoid programs leading to increased dependence wherever possible, and affirmative action falls into this category. Under these circumstances of great dependence, an agency would be expected to follow the wishes of these important suppliers of resources when they have clear preferences, particularly because affirmative action is not directly related to the accomplishment of the agency's mandated goals.

The assessment criteria used to evaluate social service agency performance are a critical part of these external contingencies. The assessment criteria normally used militate against the implementation of affirmative action programs because these programs do not help the agency score well on these criteria. Given the indeterminate nature of social service technology—as well as the technical inability of task-environment elements to adequately evaluate agency performance—social tests and extrinsic criteria such as the number and types of services delivered are usually the major assessment criteria used (Thompson, 1967). It can be seen that, although it is true that affirmative action might improve the quality of services to minorities, the assessment criteria do not measure quality. Therefore, resources are likely to be committed first to those programs that improve assessment measures and second to affirmative action. In addition, the ability to steer clear of controversial issues is often one social test used by key local government officials to judge agency performance.

In conclusion, one reason for the failure of affirmative action programs is that active support of the key task-environment entities, which control the external contingencies, has not been present. Furthermore, such failures can occur even when top agency administrators are committed to the concept of affirmative action. For affirmative action to succeed under these circumstances, it is essential that pressures exist to implement affirmative action from other external sources.

Pro-Affirmative Action Pressures

If key local governmental agencies do not place a high priority on affirmative action programs when left alone to make their own decisions, there are only two sources capable of applying sufficient pressure to make them support the implementation of affirmative action programs.

One source of pro-affirmative action pressure is organized minority groups and their supporters. Because minorities hold little power to offer incentives for change, they can usually only bring about change by exacting costs for continuing to do things in the usual way through organized pressure or disruptive tactics (Molotch & Wolf, 1970). Only in cases where minorities in an organization are sufficiently organized to pressure the agency and can exact such costs will changes be seen as beneficial to all—because the changes will reduce the turmoil. This pressure can sometimes be applied either internally, through minority caucuses and their allies, or externally, via civil rights and welfare rights groups or organizations such as the Association of Black Social Workers.

Decisions to allocate resources to programs are strongly affected by the degree to which constituencies are mobilized to exert pressure on decision makers. But an important reality of affirmative action programs is that minorities will be the only major constituency for the program because they are the chief beneficiaries; many Whites fear they may be affected adversely. Although it is true that women also benefit from affirmative action, all too often, ethnic minorities have been placed in competition with them for a limited number of positions. In many instances, ethnic rather than gender status has been given priority. Furthermore, because affirmative action is peripheral to the key measures of organizational success, this constituency will be relatively weak vis-à-vis other agency program constituencies, simply because the organization does not need it to score on assessment criteria.

Thus, minorities must be sufficiently numerous and well organized to compete with pressures from other program constituencies. Consequently, agency policies that either encourage or discourage the formation of minority group solidarity take on greater importance. One can predict that even in conditions of task-environment neutrality, no affirmative action program will be implemented (all things being equal) in the absence of well-organized minority group activity.

The only other elements in the work environment that are likely to encourage affirmative action are civil rights laws and regulations enforced by government agencies. There are numerous regulations requiring affirmative action programs in one form or another, but there can be great variations in the extent to which enforcement of the laws take place. The kind of sanctions that can be imposed—and the willingness of officials to impose these sanctions—also greatly vary. There is a wide range of official discretion in enforcing such laws, and perceptions of the federal government attitude toward civil rights can be an elusive but, nevertheless, important factor in determining local governments' reactions to such laws (Kimberly, 1975).

Furthermore, local officials charged with carrying out these regulations may respond differentially to government enforcement activity. Some may implement affirmative action provisions without any government action; others may hurry to respond at the slightest hint of government dissatisfaction (but not until then); still others might not move until the stiffest sanctions are imposed. Although the source of some of the local officials' resistance to affirmative action might be resentment of federal government interference, it seems reasonable to assume that their resistance is a measure of the officials' opposition to the concept itself. Most likely, agency administrators will use the response of local officials as an indicator of their support for affirmative action and will act accordingly.

Clearly, then, government intervention is in the form of imposing punishment on agencies for not adopting an affirmative action program and not in the form of providing positive reinforcement. Consequently, under circumstances in which the task-environment support does not exist and in which minority groups are not strong enough to exert countervailing pressure, an affirmative action program will not get implemented unless government agents enforce the regulations with sufficient pressure to overcome this local resistance.

Economic Conditions

A task-environment variable that interacts with these other factors and that profoundly affects the implementation of affirmative action is the general level of federal and state funding. If the economy is bad and this results in general funding cutbacks, then resources for affirmative action programs can only be secured by transferring existing resources. However, with an austerity budget there is little organizational slack that would allow a program (or division) to absorb the loss of resources (be it in funds or personnel) in such a transfer without severely hurting its operations. Hence, it would most likely fight such transfers vigorously.

Obviously, in times of financial need it is politically much easier for administrators to live without a program than it is for them to try to cut an already established operation. It would be very unlikely for administrators to commit funds to anything but essential services unless there were strong incentives or pressures to do so. In contrast, under good economic conditions, when agency budgets are expanding, it is much easier to add an affirmative action program because it will not interfere with anyone's ongoing operations. One can thus predict that the worse an agency's financial situation, the more its resistance to affirmative action will be. Furthermore, if such a program already exists, there will be pressures to cut it first.

In the past decade, few of these favorable external conditions have existed for prolonged periods of time. This has contributed significantly to the problems of affirmative action program implementation.

Official Contingencies

Even if one assumes that official environmental contingencies support the implementation of affirmative action programs, there are elements of the official contingencies that interact with the implementation process of affirmative action programs to cause problems. The usual structure of official contingencies in organizations inhibits affirmative action in two major ways: (a) by not rewarding the new behaviors required and (b) by altering the incentive system in such a way as to produce worker resistance. There are several common manifestations of the first problem.

When organizations change their expectations of worker behavior, there must be appropriate changes in official contingencies, or workers cannot be expected to change. Affirmative action programs are supposed to introduce new priorities in worker behavior; yet, frequently the new expectations are not accompanied by adjustments in the official incentives or assessment criteria. One way of introducing new priorities may be through new tasks and responsibilities. For example, even if affirmative action were restricted to the employment sphere, new tasks such as minority recruitment, training, and the revision of selection and promotion procedures would be necessary. Someone would have to be responsible for hearing and investigating complaints and for mediating disputes.

Although new positions are sometimes created solely to fulfill these functions, all too often these responsibilities are added on to a worker's (usually a minority's) already existing duties with no compensatory reduction in his or her previous responsibilities or increase in salary or rank to reflect the increased workload (Paulson, 1977). Furthermore, this performance will still be evaluated using the traditional criteria geared to his or her initial duties. As a consequence, the employee's affirmative action work will suffer—most workers will be concerned with fulfilling the assessment criteria that lead to organizational advancement.

A second common practice is to add a new position, but one that also has some traditional organization function associated with it, such as a combined personnel manager-affirmative action coordinator. Two consequences result from such a strategy. First, because the traditional functions of the job are more essential for the organization's ongoing needs and its successful performance, those functions are likely to be encouraged more than the affirmative action functions. Secondly, there are likely to be conflicts among the goals, roles, and procedures of the two functions. Such conflicts would likely be resolved to the detriment of affirmative action because alternative action has lowest priority. Personnel managers who are assigned affirmative action responsibilities, for example, would be placed in the position of evaluating their own operations and thus would be expected to make changes that might result in more work for themselves without any increased recognition or reward.

When affirmative action programs include an examination of an agency's service delivery and ongoing operations to enhance their access and effectiveness to minority clients, these usually result in changes in worker behaviors and priorities. But such changes are often not accompanied by changes in the standard operating procedures nor in the assessment criteria. Consequently, workers trying to be more responsive to minority clientele may find that they are in conflict with normal agency operations.

Once standard operating procedures become adopted by an organization, they frequently assume quasi-legal status and, therefore, compliance with them becomes the basis of rewards. As a result, workers will be reluctant to risk modifying or ignoring such procedures for affirmative action purposes (Landau, 1973). In such cases, affirmative action is officially discouraged in two ways. First, there are no built-in rewards for affirmative action-oriented behavior. Second, if workers modify procedures with affirmative action in mind, they might be punished for "violating" agency policy.

In short, there are usually no institutional rewards for workers in any agency to engage in affirmative action-related activities (Katz & Proshansky, 1987), such as recruiting minorities or providing service to minority communities. Therefore, such behaviors will generally be infrequent or otherwise weak (Molotch & Wolf, 1970). Also, if assessment criteria encourage the use of existing standard operating procedures that happen to conflict with achieving equal benefits to minorities, then achieving such benefits will be of lesser importance. Workers' commitments to minorities will be at best secondary to those of their profession and career (Blau, 1963). The commitments will only be met if there is any energy left over after these primary tasks are finished.

A clear hypothesis that emerges from this analysis is that unless the behaviors required to carry out an affirmative action program are explicitly reinforced by changes in the official contingency system and assessment criteria, there is a low probability that they will be carried out or be successful.

Organizational resistance to affirmative action programs can be generated by the official contingencies both directly and indirectly. Personnel practices are a major component of both official contingencies and affirmative action. Affirmative action programs can thus directly change official contingencies by modifying the practices affecting the previous distribution of promotions, assignments, and merit increases between minorities and Whites. This could make minorities an increased competitive threat in the view of the existing majority staff and encourage their resistance to the plan.

When an affirmative action program is restricted to employment, unintended consequences are likely to occur. For example, strategies for increasing the percentage of minorities may raise fears among existing workers. Past abuses—perceived or real—such as favoritism, reverse racism, or the lowering of standards (as preferential treatment for minorities who meet the qualifications) might reoccur. This is not inevitable, because there can be a clear balance between providing equal or accelerated opportunities for minorities without sacrificing the legitimate interests of existing employees. For employees not to react in terms of their worst fears, administrators must thoroughly explain the affirmative action program to all staff and involve them in a realistic assessment of its effect on the current contingencies.

The official contingencies and intrinsic task characteristics can interact in a number of ways that cause increased uncertainty as a consequence of steps taken to implement affirmative action. This frequently results in increased worker resistance to the program. As a long-term process, affirmative action program implementation can produce ongoing changes in the contingencies and the methods of carrying out official tasks, as well as in the balance of power in the composition of the work force. Each of these changes could be a considerable source of frustration for the work force as well as a considerable source of continuous uncertainty.

The organizational literature emphasizes the importance of reducing uncertainty among individuals and in the organization as a whole. A change that will increase uncertainty will generally be opposed, unless it brings definite benefits that compensate for the change. Because standard operating procedures serve to reduce uncertainty and thus are a form of security for workers, most changes will be resisted (Crozier, 1964). Once rules become adopted by an organization, they frequently assume quasilegal status and compliance with them becomes the basis of rewards (Landau, 1973). As a reflection of goals and priorities, these procedures become built into organizations so that people construct their activity around this reality (Perrow, 1970). Once a worker "learns the ropes" and knows how to get the most reward for the least effort, he or she will not welcome any change in the rules (Perrow, 1970).

An affirmative action program might change the organizational environment from one in which a worker knows what is expected of him to one in which he is faced with having to learn things all over again. Additionally, the rules for obtaining organizational rewards and escaping punishment are unclear in the new environment. Thus, the job becomes not only more uncertain and aversive, but also more difficult. Specifically, changes in decision premises or procedures that would make the organization more responsive to the different life-styles or circumstances of clients (or minority employees) will be resisted unless workers can see that the change will make things easier for them. Often then, racism is fundamentally the result of past priorities being applied to ongoing situations (Molotch & Wolf, 1970). When making changes in the premises or procedures, organization administrators frequently do not take this history into account, thus encouraging workers' resistance.

Unofficial Contingencies

Because its importance in decision making and intraorganizational power struggles has been recognized, the informal organization has been receiving more attention of late. Affirmative action programs also affect the unofficial contingencies that shape these informal organization dynamics. For instance, it is inherent in affirmative action programs that some realignment of coalition making will occur (Cyert & March, 1963). If one of the aims of the program is to enable minorities to influence agency policies and procedures, minorities would need to be included in certain decisions where they had previously been excluded. This granting of more power to minorities might result in some other individual or group losing power. It would certainly involve a change in the composition of the decision-making coalitions, resulting in a realignment of power in the organization (Crozier, 1964; Thompson, 1967). This realignment would likely be resisted by the majority of coalition members directly benefiting from such a change—if for no other reason than the uncertainty it would create.

This change in the decision-making coalitions would have implication for internal power struggles. It is conceivable that the implementation of affirmative action would become politicized. It would be used by various groups who thought they could gain by the changes and opposed by those who stood to lose. As described by Crozier (1964), many such struggles concern the control of uncertainty as a source of informal power. In such cases, the ambiguity or specificity of procedures and contingencies that limit uncertainty are of major importance. The procedural and contingency changes produced by affirmative action, then, could provide new opportunities for groups dissatisfied with the negotiated environment existing in the organization under the status quo. Because such changes are more likely to benefit those who want to gain power rather than those who already possess it, the people most likely to support affirmative action will have the least ability to see that it has been implemented. One reason affirmative action programs have not been implemented expeditiously is because implementation plans have not taken into account the current decision-making coalitions and intergroup power struggles.

Affirmative action affects not only the unofficial contingencies but also the existing informal organization dynamics; such dynamics can be crucial in determining the success of the program. It is the informal contingencies operating in work groups that are the most important because social reinforcement can shape worker behavior—either to aid or to sabotage the implementation of the program. Such groups as union locals and professional associations might have a similar effect.

A less explicit role these contingencies play is in the agency socialization process. Molotch and Wolf (1970) stressed the importance of improving the socialization process for minorities in organizations to maximize their chances for success. As the best vehicle for agency socialization of new workers, the informal group contingencies could become the crucial element in an individual minority's success. The degree to which official contingencies explicitly shape the informal contingencies in the direction of supporting the program and proper socialization will thus be very important in eliminating implementation barriers. The willingness of administrators to let minorities organize themselves on their behalf is part of this.

Intrinsic Task Characteristics

Affirmative action is usually regulated by federal, state, and local statutes and regulations. These regulations usually require extensive prescribed procedures and documentation to ensure that the legislative intent has been carried out in the program's implementation. These procedures, however, require organizational effort and resources. The additional time and effort required to implement these regulations are all too often added to a worker's ordinary duties and, therefore, are likely to be aversive to most workers—most of whom naturally would prefer their jobs to be simpler. Furthermore, paperwork and procedures in and of themselves are inherently aversive to most workers; therefore, workers are not likely to respond favorably to the detailed requirements of many affirmative action plans. In short, many of the processes required to implement affirmative action programs are likely to be resisted unless substantial new resources are added, and existing workers do not have to implement these additional procedures.

Decision-Making Process

There is still another aspect of organizational activity, reinforced by all the contingency systems, that militates against the successful establishment of affirmative action programs. This is the normal decision-making process in organizations.

Studies of organizational decision making have suggested that organizations generally make decisions and search for alternative ways of doing things only in response to problems (e.g., Cyert & March, 1963). Thus, it is unlikely that an organization would spontaneously or unilaterally make a decision to implement an affirmative action program. This finding corroborates the assertion that external or internal pressure and support would be necessary. For example, if a civil service department that has always relied on applicants, learning about vacancies on their own—and that department has had no problem filling vacancies with qualified personnel before—it will not implement a minority recruitment program, unless some external force makes such recruitment a "problem" for the department.

Furthermore, any decision is likely to be related to the way the organization has previously solved such problems and will reflect the stereotyped perceptual biases of the personnel and the organization's communications systems (Landau, 1973). Consequently, it would be unlikely for the organization to choose a solution involving major changes—such as a comprehensive affirmative action plan—when alternatives involving only minor adjustments are available. This is true even if such adjustments would only alleviate the problem on a short-term basis and not provide a long-term solution (Cyert & March, 1963). For example, a small concession to minorities might be made that had a momentarily calming effect but would not alter any of the basic ways in which the agency treats minorities. Inevitably, then, other problems will arise later on a regular basis, problems that will also be resolved by a specific short-term solution. The organization responds to each problem incrementally, treating it as a separate and distinct entity, rather than as a part of a more fundamental problem requiring more drastic solutions. The comprehensive study of organizational practices as they affect minorities and the subsequent adoption of comprehensive measures to form an affirmative action program—which would eliminate any systematic racial inequities—contradict the way most organizations make decisions and solve problems. Affirmative action programs are thus less likely to be adopted than some more incremental alternatives.

Making Affirmative Action Work

Our discussion thus far has shown that there are numerous obstacles to the successful implementation of an affirmative action program. These implementation problems cannot be overcome if they continue to go unrecognized and underestimated, and positive steps to alleviate them are not forthcoming. Our analysis, however, suggests what some of the most important steps might be for making affirmative action work.

Because task-environment support is so essential and is not automatically forthcoming, more attention must be paid to the role of the federal government in encouraging such support. A joint carrot-stick approach seems to be in order. On the one hand, more recognition of the costs involved in carrying out affirmative action is necessary. Legislation providing funding for such costs, either through their inclusion in ongoing agency budgets or through special restricted grants, is essential. In those cases in which no efforts are being made to implement affirmative action, current laws must be strongly and quickly enforced. Otherwise, affirmative action will be viewed as a low priority, and efforts to achieve the high priority objectives of local governments will be diluted.

Worker cooperation must also be encouraged through official contingencies. New behavioral expectations must be made clear and explicit; adjustments must be made in the workload, assessment criteria, and rewards to reflect additional assignments and expected changes in behavior patterns. Care must be exercised to ensure that the new expectations are explicit; otherwise, workers will be caught in a double bind and will engage in informal actions to minimize such conflict. This situation would be counterproductive to goal attainment (Blau, 1963).

Task-environment and official agency support are necessary, but not sufficient, conditions for successful affirmative action implementation. Uncertainty and the aversive aspects of the new behavioral expectations must be minimized. This goal can be done through careful job redesign and additional training, but only if administrators allow for worker input and feedback in the planning and implementation phases. Widespread communication about content, process, and consequences of the affirmative action program implementation will be a necessity if resistance and morale problems caused by uncertainty are to be reduced.

Finally, the importance of informal networks to the success of the program implementation process should not be overlooked. Such networks are an importance source of redundancy for obtaining feedback on workers' misconceptions and concerns and can warn administrators of the need for either further explanation of the program or a different incentive approach. The agency must also reinforce the formation of informal ties among the groups that must cooperate if the implementation is to be successful. In addition, management should solicit the support of unions, professional associations, and other groups that act as more structured informal groups in the organization. Most important, the development of group solidarity among minorities must not be discouraged; if necessary, help should be provided to augment the socialization process for new minority employees. This is critical to their successful organizational careers.

The time has passed when program implementation can be taken for granted. The inherent nature of affirmative action programs itself increases the likelihood that problems will result. If these problems are explicitly recognized in advance, and the kinds of steps outlined here are taken, then there is no reason why these obstacles cannot be minimized and affirmative action programs successfully implemented.

CONCLUSION

Institutional racism is a social problem that is prevalent throughout American society. For a problem of this magnitude to be corrected, it is essential that we have a comprehensive and accurate understanding of the problem. As we have demonstrated, traditional explanations of racism have not successfully accounted for the persistence and pervasiveness of the problem. Even the more contemporary explanations have not provided frameworks useful for understanding and correcting specific organizational incidences of racism. We believe behavioral analysis adds a powerful tool in both understanding the phenomenon of institutional racism and in developing strategies to resolve the problem (see, for example, Hauserman, Walen, & Behling, 1973). Recognition of the fact that racism is not an individual problem that can be resolved by changing individual attitudes and behaviors is essential. Rather, racism must be viewed as an institutional and societal problem maintained by incentives that reinforce White privilege and fail to adequately sanction policies and practices that collectively result in outcomes negatively affecting minorities.

REFERENCES

Alstyne, C. V., & Elliott, S. (1977). Affirmative inaction: The bottom line tells the tale. *Change*, 9(8), 39–41.

Baeyens, F., Crombez Van den Bergh, O., & Eelen, P. (1988). Once in contact always in contact: Evaluative conditioning is resistant to extinction. *Advances in Behavior Research and Therapy*, 10, 179–199.

Baron, H. (1969). The web of urban racism. In L. Knowles & K. Prewitt (Eds.), *Institutional racism in America*. Englewood Cliffs, NJ: Prentice-Hall.

Bernard, J., & Sontag, L. W. (1947). Fetal reactivity to tonal stimulation: A preliminary report. *Journal of Genetic Psychology*, 70, 205–210.

Billingsley, A., & Giovannoni, J., (1972). *Children of the storm: Black children and American child welfare*. New York: Harcourt Brace Jovanovich.

Blanford, D. H., & Sampson, G. L. (1964). Induction of prestige suggestion through classical conditioning. *Journal of Abnormal and Social Psychology*, 69, 332–337.

Blau, P. (1963). *The dynamics of bureaucracy*. Chicago: University of Chicago Press.

Blauner, R. (1972). *Racial oppression in America*. New York: Harper & Row.

Braun, D. (1991). *The rich get richer: The rise of income inequality in the US and the world*. Chicago: Nelson-Hall.

Brethower, D. M. (1972). *Behavioral analysis in business and industry: A total performance system*. Kalamazoo, MI: Behaviordelia.

Briggs, H. E. (in press). Cultural diversity: A latter day trojan horse. *Psychology: A Journal of Human Behavior*.

Chapman, M. (Ed.). (1993). *Social and biological aspects of ethnicity*. New York: Oxford University Press.

Crozier, M. (1964). *The bureaucratic phenomenon*. Chicago: University of Chicago Press.

Cyert, R. M., & March, J. G. (1963). *A behavioral theory of the firm.* Englewood Cliffs, NJ: Prentice Hall.

Dovidio, J. F., & Gaertner, S. L. (1983). Race, normative structure, and help-seeking. In B. DePaulo, A. Nadler, & Fisher, J. D. (Eds.). *New directions in helping* (pp. 285–302). New York: Academic Press.

Doyo, M. C. (1971). Establishing and changing meaning by means of classical conditioning using the paired-associate method. *Philippine Journal of Psychology, 4,* 117–124.

Duckitt, S. (1992). Psychology and prejudice: A historical analysis and integrative framework. *American Psychologist, 47,* 1182–1193.

Farrell, W. C., & Jones, C. K. (1988). Recent racial incidents in higher education: A preliminary perspective. *The Urban Review, 20,* 211–226.

Fredrickson, G. (1971). *The black image in the white mind: The debate on afroamerican character and destiny.* New York: Harper & Row.

Gaines, S. O., & Reed, E. S. (1995). Prejudice: Allport to DuBois. *American Psychologist, 50,* 96–103.

Gale, E. N., & Jacobson, M. B. (1970). The relationship between social comments as unconditioned stimuli and fear responding. *Behavior Research and Therapy, 8,* 301–307.

Gibbs, J. T. (1988). *Young, black and male in America: An endangered species.* Dover, DE: Auburn House.

Gossett, T. (1965). *Race: the history of an idea in America.* New York: Schocken.

Gould, S. J. (1981). *The mismeasure of man.* New York: W. W. Norton.

Greenberg, J., & Pyszczynski, T. (1985). The effect of an overheard ethnic slur on evaluations of the target: How to spread a social disease. *Journal of Experimental Social Psychology, 21,* 61–72.

Greenhaus, J. H., & Parasuraman, S. (1993). Job performance attributions and career advancement prospects: An examination of gender and race effects. *Organizational Behavior and Human Decision Processes, 55,* 273–297.

Gross, N., Giacquinta, J. B., & Bernstein, M. (1971). *Implementing organizational innovations.* New York: Basic.

Hacker, A. (1995). *Two nations: Black and white, separate, hostile, unequal.* New York: Ballantine.

Hall, W. T. (1992). Bias among African-Americans regarding skin color. *Research on Social Work Practice, 2,* 479–486.

Harver, J. C. (1977). Black progress and reality. *Public Administration Review, 37,* 549–553.

Hauserman, N., Walen, S. R., & Behling M. (1973). Reinforced racial integration in the first grade: A study in generalization. *Journal of Applied Behavior Analysis, 6,* 193–200.

Howitt, D., & Owusu-Bempah, J. (1990). The pragmatics of institutional racism: Beyond words. *Human Relations, 43,* 885–899.

Katz, I., & Proshansky, H. M. (1987). Rethinking affirmative action. *Journal of Social Issues, 43*, 69–104.

Kerner, O. (1968). *Report of the National Advisory Commission on Civil Disorders.* New York: Bantam.

Kimberly, J. R. (1975). Environmental constraints and organizational structure: A comparative analysis of rehabilitation organizations. *Administrative Science Quarterly, 20*, 1–10.

Kirkland, S. G., & Pyszczynski, T. (1987). Further evidence of the deleterious effects of overheard derogatory ethnic labels: Derogation beyond the target. *Personality and Social Psychology Bulletin, 13*, 216–227.

Kisilevsky, B. S., & Muir, D. W. (1991). Human fetal and subsequent newborn responses to sound and vibration. *Infant Behavior and Development, 14*, 1–26.

Kisilevsky, B. S., Muir, D. W., & Low, J. A. (1992). Maturation of human fetal responses to vibroacoustic stimulation. *Child Development, 63*, 1497–1508.

Knowles, L., & Prewitt, K. (1969). *Institutional racism in America.* Englewood Cliffs, NJ: Prentice-Hall.

Kunkel, J. (1970). *Society and economic growth.* New York: Oxford University Press.

Landau, M. (1973). On the concept of a self-correcting organization. *Public Administration Review, 33*, 533–542.

Lepper, M. M. (1976). The status of women in the United States. *Public Administration Review, 36*, 365–368.

Luthans, F., & Kreitner, R. (1974). *Organizational behavior modification.* Glenview, IL: Scott, Foreman & Co.

Mager, R., & Pipe, P. (1970). *Analyzing performance problems.* Belmont, CA: Fearon Publishers.

Miller, A. W. (1966). Conditioned connotative meaning. *Journal of General Psychology, 50*, 319–328.

Molotch, H., & Wolf, L. (1970). *Bureau of Institutional Analysis: Pilot research project on white racism in one place, report of preliminary findings.* Santa Barbara, CA: Community and Organizational Research Institute.

Molotch, H. & Wolf, L. (1971). *Report on white racism in one place pilot research project.* Santa Barbara, CA: Community and Organizational Research Institute, University of California at Santa Barbara.

Nigro, L. G. (1974). Affirmative Action in public employment. *Public Administrative Review, 34*, 234–246.

Paulson, R. I. (1977). *Goal displacement in a public welfare organization.* Unpublished doctoral dissertation, School of Social Welfare, University of California at Berkeley.

Perrow, C. (1970). *Organizational analysis: A sociological view.* Belmont, CA: Brooks/Cole.

Platt, A. M. (1990). Racism in academia: Lessons from the life of E. Franklin Frazier. *Monthly Review, 4*, 29–45.

Prager, J. (1973). *The minds of white folk: An analysis of racism in America.* Unpublished manuscript.

Reynolds, V., Falger, V. S., & Vine, I. (Eds.). (1986). *The sociobiology of ethnocentrism: Evolutionary dimensions of xenophobia, discrimination, racism, and nationalism.* Athens, GA: University of Georgia Press.

Schwartz, B., & Disch, R. (1970). *White racism: Its history, pathology and practice.* New York: Dell.

Staats, A. W., & Staats, C. K. (1958). Attitudes established by classical conditioning. *Journal of Abnormal and Social Psychology, 57,* 37–40.

Staats, C. K., & Staats, A. W. (1957). Meaning established by classical conditioning. *Journal of Experimental Psychology, 54,* 74–80.

Staples, R. (1988). Racial ideology and intellectual racism: Blacks in academia. *The Black Scholar, 15*(2), 2–17.

Steno, S. M. (1982). Differential treatment of minority children in service systems. *Social Work, 27,* 39–45.

Stewart, D. W. (1976). Women in top jobs: An opportunity for federal leadership, *Public Administration Review, 36,* 357–364.

Tabb, W. (1970). *The political economy of the black ghetto.* New York: W.W. Norton.

Thompson, J. D. (1967). *Organizations in action.* New York: McGraw-Hill.

Tossi, H. L., & Hammer, W. C. (1974). *Organizational behavior and management: A contingency approach,* Chicago, IL: St. Clair Press.

Weigel, R. H., & Howe, P. W. (1985). Conceptions of racial prejudice: Symbolic racism reconsidered. *Journal of Social Issues, 41,* 117–138.

Wellman, D. (1977). *Portraits of white racism.* Cambridge, England: Cambridge University Press.

Williams, J. (1984). Closed doors. In J. H. Skolmzk & E. Currie (Eds.), *Crisis in American institutions* (pp. 182–187). Glenview, IL: Scott Foresman & Co.

Williams, W., & Elmore, R. F. (Eds.). (1967). *Social program implementation.* New York: Academic Press.

Wulczyn, F. (1991). Caseload dynamics and foster care reentry. *Social Service Review, 64,* 133–156.

Zwerling, C., & Silver, H. (1992). Race and job dismissals in a federal beaurocracy. *American Sociological Review, 57,* 651–660.

7

PRODUCTIVITY IN THE WORKPLACE

JON S. BAILEY and JOHN AUSTIN

In this era of global competition, rightsizing, and downsizing, companies, executives, and managers consider positive attitude, loyalty, and undying commitment as essential qualities of the good employee. We do not fault managers for emphasizing these traits; they are undeniably important. However, simply identifying these traits and then seeking them in employees may not be the best strategy for increasing productivity. Why *do* some employees have a more positive attitude? Why *are* some employees more loyal, committed, productive, and dependable than others? Many managers would probably answer these questions by saying that good employees just have the right attitude. However, we would offer an alternative view: The answer lies in observable, employee *behavior*, not attitude.

CURRENT PROBLEMS AND APPROACHES

To stay competitive in today's global economy, company executives must be prepared to critically evaluate every aspect of their operations, from organizational tables to paper clip-purchasing practices. Efficiency and effectiveness are not optional; they are required for survival. Often lost in the rush to incorporate the latest management fad, such as total quality management (Capezio & Morehouse, 1993; Gabor, 1990; Walton, 1986,

1990), empowerment (Covey, 1989), or reengineering (Hammer & Champy, 1993), is the realization that business runs on human behavior. Understanding how to optimize human behavior is the major challenge at hand.

Not all of the business world is inundated with fad and hypothetical quick-fixes, however. Many social scientists are studying organizational productivity in laboratories and field settings, but, again, the problem is that most do not focus on behavior. In fact, organizational productivity is a hot topic in the world of academe, where research is ongoing in such areas as organizational citizenship (Posdakoff & MacKenzie, 1994), satisfaction (Abramis, 1994), quality of work life (Maupin, 1990), improvement of productivity through cultural change (Schneider, 1995), and transformational leadership (Bass & Avolio, 1994).

Some may argue that these researchers are studying behavior, but we would retort that they are not studying behavior in the same manner as we are. Most of the extant research is primarily descriptive in nature (Basu & Green, 1995; Jones, 1995), and when solutions *are* evaluated in real business settings, the data are collected primarily through interviews, ratings, and surveys (Gyan-Baffour, 1994; Smither, London, Vasilopoulos, & Reilly, 1995). In short, it may be nice to know descriptions of and have theories about organizational phenomena, but to change an organization's bottom line, we must change what its people do.

The one thoroughly researched and well-documented approach to improving performance in the workplace that focuses on behavior is Performance Management (PM). In this chapter, we will (a) explain the history and background from which Performance Management developed, (b) discuss measurement and intervention issues, (c) provide a summary of the PM research, (d) discuss evaluation issues, and (e) provide a description of a diagnostic system that managers can use to solve performance problems.

Performance Management

Performance Management[1] (Daniels, 1989) refers to the use of behavior analysis in business, industry, and government. In his seminal text, *Performance Management*, Daniels defined PM as "the systematic, data-oriented approach to managing human behavior in the workplace that relies on positive reinforcement as the major way of maximizing perform-

---

[1] When researchers first began to publish studies demonstrating the effective use of behavior analysis in organizations, the technology was named *organizational behavior modification* (OB Mod.; Luthans & Kreitner, 1975; Luthans & Schewizer, 1979). Today, this name is primarily used among academics employed in business departments. During the 1970s, the phrase *organizational behavior management* (OBM) (Frederiksen, 1982; Frederiksen and Johnson, 1981) replaced OB Mod. as the name of choice for behavior analysts who work in organizational settings. The seminal publication in the field was then also named the *Journal of Organizational Behavior Management* (JOBM); and OBM has

ance" (p. 4). PM is easily distinguished from other management methods by its paradigm, its focus on the bottom line, and its science-based methodology.

Few management researchers use the behavioral methodology paradigm, even though it is simple to use. Furthermore, studies that have used this paradigm can be read, understood, and implemented by managers without any high-level knowledge of statistics or behavioral science.

Most scientific research on management techniques is highly theoretical, as that is what is reinforced by the largest circulating journals in the field. They are, therefore, not bottom-line oriented. As discussed above, many studies lose focus of the primary goal: to change the way organizations and consequently, people, work. This, of course, requires its share of theory, but theories and models are tools, not an end in themselves.

Managers, like everyone, are influenced by the media. If a book about management is on the *New York Times'* best-seller list, many managers will buy the book. This is not necessarily bad. But the blind application of the techniques described in such a book is hazardous. Without science-based interventions, it is not possible to know the effects of implemented (perhaps acclaimed) programs. Most popular management techniques are not based on data; rather, they are trendy and hypothetical. *In Search of Excellence* (Peters & Waterman, 1982) provides a great example of such techniques. In 1982, Peters and Waterman identified 43 companies that met their criteria for excellence. By 1984, 14 of these 43 no longer met the criteria ("Who's Excellent Now," 1984). Was this because, 2 years later, the practices the authors recommended were no longer useful? Perhaps, but it could also be that these highly touted businesses did not know what it really takes to be successful. Only the behavioral methodology, combined with a focus on the bottom line and a basis in science, can lead to systematic and tangible solutions for managers.

The operant model is the paradigm of choice for behavior analysts (and, therefore, performance managers). The basics of this model were set forth primarily by the research of B. F. Skinner (1938, 1953, 1971). The model holds that behavior is largely a function of antecedent stimuli, reinforcement history (which resides in the person), and the consequences that the person's behavior produces when operating on the environment. More specifically, the context and temporal relation in which stimuli and behavior occur can be analyzed in the workplace using a four-term contingency model as shown in Figure 1.

---

remained popular among academics in both psychology and business departments who practice behavior analysis. More recently, however, the founder of JOBM, Aubrey Daniels, has proposed a new name for the field—performance management (Daniels, 1989). The new name was proposed primarily because it remains adequately descriptive of the field while being more acceptable to potential consumers than OBM or OB Mod. Each of the three terms are used fairly interchangeably in the current literature.

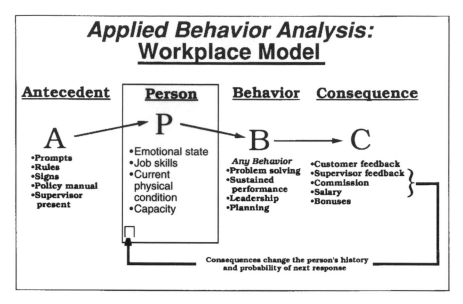

Figure 1. The four-term contingency for behavior analysis.

Antecedents (A) are those stimuli that precede a person's (P) behavior (B). Consequences (C) are those stimuli that follow a behavior. A behavioral analysis of any situation takes into account those antecedents and consequences that are functionally relevant to the target behavior of interest. In a business setting, the performance manager seeks to use this knowledge of contingencies (antecedents, consequences, and their effects on behavior) to the benefit of employees, managers, and the organization. Once the contingencies influencing behavior in any given setting are understood, these contingencies can be rearranged to make the environment more supportive of the behaviors in which both employees and managers wish to engage. It is important to note that the role of consequences is to change the reinforcement history of the person so they will have a greater probability of engaging in the desired behavior in the future. This is shown by the arrow in Figure 1.

This four-term contingency (otherwise known as the APBC model of behavior) is something that is easily taught and handily remembered. And, as shown by extensive empirical research, it is almost always effective when properly applied. In addition, the model provides employees at every level of the organization a way of making sense of the complexity of work behavior. Using this visual aid, supervisors can see that if they want to change the performance of an employee, they will need to provide either additional antecedents (prompts, rules, or instructions) or consequences that can shape the desired behavior. Labeling an employee as lazy does little good in changing the person's behavior; adding effective prompts and appropriately timed reinforcers could well begin the process of turning the person into a productive employee.

To properly apply the model to a work situation or performance problem, however, one first needs to know some PM basics. What makes PM so different from many of today's popular management techniques is its devotion to (a) frequent, objective, and quantifiable performance measurement of target behaviors, (b) research-based intervention, and (c) ongoing evaluation of interventions.

Performance Measurement

It should be obvious that, because there are so many differing types of work behavior, there are equally as many ways to measure that behavior. As a result, there is no one correct way to measure behavior at work. There are a few items to keep in mind, however.

When measuring work behavior, it is important to remember that what is being measured is always behavior, and that behavior has certain identifiable characteristics. Performance managers (individuals who use these management techniques) are interested in how people feel and think, and these are as much behaviors as turning a screw or filing a report. However, asking employees to describe their performances or their levels of job satisfaction has inherent problems, not limited to unreliability and difficulty in definition. Therefore, it is typical for performance managers to use objective and more reliable units of measurement and target behaviors. Some typical qualities of behaviors chosen for PM intervention follow:

1. Behavior is observable and can be operationally defined. If two independent observers were to measure the behavior at the same time, they would always find the same results.
2. Behavior is quantifiable. Managers can count instances of behavior and use the data to solve performance problems.
3. Behavior is labile. Behavior—especially work behavior— changes from day to day and, therefore, must be measured frequently and consistently for the data to be an accurate representation of reality.

Systematic, Data-Based Interventions

Performance Management techniques have demonstrated effectiveness in modifying varied behaviors in numerous settings. To say that the effectiveness of the techniques has been demonstrated is to say that they have been experimentally evaluated. The performance manager does not implement the newest management technique because it has received critical acclaim; rather, the performance manager's decisions of implementation and change are data-driven. The effective performance manager collects data and empirically determines the ways to maximize performance. In this section, I will describe some of the activities upon which such evaluation has taken place. In the next section, I will discuss more explicitly the methods by which techniques are often evaluated.

PM has demonstrated success with individuals in many diverse activities, from manufacturing line work to sales to other, more creative endeavors. Some of these include (a) a reduction of machine set-up time in a rubber manufacturing company (Wittkopp, Rowan, & Poling, 1990); (b) an improvement in the use of statistical process control in a machine shop (Henry & Redmon, 1990); (c) an increase in innovation in a public utility company (Smith, Kaminski, & Wylie, 1990); (d) an increase in the effectiveness of performance management training in city government (Nordstrum, Lorenzi, & Hall, 1990); (e) an increase in functional sales behaviors among salespersons (Luthans, Paul, & Taylor, 1985); (f) an increase in the number of on-time completions by engineers (McCuddy & Griggs, 1984); (g) an increase in the safety behavior and productivity of roofers (Austin, Kessler, Riccobono, & Bailey, in press); and (h) an increase in the number of contacts and followups for real estate agents (Anderson, Crowell, Sucec, Gilligan, & Wikoff, 1982).

According to operant reinforcement theory, reinforced behaviors are more likely to occur again (Skinner, 1938, 1953). Therefore, the primary goal of the performance manager is to create those contingencies in the work environment that help to make the desired behavior reinforcing to the employee (or whomever the target population may be). Such positive conditions have been created through the manipulation of antecedents and consequences such as training (Brown, Malott, Dillon, & Keeps, 1980; Komaki, Barwick, & Scott, 1978), prompts and information (Austin, Hatfield, Grindle, & Bailey, 1993; Carter, Hansson, Holmberg, & Melin, 1979; Greene & Neistat, 1983; Runnion, Watson, & McWhorter, 1978), goal setting (Eldridge, Lemasters, & Szypot, 1978; Komaki et al., 1978), written or verbal performance feedback (Henry & Redmon, 1990; Silva, Duncan, & Doudna, 1981; Wittkopp et al., 1990), written or verbal praise (Gaetani & Johnson, 1983; Komaki, Blood, & Holder, 1981), and various forms of contingent reinforcement (Foxx & Schaeffer, 1981; Newby & Robinson, 1983; Smith et al., 1990).

Although there are a wide variety of behavior-change strategies, performance feedback is clearly the most widely used performance management intervention. Feedback has been generally defined as information that is given to employees regarding the quantity or quality of their past performance (Prue & Fairbank, 1981). In their review of all the articles published in the *Journal of Organizational Behavior Management* from 1977 to 1986, Balcazar, Shupert, Daniels, Mawhinney, and Hopkins (1989) reported that 50% of all studies published used feedback as at least one independent variable. It has been suggested that feedback is often the intervention of choice because of its low cost, simplicity, and flexibility (Prue

& Fairbank, 1981). In addition, feedback has been demonstrated to be effective in a variety of areas, such as improving occupational safety compliance (Chhokar & Wallin, 1984; Sulzer-Azaroff, Loafman, Merante, & Hlavacek, 1990), increasing suggestive selling at a restaurant (Johnson & Masotti, 1990; Ralis & O'Brien, 1986), and teaching fire evacuation skills to adults with mental retardation (Fox & Sulzer-Azaroff, 1989).

Most studies of PM have been focused on providing demonstrations and systematic replications; however, some research has examined other, more complex issues and techniques while maintaining the all-important focus on behavior. For example, Wolf and colleagues (1995) and Malott and colleagues (1995) have described in detail their approach to developing, maintaining, and improving large-scale data-based programs; LaFleur and Hyten (1995) provided a performance analysis and improvement of quality service for a hotel banquet staff; Cole and Hopkins (1995) demonstrated that the relationship between self-efficacy and performance (Bandura, 1986) varies with environmental manipulations; and Mawhinney (1992) discussed the impact of metacontingencies on organizational effectiveness. These are some of the state-of-the-art studies in the field. Intense analyses of (a) larger-scale programs, (b) diagnosis and analysis of performance problems, and (c) complex organizational phenomena must be conducted in the future, however.

Experimentation and Evaluation

Managers and employees in many organizations today feel the need to make immediate changes and see immediate effects from the selected interventions. This is understandable because, as already mentioned, today's competitive markets are placing more and more pressure on all parts of organizations. In the absence of reliable data collection and consistent evaluation; however, the problem exists that the more one wants to see change, the more likely one is to perceive that change. When managers are left to their perceptions and gut feelings, they are playing a risky and unnecessary game of chance.

These games of chance can be avoided through properly controlled evaluations. After deciding on the most appropriate intervention (which will be discussed in the next section of this chapter), one needs to know whether the intervention of choice really had the desired effect(s). There are several ways to evaluate interventions, but two commonly used methods are the reversal design and the multiple baseline design. (See Baer, Wolf, & Risley, 1968 or Bailey & Bostow, 1979 for a more thorough explanation of these designs.)

The reversal design gets its name from the effort made to show a reversal effect in the behavior being targeted. If it can be demonstrated that the behavior changes in the intended direction when the intervention is in place, and that the behavior changes back to or near the original levels when the intervention is not in place, then the intervention is effective. Another way to view the reversal design is to imagine using the intervention to turn the behavior on and off like a water faucet: When the intervention is being used, the behavior is on (it occurs as desired), whereas when the intervention is not being used, the behavior is off (it occurs about as it did before the intervention was ever used). If the water faucet analogy works, the intervention was probably effective; if not, it is time to look for a new intervention.

The multiple baseline design is most useful when the reversal design is not feasible. For example, when there are potentially large sums of money to be lost as a result of removing the intervention (as in some gain-sharing plans), naturally one would seek to avoid its removal. Also, if removal could result in the personal injury of employees or an increase in danger associated with the work place, it is better to simply leave the intervention in place. But, leaving the intervention in place does not mean the intervention's effectiveness cannot be evaluated.

The purpose of the multiple baseline is to show the effects of an intervention through the sequential, time-staggered introduction of the intervention across different places (Plant A, Plant B, and so forth), different departments within one organization, different work crews or individual employees, or different measurable work behaviors. If, for instance, employee A receives the intervention in week 1 (before employees B and C), and there is some effect on the first employee's behavior but no effect on the other employees' behavior, and the same effect happens when the intervention is presented to employees B and C, respectively, then the intervention was probably effective. In other words, if one can show that

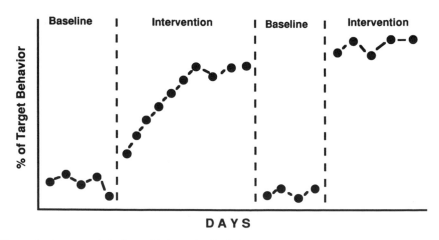

Figure 2. A reversal design with hypothetical data.

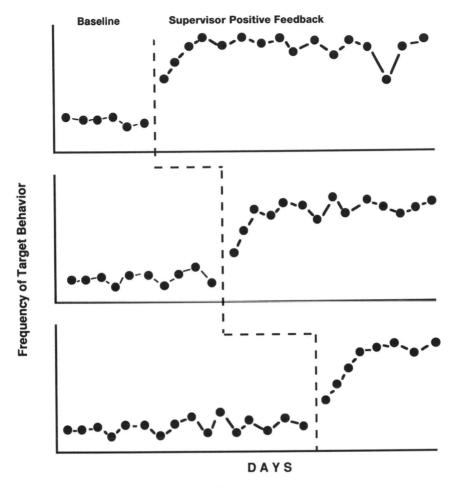

Figure 3. A multiple-baseline design with hypothetical data.

although the employees work together and do about the same job, the intervention worked for each of them, then that intervention is probably effective.

DIAGNOSING PERFORMANCE PROBLEMS: NEW STRATEGIES FOR MANAGEMENT

Diagnosing organizational problems has recently become a concern for industrial and organizational psychologists (Howard, 1994a) and many models and methods are currently being offered (Bray, 1994; Howard, 1994b; Lawler, 1994; Zemke, 1994). These approaches, however, are largely theoretical in nature and frequently overlook critical environmental variables affecting individual employee performance (Burke, 1994; Rogers & Byham, 1994; Walton & Nadler, 1994).

Performance Management, on the other hand, has many of the answers that corporate America wants, and PM can provide systematic, data-based recommendations that can have significant and profound effects on human performance in almost any size organization or company. To put the power of Performance Management to work, it is necessary to discover why the current performance is not optimal. To this end, we may follow the Performance Management flowchart of specific steps for problem solving as shown in Figure 4. First, a performance problem is selected. Then the specific performance is pinpointed that will be targeted for analysis. A general manager of a retail chain may, for example, select customer service as the performance. This would then be pinpointed to the specific performance of cashiers when customers are checking out (Daniels, 1989). An alternative specific performance could have been pinpointed, such as sales representatives who were rude to customers on the floor, or unnecessary delays in assisting patrons at the customer service desk. For whatever specific performance is pinpointed, reliable and valid measures are always developed and the data graphed for easy, visual evaluation (Daniels, 1989). Analyzing and diagnosing performance problems becomes the next key step. Fortunately, we have a relatively sophisticated behavioral model that allows us to analyze pivotal aspects of the environment to determine what changes need to be made.

Basic Diagnostic Questions

One strategy that has paid off in consulting with several dozen businesses over the past 10 years involves asking a series of questions to determine what type of intervention is most appropriate to solve a given performance problem. Although the exact order is probably not fixed, we have learned to start with questions that involve individual employees and work toward those that might affect a larger group. A flowchart showing the questions and specific interventions is shown in Figure 5.

Diagnostic Question 1. Does the Employee Have a Personal Problem That Requires Counseling or Other Assistance?

First-line supervisors confront and have to deal with variable employee performance every day. One not-so-recent observation by the primary author suggests that these supervisors need to be trained to watch for clinical symptoms of personal problems in employees. These range from possible effects of drug or alcohol abuse to signs of stress in the family resulting from divorce, child custody battles, or economic woes. Most su-

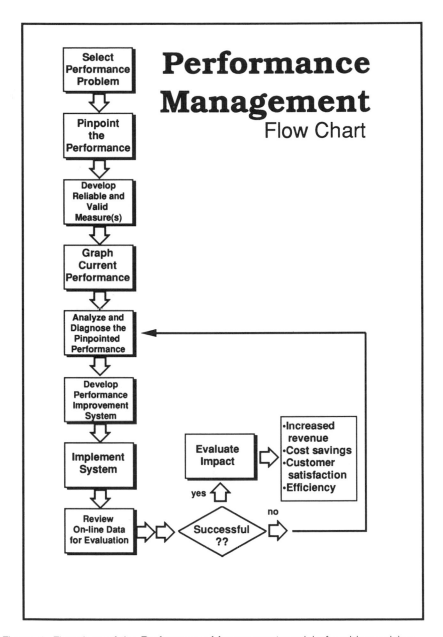

Figure 4. Flowchart of the Performance Management model of problem solving.

pervisors will not be prepared to provide the necessary counseling for such employees, but they can, at least, be trained to watch for symptoms and understand the referral process for appropriate clinical treatment. It is clearly inappropriate for supervisors to assume that every deviation from

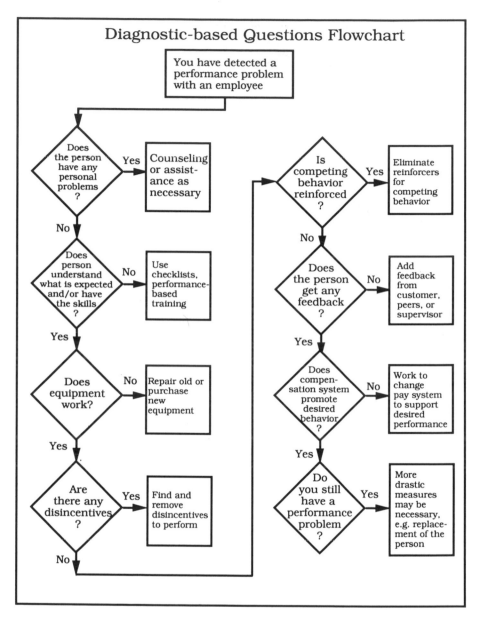

Diagnostic-based Questions Flowchart

You have detected a performance problem with an employee

Does the person have any personal problems ? — **Yes** → Counseling or assistance as necessary

No

Does person understand what is expected and/or have the skills ? — **No** → Use checklists, performance-based training

Yes

Does equipment work? — **No** → Repair old or purchase new equipment

Yes

Are there any disincentives ? — **Yes** → Find and remove disincentives to perform

No

Is competing behavior reinforced ? — **Yes** → Eliminate reinforcers for competing behavior

No

Does the person get any feedback ? — **No** → Add feedback from customer, peers, or supervisor

Yes

Does compensation system promote desired behavior ? — **No** → Work to change pay system to support desired performance

Yes

Do you still have a performance problem ? — **Yes** → More drastic measures may be necessary, e.g. replacement of the person

Figure 5. A flowchart showing how a performance manager diagnoses behavior problems in the workplace.

accepted work standard is due to lack of motivation, skill, or loyalty to the company. It would clearly be inappropriate for such supervisors to discipline employees who have a legitimate reason for poor performance.

*Diagnostic Question 2. Does the Person Understand What Behavior Is
Expected, and Do They Have The Skill to Perform That Behavior?*

It is important to make sure the performance problem noted is not
due to a simple misunderstanding about what is expected. The answer to
this question may be reached most easily by asking, "Has the person *demonstrated* the behavior has previously?" If not, then training or retraining
is in order. If the person has previously demonstrated the correct performance, the supervisor will need to look for some other cause. The poor or
unacceptable performance may possibly be due to the employee's belief that
a higher quality performance is not expected (perhaps gleaned from peers).
Certainly the simplest and least expensive intervention involves informing
employees exactly what is expected. A recent project carried out by Davis
(1994) in a local dental office illustrates this point. The dentist was dis-
pleased with the way his patients' needs were being met by his clinical
staff, but he had been unable to effect changes in his staff's behavior. A
baseline analysis showed that the desired behaviors existed in only a dismal
10% of occurrences. When it was discovered that the dentist had never
explicitly informed the staff about his specific standards, a complete checklist with the desired skills was developed and presented to the dental assistants and hygienists in checklist form. In addition, staff members were
given criterion-based training. Within a few days, they accomplished more
than 90% of the required behaviors.

*Diagnostic Question 3. Does the Equipment Work? Is It in Good Repair? Is
the Environment Conducive to Top Performance?*

Before accusations about an employee's performance are presented to
the employee, a check of the working conditions should be done to make
sure that all equipment is operating according to specifications. High expectations for performance can only be achieved if the tools, equipment,
and environment have been properly brought up to standard. Supervisors
should establish whether there is an "exemplar" employee (Gilbert, 1978)
who can perform up to the standard using the equipment available to
everyone else. If there is such a person, then it is possible to conclude that
the performance problem is due to some other source than faulty equipment. If no one can perform to standard using the equipment, then repair
or replacement becomes the focus of the intervention. In the quality management literature, considerable credence is given to the strategy of involving workers in the analysis and design of equipment and environments
(Walton, 1986). For example, one agribusiness, for which we were consultants, was experiencing problems in its mushroom harvesting operations.
The quality of mushroom picking was less than desired by management,
which tended to blame the workers for sloppy work. Our examination of

the problem revealed, however, that the knives the workers used to slice the stems of the mushrooms were often in disrepair. There was no routine way for the employees to sharpen these knives. We recommended to the company that—before it implemented other interventions that would involve costly retraining of farm workers—it sharpen the scalpel-looking tools at the end of each shift so as to be ready for the next day's work. This solution had evaded the company's managers largely because they did not take the time to ask the workers about ways to improve the quality of their work. Similar strategies would no doubt pay off in a wide variety of work settings and support the overall strategy of seeking to optimize the work environment.

Diagnostic Question 4. Are There Any Disincentives for Performing the Task?

Inherent in every task is some built-in or automatic effort, whether it be physical, mental, or emotional. Dealing with angry customers on the phone, carrying out essential preventive maintenance tasks on equipment, or retrieving the latest financial data for an annual report all have some disincentive or response effort associated with them. By considering this variable, supervisors may begin to understand why workers do not carry out tasks with care 100% of the time.

In a state government office that promoted tourism, representatives had to plan trips to major cities to stage promotional meetings for travel agents, association executive directors, feature writers, and corporate sponsors. Considerable waste of fiscal resources resulted from lack of advance planning on the part of these representatives. Bulky displays shipped by air freight at the last minute cost 10 times what standard, but slow, trucking costs would be. Printing costs for five-color brochures were exorbitant because of rush orders, whereas placing them in a timely fashion would have meant huge savings. A detailed diagnosis of the problem revealed that planning ahead was just too much trouble for these highly paid state ambassadors. Accomplishing these and other savings involved skills in project-task analysis and deadline-meeting that were simply not part of their daily repertoire. (Acquiring these skills was apparently too much trouble for them.) Our behavioral consultants showed their supervisor how to use project-planning boards to illustrate the task-analysis process and to make the advance planning process simple. Weekly deadlines for completion of the planning steps were also added and enforced; within 6 months these state representatives were able to plan their complex promotional trips effectively, and costs were reduced significantly.

Diagnostic Question 5. Is a Competing Behavior Being Reinforced?

This may seem odd but it appears to happen often. Although management desires a certain behavior (e.g., phoning potential customers to arrange appointments), an employee may discover another, more powerful reinforcer (e.g., talking on the phone to his or her friends). In one state government office in which the first author consulted on a problem that involved a low volume of work and a high error rate, employees had their FM radio tuned to a station that offered prizes throughout the day to listeners who called in (". . . be the 10th caller and give us the name of the first Elvis gold record and win a trip to Graceland"). Attentive listening to the radio and making calls to the station effectively competed with the task of reviewing equipment requisitions for state contracts. The employees simply could not pay attention to the details of the task of matching equipment model numbers with bid specifications for a myriad of contracts while debating among themselves about top-40 artists and their musical accomplishments. Because responding correctly to the contests paid off handsomely (although intermittently), employees were much more attentive to this task and less concerned about their assigned work (especially since they were state employees who were virtually immune from immediate consequences for poor quality work). The solution was obvious—but somewhat painful and awkward for the supervisor, who desperately wanted these employees to like her. The radio had to go, and the supervisor moved her desk into the same room as the employees. She set up a new system of checking each batch of requisitions as they were turned in rather than spot checking them at the end of the week. Performance improved dramatically in a few days with the friendly relationship between supervisor and employees the only casualty.

Diagnostic Question 6. Does the Person Get Any Feedback?

Clearly one of the most important findings in the growing PM literature is the significant role positive consequences play in the motivation of human performance. Many employees in today's workplace rarely, if ever, see any immediate, observable, positive effects of their efforts. A large percentage are isolated from the consumer and might easily conclude that going to great lengths to produce a quality product does not pay off. Supervisors (surprisingly) and coworkers (not so surprisingly) rarely give feedback. Annual performance ratings, of course, do not come close to approximating the type of immediate feedback employees need to maintain quality performance—the time delays are simply too great.

Certainly the least expensive solutions would involve including employees in a customer-driven feedback loop. Training supervisors to provide timely positive feedback, praise, and approval may also be necessary. Supervisors who want to motivate their employees maximally should arrange their schedule so that they can monitor employee performance daily and provide verbal, written, or graphic feedback (Daniels, 1989). To be effective, feedback should be personal, descriptive, immediate, and possibly even presented in the form of a graph.

Diagnostic Question 7. Does the Behavior Produce Any Important Positive Consequence?

Most employees will say that the most important positive consequence for them is their paycheck and, as many executives are beginning to discover, the traditional method of compensation may be a major culprit in poor performance (McCoy, 1992). In behavior analysis we have learned that, as a general rule "you get what you reinforce." This simple observation is especially true in organizations in which employees are paid by the hour or on salary rather than by the newer behavior-based incentive plans. Morale problems invariably result when people are asked to perform difficult, detailed, time-consuming tasks that have great economic benefit to the company or organization but for which they receive no meaningful compensation. Corporate executives interested in making significant gains in employee productivity need to review their current compensation systems to see if these systems reinforce the desired behavior. In a recent survey of 144 companies, it was found that greater employee involvement and significant quantifiable improvements in productivity were seen with the application of cash-based group-incentive plans (Towers Perrin survey as cited in McCoy, 1992).

Completing the Performance Management Flowchart

Once a tentative diagnosis of the performance problem is made, a performance improvement system (see Figure 4) can be devised to match the hypothesized cause. We have discovered that in a great many businesses, managers consistently rely on their favorite interventions and rarely take the time to think about all of the possible causes of a performance problem. Employees who actually need training may be told to sign a statement indicating that they have read the policy and procedure manual. Others who are starved for feedback from their supervisors are sent off for more training. Using the diagnostic method described here should ensure a closer match between the cause and the solution that is implemented; however, future research needs to be conducted in this area. Performance Management interventions are systematic in that they are carefully thought through, written out, explained to all concerned, and are applied over a considerable period of time, so that they can be evaluated carefully using baseline data for comparison purposes.

We strongly discourage impromptu interventions by frustrated managers. Use of a systematic intervention, one that is based on the likely causes of a performance problem and evaluated with data as shown in

Figure 4, is the standard accepted practice of PM. The payoff for such an intervention is a technology of performance improvement that is replicable and has scientific merit.

CONCLUSION

Significantly improving human performance in the 1990s requires a detailed understanding of the basic principles of behavior and of the extensive applied behavior analysis research that has been carried on over the past 25 years. In that time, we have learned the importance of antecedent events in setting the occasion for optimal performance. The role of consequences in motivating human behavior is also well understood. To find the most effective way of changing behavior in complex organizations today, we recommend a diagnostic approach that takes a wide variety of factors into account. An individual employee's performance might be unacceptable for any number of reasons and finding the likely cause should lead to an appropriate intervention. We believe this approach is appropriate for almost any size organization and that every manager and supervisor can benefit from considering many possible reasons for less-than-optimal performance. Carrying through with a diagnostic assessment and implementing the most appropriate intervention puts the supervisor in an ideal position to learn more about human behavior and to improve the working conditions of the employees as well as the bottom line for the company.

REFERENCES

Abramis, D. J. (1994). Work role ambiguity, job satisfaction, and job performance: Meta-analyses and review. *Psychological Reports, 75,* 1411–1433.

Anderson, D. C., Crowell, C. R., Sucec, J., Gilligan, K. D., & Witkoff, M. (1982). Behavioral management of client contacts in a real estate brokerage: Getting agents to sell more. *Journal of Organizational Behavior Management, 4,* 67–95.

Austin, J., Hatfield, D. B., Grindle, A. C., & Bailey, J. S. (1993). Increasing recycling in office environments: The effects of specific, informative cues. *Journal of Applied Behavior Analysis, 26,* 247–253.

Austin, J., Kessler, M. L., Riccobono, J. E., & Bailey, J. S. (in press). Using feedback and reinforcement to improve the performance and safety of a roofing crew. *Journal of Organizational Behavior Management.*

Baer, D. M., Wolf, M. M., & Risley, T. R. (1968). Some current dimensions of applied behavior analysis. *Journal of Applied Behavior Analysis, 1,* 91–97.

Bailey, J. S., & Bostow, D. E. (1979). *A handbook of research methods in applied behavior analysis*. Tallahassee: Behavior Management Consultants.

Balcazar, F. E., Shupert, M. K., Daniels, A. C., Mawhinney, T. C., & Hopkins, B. L. (1989). An objective review and analysis of ten years of publication in the Journal of Organizational Behavior Management. *Journal of Organizational Behavior Management, 10,* 7–38.

Bandura, A. (1986). *Social foundations of thought and action: A social cognitive view.* Englewood Cliffs, NJ: Prentice-Hall.

Bass, B. M., & Avolio, B. J. (Eds.). (1994). *Improving organizational performance through transformational leadership* (pp. 152–171). Thousand Oaks, CA: Sage.

Basu, R., & Green, S. G. (1995). Subordinate performance, leader-subordinate compatibility, and exchange quality in leader-member dyads: A field study. *Journal of Applied Social Psychology, 25,* 77–92.

Bray, D.W. (1994). Personnel-centered organizational diagnosis. In A. Howard (Ed.), *Diagnosis for organizational change.* New York: Guilford.

Brown, M. G., Malott, R. W., Dillon, M. J., & Keeps, E. J. (1980). Improving customer service in a large department store through the use of training and feedback. *Journal of Organizational Behavior Management, 2,* 251–265.

Burke, W. W. (1994). Diagnostic models for organization development. In A. Howard (Ed.), *Diagnosis for organizational change* (pp. 53–84). New York: Guilford Press.

Capezio, P., & Morehouse, D. (1993). *Taking the mystery out of TQM.* Hawthorne, NJ: Career Press.

Carter, N., Hansson, L., Holmberg, B., & Melin, L. (1979). Shoplifting reduction through the use of specific signs. *Journal of Organizational Behavior Management, 2,* 73–84.

Chhokar, J. S., & Wallin, J. A. (1984) A field study of the effect of feedback frequency on performance. *Journal of Applied Psychology, 69,* 524–530.

Cole, B. L., & Hopkins, B. L. (1995). Manipulations of the relationship between reported self-efficacy and performance. *Journal of Organizational Behavior Management, 15,* 95–136.

Covey, S. R. (1989, May). Basic principles of total quality. *Executive Excellence, 6,* 17–19.

Daniels, A. C. (1989). *Performance management.* Tucker, GA: Performance Management Publications.

Davis, A. (1994). *Improving quality of service in a dental office.* Unpublished manuscript, Society for Performance Management, Florida State University, Tallahassee.

Eldridge, L., Lemasters, S., & Szypot, B. (1978). A performance feedback intervention to reduce waste: Performance data and participant responses. *Journal of Organizational Behavior Management, 1*, 258–266.

Fox, C. J., & Sulzer-Azaroff, B. (1989). The effectiveness of two different sources of feedback on staff teaching of fire evacuation skills. *Journal of Organizational Behavior Management, 10*, 19–35.

Foxx, R. M., & Schaeffer, M. H. (1981). A company-based lottery to reduce the personal driving of employees. *Journal of Applied Behavior Analysis, 14*, 273–285.

Frederiksen, L. W. (1982). Organizational behavior management: An overview. In L. Frederiksen (Ed.), *Handbook of Organizational Behavior Management* (pp. 1–8). New York: Wiley-Interscience.

Frederiksen, L. W., & Johnson, R. P. (1981). Organizational behavior management. In M. Hersen, R. Eisler, & P. Miller (Eds.), *Progress in behavior modification* (pp. 67–118). New York: Academic Press.

Gabor, A. (1990). *The man who discovered quality.* New York: Penguin.

Gaetani, J. J., & Johnson, C. M. (1983). The effect of data plotting, praise, and state lottery tickets on decreasing cash shortages in a retail beverage chain. *Journal of Organizational Behavior Management, 5*, 5–15.

Gilbert, T. F. (1978). *Human competence: Engineering worthy performance.* New York: McGraw-Hill.

Greene, B. F., & Neistat, M. D. (1983). Behavior analysis in consumer affairs: Encouraging dental professionals to provide consumers with shielding from unnecessary x-ray exposure. *Journal of Applied Behavior Analysis, 16*, 13–27.

Gyan-Baffour, G. (1994). Advanced manufacturing technology, employee participation, and economic performance: An empirical analysis. *Journal of Managerial Issues, 6*, 491–505.

Hammer, M., & Champy, J. (1993). *Reengineering the corporation.* New York: HarperCollins.

Henry, G. O., & Redmon, W. K. (1990). The effects of performance feedback on the implementation of a statistical process control (SPC) program. *Journal of Organizational Behavior Management, 11*, 23–46.

Howard, A. (1994a). *Diagnosis for organizational change.* New York: Guilford Press.

Howard, A. (1994b). Toward integrated organizational diagnosis. In A. Howard (Ed.), *Diagnosis for organizational change* (pp. 239–268). New York: Guilford Press.

Johnson, C. M., & Masotti, R. M. (1990). Suggestive selling by waitstaff in family-style restaurants: An experiment and multisetting observations. *Journal of Organizational Behavior Management, 11*, 35–54.

Jones, J. W. (1995). Are retailers fully prepared for the holiday shopping season? *Journal of Business and Psychology, 9*, 299–313.

Komaki, J., Barwick, K. D., & Scott, L. R. (1978). A behavioral approach to occupational safety: Pinpointing and reinforcing safe performance in a food manufacturing plant. *Journal of Applied Psychology, 53*, 434–445.

Komaki, J., Blood, M. R., & Holder, D. (1981). Fostering friendliness in a fast food franchise. *Journal of Organizational Behavior Management, 2*, 151–164.

LaFleur, T., & Hyten, C. (1995). Improving the quality of hotel banquet staff performance. *Journal of Organizational Behavior Management, 15*, 69–94.

Lawler, E.E. (1994). Effective reward systems: Strategy, diagnosis, and design. In A. Howard (Ed.), *Diagnosis for organizational change* (pp. 210–238). New York: Guilford Press.

Luthans, F., & Kreitner, R. (1975). *Organizational behavior modification*. Glenview, IL: Scott, Foreman.

Luthans, F., Paul, R., & Taylor, L. (1985). The impact of contingent reinforcement on retail salespersons' performance behaviors: A replicated field experiment. *Journal of Organizational Behavior Management, 7*, 25–35.

Luthans, F., & Schewizer, J. (1979). OB Mod. in a small factory: How behavior modification techniques can improve total organizational performance. *Management Review 13*, 43–50.

Malott, R. W., Vunivich, P. L., Boettcher, W., & Groeger, C. (1995). Saving the world by teaching behavior analysis: A behavioral systems approach. *The Behavior Analyst, 18*, 341–354.

Maupin, R. J. (1990). Redesigning management consulting practices. *Leadership & Organization Development Journal, 11*(4), 3–9.

Mawhinney, T. C. (1992). Evolution of organizational cultures as selection by consequences: The gaia hypothesis, metacontingencies, and organizational ecology. *Journal of Organizational Behavior Management, 12*, 1–26.

McCoy, T. J. (1992). *Compensation and motivation*. New York: American Management Association.

McCuddy, M. K., & Griggs, M. H. (1984). Goal setting and feedback in the management of a professional department: A case study. *Journal of Organizational Behavior Management, 6*, 53–64.

Newby, T. J., & Robinson, P. W. (1983). Effects of grouped and individual feedback and reinforcement on retail employee performances. *Journal of Organizational Behavior Management, 5*, 51–68.

Nordstrum, R. R., Lorenzi, P., & Hall, R. V. (1990). A behavioral training program for managers in city government. *Journal of Organizational Behavior Management, 11*, 189–213.

Peters, T. J., & Waterman, W. H., Jr. (1982). *In search of excellence: Lessons from America's best-run companies*. New York: Englewood.

Posdakoff, P. M., & MacKenzie, S. B. (1994). Organizational citizenship behaviors and sales unit effectiveness. *Journal of Marketing Research, 31*, 351–363.

Prue, D. M., & Fairbank, J. A. (1981). Performance feedback in organizational behavior management: A review. *Journal of Organizational Behavior Management, 3*, 1–16.

Ralis, M. T., & O'Brien, R. M. (1986). Prompts, goal setting, and feedback to increase suggestive selling. *Journal of Organizational Behavior Management, 8*, 5–18.

Rogers, R. W., & Byham, W. C. (1994). Diagnosing organization cultures for re-alignment. In A. Howard (Ed.), *Diagnosis for organizational change* (pp. 179–209). New York: Guilford Press.

Runnion, A., Watson, J. O., & McWhorter, J. (1978). Energy savings in interstate transportation through feedback and reinforcement. *Journal of Organizational Behavior Management, 1*, 180–191.

Schneider, W. E. (1995). Productivity improvement through cultural focus. *Consulting Psychology Journal: Practice and Research, 47*, 3–37.

Silva, D. B., Duncan, P. K., & Doudna, D. (1981). The effects of attendance-contingent feedback and praise on attendance and work efficiency. *Journal of Organizational Behavior Management, 3*, 59–69.

Skinner, B. F. (1938). *The behavior of organisms.* New York: Appleton-Century-Crofts.

Skinner, B. F. (1953). *Science and human behavior.* New York: Macmillan.

Skinner, B. F. (1971). *Beyond freedom and dignity.* New York: Knopf.

Smith, J. M., Kaminski, B. J., & Wylie, R. G. (1990). May I make a suggestion?: Corporate support for innovation. *Journal of Organizational Behavior Management, 11*, 125–146.

Smither, J. W., London, M., Vasilopoulos, N. L., & Reilly, R. R. (1995). An examination of the effects of an upward feedback program over time. *Personnel Psychology, 48*, 1–34.

Sulzer-Azaroff, B., Loafman, B., Merante, R. J., & Hlavacek, A. C. (1990). Improving occupational safety in a large industrial plant: A systematic replication. *Journal of Organizational Behavior Management, 11*, 99–120.

Walton, E., & Nadler, D.A. (1994). Diagnosis for organization design. In A. Howard (Ed.), *Diagnosis for organizational change* (pp. 85–105). New York: Guilford Press.

Walton, M. (1986). *The Deming management method.* New York: Dodd, Mead.

Walton, M. (1990). *Deming management at work.* New York: Putnam.

Who's excellent now? Some of the best-sellers picks haven't been doing so well lately. *Business Week*, p. 76(3).

Wittkopp, C. J., Rowan, J. F., & Poling, A. (1990). Use of a feedback package to reduce machine set-up time in a manufacturing setting. *Journal of Organizational Behavior Management, 11*, 7–22.

Wolf, M. M., Kirigin, K. A., Fixsen, D. L., Blase, K. A., & Braukmann, C. J. (1995). The family teaching model: A case study in data-based program development and refinement (and dragon wrestling). *Journal of Organizational Behavior Management, 15,* 11–68.

Zemke, R.E. (1994). Training needs assessment: The broadening focus of a simple concept. In A. Howard (Ed.), *Diagnosis for organizational change* (pp. 139–151). New York: Guilford.

8

SEXISM

PATRICIA M. DALY

INDIVIDUAL BEHAVIOR AND CULTURAL PRACTICES

Malagodi and Jackson (1989) noted distinctions between *troubles* and *issues* in a manner useful to this chapter. Troubles are individual and personal. They are explained by the contingencies operating at the individual level. An employee who is paid less than other employees for comparable work because she is female has a personal trouble. An issue, on the other hand, is a trouble experienced by a group of people. It is not explainable at the level of individually operating contingencies. Issues are understood within a broader cultural context. As a group, college-educated women earn approximately 60% of what their male counterparts earn (U.S. Bureau of Census, 1991). This is an issue. The solution to issues requires analysis at both individual and cultural levels. It is important to consider women's issues at the cultural level. As Malagodi and Jackson (1989) warned:

Members of a culture, be they ordinary people or people in power, are not led to examine seriously, to challenge, or to change even personal-orbit local contingencies—let alone broad social-system metacontingencies—when widespread personal problems that occur within that system are viewed as troubles arising out of common human failings rather than as issues arising out of fundamental failures of the culture's political, economic, legal, religious, educational, mental-health, and other institutions of social control. (p. 27)

The purpose of this chapter is to use a behavior analytic approach to define sexism, to explore its extent in our culture, and to analyze potential sources of, and explanations for, its continuance. Nonviolent sexist behavior is analyzed both as individual behavior maintained by contingencies of reinforcement and as cultural practices that may have had survival value in the past, but no longer do. Further, major feminist schools of thought on sexist behavior are described, and suggestions for behavioral interventions to combat sexism are presented.

Sexism Defined

Women's issues are conceptualized here as a continuum of behavior collectively labeled sexism. Sexism is a socially acquired repertoire, one which reflects specific societal values. It is defined as a response class emitted by men and women that produces consequences ranging from denying women access to reinforcers and restricting their opportunities to acquire and emit certain repertoires, to endangering their health and lives. Examples of sexist behaviors according to this definition include the writing and purchasing of elementary school textbooks and tests that underrepresent girls in active, interesting, and exciting roles. This practice contributes to the teaching of gender-specific roles, which limit girls' access to reinforcers. The middle of the definitional continuum describes behaviors that discourage women from considering and persevering in certain career and job choices. These behaviors include differential treatment of boys and girls in math and science classes in elementary and secondary schools; the creation of work environments hostile to women, primarily through the sanction of sexist language; the expectation that women will do the majority of child care and childrearing activities; and the induction of men to upper-level administrative positions through the use of "good-old-boy" networks that exclude women. The last level on the definitional continuum contains behaviors that harass women and threaten their safety and even their lives. It is, however, beyond the scope of this chapter to analyze violence toward women.

Prevalence of Sexism

Sexist behaviors are institutionalized and prevalent. The major institutions that teach sexism are the family and schools. The development of sexist repertoires in the home is described later. Research on sexist behaviors in education has focused on the portrayal of male and female characters in stories and on the differential treatment of boys and girls in classrooms.

Researchers analyzed the ratio of male-to-female characters in children's stories and textbooks during the 1970s and 1980s. In the 1970s, boys or men were the main characters in 61% to 75% of the stories examined (Britton & Limpkin, 1977; Graebner, 1972). Animals and objects—not identifiable by gender ("other")—constituted 23% of main characters. Male roles included doctors, science teachers, military officers, ministers, and writers, whereas female roles were those of teachers, nurses, clerks, stewardesses, and cooks (Hitchcock & Tompkins, 1987). Hitchcock and Tompkins also examined six major series of basal readers for changes in ratio between male and female characters. Boys or men were the main characters in 18% of the stories; girls or women were the main characters in 17%. The category of other rose to more than 60%. The researchers concluded that writers and publishers were not increasing representation of girls in nontraditional roles. They were effectively sidestepping the issue by creating larger numbers of characters with no gender identification. Findings for math texts' use of story-problem characters parallel those for reading (Nibbelink, Stockdale, and Mangru, 1986).

The research of Sadker and Sadker (1985) produced much evidence of differential treatment of boys and girls in classrooms. Boys talked more than girls in elementary, secondary, and postsecondary classrooms. There was widespread sex segregation in classrooms at all educational levels. Teachers were more likely to punish girls than boys for calling out answers during class discussion. Boys received more praise from teachers and were criticized more than girls. In vocational settings, teachers gave male students extended directions on how to complete tasks for themselves. Teachers were more likely to do a task for female students. This last finding was as prevalent in early childhood classes in arts and crafts projects as it was in the Coast Guard Academy, where instructors explained to males how to operate equipment and operated it for female students.

The education experienced by women students at the university level also differs considerably from that of men because of the prevalence of sexist behaviors. Myers (1993) noted that 70% of women college students experienced either sexual or gender harassment on campus. Examples included degrading statements about their clothing, body, or sexual behavior.

If students learn what is taught, what male students learn is significantly different from what females learn. The absence of nontraditional models for boys and girls in textbooks maintains specific values of the culture relative to what men and women should and should not seek or expect. The cost of maintaining these values will be addressed later in this chapter. Thus, there is ample evidence that sexist behavior is a dominant practice in education.

There is also evidence that work environments are less than supportive to women in nontraditional careers or jobs. Apart from pay inequities (Ostertag & McNamara, 1991), women experience varying levels of discrimination, ranging from sexist language to harassment in the workplace. Myers (1993) detailed the prevalence of these behaviors with data suggesting that more than 50% of all women working in the private sector "reported negative consequences . . . for refusal to comply with sexual propositions" (p. 83). Some effects of these sexist behaviors include interference with the ability to do the job and an uncomfortable work environment for women. Sutherland (1987) documented the differential treatment of women by employers, especially in jobs typically held by men. Further, women occupied lower positions and lower status jobs, engaged more in part-time work, and were more likely to become unemployed in times of economic stress.

Social Costs of Sexism

The personal and social costs of sexist behaviors are inestimable. Chronic underrepresentation of women in the sciences, medicine, law, administration, and almost all top-level government positions results in a paucity of models for these careers (Fox Keller, 1985). This in turn ensures the difficulties experienced by those women who break the mold and accomplish nontraditional goals. The absence of women in rank-and-file jobs affects the choices of problems researched in science and medicine. For instance, it is only since 1993 that federal funding for large-scale medical research into breast cancer, a major cause of death in women, has been made available. Further, the research on heart disease, the number-one killer of women in the United States, has yet to include large numbers of women participants. Because many women have primary child-care responsibilities and lower paying jobs, more women-headed single parent families are at or below poverty level than similar families headed by men (U.S. Bureau of Census, 1991). The waste of talent and underdevelopment of skills is most evident and most difficult to document in the prevalent belief that women are and should be the primary homemaker and parent. The energy and time these roles require detract from that needed to pursue a demanding, better paying career (Favell, 1989). The negative outcomes of sexist behaviors have been brought to public attention by feminist special interest groups. As a result, in the past decade major changes in policy and practice have been made.

Existing Knowledge and Conceptual Base for Combating Sexism

Most of the work to identify and combat sexist behavior has grown and developed into a new discipline called feminism. Feminism, not unlike psychology, has many philosophies reflecting its multiple sources. It is not possible to reduce feminist theory to a couple of paragraphs without making some very difficult choices. However, it is appropriate to attempt to describe briefly the major types of feminisms, with their concomitant social agendas and some of their better known advocates. An excellent overview is provided by Tong (1989), from which the following summaries are drawn (pp. 1-11). Seven theoretical approaches to feminism can be distinguished. They are:

1. Traditional Liberal Feminism identified with Mary Wollstonecraft (1975) and John Stuart Mill (1869/1970).

   Basic premises: Custom and law prevent women from developing their full potential through educational opportunities. With equal educational opportunity and civil rights, women will achieve in ways comparable to men.

2. Marxist Feminism identified with Engels (1972), Bentson (1969), Dalla Costa and James (1972).

   Basic premises: As long as class distinctions exist and the majority of private property is owned by men, women will never have equal educational or economic opportunities. With the abolition of private ownership, women will no longer be economically dependent on men and will be able to achieve equality.

3. Radical Feminism identified with Firestone (1970), Rich (1979), Millett (1970), French (1985), and Daly (1978).

   Basic premises: Neither Marxist nor traditional liberal Feminism go far enough. Women are oppressed by all societal institutions, which are male-dominated and patriarchal. All institutions as we know them must be abolished. This includes the biological family. Biology is a fact women and men must overcome, not accept as the basis for gender-role differences.[1]

4. Psychoanalytic Feminism identified with Dinnerstein (1977) and Chodorow (1978).

   Basic premises: Freud's theories, particularly that of the oedipal complex, inform psychoanalytic feminism. Women-dominated childrearing forces boys to give up their first love object, the mother, to avoid castration at the hands of the father. In this way, boys become fully integrated into the dominant male culture. Girls, on the other hand, do not completely separate from their mothers, so they never become fully integrated. The only solution is dual parenting, in which men and women take equal shares in disciplining and nurturing.

5. Existential Feminism identified with Simone de Beauvoir (1949/1974).

---

[1] In B. F. Skinner's *Walden Two* (1948), social arrangements, particularly child rearing practices, are closest to those advocated by the radical feminist perspective.

Basic premises: Woman is the *other* in relation to man, who is the *self*. In other words, women are always second-class citizens and outsiders; they are "objects" whose meanings are interpreted for them by men. Only women themselves can transcend the definitions and labels of femininity coined by men by working, by becoming intellectuals, and by socially transforming society.

6. Socialist Feminism associated with Mitchell (1974), Hartmann (1981), and Jaggar 1983).

Basic premises: Socialist feminism differs from Marxist feminism by adding notions from radical and psychoanalytical feminisms to the Marxist position. Socialist feminists attempt to completely explain the origins of women's oppression by both analyzing capitalism and patriarchy as distinct forms of oppression (dual-systems theorists) and by analyzing capitalism and patriarchy together as one indistinguishable system (unified-systems theorists).

7. Postmodern Feminism identified with Derrida (1978), Lacan (1977), Cixous (1981), and Irigaray (1985).

Basic premises: Postmodern feminists reject the notion that one unifying concept, however complex, can explain women's oppression. Women's experiences of oppression differ across racial, class, and cultural lines. The more and diverse feminist thought that can be generated, the better.

The following are some common concerns feminists from all these theoretical approaches share. Feminist scholars tend to have an interest in praxis (providing a direct connection between a theoretical position and the practices and behaviors related to that position) in which women and men are reeducated to examine existing scholarship from a feminist point of view (Luke & Gore, 1992). Feminists have identified sexist practices in the lives of women through the organization of community-based, consciousness-raising groups. Women's studies departments have been established on campuses where feminist scholarship is critiqued and where the once little-known works written and composed by women are the major focus. Notions of male power and female disempowerment are examined. Many feminists have sought to locate the causes of women's oppression by men (Nicholson, 1990). Other feminists like hooks (1989, 1984), Rich (1986), and Ellsworth (1989) consider oppression of women to have many levels, depending on the influence of racism and classism. These writers claim all women experience varying degrees of each "-ism"; therefore, no two women's experiences of oppression are exactly alike.

Whatever particular forms of feminism now exist, the public arm of this movement, the National Organization for Women, has lobbied extensively and successfully for legislative changes on women's behalf. For example, public attention has been focused on the uses and effects of sexist language, so that now most publishing criteria require nonsexist language guidelines to be followed. Affirmative action procedures exist in all public sources of employment in a deliberate attempt to alter hiring biases. It is undeniable that feminist political action networks have brought about significant changes in language and practices in public settings. It is likely such changes will continue, though not without resistance (Faludi, 1991). It is a problem that the analyses by many feminists of sexist behavior cause a strong element of blame directed toward men. This in turn has made it easier to stereotype as man-haters those women who call themselves feminists. hooks (1984) suggested that people advocate feminism rather than call themselves feminists. This allows a person to belong to any discipline and espouse feminist values, for instance, to be a behaviorist and advocate feminism.

Feminists acknowledge that human behavior must change for women to be treated equitably. Behavior change is certainly the domain of behavior analysts, some of whom have examined the contributions of women to the field (Favell, 1989; Myers, 1993; Poling et al., 1983). To date, however, this community has not considered sexist behavior to be a major research topic. With the current interest of several behavior analysts in the possible contributions of cultural anthropology to behavior analysis (Glenn, 1988; Malagodi, 1986; Malagodi & Jackson, 1989; Malott, 1988), there is the potential to analyze sexist behavior as cultural practices that, at one time, had materialistic outcomes. That is to say, such behavior had useful practical consequences at some point in human evolution. Perhaps such an analysis can be conducted without blame.

Behavioral Analysis of Sexism

The domain of behavior analysis is the explanation, prediction, and control of individual human behavior. Determinants of individual human behavior are sought in the contingencies of behavior operating in the immediate environment, coupled with the unique history of the individual with those contingencies or ones similar to them. A person acquires a repertoire through a combination of contingency-developed and rule-governed behavior. With respect to verbal sexism, an individual's sexist behavior is maintained largely by the verbal community's contingencies of reinforcement. A worker who whistles and makes obscene comments to a woman walking past is reinforced by the verbal approval of his colleagues. He may be considered a suspect member of that community if he does not engage in this behavior where it is accepted practice. How does a person acquire a sexist repertoire? The verbal community into which an individual is born reinforces and explicitly teaches sexist repertoires to a greater or lesser extent. The models for sexist behaving that are most prevalent are in both written and visual media.

The home is the first place where sexist behavior is conditioned and maintained. When aggressive behavior by girls is punished more severely than similar behavior by boys, boys learn to behave more aggressively. When boys are expected to do certain chores and not others (e.g., take out the trash and not do dishes), they learn that certain tasks are gender-specific. A man can often articulate these differences as rules when challenged to participate in atypical tasks by saying: "That's women's work." This statement represents a rule specifying that only women may do certain work and that men are likely to be punished for doing that work. The punishers are most often the verbal community such as the man's friends, his family, even his wife. In short, sexist behaviors can be explained by the contingencies of reinforcement, by the avoidance of punishing situations, and by rule-governed behavior. But this analysis does not account for the generational presence of the type of verbal community described above. Why did such sexist verbal communities develop, and how are they maintained across generations? Only by using the notion of the metacontingency (Glenn, 1986), defined next, can such behaviors be understood and changed.

Cultural Practices: Definitions and Types

The domain of cultural anthropologists is cultural practices, their development, maintenance, and change. Cultural practices involve the interrelated behavior of two or more people and the environments in which those practices occur. Among the many types of cultural anthropologies, cultural materialism, as exemplified in the works of Harris (1980, 1981, 1983), has been described as the most compatible with radical behavior analysis (Malagodi, 1986).

Harris (1979) identified three levels of cultural practices—infrastructural, structural, and superstructural. Infrastructural practices are primarily productive and reproductive in nature. In other words, cultural practices that produce population increases, decreases, or control are infrastructural, as are practices that feed and protect people. Examples of infrastructural practices might be different types of farming, food processing, and birth control. These are key practices because changes in these affect changes in practices at the other two levels. Harris believes that infrastructural practices determine the forms and limits of practices in structure and superstructure (Malagodi & Jackson, 1989).

The second type of cultural practice consists of a culture's structure. Here are found major institutional practices such as education, political organizations, family systems, military, police, and religions. These are built on infrastructural practices and they change in response to them, though not immediately. An example here might be the structural practice of education in terms of the typical school year. When societies, including the

United States, were agriculturally based, students could not attend school during the summer because extra labor was needed to harvest crops. Harvesting is an infrastructural practice. Now, with the advent of mechanization and the exodus from rural to urban areas, additional labor is not required on the same scale. (Child labor laws may have also influenced the change from using children to hiring adults when necessary.) But for most students, the school year remains the same, despite changes in the relevant infrastructural practices. The no-summer school year now has other outcomes besides the original one. In many families, both parents work and rarely share the school-year schedule. Child care has become a pressing problem during the summer. The impetus for changing to a 12-month school year is strong and, in some locations, has already been successful. This example illustrates the interconnectedness of cultural practices as well as the delay between changes in one level and their effects at the second level.

The third level of cultural practices compose the superstructure. Practices related to literature, art, games, sport, advertising, rituals, myths, and ideologies are superstructural.

Glenn (1988) interpreted a cultural practice to be "a set of interlocking contingencies of reinforcement in which the behavior and behavioral products of each participant function as environmental events with which the behavior of other individuals interacts" (p. 167). The behavior of each individual participating in the practice influences that of some other individuals in the same practice and is influenced in turn by the behavior of the others. The cultural practice becomes a metacontingency when the practice has outcomes that contribute to or adversely affect the survival of the culture. The outcomes of the practice are the result of the combined behavior of all individuals engaged in the practice. Consider child care by women as a cultural practice. Although the specific behaviors engaged in by each mother may differ slightly or significantly from each other (e.g., the type and amount of foods used, clothes worn by the children, time spent with children, medical care provided), the result of the aggregate behavior of mothers in all variations of this practice might be children ready to benefit from formal education in varying degrees. Other participants in this cultural practice may be other family members, pediatricians (and other medical personnel), social service agencies, and welfare. If enough children are not prepared to benefit from formal education at the usual age in a given community, child care practices may be examined and changed.

A fundamental principle of Harris' cultural materialism is the belief that cultural practices have materialistic origins (Malott, 1988). That is, cultural practices such as premodern traumatic abortion and female infanticide developed because they had survival value for the cultures in which they flourished (Glenn, 1988).

One last concept merits discussion. If metacontingencies have out-comes that are remote, small, and cumulative, how do they affect the be-havior of the participants in the practice? What is the connection between remote outcomes and the probability of behaving in certain ways? Malott (1988) made a case for the intervention of rules and rule-governed be-havior as this link. Basically, direct-acting contingencies affect the future probability of behavior regardless of whether the person knows (can state verbally) the contingency as a rule. For example, if you reverse your car without looking first and hit a harder object than your car, you will be less likely to do the same behavior again in the near future. Indirect-acting contingencies cannot control behavior because their outcomes are too re-mote, too far removed in time, or too small to be significant. An example of an indirect-acting contingency might be the effects of smoking. All the long-term effects of smoking are negative, and many of them are life-threatening, but one does not get cancer by smoking a pack of cigarettes. There is no immediate strong negative effect. Malott suggests that indirect-acting contingencies work only when direct-acting contingencies operate as part of them or in their place. For behavior to be rule-governed, the behaver must be able to articulate the rule. If the rule is hard to follow, regardless of its ultimate benefits, it will not control behavior. The substi-tution of an easy-to-follow rule for a hard-to-follow rule would control the behavior by establishing "the stimuli associated with noncompliance as an aversive condition; and a reduction of those aversive stimuli in turn rein-forces compliance" (p. 190). Malott further suggested that religious organ-izations frequently provide the easy-to-follow rules by providing the threat of supernatural punishment for noncompliance. This form of compliance is dependent on the existence of a prerequisite repertoire of effective con-trol by rules stated by others.

Sexist Behavior as Cultural Practices

The expectation that child rearing is women's work disadvantages women in many ways. The amount of time and energy they can give to their careers is reduced. A disproportionate share of homemaking and child care is still the lot of professional women in general (Pizurki, Meija, Butter, & Ewart, 1987). Doing certain household chores and not others because of gender is sexist behavior. How might this be described as a cultural practice? Child rearing and labor division can be analyzed as interrelated cultural practices. It is true that this analysis might apply only to certain cultures and not to others.

The cultural practice of child rearing by women probably had many determinants. Clearly, women became associated with child rearing because of their biological role in reproduction. The fact that infants and toddlers who were breastfed had a lower mortality rate than those who were not breastfed may be another reason. This connection may not have been noticed explicitly, because the outcome of the practice was gradual and cumulative. Another outcome of the practice of lactation was the decreased likelihood of becoming pregnant. This connection certainly existed as a rule and may have maintained the behavior. The materialistic outcomes of this cultural practice included healthier children and healthier mothers—it clearly had survival value. Whether religious easy-to-follow rules enabled such practices to be maintained is unclear. Certainly in Western European countries in preindustrialization times, the Roman Catholic church had clear expectations for what women could and could not do. The church certainly supported the role of women in child rearing.

Cultural practices rarely exist in isolation but intertwine with other related cultural practices. Just as there are clear biological origins for the practice of child rearing by women, some cultural practices most likely developed because of male biology also. In times when even the simplest activities of providing heat and food required physical strength, men had a clear advantage. Cultures that provided better food, heat, and protection because of their superior strength tended to survive better than those that did not. So there is a possible biological explanation for some division of labor between the genders. These activities reduced the likelihood that men would be available for child rearing. They also increased the probability that rules were developed identifying specific tasks to be the exclusive domain of men or women.

A third practice that contributed to women-centered child care and gender role differentiation relates to property ownership and legal inheritance procedures (Rich, 1986). Whereas it was clear who the mother of a child was because it was physically possible to prove, it was not possible until very recently to prove paternity. With men typically the protectors of the property, it became important to identify who their inheritors were. When women were kept in a residence with her children—away from the possibility of having children by other men—a man's inheritance was assured.

With women raising children and men engaged in political matters outside the home, other rules were easier to provide to keep women from entering the realm of male political power. Women might be more likely to stay in the home if they believe it unsafe physically for them to go outside without the protection of their husband. This is a much simpler rule to follow with potentially immediate consequences than an inheritance rule. And the outcomes of all three practices—woman-centered child rearing, men-centered war and protection, and property transfer practices—all had survival value.

Once practices are established, the behavior of individuals in the practices is explained by the contingencies of reinforcement. The practice is taught to new members and thus maintained generationally. Individual exceptions to the practice, women who did not have children or who became soldiers and did not assume typical female roles, did not affect the outcomes of the practices because most women participated. Practices become self-sustaining as long as certain conditions remain unchanged. These conditions are the outcomes of infrastructural practices. As long as there are enough children born to replace population losses and enough food to feed those children, the cultural practices remain unchanged. When something happens to change the balance of population and food production, practices at the structural level change. The problem with this scenario is that when the outcomes of the original practices no longer have survival value and are so remote and small that they are not articulated or have weak control over behavior, damaging practices can be maintained.

Changes in Survival Value of Cultural Practices

As previously stated, practices that develop in response to contingencies can be maintained after the original contingencies no longer apply. This may happen for at least a couple of reasons. First, the connection between the outcomes and the practice may not be articulated. The rule is never stated. If the outcome is negative, ignorance of it will not promote change in the practice. For example, from the mid-1940s to the mid-1960s the drug DES (diethylstilbestrol) was commonly administered to pregnant women with a history of miscarriage and other problems (Boston Women's Health Book Collective, 1984). One long-term outcome of the DES was an increased incidence of cancer in the daughters of women who took the drug. This connection was not known to the consumers of the drug—their ignorance of it allowed administration of the drug to continue. Second, practices may have multiple outcomes in complex societies. Some of these may be positive and some, negative. Clear statements of contingent relationships may be confusing because they seem to contradict each other. It is interesting to examine some of the massive changes in cultural practices relative to women that occurred during and after World War II as an example of deliberate cultural engineering.

When most of the male work force was inducted into the armed forces during this war, production on the home front had to be maintained by those men not drafted and by women. In the course of a few short years, the roles of women changed dramatically. Jobs typically held by men became open to women, and women were actively encouraged to engage in them. Operating heavy machinery, steel work, welding, and other heavy industry production processes were suddenly the work of patriotic women. The infrastructural cultural practices of reproduction and production changed. The changes in metacontingencies were articulated by government spokespersons, in cinema newsreels, and in other news media. Explicit rules specifying the connection between women working and industrial output were stated. Even in entertainment practices changed. For instance, women's baseball teams had only tentative public approval before the war years. During the war, however, the first (and only) professional women's baseball league was established (Gregorich, 1993). A second drastic change in cultural practices occurred at the end of the war when the working population reverted to its prewar status. Women were urged—and indeed forced—to give up their jobs to the returning men. Once again, certain jobs were men's work and child rearing was women's major task. The use of media to encourage women to be satisfied with a return to the home was well documented by Friedan (1963) and was discussed by Faludi (1991). This example of immediate and pervasive change was made possible by the explicit connection made between old cultural practices, no longer possible, and the desired outcomes. To meet the desired outcomes, new practices were designed and implemented. Most cultural practices do not change this suddenly even when their outcomes cease to have survival value. This is an example of deliberate cultural engineering.

It is likely that what are now called sexist practices—which once may have had survival value—no longer benefit the cultures in which they exist. Apart from the example of wartime-emergency cultural behavior changes, the connection between sexist practices and their outcomes is more difficult to state in rule form. Changes in infrastructural practices have occurred that have removed the need for the maintenance of the sexist practices of child care and gender role differentiation. The lack of survival value of these practices is best articulated by the various feminist theories.

Major economic changes have occurred in the past 150 years that have broken the connection between existing practices and their survival contributions to society. With mechanization and the development of electronic tools, the need for excessive physical strength has diminished almost to the point of disappearing. Hence, women can physically do most of the tasks men do. Advances in medical care and birth control in non-third world countries have removed the need for women to lactate for lengthy periods of time (Kamal, 1987). Finally, the verbal community itself has changed in no small measure due to the rise of feminism. What feminists have done for the collective consciousness of women is to tact the contingencies that affect their lives. In their consciousness-raising groups, feminists assist other women in identifying and articulating "oppressive" practices in their lives (Shakeshaft, 1989). Feminists labeled punitive contingencies for women and for men. This process is akin to taking the first few courses in applied behavior analysis and then seeing human behavior, describing it, and explaining it, differently from before. It is acquiring a different verbal repertoire. Women have become more articulate about the roles they are expected to play and have become aware of the roles they could play. When the difference between these scenarios is large and negative, women have expressed anger and outrage (hooks, 1989). For many women now, with their new repertoires, old models no longer suffice. Women label sexist behavior to be clearly disadvantageous to them. And with these changes came other problems.

Positive teaching practices need to be used when shaping new non-sexist repertoires. Some new verbal repertoires are acquired in a male-blaming atmosphere. Major changes in verbal behavior and physical behavior are suddenly expected of men. Women entered the work force in larger numbers, and child care has become an economic issue and a moral one (Faludi, 1991; hooks, 1984). Women are exposed to rules that specify the harmful consequences of their working full time and not providing traditional homes for their children. There is an atmosphere of threat and unease in some public forums in which women's issues are discussed. Some efforts to change sexist behavior and attitudes encounter strong resistance. If behavior analysts could be persuaded that sexist behavior in all forms no longer has survival value for the cultures in which it is practiced as normal behavior, positive behavior change efforts could be designed and would be more successful.

Implications for Intervention and Prevention

Some sexist repertoires are more amenable to change than others because of their accessibility and their public nature. For example, it is easier, relatively speaking, to change educational institutions than family institutions because education takes place in a more public arena, and the preparation of teachers is an ideal stage for intervention. Family institutions, on the other hand, are far more difficult to influence and are more resistant to change. The notion of the privacy (and even sacredness) of family life prohibits access in many instances to opportunities to change practices in the home. It also severely limits accountability mechanisms. In other words, whereas you can require changes in behavior for grades at university (admittedly not the ideal contingency), you have no such leverage when working with families on issues like sexist behavior. Intervention at the preservice, teacher-preparation level has the potential to influence both educational and family practices for, at least, college students. Other public arenas, such as advertising, are prime targets for intervention to change sexist behaviors. The consumer has the ultimate power to buy or not to buy and to let the manufacturer know when its advertising or product is sexist. So, although institutions that transmit culture are changeable, some are more accessible than others.

Behavior analysts have the potential to affect sexist behaviors in several ways. Behavior analysts have extensive experience in planning and bringing about successful behavior change in many individuals (see, for example, Geller's, 1992 work on safety belt usage). If specific sexist repertoires are identified in behavioral terms, interventions can be designed to change those repertoires. Here are some examples of several sexist practices and suggestions for changing them.

Toy Selection

Selecting toys purely on the basis of a child's gender rather than a child's interest (e.g., buying building blocks and computer games for boys and dolls and needlework for girls) is sexist behavior. Several interventions can be tried here to change the behavior of day care workers, parents, and toy manufacturers. University preservice early childhood programs could specifically address the issue of toy selection and use. However, many child-care workers do not have postsecondary educations. Workshops could be offered to child-care workers as part of their training. This training will improve in quality only when parents demand it, however, so parents will have some say in what that education might contain. Community centers could offer parent workshops to make them aware of sex bias in toy selection and to suggest ways parents could influence toy manufacturers. Ultimately, toy manufacturers care about profits and their reputations. The power of purchasing can be used judiciously. In other words, purchasers of toys should differentially reinforce nonsexist toy manufacture and advertising.

Chores

Traditional gender roles have boys doing outdoor chores and girls doing indoor chores. Boys take out the trash, and girls wash dishes. Parent education, particularly by other parents through modeling, is a suggested intervention for this practice. Labeling chores only as individual or cooperative might help prevent using male and female designations.

Teacher Behaviors

Examples of sexist behaviors by teachers include using low-level questions for girls and high-level for boys, giving more help to girls and expecting boys to complete tasks more independently, asking questions more frequently of boys than girls, and asking gender-specific questions (e.g., "What do the girls think?") when it is not warranted. Interventions at teacher preservice and inservice levels might be awareness workshops in which sexist behaviors are discriminated from nonsexist options, alternatives to sexist behaviors are shaped and modeled, and self-management skills are taught to enable teachers to monitor and change their own behaviors.

Car Sales

Women pay more than men for the same cars. Some car dealers will not allow women to test drive cars if their husbands are not present, a practice which implies the decision to buy is influenced more by the husband than by the wife. Specific technical aspects of cars are discussed with men but not with women. This occurs even though individual interests of men and women vary considerably in this area. To change these behaviors, men and women should withhold reinforcers from car dealers who engage in them by buying cars from nonsexist dealers. Both women and men should be encouraged to write letters to sexist sales staff, informing them that their sexism was the reason a purchase was not made. Workshops on how to change sexist verbal behavior should be provided to dealers.

Behavior analysts can influence sexist practices in other ways. Behavior analysts have articulated coercive practices and their consequences (Sidman, 1989). Existing interventions for sexist behavior can be analyzed in terms of their level of coercion. When there is strong countercontrol exerted it is usually in response to contingencies perceived as coercive. Perhaps the acknowledgment of the costs of sexist behavior to men as well as women might make antisexist interventions the domain of both. Feminist practices have occasioned anger and resentment among men and women and have failed to attract large numbers of both genders for that reason. Consider the following simple example of using coercion to change a sexist repertoire. A colleague teaching a women's studies class used an interactive pedagogical approach. Students' comments were actively solicited in class. All class members were given a metal button that emitted a loud click when squeezed. Students were told to click whenever they judged a peer's comment to be sexist. In a short time, comment frequency was reduced, and students complained of feeling excessive anxiety. In such a situation, some students would opt for a class environment that did not punish their verbal behavior. Rather than change their repertoires, others would make no further comments. The generation of a more risk-free, nurturing classroom might support more dramatic changes in verbal behavior without generating collateral negative emotions.

From the writings of B. F. Skinner (1949) comes a unique vision of a nonsexist society in *Walden Two*. The living experiment of Communidad Los Horcones, established in 1973, is an ideal testing ground for small community cultural engineering. An examination of this community's success in changing sexist behavior might be instructive for applications to other small communities.

Behavior analysts participate in many cultural practices as parents, teachers, scientists, and so forth. Turning the behavior analytic lens on sexist practices they experience or participate in might have interesting results.

Finally, behaviorists interested in combining behavioral with cultural analyses could do culture-specific investigations of current sexist practices. Outcomes of these practices in terms of their survival value need to be identified and articulated.

A behavior analytic examination of sexism is potentially useful in several ways. It could provide explanations for sexist practices at the cultural level without allocating blame. No one is presented as the villain, the aggressor, or the power-hungry male determined to keep women in disadvantaged positions in society—although all such types exist. Sexism as cultural practices are explained like all other cultural practices; they probably developed in response to situation-specific contingencies and evolved into practices. Some of these practices became rules. Despite the passage of time, the invention of tools, industrialization, computerization, and other major changes, these rules were transmitted from one generation to the next. They did so even when their original, practical usefulness had changed or, as in many cases, had disappeared. Thus, contingency-developed behavior became rule-governed behavior, and the rules became tradition completely out of touch with the contingencies that generated them. Sexism as cultural practice has outcomes in the modern age that, ultimately, disadvantage all members of society.

A behavior analytic explanation has implications for interventions to change sexist behavior. With a keen understanding of the power of consequences over future probability of behavior, behaviorists can design change projects that use predominantly positive interventions. For such interventions, there is less likelihood of countercontrol and resistance to change. To design improved cultural practices that have survival value, behavior analysts must understand sexism as both an individual behavioral repertoire and a cultural practice.

REFERENCES

Benston, M. (1969). The political economy of women's liberation. *Monthly Review*, *24*, 13–27.

Boston Women's Health Book Collective (1984). *The new our bodies, ourselves.* New York: Simon & Schuster.

Britton, G. E., & Limpkin, M. C. (1977). For sale: Subliminal bias in textbooks. *The Reading Teacher*, *31*, 40–45.

Chodorow, N. (1978). *The reproduction of mothering.* Berkeley, CA: California University Press.

Cixous, H. (1981). Castration or decapitation? *Signs: Journal of Women in Culture and Society*, *7*, 41–55.

Dalla Costa, M., & James, S. (1972). *The power of women and the subversion of the community.* Bristol, England: Falling Wall Press.

Daly, M. (1978). *Gyn/Ecology*. Boston: Beacon Press.

de Beauvoir, S. (1974). *The second sex*. New York: Vintage Books. (Original work published 1949)

Derrida, J. (1978). *Spurs: Nietzsche's styles* (B. Harlow, Trans.). Chicago: University of Chicago Press.

Dinnerstein, D. (1977). *The mermaid and the minotaur: Sexual arrangements and human malaise*. New York: Harper Colophon.

Ellsworth, E. (1989). Why doesn't this feel empowering? *Harvard Educational Review, 59*, 297–324.

Engels, F. (1972). *The origin of the family, private property, and the state*. New York: International Publishers.

Faludi, S. (1991). *Backlash: The undeclared war against American women*. New York: Crown Publishers.

Favell, J. (1989, May). *What I think I hear you saying . . . women in ABA speak out*. Paper presented at the 1989 annual breakfast of the Association for Behavior Analysis, Milwaukee, WI.

Firestone, S. (1970). *The dialectic of sex*. New York: Bantam Books.

Fox Keller, E. (1985). *Reflections on gender and science*. New Haven, CT: Yale University Press.

French, M. (1985). *Beyond power: On women, men, and morals*. New York: Summit Books.

Friedan, B. (1963). *The feminine mystique*. New York: W. W. Norton.

Geller, S. (1992). Applications of behavior analysis to prevent injuries from vehicle crashes. In S. S. Glenn (Ed.), *Cambridge Center for Behavioral Studies Monograph Series, Monograph #2*.

Glenn, S. (1986). Metacontingencies in Walden Two. *Behavior Analysis and Social Action, 5*, 2–8.

Glenn, S. (1988). Contingencies and metacontingencies: Toward a synthesis of behavior analysis and cultural materialism. *The Behavior Analyst, 11*, 161–179.

Graebner, D. (1972). A decade of sexism in readers. *The Reading Teacher, 26*, 52–58.

Gregorich, B. (1993). *Women at play: The story of women in baseball*. New York: Harcourt Brace.

Harris, M. (1979). *Cultural materialism*. New York: Random House.

Harris, M. (1980). *Cultural materialism: The struggle for a science of culture*. New York: Random House.

Harris, M. (1981). *Why nothing works*. New York: Simon & Schuster. (Originally published in 1981 as *America Now*)

Harris, M. (1983). *Cultural anthropology*. New York: Harper & Row.

Hartmann, H. (1981). The family as the locus of gender, class, and political struggle: The example of housework. *Signs: Journal of Women in Culture and Society, 6*, 366–394.

Hitchcock, M. E., & Tompkins, G. E. (1987). Basal readers: Are they still sexist? *The Reading Teacher, 41*, 288–292.

hooks, b. (1989). *Talking back.* Boston: South End Press.

hooks, b. (1984). *Feminist theory: From margin to center.* Boston: South End Press.

Irigaray, L. (1985). *Speculum of the other woman* (G.C. Gill, Trans.). Ithaca, NY: Cornell University Press. (Original work published 1974)

Jaggar, A. (1983). *Feminist politics and human nature.* Sussex: The Harvester Press.

Kamal, S. (1987). Seizure of reproductive rights? A discussion on population control in the third world and the emergence of the new reproductive technologies in the west. In P. Spallone & D. L. Steinberg (Eds.), *Made to order: The myth of reproductive and genetic progress.* New York: Pergamon Press.

Lacan, J. (1977). *Ecrits: A selection* (A. Sheridan, Trans.). New York: W. W. Norton. (Original work published 1966)

Luke, C., & Gore, J. (Eds.). (1992). *Feminisms and critical pedagogy.* New York: Routledge.

Malagodi, E. F. (1986). On radicalizing behaviorism: A call for cultural analysis. *The Behavior Analyst, 9*, 1–17.

Malagodi, E. F., & Jackson, K. (1989). Behavior analysts and cultural analysis: Troubles and issues. *The Behavior Analyst, 12*, 17–33.

Malott, R. (1988). Rule-governed behavior and behavioral anthropology. *The Behavior Analyst, 11*, 181–203.

Mill, J. S. (1970). *The subjection of women.* Cambridge MA: MIT Press. (Original work published 1869)

Millett, K. (1970). *Sexual politics.* Garden City, NY: Doubleday.

Mitchell, J. (1974). *Psychoanalysis and feminism.* New York: Vintage Books.

Myers, D. L. (1993). Participation by women in behavior analysis II. (1992). *The Behavior Analyst, 16*, 75–86.

Nibbelink, W. H., Stockdale, S. R., & Mangru, M. (1986). Sex-role assignments in elementary school mathematics textbooks. *Arithmetic Teacher, 34*, 19–21.

Nicholson, L. (Ed.). (1990). *Feminism/postmodernism.* New York: Routledge.

Ostertag, P. A., & McNamara, J. R. (1991). Feminization of psychology: The changing sex ratio and its implications for the profession. *Psychology of Women Quarterly, 15*, 349–369.

Pizurki, H., Meija, A., Butter, I., & Ewart, L. (1987). *Women as providers of health care.* Geneva: World Health Organization.

Poling, A., Grossett, D., Fulton, B., Roy, S., Beecher, S., & Wittkoopp, C. (1983). Participation by women in behavior analysis. *The Behavior Analyst, 6*, 145–152.

Rich, A. (1979). *On lies, secrets, and silence: Selected prose, 1966–1968.* New York: W. W. Norton.

Rich, A. (1986). *Of woman born.* New York: W. W. Norton.

Sadker, M., & Sadker, D. (1985). Sexism in the classroom. *Vocational Education Journal, 7*, 30–32.

Shakeshaft, C. (1989). *Women in administration.* New York: Sage.

Sidman, M. (1989). *Coercion and its fallout.* Boston: Authors Cooperative.

Skinner, B. F. (1948). *Walden two.* New York: MacMillan.

Sutherland, M. B. (1987). Sex differences in education: An overview. *Comparative Education, 23*, 5–9.

Tong, R. (1989). *Feminist thought: A comprehensive introduction.* Boulder, CO: Westview Press.

U.S. Bureau of Census. (1991). *Current population reports, consumer income series* (Series P-60, No. 166). Washington, DC: Author.

Wollstonecraft, M. (1975). *A vindication of the rights of woman.* New York: W. W. Norton. (Originally published 1792)

III

CHANGE IN PRIVATE RELATIONSHIPS

9

CHILD MALTREATMENT

MARK A. MATTAINI, BRENDA G. McGOWAN,
and GLADYS WILLIAMS

Among the most publicly visible and troubling of contemporary social problems is the abuse and neglect of children. Abuse and neglect are closely linked with problems discussed in other chapters of this volume, including drug and alcohol abuse and battering, and comprehensive action to address these multiple issues is commonly necessary for maximum effect. Between 1,200 and 5,000 children die each year from maltreatment (U.S. Department of Health and Human Services, 1990), and as will be discussed here, tens of thousands of others are severely damaged, sometimes for life. Of all the issues discussed in this book, child maltreatment is often the most difficult to understand, and tends to elicit strong emotional reactions; it also can have effects on society that last for generations.

A careful behavioral analysis can be of significant help in understanding the disturbing patterns involved in the physical, emotional, and sexual abuse of children. The lack of physical, emotional, and other caretaking behaviors found among those who neglect children can also be better understood through behavior analysis. Although abuse and neglect often co-occur, differences between these two phenomena are important. As will be seen, some of the environmental determinants are common to all forms of maltreatment, but others are not. Therefore, careful disentanglement is required. Given the limitations of a single chapter, the primary emphases in this chapter will be on physical and emotional abuse and neglect. Sexual abuse (a somewhat different issue) will also be briefly considered, and references to other behavioral work in that area will be provided.

Child maltreatment is not a simple or private affair, affecting as it does large numbers of children, and families, as well as society as a whole. We begin with a discussion of definitions (which can be slippery here), epidemiology, and the personal and social costs of the problem. We then turn to what is known about the causes, course, and treatment of maltreatment. The heart of the chapter consists of detailed analyses of the contingencies (antecedents and consequences) that maintain maltreatment, and their implications for prevention and intervention. Finally, we briefly present a single-case study tracing work with a high-risk family.

THE PROBLEM OF CHILD MALTREATMENT

Although child maltreatment is frequently described as a current crisis or epidemic, it is not a new social problem. Reports of infanticide and child abuse and neglect go back to the earliest days of recorded history (Boswell, 1990). The American Humane Association and local Societies for the Prevention of Cruelty to Children were founded more than a century ago. New York State passed a statute in 1874 related to protective services for children (Daro, 1988). Participants at the first White House Conference on Children in 1909 debated the merits of foster care versus in-home services for children who were victims of maltreatment. In response to publication of an article in a medical journal in 1962 about the "battered child syndrome" (Kempe, Silverman, Steele, Droegemueller, & Silver, 1962), every state, as well as the District of Columbia, passed mandatory child abuse reporting laws between 1963 and 1967.

What *is* relatively new is that there is now extensive publicity about the pervasiveness and damaging effects of child maltreatment in American society and widespread public recognition of the principle that children are entitled to some minimally acceptable level of parental care. There is also increasing professional acknowledgment of the limitations of available knowledge regarding the prevention and treatment of child abuse. Current concerns about this problem reflect the dramatic increase in reported incidents of child abuse and neglect during the past two decades. But the extensive policy, research, and service attention now devoted to the problem of child abuse and neglect is also a consequence of the passage of the Child Abuse Prevention and Treatment Act (1974), federal legislation broadening the concept of child abuse and establishing standards for the reporting and investigation of cases of child maltreatment. The National Center for Child Abuse and Neglect (NCCAN), which has served as a catalyst for extensive federal and state research activity, was established as a result of this legislation.

Definitional Issues

Child maltreatment is not a unitary phenomenon. The term is commonly used to refer to a wide range of parental acts of commission (child abuse) and omission (child neglect) that result in some harm to or endangerment of a person under the age of 18. However, child abuse and neglect are legal and social constructs, not biological conditions, so definitions tend to change with shifting social mores. Legal and professional definitions of what does and does not constitute specific types of child maltreatment have evolved over time with the changing understanding of the developmental needs of children and the components of adequate parenting. State statutes vary considerably in relation to definitions of different types of child abuse and neglect; there is significant variation among different ethnic and cultural groups regarding what is seen as child maltreatment.

Despite these variations, there are four generally recognized categories of child maltreatment, each encompassing a range of behaviors: a) physical abuse, b) neglect, c) sexual abuse, and d) emotional maltreatment. *Physical abuse* includes any behavior that inflicts physical injury on a child, such as beating or scalding. *Neglect* refers to the failure of the parent or other legally responsible caretaker to provide for a child's basic physical, educational, medical, or supervisory needs. *Sexual abuse* includes incest, sexual assault, fondling, exposure, and inappropriate sexual stimulation. *Emotional maltreatment* includes acts that result in impairment of a child's emotional or mental health such as "verbal abuse and belittlement, symbolic acts designed to terrorize a child, and lack of nurturance or emotional availability by caregivers" (National Research Council [NRC], 1993, p. 60).

Although broad definitions such as these often suffice for medical and mental health practitioners concerned about diagnosis and treatment, research has been hampered by the lack of clear operational definitions. For example, there are differences regarding the frequency and severity of behaviors defined as abusive, debates about whether child maltreatment should include acts that endanger a child or only those that result in demonstrable harm, and questions posed about how the developmental level of the child and the intent of the perpetrator should be evaluated. These differences, like the variations in state statutes, limit the comparability and aggregation of data on the problem of child maltreatment.

Legal and Service Framework

All 50 states now have mandatory child abuse reporting laws. Although there are some variations from state to state regarding actual reporting requirements and evidentiary standards, licensed mental health professionals, as well as a range of other mandated reporters, are generally under legal obligation to report to a central state child protective agency all situations in which they have professional reason to suspect child maltreatment. The state agency in turn is responsible for investigating the alleged abuse or neglect, determining whether there is sufficient evidence to substantiate the complaint. If the allegations are substantiated, the state agency is charged with taking whatever actions seem necessary to protect the child. Such actions can include filing a formal child abuse complaint in court, removing the child from the home, or providing supportive services and counseling to the parent(s) so the child can remain at home.

The recent dramatic increase in reported child maltreatment has occured without a proportionate increase in prevention or treatment resources. As a result, state courts and social service agency employees often claim that they are overwhelmed by the numbers of child abuse reports they must process and that they lack the resources and research knowledge required to deal effectively with these very troubling situations (Kamerman & Kahn, 1990). Although state laws require investigation of alleged maltreatment and protection of any child at risk, they do not mandate treatment for the victim or the perpetrator of abuse; nor do they mandate services aimed at prevention of child abuse. Consequently, in many areas of the country, child welfare authorities have essentially abdicated responsibility for prevention and treatment efforts, allowing this burden to be assumed by schools, voluntary social agencies, hospitals, and mental health clinics.

Epidemiology

It is impossible to present reliable national data regarding the incidence and prevalence of child maltreatment for several reasons. First, most figures are compiled on the basis of official reports of the suspicion of child abuse to state child protective agencies and state substantiation of these reports. Yet states vary in their definitions of different types of child maltreatment, ways in which reported incidents are counted, policies regarding which reports are officially accepted, and procedures and standards for substantiation.[1] Second, official reports do not encompass the large but unknown numbers of unreported child maltreatment.[2] Third, state data generally refer to the total number of reports of abuse in a given year, not to the total number of children affected. Thus it is impossible to obtain

---

[1]Although Child Abuse Prevention and Treatment Act (1974) stipulated that NCCAN investigate the national incidence of child maltreatment, and the Child Abuse Prevention, Adoption and Family Services Act (1988) required that NCCAN establish a national data collection and analysis system, states are still not required to use the same data reporting systems.
[2]Repeated research has demonstrated that children, parents, lay persons, and mandated reporters all frequently fail to identify or report actual incidents or suspicions of child maltreatment (NRC, 1993).

an unduplicated count or to distinguish incidence clearly from preva-lence.[3]

The best available current data derive from two sources: The National Child Abuse and Neglect Data System (NCANDS) and the National Center on Child Abuse Prevention Research, a program of the National Committee to Prevent Child Abuse (NCPCA). The former, developed by NCCAN in consultation with a state advisory committee in response to a 1988 Congressional mandate, has conducted two national surveys. The latter is a voluntary organization that has conducted annual surveys of all 50 states and the District of Columbia since 1986.

The latest survey by NCPCA estimated that more than 2.9 million children in the United States were reported as victims of maltreatment in 1993.[4] This number represents 45 children per every 1,000 in the population, a 50% increase from 1985 survey data, when 30 children per 1,000 were reported as maltreated. Of the total number reported, 34% (N = 1,016,000) were confirmed or substantiated by child protective services.[5] The total number of reports in 1993 represented an average 2.5% increase from 1992, much less than the average 8.4% rise from 1991 to 1992 and the steady growth from 1988 to 1993 of about 6% each year. It is too early to determine whether this pattern suggests that child maltreatment patterns have begun to stabilize (McCurdy & Daro, 1994).

The NCPCA survey does not present any demographic data on the substantiated cases, but the most recent survey by NCCAN conducted in 1991 provides some additional information about this population.[6] Although the median age of the child victims in this survey was 7 years, the percentages ranged fairly evenly across the age spectrum, with the highest proportion (7.6%) under the age of one and the portion of each age decreasing quite consistently until the age of 18. Fifty-three percent of the victims were girls, and 46% were boys. The NCCAN survey described 55% of the child victims as White, 26% as Black, and 9% as Hispanic. It is presumed, however, that the total proportion of Hispanics is somewhat larger, because states with large Hispanic populations were unable to report on this item due to limitations in their collection procedures (NCCAN, 1993).

---

[3]Some indication of the enormity of this problem is given in a Massachusetts study, which demonstrated that by removing duplicated counts, the total number of reported cases in a single year was reduced by 31% and the total number of substantiated cases by 10%. The percentage of duplicated reports was much higher for child neglect (25%) than for physical abuse (14%), sexual abuse (14%), and emotional maltreatment (10%) (Massachusetts Office of Policy and Programs, as cited in NCCAN, 1993).

[4]For a full discussion of the number of states responding to each question and the procedures used to make national estimates, see McCurdy and Daro, 1994.

[5]It is interesting to note that contrary to popular perception, less than 1% of substantiated cases occurred in day care centers or foster care settings (McCurdy & Daro, 1994).

[6]For a full discussion of the number of states responding to each question and the procedures used to make national estimates, see NCCAN, 1993.

Case Characteristics

An estimated total of 1,299 child maltreatment fatalities were reported in the NCPCA survey for 1993, 42% of which involved children who had had prior contact with child protective services. This phenomenon has risen steadily since 1985 (McCurdy & Daro, 1994).

Among the total reported cases, 47% involved reports of neglect; 30% involved physical abuse; 11% involved sexual abuse; and 2% involved emotional maltreatment. Another 10% involved behaviours described as "other." However, physical abuse represented significantly less of the substantiated cases (25%), and sexual abuse, considerably more (15%). The key presenting problems identified in these cases were as follows: substance abuse, 63%; lack of support from family and community sources, 39%; and economic stress, 35%. Other problems noted by a significant number of states were lack of knowledge of child care, lack of parenting skills and inappropriate child management techniques, domestic violence, and fragmented families (McCurdy & Daro, 1994).

Only 22 of the states surveyed could provide any data on services offered after cases were substantiated. On average, these states provided services to 70% of the confirmed cases, but the percentages ranged from 15% to 100%. The most common services offered were case management and individual or family counseling, but 17% of the children were removed from their homes.

Populations at Risk

Although many factors have been identified as correlates of child maltreatment, no strong predictor variables have been identified. As will be discussed later in this chapter, there is now relatively strong consensus that "the etiology of maltreatment involves complex clusters of variables that interact along various dimensions of a child's ecological/transactional system" (NRC, 1993, p. 10). What can be specified on the basis of repeated studies are a number of sociodemographic marker variables including low income, unemployment, low education, spouse abuse, early childbearing, substance abuse, and health problems (Videka-Sherman, 1991).

Personal and Social Costs

Both the personal and social costs of child abuse and neglect are staggering. Repeated research has demonstrated the harmful consequences of maltreatment for children and adolescents in relation to cognitive and behavioral functioning, health, peer and adult relationships, school performance, self-esteem, and emotional stability. In addition, it has been demonstrated that children who have been maltreated are more likely during adolescence and adulthood to display increased rates of delinquent and criminal behavior, drug and alcohol dependence, physical and mental health problems, and self-destructive and suicidal behavior. Finally, adults who were maltreated as children often themselves become abusive or neglectful parents. (See Daro, 1988; NRC, 1993; and Videka-Sherman, 1991, for further discussion of these studies).

It is difficult to obtain any hard data on actual fiscal costs, but the General Accounting Office estimated in 1991 that more than $500 million is spent annually on the immediate costs of providing services such as medical care, family counseling, special education, and foster care for maltreated children (NRC, 1993). This estimate did not account for all the legal and child protective service costs associated with processing reports of child abuse and neglect, the costs of long-term treatment and foster care for maltreated children, or the lost productivity costs incurred by adults who were maltreated as children. Given these enormous costs, it is difficult not to concur with Daro (1988), who pointed out that the high costs of treatment services and their limited potential for mediating the consequences of maltreatment makes "prevention efforts appear to be a more efficient alternative" (p. 198).

THE EXISTING KNOWLEDGE AND CONCEPTUAL BASE

The understanding of child maltreatment has evolved dramatically over the past several decades. Relatively linear, single-cause models (producing disappointing results) have given way to ecological frameworks. Given the complexity of such multidimensional perspectives, it is not surprising that over time these, too, have changed, moving from almost random combinations of multiple causal factors to better specified and organic models with greater conceptual coherence and empirical support. Space permits only a cursory look at this evolution; for more detail, the reader should refer to Wolfe (1987, 1991).

The Evolution of Conceptual and Treatment Approaches

When the battered child syndrome (Kempe et al., 1962) began to be defined and labeled in the early 1960s, clinical and medical understanding of human behavior were largely rooted in psychodynamic thought. Child maltreatment (at the time framed primarily in terms of physical abuse) was viewed as an indicator of serious psychopathology, a symptom of an underlying psychiatric disorder. Substantial effort, therefore, was directed to the identification of psychopathological processes, particularly in the parent's own early development. Treatment, when it was offered, generally consisted of individual psychotherapy focused on changing underlying personality dynamics. Unfortunately, the outcome data from studies conducted in the 1970s of programs (including well-funded demonstration projects) rooted in this orientation were disappointing (Azar & Wolfe, 1989), and the search for other approaches became a priority.

During the 1970s, the connections between child maltreatment and situational factors like poverty (Gil, 1970), social isolation and chronic stress (Garbarino, 1977), and other contextual factors such as substance abuse, battering, and health problems became increasingly clear, driving the development and refinement of ecological models for understanding and treating the problem. The recognition of the relationship of larger sociocultural factors and family processes to abusive behavior was important, both in attenuating the focus on individual psychopathology and in providing support for advocacy efforts. At the same time, specifying how all of the factors associated with maltreatment interrelate in ways that could lead to specific treatment and preventive approaches became more challenging. For example, economic disadvantage is related to both abuse and neglect; however, most parents who are poor do not mistreat their children, so the effects are obviously probabilistic and indirect. The usual caveat that correlation does not necessarily indicate functional relationships becomes particularly important in such cases; association can suggest hypotheses, but only experimental data allow researchers to test causal relations.

Other, more focused approaches were developed and tested during the 1970s and early 1980s. Cognitive-behavioral treatment approaches were being applied to many problems (e.g., Beck, Rush, Shaw, & Emery, 1978; Foreyt & Rathjen, 1978; Meichenbaum & Turk, 1976) and showed particular promise for anger management (Novaco, 1974). It therefore seemed reasonable to try this approach with child maltreatment—particularly abuse, which often involves difficulty managing strong emotions. Early conceptual work (e.g., Otto & Smith, 1980) led over time to interventive protocols that produced positive results (Whiteman, Fanshel, & Grundy, 1987). Still, these interventive strategies produced only modest effects (not surprisingly, given what was known about the multidetermination of abuse), and the need to link them to more comprehensive approaches remained clear.

A range of more specific interventive strategies based on a variety of understandings of the etiology of abuse were tested during the 1970s and 1980s, and patterns began to emerge from the data. The following were among the basic findings reported in a review by Howing, Wodarski, Gaudin, and Kurtz (1989):

1. Families characterized by abuse, neglect, and sexual abuse often benefit from group services and programs that meet concrete needs.

2. Abusive parents tend to respond to individual behavioral training and parenting classes, but in-home services may need to be included. (Details of such *transfer-enhancing* strategies are discussed later in this chapter.)
3. Parents who neglect their children sometimes benefit from individual problem-solving treatment and family therapy.
4. Parents (or other adults) who engage in sexual abuse require intervention that is closely coordinated among the multiple legal and treatment agencies involved. Also, a variety of modalities (individual, group, couples, and family) commonly need to be mixed and phased for intervention to be successful.

Programs of preventive services and intensive home-based service approaches became increasingly widespread in the 1980s. Summarizing the results of these programs is difficult: Such programs are rooted in a variety of conceptual frameworks (from psychodynamic to behavioral); the client populations served are highly variable; and the intensity of services provided also covers a tremendous spectrum. It is therefore no surprise that outcome data have been equivocal, though some programs clearly help in some cases (Blythe, Salley, & Jayaratne, 1994).

Valuable as general data may be, they provide only limited guidance for specific cases. Group designs, from which such data come, necessarily average the results across cases because, in most such studies, some families do much better, some do somewhat better, some do not change much, and some deteriorate (Johnston, 1988). The need for individualized assessment that can take a holistic and integrated look at each case, therefore, remains crucial (Meyer, 1993).

One of the most conceptually and empirically appealing of the currently available multidimensional models is the social-interactional approach developed by Wolfe and his colleagues (Wolfe, 1991). This approach takes into account both contextual factors and individual behavioral patterns. Recognizing that social isolation, financial pressures, child and parent behavior, and other factors are tightly intertwined, Wolfe's group has developed a multifaceted program that includes family behavioral training and guidance in parenting, informal activity and parent support groups in a community setting, connection to needed resources and services, and the ready availability of respite care. This combined program has demonstrated promising results.

Wolfe's approach is also noteworthy for the breadth of theoretical frameworks that are brought to bear on the issue; these theories include ecological theory, developmental psychology, and attribution theory, as well as operant, respondent, and cognitive–social learning frameworks. While such a broad-spectrum approach ensures broad consideration of variables, it also mixes models in ways that can lead to conceptual and interventive confusion, and the links among these disparate approaches are not always entirely clear. Material later in this chapter will attempt to integrate such multiple factors in a conceptually consistent way.

Although abuse, neglect, and sexual abuse commonly co-occur in various mixtures, detailed analysis of their courses, etiology, and interventive strategies requires recognizing the differences and discontinuities among them. Abuse, in general, consists of patterns of behavioral excess (for example, excesses of physical punishment or shouting), whereas neglect consists of a pattern of behavioral deficits (failure to act to meet the child's physical needs, too few acts of affection, etc.). This deceptively simple dichotomy already suggests the basic behavioral strategies required to intervene. Decelerating problem behaviors (like abuse) is complicated; the most common strategy is to punish such actions, but this approach is frequently ineffective and costly (Kazdin, 1989; Sidman, 1989; Skinner, 1953). To be effective, punishment must be applied consistently and often must be rather severe; perhaps more seriously, punitive action often disrupts relationships, leading to escape, avoidance, and counteraggression. With reference to child abuse, of course, punishing the abuser also models punitive behavior, which, paradoxically, may lead to increases in abuse in some cases.

Because punishment is not generally the approach of choice, the prototypical strategy for decelerating behavior is to construct and accelerate alternatives using positive reinforcement. There are many other facets of a comprehensive approach, but this element is the kernel. By contrast, addressing neglect in general involves the direct construction of the behaviors of choice, again using reinforcement. As a general principle, the more natural the reinforcers used in the process, the more likely the new behaviors will generalize and be maintained. In the case of neglect, potentiating *the child* as a valuable source of reinforcers is often important (see the single case study reported later in this chapter).

Sexual abuse is more complicated, often involving a mix of inappropriate stimulus control and problematic patterns of consequation; intervention, therefore, needs to incorporate multiple components. An issue in all forms of maltreatment, but which has particular emotional salience in cases of sexual abuse or severe physical abuse, is that the protection of the child must always be the central and first concern.[7] Despite the ethical struggles that sexual abuse in particular tends to elicit in the public and professionals alike, the most effective approaches are likely to include an emphasis on constructing new behavioral repertoires that work for the perpetrator.

---

[7]In behavioral terms, preventing access to the child when there is significant risk is one form of manipulating structural antecedents—environmental events that permit the behavior to occur.

CHILD ABUSE

Each case is unique. Nevertheless, much of what is known of abuse has relatively broad applicability. The following analyses of the course of child abuse and of its associated behavioral contingencies apply to a range of abusive acts, ranging from severe physical abuse to acts of emotional cruelty or coercion.

The Course of Child Abuse

The natural history of patterns of child maltreatment has yet to be adequately investigated, in part because cases often are not identified until severe problems have already developed. Therefore, the material here—particularly that regarding the course of maltreatment—while rooted in available empirical evidence, should be viewed as tentative. The course of child physical and emotional abuse has been explored in somewhat more detail than has the development of neglect or sexual abuse. The presentation here generally follows Wolfe's (1991) model, with contributions from other sources as noted. Wolfe's model, which also identifies factors that may increase or decrease risks, is reproduced in Figure 1.

Wolfe suggested that the abusive process evolves from a general pattern of "reduced tolerance for stress and disinhibition of aggression" (1991,

DESTABILIZING FACTORS	COMPENSATORY FACTORS

STAGE I:
Reduced Tolerance for Stress and Disinhibition of Aggression

- Weak preparation for parenting
- Low control, feedback, predictability
- Stressful life events

- Supportive spouse
- Socioeconomic stability
- Success at work, school
- Social supports and models

STAGE II:
Poor Management of Acute Crises and Provocation

- Conditioned emotional arousal
- Sources of anger and aggression
- Appraisal of harm/loss; threat

- Improvement in child behavior
- Community programs for parents
- Coping resources

STAGE III:
Habitual Patterns of Arousal and Aggression with Family Members

- Child's habituation to physical punishment
- Parent's reinforcement for using strict control techniques
- Child's increase in problem behavior

- Parental dissatisfaction with physical punishment
- Child responds favorably to non-coercive methods
- Community restraints/services

Figure 1. Wolfe's model of the development of a pattern of abusive behavior. From D. A. Wolfe, *Child Abuse: Implications for child development and psychopathology* p. 59, 1987, copyright by Sage Publications, Inc. Reprinted with permission.

p. 40), which may develop early in the life of the abuser. Models of aggression and abuse within the family of origin may often be involved (some, but by no means all, abusers were abused themselves in early life; those who were abused as children are at increased risk for perpetrating abuse; Widom, 1989). Lack of opportunities to learn alternative ways to influence the behavior of others and what Wolfe describes as an "external attributional style"[8] also appear to be related.

In Wolfe's second stage, the parent falls into a pattern of difficulty managing particular problems (related to child behavior and other issues in which the child is not involved), and may then escalate his use of coercive tactics learned earlier in life in an effort to regain control.

This pattern potentiates abuse in the third stage, when physiological arousal becomes increasingly difficult to manage, and the parent may increasingly feel that he or she is losing control. Connections with the "power and control" model used in understanding battering (Pence & Paymar, 1993) are evident. (Both of these models are clearly comprehensible within the behavior analytic frame that will be outlined here). Because the child is likely to imitate the behavior of the parent, by the time the child is a few years old, the potential for development of a coercive spiral leading to progressive escalation on both sides is high (Patterson, 1976). This pattern may be particularly salient when the mother responds relatively indiscriminantly and noncontingently to child behavior (Dumas & Wahler, 1985). Environmental factors, in Wolfe's model, may either destabilize and exacerbate the situation, or compensate for these learned behaviors, reducing the risk. The analysis presented next will attempt to further specify the mechanisms by which this may occur.

Behavioral Analysis of Physical and Emotional Abuse

Figure 2 is a contingency diagram (Malott, 1992) tracing patterns of antecedents and consequences often associated with acts of abuse. In individual cases, there may be more than one relatively discrete class of abusive acts occurring, each embedded in its own pattern of contingent relations. (For definitions and further examples of the terms used in the diagram, refer to Chapter 1 of this volume.)

Antecedents of Abusive Acts

There are a number of classes of antecedents that are often related to abuse, including occasions, imitation and modeling, rules, structural fac-

---

[8]Within a radical behaviorist paradigm, this "style" can be redefined in rule-governed terms. Within this frame, the abuser learns inaccurate ways of understanding the causes of events—*rules* in the technical sense (e.g., "my actions don't make a difference; other forces control the outcomes I experience"; see Kunkel, 1991, for further discussion).

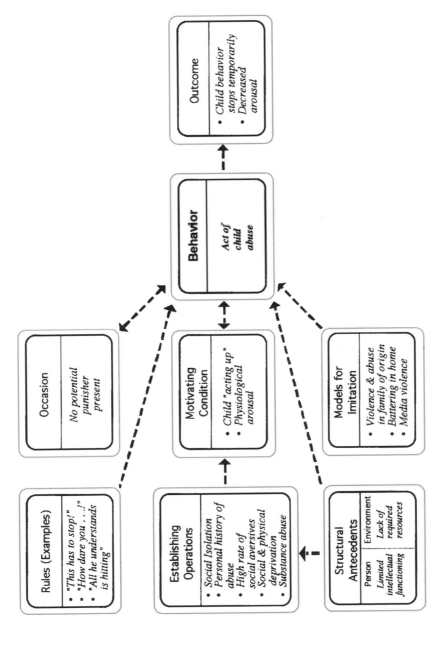

Figure 2. Factors involved in acts of child abuse.

tors, and other contextual variables. Although behavior analytic theory clarifies that behavior is ultimately shaped by its consequences over personal history, antecedents are linked with consequences in crucial ways, so management of antecedents can be extremely important.

Occasions (*discriminative stimuli*) are, roughly, cues for a behavior. Under particular conditions, experience teaches that a behavior is likely to be reinforced (and under other circumstances, it may be punished). In the case of acts of abuse, when irritating behavior on the part of the child occurs, hitting or other abusive behaviors by the caretaker may be more likely if no one else (who may observe and punish the abuse) is present, for example. Social isolation (*insularity*; Wahler, 1980) may be an important factor in several ways. Parents who are not isolated may experience approval from others for effective parenting, and disapproval for overly coercive or violent acts. A parent may therefore be less likely to act abusively in the presence of others; under these circumstances, the parent may try other ways to manage (or ignore) the child's behavior. If these are effective, they are likely to be repeated.

The literature suggests that persons who were abused themselves or who observed violence used to coercively control others may subsequently turn to abusive strategies themselves (Widom, 1989). The search for relatively universal characteristics may be of limited value; the explanation for variations often lies in the nuances of differential learning history. Still, imitation of models (*in vivo* and, under some conditions, in the media) who rely on violence and abuse to control others is probably often an important factor. Unlike nonverbal organisms, much of people's behavior is governed by rules, verbal descriptions of contingencies that may be learned from others or self-generated. Once a rule has been learned, behaviors based on it can be relatively insensitive to the actual consequences of actions (Cerutti, 1989). The sort of self-talk that may co-occur with abuse includes rules like:

- "This has to stop [or it will be intolerable]";
- "I can't let him get away with this [or he will become impossible to control and I will be miserable]"; or
- "This is awful!" [If she keeps screaming, and I don't stop her, I will be embarrassed in front of everyone].

Note that portions of such rules, particularly with regard to the consequences of behavior, are often not verbalized. Cognitive therapy relies heavily on changing these (often covert) verbal behaviors, thereby providing opportunities for the person to be exposed to contingencies that might not otherwise be experienced. (Once the overall pattern has been overlearned, abusive behavior may come to be associated with the occasion rather automatically, and the verbal component may drop out.)

Some parents do not have much opportunity to learn effective rules; successful parents often learn (both by modeling and through explicit rules) how to manage difficult child behavior from others. For example, many parents have learned that children often become cranky when they are tired, and that often the best way to manage such behavior is to put them to bed. Some parents, however, do not know this technique and they may try to deal with the problem in less effective and, occasionally, abusive ways.

"Knowing the rules" becomes even more important when the child involved is more challenging. Some children, partly for genetic and other biological reasons, are easier to manage than others. Those with more challenging temperaments (Thomas & Chess, 1977), as well as those children with developmental delays, often require more skilled parenting. Even from infancy, parents and children are involved in systems of interlocking contingencies (Bell, 1977). Parents of children with autism or who are developmentally delayed or otherwise challenging may also engage in guilty or angry self-talk (e.g., "it's not fair" or "it must be because of something I did") that can interfere with effective parenting.

Certain contextual events or conditions (*establishing operations*) potentiate the value of a reinforcer and evoke behaviors that have been associated with obtaining that reinforcer in the past (Michael, 1993). Other contextual factors (like satiation) may decrease the value of a reinforcer as well as the rate of behaviors associated with it. To give a simple example: A person who has not eaten for many hours experiences a motivating condition that we label hunger and tends to act in ways that have led to obtaining food in the past. Children with more difficult temperaments may behave in ways that are particularly aversive, increasing the likelihood of abuse. Level of aversives—from *anywhere*—experienced by a parent appears to be a crucial contextual factor associated with failures of adequate parenting (Dumas, 1989; Wahler, 1980). Such aversives apparently decrease the reinforcing effects of positive child behavior and increase the aversive affects of other actions by the child.

Other states of the body, including those associated with psychoactive substances and depression, also may change the level of physiological reactance and arousal. The occurrence of negative self-talk ("this is intolerable") may have similar potentiating effects. Given some combination of such factors, the probability of abusive acts leading to changes in child behavior increases. Irritating or aversive child behavior often is a crucial establishing operation as well as an occasion for abuse, but aversives from anywhere may potentiate abuse, given the child's availability. Generalized deprivation (often due to poverty) is a contextual factor often associated with abuse, though not a direct cause.

An important *structural* antecedent is the parent's generalized repertoire of learning rapidly and efficiently. Some persons, because of learning history, genetics, damage *in utero*, malnutrition, or other factors, do not learn as efficiently or quickly as others. This is not to suggest that parents with intellectual limitations cannot learn effective parenting strategies, but it is important to recognize that some may learn more easily than others, and some may require additional—and ongoing—environmental supports.

Consequences of Abusive Acts

Behavior is ultimately shaped by its consequences. Although the antecedents discussed can be crucial in supporting abuse, the source of their power lies in their relationships to consequences. Negative reinforcement is perhaps the most important consequation issue in most abuse, but other consequences are also involved in many cases.

When an act of abuse occurs, the motivating condition (e.g., the child's aversive behavior or an unpleasant state of physiological arousal) is, at least sometimes, reduced. This is a central factor in much physical and emotional abuse. The child acts up, the parent hits, the child stops—at least for now, at least sometimes (resulting in intermittent reinforcement). Over time, however, the pattern often changes. The child often learns—by modeling, reinforcement of random variations, or both—that when he or she increases the rate or intensity of problem behavior, the parent's aversive actions may sometimes stop.

The possible progression toward Patterson's coercive spiral then begins, with parent and child locked into a pattern of reiprocal negative reinforcement. If the parent's abusive act does lead to a temporary interruption of the aversive child behavior, the parent is likely to turn again to this strategy in the future under similar circumstances. If the child habituates to the parent's behavior and does not stop, the parent (experiencing extinction) is likely to increase the rate and intensity of abusive behavior, which may also prove effective sometimes. These are the simple but pervasive patterns present in coercive contingencies in general (Sidman, 1989) and are the heart of the matter in most abuse.

Although negative reinforcement is the most obvious process in most acts of abuse, self- or other-generated positive reinforcement may also be relevant in some cases. In an abusive family, for example, members may express approval for "shutting the child up." Approving self-talk may be self-reinforcing (e.g., "I guess I taught that child a lesson!").

Some level of self- or other-generated punishment may also follow acts of abuse. These effects may be quite powerful and protective in the beginning; however, behavior analysts have long recognized that punishment does not reduce the "tendency to behave"—because the potential reinforcers for the behavior are still active. Being aware of self-generated punishment is aversive in itself, so in many cases the person may simply stop thinking about it—"denial." So long as the child's behavior is aversive to the parent, and the parent has no other effective repertoire for managing or preventing this behavior, abuse is likely to continue and perhaps escalate.

Contingencies Associated With Alternatives to Abuse

Although contingencies associated with abuse may, at first glance, appear overwhelming, rich possibilities exist for interrupting—or better, preventing—the abuse. The most crucial task is to help the parent learn alternative ways of achieving the reinforcement currently provided by abusive acts. If the parent learns more effective ways to deal with the child's behavior, to cope with other aversives, and to reduce deprivation, abuse can be attenuated. As is almost always the case when the goal is to reduce a behavior, the most effective approaches de-emphasize punishing the undesirable behavior and focus on reinforcing more acceptable alternatives. This is as true in planning programs to prevent and treat abuse by parents as it is in parenting children.

Implications for Clinical Intervention

The contingency diagram and related analyses just discussed suggest rich possibilities for intervening at a clinical level to prevent maltreatment. At the same time, the systems and resources required to pursue these approaches may not be present. If a parent experiences high rates of uncontrollable environmental aversives that potentiate abuse, reducing those aversives is crucial, but may not be easy. If the aversives cannot be reduced, respite care may be able to interrupt dysfunctional patterns, but only if adequate respite is available. Establishing and stabilizing the necessary supports often involves work at other sociocultural levels. These topics will be discussed in later sections of the chapter; see also material related to cultural design in chapter 1 and social policy in chapter 2.

Acts of abuse are often, at root, shaped by negative reinforcement—the parent learns to escape or avoid negative situations by striking out. If an individualized assessment suggests that bringing the child's behavior under control is a crucial factor in the case, behavioral parent training is indicated. There is a wealth of data, however, that suggest that simply learning skills in a parenting group does not always lead to use of those skills at home. Persons who experience a high rate of aversive exchanges with others (usually kin and agency staff) and a low rate of positive exchanges with friends tend not to use skills they have learned, for example (Dumas, 1989; Wahler, 1980). This may be one of the reasons why the friendship and social support groups that are included in Wolfe's (1991) program can be valuable. Also, behavior learned in one setting often does not transfer well to others; this finding appears to be particularly true for parenting, because contextual factors at the clinic and in the home are very different. The following transfer-enhancing strategies outlined by Goldstein, Keller, and Erné (1985) appear important in mediating the transition:

- *overlearning* (in group, the parent practices until achieving a high, almost automatic level of mastery);
- *stimulus variability* (the parent learns to use the skills with multiple partners under multiple circumstances in the group);
- *identical elements* (skills originally learned in the group are practiced in the home with parent aides, in a way identical to how they were learned in the group); and
- *programmed reinforcement* (parent aides are trained to reinforce use of new skills in the home—which often does not occur unless this procedure is designed into the program).

Somewhat similar results were obtained by Serna, Schumaker, Sherman, and Sheldon (1991). These researchers worked with three families with adolescents. In at least two of these families, there was significant verbal abuse, and in one there was serious violence between siblings. The researchers did not find adequate generalization from the teaching setting to the home. (The interventions, consistent with other behavioral work with parent–adolescent issues, focused on increasing the use of communication and problem-solving skills, as well as increasing positive exchange.) Even when training also occurred in the home, generalization to spontaneous situations did not occur. Serna and her colleagues then implemented a package called the "family conference," a structured, self-directed format for problem-solving discussion. When families adopted this framework, excellent generalization was finally obtained. Consumer satisfaction and ratings by independent judges of the adequacy of family problem-solving were also very positive. These data suggest that it is not a simple matter to achieve lasting changes within maltreating families, but that available technologies for producing generalization and maintenance can achieve such change, if they are well designed.

The contingency diagram above suggests a number of other strategies of potential value, including the following:

1. Changing the behavior of *the child*, thus reducing the number occasions for abuse. This is one of the goals of behavioral parent training; if the child learns to get more of what he or she wants in less aversive ways, reciprocal positive effects for the family system occur. The child is then more likely to act as a significant reinforcer for the parent (as occurred in the single-case study that is reported in this chapter).
2. Learning new self-talk about what is normal for children, especially when accompanied by learning new skills.

3. Turning circumstances that are currently occasions for aversive action into cues for something else (in one popular strategy, negative behavior by one child can be used to cue paying particular attention to the appropriate behavior of a sibling).
4. Facilitating empowerment and advocacy aimed at reducing the level of impinging aversives and teaching coping strategies for reducing arousal associated with those that cannot be eliminated.
5. Providing modeling and opportunities to rehearse new approaches for managing child behavior and environmental aversives, including parent training, assertion training (Rakos, 1991), anger management, and life-sculpting.
6. Designing networks of social reinforcement, including through self-help, for learning and using noncoercive parenting strategies.
7. Designing and stabilizing social networks that provide general social reinforcement, which may reduce physiological arousal and depotentiate the consequences of abuse.

Designing and stabilizing networks of environmental reinforcement to support and maintain such changes will often be the most challenging aspect of an intervention plan. Improvements in the child's behavior can serve as one important reinforcer, but are often in themselves not sufficient, and other contingencies may need to be put in place.

CHILD NEGLECT

An analysis of child neglect shows distinct parallels, but also important distinctions, between neglect and abuse. The extent to which some of the contingencies are common provides an explanation for the frequent co-occurrence of the two forms of maltreatment, but attention to their differences is important for adequate prevention and intervention.

The Course of Child Neglect

The course of child neglect is less clearly understood than that of abuse. Current data suggest that it may involve a long-term pattern of nonresponsiveness on the part of the parent (Bousha & Twentyman, 1984), which may become even more serious if the parent sees the child as being increasingly difficult to manage. Such a pattern may lead to increasing disengagement and hopelessness on the part of the parent. The literature suggests that many neglecting parents lack the skills to attend to their children's behaviors in ways that make parenting reinforcing. This clarifies the need to find ways to increase parental sensitivity and responsiveness (Wolfe, 1991) and to potentiate child behavior and well-being as reinforcers for parents.

Long-term exposure to high levels of stress and aversives from social and environmental systems is also likely to result in increases in parental depression (Sidman, 1989), a condition which may result in the parent's being less available to the child. This condition also reduces the value of any form of reinforcement, including that provided by the child. A particularly relevant factor may be the loneliness and social isolation that often characterize families in which neglect occurs (Polansky, Gaudin, Ammons, & Davis, 1985; Polansky, Ammons, & Gaudin, 1985). Polansky and his colleagues found that neglecting mothers were subjectively more lonely, were more isolated from community members and systems, had fewer people to turn to when in need, and were viewed as less likely to reciprocate help by neighbors (a factor that led to deepening isolation). Early learning experiences are also likely to be involved; individuals who grow up in environments in which children are not valued are unlikely to learn self-talk related to the importance or reinforcement value of children. Also, these individuals are not exposed to appropriate child-care behaviors, either through imitation or through direct teaching.

Behavioral Analysis of Child Neglect

Unlike abuse—in which the central issue is an excess of problem behavior—the major issue in neglect is behavioral deficits. The child's primary caretakers either provide too few acts of physical affection or fail to act to meet the child's basic physical, emotional, educational, or other needs. For cases of neglect, the basic strategy is to prompt, shape, and reinforce appropriate behaviors, to construct new repertoires (a "constructional" approach; Goldiamond, 1974). The analyses that follow trace contingency arrangements supporting physical caretaking and acts of affection as examples. Many of these contingencies are commonly missing in cases of neglect, and preventive and interventive strategies need to be designed to establish them.

Antecedents of Acts of Physical Caretaking

What appear to be common antecedents and consequences that support acts of physical caretaking (providing food, clothing, shelther, etc.) are depicted in Figure 3. It is important to note that many of these actions involve consequences that are delayed, uncertain, and technically involve complex behavioral chains and rule-governed analogues to simple processes (Malott, 1989; Michael, 1993). Providing food, for example, involves plan-

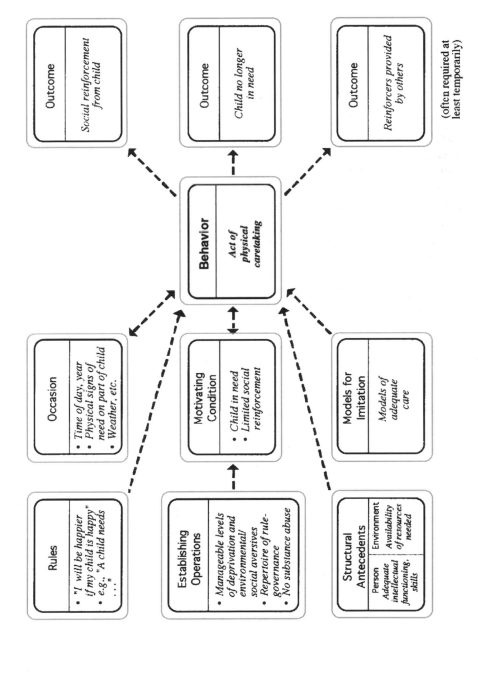

Figure 3. Contingencies associated with acts of physical caretaking.

ning ahead, purchasing, and preparing nutritious foods in adequate quantities at the right times of day. Behavior analytic programs for preventing maltreatment, like Project 12-ways (Greene, Norman, Searle, Daniels, & Lubeck, 1995; Lutzker, Frame, & Rice, 1982) are demonstrably effective in helping parents perform such complex repertoires.

Effective parents recognize situations in which a child is likely to require caretaking. In most families, certain times of day come to be associated with providing food. The clock—at noon or 6:00 p.m., for example—comes to cue food preparation. (Because personal, family, and cultural patterns differ, the clock itself may not always be the actual cue; instead, the end of a particular television show or other regular event may function more effectively as an occasion for acting.) An empty clothing drawer or a particular day of the week may function as a cue for doing laundry. Designing effective prompts may be important in many cases of neglect in which such patterns have not been established. Other important parental behaviors are even more complex and distant from their ultimate consequences, including registering the child for school, arranging inoculations, and advocating for quality education. It is likely that specifically designed cues and more immediate reinforcers may be required during the early stages of shaping such caretaking behaviors.

Effective parents have learned to be that way, often by watching how others parent. Although not true in all cases, many neglecting parents were themselves neglected as children and therefore had few models of adequate parenting to imitate. Many are also isolated (Wahler, 1980) and are not exposed to other, more effective peers. Strategies involving the provision of competent models, therefore, are often important.

Parents may not always feel like dropping what they are doing to provide caretaking for their children, and when they do so, they are often responding to rules rather than immediate preferences. Specific rules can be learned, of course, but in many cases the situation may be more complex because a generalized repertoire of following rules that point toward delayed (and sometimes uncertain) reinforcement is required if specific rules are to be followed. A competent parent learns self-instructions about what needs to be done when and why (the consequences), and environmental conditions become occasions for such rules. Those who lack a generalized repertoire of identifying and following rules pointing to distant, uncertain, and cumulative consequences, however, are likely to require more immediate reinforcers, at least for a period, to potentiate such rules.

Turning to establishing operations, available research suggests that a parent who is deprived of important reinforcers and pressed by multiple aversives is less likely to act in caretaking and nurturing ways and is more likely to act aggressively toward or ignore the child (cf. Dumas & Wahler, 1985; Wahler, 1980; Wahler, Williams, & Cerezo, 1991). Such deprivation and high levels of aversives potentiate both abuse and other ineffective parenting practices, and the connections may explain why abuse and neglect often occur together. Effective parents also come to experience child discomfort as an aversive condition that motivates action. Potentiating child well-being as an important source of reinforcement is important, but unfortunately, it is not always easy to accomplish. (We discuss this strategy further in the next section.)

Parents require certain personal and environmental resources to adequately care for their children. They need skills, of course, and some neglecting parents simply need to be taught how to parent. Many workers in the field note that those parents who have intellectual limitations are among the most challenging to work with when neglect is present, perhaps because they have difficulty learning the relatively complex rules that effective parenting involves. Crucial environmental supports required include the physical and financial resources needed to provide adequate care. Ready access to nutritious food, adequate housing, and the money required to provide (and launder) clothing facilitate caretaking. Issues of poverty and access are therefore central to achieving an adequate outcome in many cases of neglect. Connecting to necessary resources is a powerful intervention in itself and even appears to be one of the ways in which parenting classes are particularly helpful, as members tend to teach each other how to solve system problems and access resources (Brunk, Henggeler, & Whelan, 1987).

Consequences of Acts of Physical Caretaking

Parents perform acts of caretaking because of the consequences of doing so. Many of these consequences are delayed, sometimes long-delayed; this delay is clearly a central issue in neglect. If a child is in pain or deprived, and the parent acts to relieve the situation, the result is reinforcing for some parents. Parents take care of children because, for whatever reason, they find child happiness and well-being reinforcing. Although this pattern may seem natural (i.e., how things "should" be), child well-being is not a universal reinforcer. We can so far only hypothesize the causes of child well-being having differential power. A genetic connection seems unlikely, but learning history is probably crucial. Direct social reinforcement from the child is clearly one factor. In fact, interventions that help the child become a more effective reinforcer (and less punishing) are often important. Behavior analysts also know a lot about constructing conditioned reinforcers. However difficult constructing conditioned reinforcers may prove to be in practice, this strategy is likely to be critical in improving the long-term outcome in many cases of neglect. (We will elaborate further on this.)

Another critical factor in understanding many cases of neglect in the contemporary world is substance abuse. Substance abuse clearly is important at the level of establishing operations, as discussed already in relation to abuse, but it is a serious issue in other ways as well. Sobriety is required for a parent to notice the child's cues and to have the physical ability to provide adequate caretaking. With regard to consequences, however, we are faced with another problem. The matching law (McDowell, 1988) tells us, roughly, that the rate of any behavior can be predicted based on the *relative* balance of reinforcement available for that behavior versus other options.[9] Because the use of substances is closely associated with significant positive and negative reinforcement for abusers, behaviors related to obtaining and using substances compete with parenting behaviors. Action to address substance abuse, therefore, may have multiple behavioral effects related to child maltreatment (refer to the chapters in this volume addressing alcohol and drug abuse).

Antecedents of Affectionate Acts

Emotional caring is as crucial to child well-being as physical caretaking. Many of the contingencies supporting the two are similar, but given the importance of each, it is useful to look briefly at antecedents and consequences of affectionate acts as well. These patterns are summarized in Figure 4.

Seeing the child after an absence, observing the child acting appropriately, and many other situations cue behaviors like hugs, touches, smiles, and pleasant talk in adequate families. Such links may need to be explicitly designed and shaped in families in which such behaviors do not occur, both by increasing sensitivity to child behavior and by building systems of mutual reinforcement for them.

As was true for physical caretaking, models of affection are clearly important, as are rules. Because the consequences of affectionate acts (once patterns of mutuality are shaped) may be more immediate in the area of affection than in some other areas of caretaking, affectionate behavior may in some cases be an easier repertoire to learn. But it will take some time for a "culture of caring" to stabilize in a family, and specific action (including modeling, rehearsal, teaching new self-talk, and social reinforcement from persons significant to the client) may be required to establish it. Reinforcer sampling may also be a crucial factor in building affectionate repertoires. A parent who learns that affectionate acts pay off—by producing reciprocation and other positives—and that those outcomes are satisfying is likely to increase the rate of such acts. Experiencing acts of affection from anywhere, in fact, may be helpful in establishing their value.

---

[9]More precisely, the rates of concurrently available behaviors vary proportionately with the reinforcement available for each, and noncontingent reinforcement tends to reduce the rates of all behavior. Mathematical statements of this rule have proved quite robust in the laboratory and also appear to capture events in applied settings well (McDowell, 1980, 1982, 1989; McDowell, Bass, & Kessel, 1983; McDowell & Wixted, 1988; McDowell & Wood, 1984).

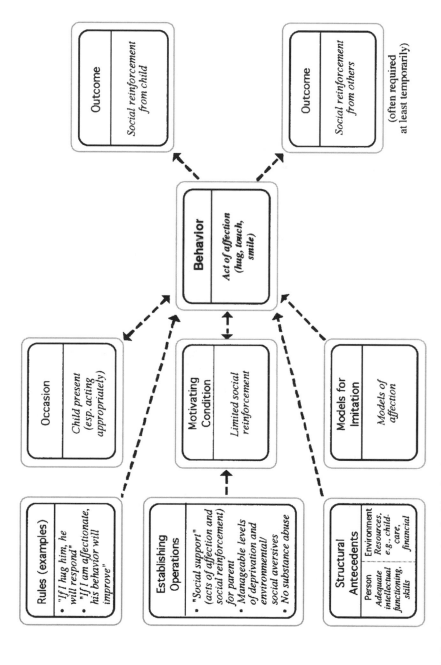

Figure 4. Contingencies associated with affectionate acts.

Consequences of Affectionate Acts

As with any other behavior, affection is shaped by its consequences. Not all of the consequences associated with positive parenting practices are immediate. Parents must sometimes set limits for children (a practice that involves modifications of both antecedents and consequences), and the child is not likely to respond with affection at those moments. Although parental affection is ultimately likely to be reciprocated, it may not be for some time, and other consequences from professionals, significant members of the social network, and the parent may need to be used to shape the behavior.

In natural settings, parents are affectionate partly in response to the positive reinforcement provided by the child, but also in response to learned self-talk about the importance of physical acts of caring. If the child looks unhappy, relief from that learned negative situation may also be reinforcing. Like any active behavior, acting warmly requires some effort and is, therefore, at least mildly costly. It is therefore important to think through potential sources of reinforcement as well as the intermediate steps that may be required to potentiate those sources.

Clinical Implications: Constructing Caring, and Caretaking, Behaviors to Prevent Neglect

In cases in which the parent is not providing adequate care (physically or emotionally), the challenge is to build *and maintain* new repertoires of caring and caretaking behavior. From this statement, the basic paradigm for intervention is clear: When there is a need to increase the rate of behavior, reinforcement—preferably positive—is the primary technology of choice. The details are crucial here. When possible, the final interventive goal is to potentiate *natural* sources of reinforcement, like that provided by the child. Many neglecting parents have deficits in noticing and responding to positive behaviors—as well as positive changes in behavior—on the part of their children. This is one of the areas for which a promising treatment package is available (Wolfe, 1991).

Once some parents learn to attend to their children more closely, positive child behavior, especially positive behaviors directed back at the parents, may prove reinforcing. When child behaviors are not adequately reinforced, and experience suggests they sometimes are not, the ultimate goal is to potentiate positive child behavior as a conditioned reinforcer. Theory tells us how to do so, essentially by temporarily pairing positive child behaviors with other reinforcers, including positive attention from respected persons. Clinically, this approach suggests the importance of reinforcing parental observation of and response to positive behavior on the part of the child. It may also be helpful to use charting, linked if necessary to temporary artificial reinforcers, and apply transfer-enhancing strategies to encourage the parent to observe and respond at home. The ultimate goal in most cases is to withdraw these extrinsic supports over time. However, in some cases (for example, working with parents with developmental disabilities) support may need to be maintained through the critical periods of the child's life, perhaps by incorporating natural helpers into the intervention plan.

As with abuse, the contingency diagrams suggest other strategies as well. Space precludes full discussion here, but a partial list includes:

1. Establishing networks of meaningful social support for sensitive parenting. (The importance of this strategy cannot be overstated; absent this, any program will probably fail).
2. Using modeling and rehearsal to teach parents how to observe and adequately respond to child behavior.
3. Specifying clearly the rules regarding what behaviors to observe and what to respond to, and the consequences for doing so.
4. Establishing everyday events (the end of a television show, bedtime) as occasions for attending to the child in particular.
5. Reducing contact with or the effects of contextual variables that may depotentiate or compete with the child as reinforcers (substance abuse, gambling).

Looking at the contingency diagrams tracing factors associated with physical and emotional caretaking in Figures 3 and 4, the effects of multiple severe aversives from the environment and the physiological effects of overall deprivation (including what is experienced emotionally as depression), are highly salient. These effects are ignored at the peril of the program—and the child. We cannot fix poverty, but we can provide lifestyle enrichment and reduction of aversives (by emphasizing life-sculpting and empowerment strategies that bring these possibilities increasingly under the control of the parent). Individual advocacy at the case level and class advocacy at policy levels should also be among the first strategic directions pursued.

Many cases of abuse also involve neglect. There is no theoretical reason to expect that reducing abuse will always increase caring and caretaking behaviors. Progress in one may facilitate progress in the other, but it may be necessary to apply both the interventions discussed with regard to abuse *and* those associated with enhanced caretaking in many cases. An example is found in the single case study reported later in this chapter, in which improved parenting led to improved child compliance but did not result in increased parental affection. The rate of affectionate acts increased dramatically, however, when this class of behaviors was specifically targeted; once the child responds, a self-perpetuating cycle may emerge (Williams & Mattaini, 1996).

SEXUAL ABUSE

Sexual abuse, like physical and emotional abuse and neglect, can have profoundly negative consequences for the child, the family, and society. The material that follows may help in understanding a pattern of behavior that is often seen not only as repugnant but also as inexplicable. The basic principles of behavior analysis and change apply here as well, however.

The Course of Sexual Abuse

We are coming to know something about effective treatment for persons who sexually abuse children (e.g., Maletzky, 1991; Salter, 1988). Yet, despite widespread theorizing, little solid information exists about how the problem develops. We are therefore forced to turn to a largely theoretical analysis here. Some things are clear: sex, like food and water, is a primary reinforcer with deep biological roots. The problem in sexual abuse is that sexual behavior occurs under undesirable circumstances and that sexual behavior with an inappropriate person or class of persons is reinforcing. (What is inappropriate here is defined based on outcomes for those involved as well as the larger society).

There are several possible explanations for how such patterns emerge. If the incest taboo (and perhaps the general prohibition against sex with children) is largely a social construction, as suggested by some anthropologists (e.g., Harris, 1989), the sexual abuser may not have had the learning experiences necessary to shape it. Or it may be that sexual activity with more appropriate partners is, for reasons of learning history, too anxiety-provoking for some, so they turn to less threatening persons. Achieving control over environmental events is probably an issue for some. Perhaps there is a biological component in some cases, producing a condition of hypersexuality (Maletzky, 1991).

Behavioral Analysis of Sexual Abuse

Sexual behavior—even inappropriate sexual behavior—leads to primary reinforcement; therefore, such behavior is not easy to eliminate. Redirection may, in some cases, be a more reasonable strategy. Because of the respondent nature of some sexual behavior, an analysis that focuses exclusively on operant antecedents and consequences is not adequate to a complete understanding of the phenomenon. Nevertheless, most of the behaviors leading to acts of sexual abuse as well as sexually abusive acts themselves are operant, shaped by their consequences, and embedded in contingent relationships with antecedents. Relapse prevention is therefore likely to require extensive focus on operant contingencies.

Antecedents of Acts of Sexual Abuse

Discrimination of appropriate occasions for sexual behavior is a core issue in sexual abuse; sexual behavior is abusive when it occurs with a person who is developmentally unprepared for it (and unable to give genuine consent) and who may be damaged by the experience. Although counterconditioning approaches may lead to reduced sexual arousal associated with children, a relapse prevention model (Marlatt & Gordon, 1980, 1985) suggests that identifying high-risk situations (those which previously have been occasions for the behavior) and developing plans for coping with them is likely to be important in the treatment of any behavior problem that appears to involve impulsive behavior, including sexual offenses. Interventions that associate alternative cues (adults) with reinforcement may also be valuable.

Consequences of Acts of Sexual Abuse

As with physical and emotional abuse, the goal in sexual abuse is to prevent or reduce the probability of a behavior that has previously resulted in reinforcement, an intrinsically difficult challenge. A common and understandable response is to turn to punishment. But because the outcome of the abuse remains potentially reinforcing, the risk of relapse remains high when the perpetrator has learned or believes (self-talk) that punishment is unlikely. Incarceration alone is unlikely to lead to lasting results, given the powerful effects of sexual reinforcement, and the low probability of detection for any particular offense. Incarceration does, of course, prevent the perpetrator from committing further offenses while in jail. It can also provide opportunities to offer treatment interventions. The threat of incarceration may be useful in motivating participation in treatment.

Strategies that go beyond punishment, however, are often required, including potentiating and building repertoires to access more appropriate sources of sexual reinforcement. Reinforcement strategies for taking active relapse prevention steps are also needed. Adding even modest reinforcement strategies have been found to enhance results in cases in which counterconditioning techniques have led to sluggish and uneven results (Maletzky, 1991). If arousal, and ultimately sexual behavior, with more appropriate persons leads to alternative sources of reinforcement, theory would strongly suggest that relapse prevention may be enhanced.

Treating Perpetrators of Sexual Abuse

Our discussion thus far has sketched in broad strokes some of the approaches that may be important in working with perpetrators of sexual abuse. Respondent techniques (covert sensitization, aversion techniques, negative practice and reconditioning; Maletzky, 1991), used in conjunction with reinforcement strategies that may be helpful in relapse prevention and the development of more acceptable social and sexual adjustments, may be essential.

Because of the complexities involved in mixing and phasing respondent and operant techniques, this is a specialty area that cannot be presented in-depth here. For general practitioners, however, recognition of several critical principles drawn from a functional analysis of the behavior may be helpful in situations in which they are working as part of an interventive team. They may also be helpful to those practitioners working in situations in which there is no access to resources beyond incarceration. Based on these principles, effective treatment must include:

1. Reducing opportunities for the sexual abuser to act on sexual urges. This approach is often the first crucial strategy, frequently requiring that legal steps be taken to ensure that the perpetrator does not have contact with potential victims (including court orders of no contact and, when necessary, incarceration). Note that in this case, incarceration is not viewed as an effective (punishing) consequence, but rather as a way of manipulating structural antecedents. In some cases, later in treatment, changes in jobs or living situations may also be useful.

2. Emphasizing changes in establishing operations. At least until changes have occurred, acts of sexual abuse, however horrifying to others, are reinforcing to the perpetrator. Depotentiating these reinforcers and establishing others is therefore likely to be required to achieve long-term change.

3. Developing a range of alternative behaviors in which the person can engage when faced with occasions for the problem behavior. These alternative behaviors and reinforcers for their use are important in relapse prevention.

4. Developing a stable network of social reinforcement. As in each of the other analyses above, this strategy is likely to be important to maintain changes. Learning new behavior, although not trivial, ordinarily is only the first step; establishing clear, predictable consequences for using those new skills is the *sine qua non* for lasting change. Networks of social reinforcement, including groups, may prove valuable here.

As with physical and emotional abuse and neglect, the effects of sexual abuse on children can be profound. The discussion in this chapter focuses particularly on the parent; however, the reader may also find it important to become familiar with the literature around treatment of victims and survivors of abuse (Helfer & Kempe, 1987; Salter, 1988).

PROGRAMMATIC AND COMMUNITY RESPONSES

The preceding analyses of abuse, neglect and sexual abuse, while tentative and incomplete, offer a good deal of direction for clinical practice in cases in which these behaviors are present. In this section, we will sketch some of the implications for program design and preventive efforts. Potential programmatic and community responses flow directly and organically from the functional analyses already presented. It is difficult for an individual clinician to implement many of the suggestions we have made without substantial programmatic supports. For work with situations of abuse, for example, even establishing a parenting skills group may be an organizational challenge; ensuring support for home-based transfer-enhancing techniques may be even more so. Unfortunately, half full in this case often means empty. Practitioners therefore need to track most of the relevant contingencies for the population they serve and consciously decide, based on data when possible, which contingencies they can safely disregard and which must be addressed no matter how difficult.

An additional challenge is that, although a standardized package of skills may be helpful for many clients, there will always be idiosyncracies associated with each client, and for some, a significantly different package may be required. One step that can be taken to ensure this modification occurs, even in bureaucratic settings, is the establishment of outcome-based incentives that encourage staff analysis and creativity. (See chapters 1, 5, and 7 in this volume for further discussion of systemic approaches to organizational behavior management.)

Community-level preventive and intervention efforts should also be designed based on an understanding of the contingency network within which the problems occur. For several decades, there has been an extended and largely meaningless debate, for example, as to whether child abuse is rooted in individual behavior or in economics. Looking at the contingency diagrams presented in Figures 2, 3, and 4, it is quite clear that interactions are only to be expected—child maltreatment is individual behavior, but the central contingencies are environmental. Generalized deprivation and high rates of aversives are establishing operations that potentiate the consequences of abuse, for example. It may be useful to trace patterns of causation that show the connections clearly. An an example, a conceptual causal chain drawn from the literature is shown in Figure 5.

In sketching it out in this way, an obvious research and analytic strategy emerges, rooted in path analysis and other forms of causal modeling, which may ultimately help in identifying those strategic directions likely to be most potent.

In the meantime, efforts at prevention ought to target, whenever possible, as many of the relevant contingencies as possible, especially those

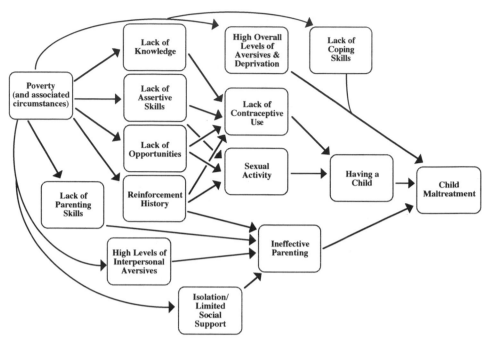

Figure 5. Hypothesized causal chain, child maltreatment. From "Generalist Practice," by M. A. Mattaini in *The Foundation of Social Work Practice: A Graduate Text* (p. 237), edited by C. H. Meyer and M. A. Mattaini, 1995, Washington, DC: NASW Press. Copyright 1995 by NASW Press. Adapted with permission.

that appear earliest in the causal chain (e.g., deficits in parenting skills and specific knowledge). Creative approaches to community education that teach new rules and provide new models to imitate are needed. A particular challenge is to find ways to make these courses so attractive that parents (especially high-risk parents) want to attend, rather than feeling coerced to do so by external systems. Other skills-training approaches may also help; teaching assertive skills, for example, can be inexpensive, and may have effects that resonate systemically through client lives (for a behavior analytic model of assertion training, refer to Rakos, 1991). Acting to reduce or attenuate the effects of poverty and high levels of environmental stress, while building networks of reinforcement on a community level, is also critical. Note that well-designed welfare reform, violence prevention, and similar efforts, therefore, are intimately related to child maltreatment (for a behavior analytic perspective on welfare reform, see Opulente & Mattaini, 1993).

Teaching skills and knowledge (the rules) may be possible in many naturally occurring settings, such as youth programs, churches, and schools. Youth are more likely to attend if offered incentives like opportunities to use video equipment, to meet sports figures, or to obtain chances in a drawing (Mattaini, 1993); once they are present, an effective presentation can often engage them. Behavior analysts are just beginning work to think through the design of data-based modules using media, in-person training, and networks of community reinforcement targeted toward particular groups (teens, parents, teachers, policy-makers, social workers, and other service providers) to establish networks of cultural practices that offer alternatives to abuse and neglect. Designing such modules so as to make them highly reinforcing will require creativity, but is possible. Imagine a situation in which there is a waiting list for participants in these programs, not because so many people have been court-mandated or otherwise required to attend, but because the program has the reputation for being fun and valuable—a challenging but highly worthwhile scenario to pursue.

CASE EXAMPLE

The following single-case study, which is reported in more detail elsewhere (Williams & Mattaini, 1996), provides an example of many of the principles discussed so far. The study involved a low-income family that consisted of a 36-year-old mother (who spoke only Spanish), a father who worked double shifts and was seldom at home, and two sons, aged 4 and 5. The 4-year-old had been placed in a special-needs preschool (a CABAS school; see Greer, this volume) because of his noncompliant and aggressive behavior at home and in social settings; after 1 week in the school program, he was described by his teacher as well behaved. His mother continued to complain persistently about the child's behavior at home, however, and she demonstrated a high level of criticism and little or no affection toward the child. Observers particularly noted the high rate of negative comments she made about her child. No physical punishment or abuse was observed. Given the high rate of aversive exchange that was observed, however, both emotional and physical abuse were potentially probable. Although the child was adequately cared for physically, the obvious lack of affection from his mother also reflected potential emotional neglect. Especially in light of the child's young age, staff working at the school saw him as being at very high risk for maltreatment.

The design selected was a multiple baseline across settings. Baseline data collection began during the summer, but was interrupted due to scheduling problems. Additional baseline data, therefore, was collected in September, with intervention occurring over an 8-week period from September through the following November. Data collection and intervention occurred in the family home during the early morning hours. Three settings, each of which was somewhat challenging for the child and mother, were selected: putting away toys, playing with the boy's brother, and mealtime. Sessions were videotaped; observational data were later recorded from the tapes. (Reliability, with a second Spanish-speaking observer rating 25% of the tapes, averaged 84% across settings and conditions.)

The behaviors of interest included the mother's provision of clear and unclear commands, the child's rate of compliance, and the mother's use of inadequate consequences (including verbal or physical punishment and lack of positive reinforcement or positive correction when indicated; see full report for operational definitions) and appropriate consequences (positive reinforcement, or positive forms of correction for noncompliance). The levels of reprimands—a subset of particularly aversive inadequate consequences—and the levels of contingent physical affection—a subset of appropriate consequences—were also recorded. The rationale for selection of these targets was that improving the rates of child compliance and maternal use of positive reinforcement (including physical affection) were expected to have multiple benefits, including breaking the existing coercive pattern of exchanges, and increasing reciprocal positive transactions. At the same time, reducing the rates of punishment and other aversive behaviors from the mother (and the child) was also expected to reduce the risk for maltreatment. The mother could learn to obtain the consequences she wanted (child compliance and escape from aversive child behaviors) in ways that were more effective while placing the child at decreased risk.

The intervention package applied (Treatment 1, Figures 6 and 7) included prompting, modeling, training in new rules (in part using readings and quizzes), positive reinforcement, fading of instruction and thinning of reinforcement over time, and feedback on videotaped sessions. Intervention was provided in the home, in part to be responsive to reality pressures faced by the family, and in part to eliminate the need to train for generalization. As is usual in clinical applications of multiple baseline designs, training in each setting was initiated after relatively stable change was obtained in the previous setting. The settings chosen (putting away toys—a representative example in which compliance is essential—playing with brother, and mealtimes) had been identified as particularly problematic. The mother was first given written materials (in Spanish) about each skill to be learned. She completed a quiz on each of these skills. Then, on each visit by the behavioral trainer, the video camera was set up and the occasion for behavior arranged (for example, by putting the mother and child in an area where there were toys spread around). The mother was instructed to have the child put away the toys. Appropriate vocal and physical actions were demonstrated by the trainer, and the mother was prompted to the extent necessary until she was independently demonstrating the skill. Extensive verbal reinforcement from the trainer was provided.

Some of the findings are portrayed in Figure 6 and Figure 7, which demonstrate the variability expected in natural settings, yet suggest relatively persuasive results. Other data included in the full report indicate that child compliance improved substantially, as did the mother's ability

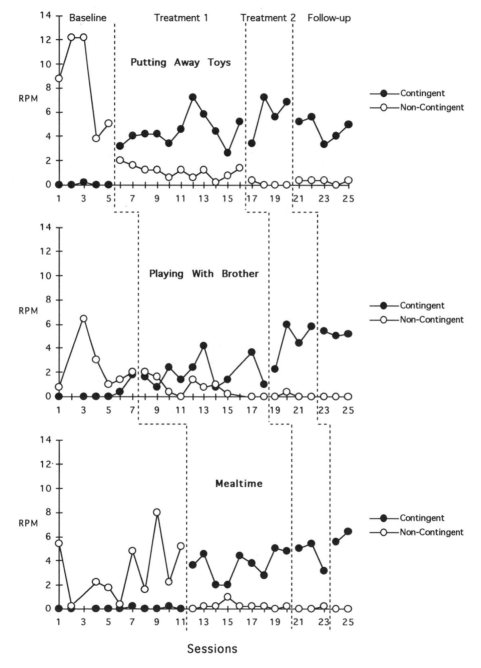

Figure 6. Rates per minute of contingent and noncontingent consequences provided by mother under varying conditions.

to provide appropriate commands (occasions for compliant behavior); our main interest here, however, is in changes in consequences provided by the mother. Note in Figure 6 that the mother's rates per minute of appropriate (contingent) and inadequate (noncontingent) consequences for child behavior responded to the intervention package as expected; in each setting, the previously high rate of inadequate consequation dropped to near zero, whereas appropriate consequation increased from near zero to a substantial rate in each setting when training was implemented there. This change is important because effective consequation leads to effective management of child behavior; noncontingent, relatively random consequences lead to out-of-control behavior, which in turn may potentiate abuse.

These results indicate that the ratio of positive reinforcement to punishment and other problematic consequences shifted dramatically. The rate of reprimands specifically dropped in concert with the overall rate of inappropriate consequences (see Figure 7). It is important to note also that, although other forms of reinforcement increased, the rate of physical affection *did not* increase when the compliance training package was provided. A second treatment condition (Treatment 2 in the figures), therefore, was initiated, in which the mother was specifically prompted and reinforced for the use of physical affection as a form of reinforcement. When this class of behaviors was targeted, its rate increased from near zero to 2 or more times per minute in each setting.

This is not a complete description of the case, and reports follow up after 2 months. Additional follow-up data is being collected, although interpretation will be complicated by ongoing services and other improvements in the family living situation. The mother has now enrolled in additional parenting classes at the school, and she recently moved to a new neighborhood where she feels more comfortable; both of these events are likely to decrease insularity, an important consideration in this case. The school is also planning to initiate a parents' group for Spanish-speaking mothers, a program that may also be helpful for this mother, and the parent worker is also exploring with the mother other ways to build additional social connections.

Note that the simple data presented here suggest that if behavioral consultation begins before patterns of severe maltreatment are firmly established, relatively inexpensive and rapid interventions may have substantial effects. The child became more compliant, but more important, the rate of aversives from the mother dropped dramatically, while the rate of positive reinforcement increased, leading to a significantly altered relationship. By informal observation, the mother no longer described her child as bad and, in fact, came to enjoy spending time with him. The child became substantially more reinforcing to his mother, which was a particularly desirable outcome, because reinforcement from the child may be

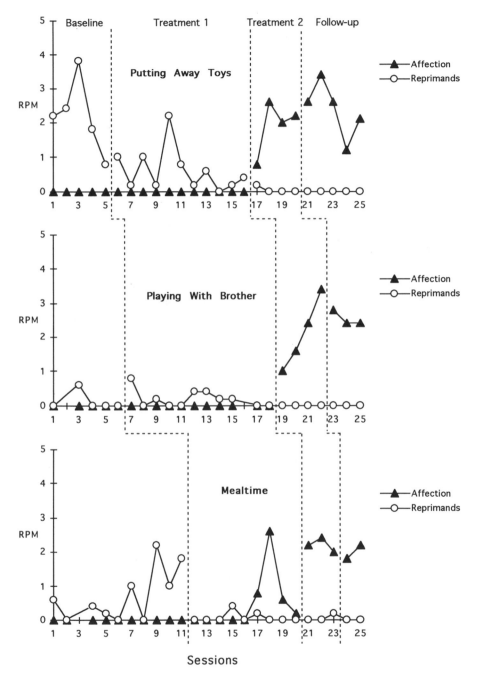

Figure 7. Rates per minute of maternal reprimands and acts of physical affection under varying conditions.

important in the mother's maintaining appropriate parenting over time. As a result of her involvement in parenting classes, the mother is now working with the child on programs targeting social and academic work at home. Staff, who once were inclined to avoid this woman because of her high rate of negative comments about her child, now report that she describes him as a "good boy," and that the child even reminds her to praise him!

CONCLUSION

We have a good deal of knowledge about how to make a difference in the level of child maltreatment in society. What is largely missing, however, is an integrated plan for applying what we know effectively and broadly. The following suggestions are practical next steps in this direction.

The Development and Dissemination of Tested Packages

Systematizing what is known into interventive packages that are demonstrably effective in community settings appears to be critical. It is not realistic to expect every parent, or every child-protective services worker to independently design effective strategies based on the principles outlined here. Such packages need to be reasonably inexpensive, flexible enough that they can be applied in ways that fit the specifics of the situation and do not require high levels of precision on the part of those implementing them, and consistent with local values and with what Fawcett and his colleagues have identified as essential principles in community practice (Fawcett, Mathews, & Fletcher, 1980). Packages developed need to include strategies for attracting people to use them, drawing on what we know of the use of incentives, mass media, and marketing strategies.

The sensible way to produce adequate packages is to develop and test them in an iterative way before they are widely disseminated. This has not always been standard practice; some parenting programs, for example, have not been carefully tested or modified for effectiveness before they were marketed. This is an ethically questionable practice. Packages could be developed for multiple target groups, not only for persons currently known to be involved in maltreatment, but also for others who may be at risk (including teens). Those who work—or live—with perpetrators of maltreatment could also be targeted.

Policy Considerations

At several points in this chapter, areas where larger sociocultural considerations intersect with the treatment of children have been identified.

The provision of service networks with adequate resources to teach families new skills without labeling them as deviant is a clear example. Given an apparent political shift toward further limiting government programs and funding, it is clearly important that cuts not be made without attention to their effects on children. The dangers of increasing levels of deprivation and uncontrollable aversives are particularly crucial to consider. Prevention programs, both for those who may be at risk and for families in which early problems have already emerged, offer many opportunities for addressing the factors identified in this chapter, but are often at high risk themselves. Government in a democracy is ultimately the people, and we as individuals and collectively have ultimate responsibility for the well-being of our children. This responsibility can best be addressed through effective partnerships between government agencies, private organizations, families, and individuals. At a time when cutting budgets is a major focus of many in government, our collective responsibility to children continues to be an ethical and moral imperative that cannot be neglected.

A number of specific areas in which social policy may affect the rate and severity of child maltreatment also emerge from this analysis. For example:

- Deprivation is associated with maltreatment. Adequate, politically acceptable approaches for making sufficient resources available to all families for a life of dignity are therefore needed. A particularly important form of deprivation is the social isolation and insularity commonly associated with child maltreatment. Attention to building stable, interlocking networks of social reinforcement for at-risk parents must also be a priority.
- Substance abuse is associated with child maltreatment. Support for effective prevention and treatment of substance abuse also represents an important means toward preventing maltreatment.
- Employment is an important source of tangible and intangible reinforcement, and income from employment empowers people to take control of many aspects of their social environment (reducing aversives and increasing reinforcers). Policy aimed at maximizing opportunity, therefore, is also organically tied to prevention of maltreatment. The availability of adequate employment opportunities and the skills needed to obtain and maintain fulfilling work are valuable not only in their own right but also for the multiple effects they may have on the family.
- Many service systems now rely heavily on aversive control, and parents, not surprisingly, try to avoid involvement with

them. New creative approaches that reduce the costs and increase the incentives for parents to ask for help before problems become severe should be supported.

Critical Areas for Further Research

There is much that is not yet known about child maltreatment and the factors associated with it; the research agenda is long (NRC, 1993). The discussion in this chapter suggests several areas for further work that may be of particular importance, however. Much of the material presented here is tentative, based on nomothetic data failing to capture the specific interactions that occur in cases among the behaviors of interest and the antecedents and consequences that shape them. There is a critical need for a large number of intensive single-case studies like the one just presented that can help us identify more precisely the contingencies operative in particular clusters of cases. Such research need not be expensive and can often be conducted by individual practitioners and programs. Both aggregate and nonaggregated results of such studies—given a structure to collect this information—have much to tell us in capturing the crucial contingencies associated with child maltreatment. These studies are the basic research on which preventive and interventive work depend.

Further investigation of what constitutes the most effective and most efficient preventive and interventive packages is clearly needed. As with other social problems of interest, the best packages are likely to be those that are based on a coherent understanding of the behaviors of interest, rather than a random, scattershot approach. The relative costs and benefits of packages aimed broadly at the population, versus those that are more tightly targeted, also need to be identified.

Child maltreatment occurs more commonly in some families, societies, and groups than in others. This phenomenon suggests the need to examine particular practices (behaviors supported by networks of social contingencies) that may be associated with the incidence and prevalence of abuse and neglect as well as the need to experiment with ways to introduce and stabilize more effective practices at the level of the family, the community, and the nation. This is, ultimately, a question of cultural design (see Chapter 1). As Specht suggested, "We must have a vision . . . that enables us to direct our energies to the creation of healthy communities. That is how we make healthy people" (Specht, 1990, p. 356).

REFERENCES

Azar, S. T., & Wolfe, D. A. (1989). Child abuse and neglect. In E. J. Mash & R. A. Barkley (Eds.), *Behavioral treatment of childhood disorders* (pp. 451–489). New York: Guilford.

Beck, A. T., Rush, A. J., Shaw, B. F., & Emery, G. (1978). *Cognitive therapy of depression*. New York: Guilford.

Bell, R. Q. (1977). Socialization findings reexamined. In R. Q. Bell & L. V. Harper (Ed.), *Child effects on adults*. Hillsdale, NJ: Erlbaum.

Blythe, B. J., Salley, M. P., Jayaratne, S. (1994). A review of intensive family preservation services research. *Social Work Research, 18*, 213–224.

Boswell, J. (1990). *The kindness of strangers*. New York: Vintage.

Bousha, D. M., & Twentyman, C. T. (1984). Mother-child interactional style in abuse, neglect, and control groups: Naturalistic observations in the home. *Journal of Abnormal Psychology, 93*, 106–114.

Brunk, M., Henggeler, S. W., & Whelan, J. P. (1987). Comparison of multisystemic therapy and parent training in the brief treatment of child abuse and neglect. *Journal of Consulting and Clinical Psychology, 55*, 171–178.

Cerutti, D. T. (1989). Discrimination theory of rule-governed behavior. *Journal of the Experimental Analysis of Behavior, 51*, 259–276.

Child Abuse Prevention, Adoption and Family Services Act (1988). 42 U.S.C. § 5105.

Child Abuse Prevention and Treatment Act (1974). 42 U.S.C. § 5101.

Daro, D. (1988). *Confronting Child Abuse: Research for Effective Program Design*. New York: Free Press.

Dumas, J. E. (1989). Let's not forget the context in behavioral assessment. *Behavioral Assessment, 11*, 231–247.

Dumas, J. E., & Wahler, R. G. (1985). Indiscriminate mothering as a contextual factor in aggressive-oppositional child behavior: "Damned if you do, damned if you don't." *Journal of Abnormal Child Psychology, 13*, 1–17.

Fawcett, S. B., Mathews, R. M., & Fletcher, R. K. (1980). Some promising dimensions of behavioral community technology. *Journal of Applied Behavior Analysis, 13*, 505–518.

Foreyt, J. P., & Rathjen, D. P. (1978). *Cognitive behavior therapy: Research and application*. New York: Plenum.

Garbarino, J. (1977). The human ecology of child maltreatment: A conceptual model for research. *Journal of Marriage and the Family, 39*, 721–735.

Gil, D. G. (1970). *Violence against children: Physical child abuse in the United States*. Cambridge, MA: Harvard University Press.

Goldiamond, I. (1974). Toward a constructional approach to social problems. *Behaviorism, 2*, 1–84.

Goldstein, A. P., Keller, H., & Erné, D. (1985). *Changing the abusive parent*. Champaign, IL: Research Press.

Greene, B. F., Norman, K. R., Searle, M. S., Daniels, M., & Lubeck, R. C. (1995). Child abuse and neglect by parents with disabilities: A tale of two families. *Journal of Applied Behavioral Analysis, 28*, 417–434.

Harris, M. (1989). *Our kind*. New York: HarperCollins.

Helfer, R. E., & Kempe, R. S. (1987). *The battered child* (4th ed.). Chicago: University of Chicago Press.

Howing, P. T., Wodarski, J. S., Gaudin, J. M., Jr., & Kurtz, P. D. (1989). Effective interventions to ameliorate the incidence of child maltreatment: The empirical base. *Social Work, 34,* 330–338.

Johnston, J. M. (1988). Strategic and tactical limits of comparison studies. *The Behavior Analyst, 11,* 1–9.

Kamerman, S. B., & Kahn, A. J. (1990). Social services for children, youth and families [Special Issue]. *Children and Youth Services Review, 12* (1, 2).

Kazdin, A. E. (1989). *Behavior Modification in Applied Settings* (4th ed.). Homewood, IL: Dorsey.

Kempe, C.H., Silverman, F. N., Steele, B. F., Droegemueller, W., & Silver, H. K. (1962). The battered child syndrome. *Journal of the American Medical Association, 181,* 17–24.

Kunkel, J. H. (1991). Apathy and irresponsibility in social systems. In P. A. Lamal (Ed.), *Behavioral analysis of societies and cultural practices* (pp. 219–240). New York: Hemisphere.

Lutzker, J. R., Frame, R. E., & Rice, J. M. (1982). Project 12-Ways: An ecobehavioral approach to the treatment and prevention of childhood abuse and neglect. *Education and Treatment of Children, 5,* 141–155.

Maletzky, B. M. (1991). *Treating the sexual offender.* Newbury Park, CA: Sage.

Malott, R. W. (1989). The achievement of evasive goals: Control by rules describing contingencies that are not direct acting. In S. C. Hayes (Ed.), *Rule-governed behavior: Cognition, contingencies, and instructional control* (pp. 269–322). New York: Plenum.

Malott, R. W. (1992). Saving the world with contingency diagraming. *The ABA Newsletter, 15,* 45.

Marlatt, G. A., & Gordon, J. R. (1980). Determinants of relapse: Implications for the maintenance of behavior change. In P. O. Davidson & S. M. Davidson (Eds.), *Behavioral medicine: Changing health lifestyles* (pp. 410–451). New York: Brunner/Mazel.

Marlatt, G. A., & Gordon, J. R. (1985). *Relapse prevention: Maintenance strategies in the treatment of addictive behaviors.* New York: Guilford.

Mattaini, M. A. (1993). Behavior analysis in community practice. *Research on Social Work Practice, 3,* 420–447.

Mattaini, M. A. (1995). Generalist practice. In C. H. Meyer & M. A. Mattaini (Eds.), *The foundations of social work practice: A graduate text* (pp. 225–245), Washington, DC: NASW Press.

McCurdy, K., & Daro, D. (1994, April). *Current trends in child abuse reporting and fatalities: The results of the 1993 annual fifty state survey.* Chicago: National Center to Prevent Child Abuse.

McDowell, J. J. (1980). An analytic comparison of Herrnstein's equations and a multivariate rate equation. *Journal of the Experimental Analysis of Behavior, 33,* 397–408.

McDowell, J. J. (1982). The importance of Herrnstein's mathematical statement of the law of effect for behavior therapy. *American Psychologist, 37*, 771–779.

McDowell, J. J. (1988). Matching theory in natural human environments. *The Behavior Analyst, 11*, 95–109.

McDowell, J. J. (1989). Two modern developments in matching theory. *The Behavior Analyst, 12*, 153–166.

McDowell, J. J., Bass, R., & Kessel, R. (1983). Variable-interval rate equations and reinforcement and response distributions. *Psychological Review, 90*, 364–375.

McDowell, J. J., & Wixted, J. T. (1988). The linear system theory's account of behavior maintained by variable-ratio schedules. *Journal of the Experimental Analysis of Behavior, 49*, 143–169.

McDowell, J. J., & Wood, H. M. (1984). Confirmation of linear system theory prediction: Rate of change of Herrnstein's *k* as a function of changes in reinforcer magnitude. *Journal of the Experimental Analysis of Behavior, 41*, 183–192.

Meichenbaum, D., & Turk, D. (1976). The cognitive-behavioral management of anxiety, anger and pain. In P. O. Davidson (Ed.), *The behavioral management of anxiety, depression and pain* (pp. 1–34). New York: Brunner/Mazel.

Meyer, C. H. (1993). *Assessment in social work practice.* New York: Columbia University Press.

Michael, J. L. (1993). *Concepts and principles of behavior analysis.* Kalamazoo, MI: Society for the Advancement of Behavior Analysis.

National Center on Child Abuse and Neglect. (1993, May). *National Child Abuse and Neglect Data System, Working Paper 2, 1991 Summary Data Component.* Washington, DC: USDHHS, Administration on Children, Youth and Families.

National Research Council. (1993). *Understanding Child Abuse and Neglect.* Washington, DC: National Academy Press.

Novaco, R. (1974). *A treatment program for the management of anger through cognitive and relaxation controls.* Unpublished doctoral dissertation, Indiana University, Bloomington, IN.

Opulente, M., & Mattaini, M. A. (1993). Toward welfare that works. *Behavior and Social Issues, 3*, 17–34.

Otto, M. L., & Smith, D. G. (1980). Child abuse: A cognitive behavioral intervention model. *Journal of Marriage and the Family, 6*, 425–429.

Patterson, G. R. (1976). The aggressive child: Victim and architect of a coercive system. In E. J. Mash, L. A. Hamerlynck, & L. C. Handy (Eds.), *Behavior modification and families* (pp. 267–316). New York: Brunner/Mazel.

Pence, E., & Paymar, M. (1993). *Education groups for men who batter.* New York: Springer.

Polansky, N. A., Ammons, P. W., Gaudin, J. M., Jr. (1985). Loneliness and isolation in child neglect. *Social Casework, 66*, 38–47.

Polansky, N. A., Gaudin, J. M., Jr., Ammons, P. W., & Davis, K. B. (1985). The psychological ecology of the neglectful mother. *Child Abuse and Neglect, 9,* 265–275.

Rakos, R. F. (1991). *Assertive behavior: Theory, research, and training.* New York: Routledge.

Salter, A. C. (1988). *Treating child sex offenders and victims: A practical guide.* Newbury Park, CA: Sage.

Serna, L. A., Schumaker, J. B., Sherman, J. A., & Sheldon, J. B. (1991). In-home generalization of social interactions in families of adolescents with behavior problems. *Journal of Applied Behavior Analysis, 24,* 733–746.

Sidman, M. (1989). *Coercion and its fallout.* Boston: Authors Cooperative.

Skinner, B. F. (1953). *Science and human behavior.* New York: Free Press.

Specht, H. (1990). Social work and the popular psychotherapies. *Social Service Review, 64,* 345–357.

Thomas, A., & Chess, S. (1977). *Temperament and development.* New York: Brunner/Mazel.

U.S. Department of Health and Human Services. (1990). *Child abuse and neglect: Critical first steps in response to a national emergency.* Washington, DC: U.S. Government Printing Office.

Videka-Sherman, L. (1991). Child abuse and neglect. In A. Gitterman (Ed.), *Social work practice with vulnerable population* (pp. 345–381). New York: Columbia University Press.

Wahler, R. G. (1980). The insular mother: Her problems in parent-child treatment. *Journal of Applied Behavior Analysis, 8,* 27–42.

Wahler, R. G., Williams, A. J., & Cerezo, A. (1991). The compliance and predictability hypotheses: Sequential and correlational analyses of coercive mother-child interactions. *Behavioral Assessment, 12,* 391–407.

Whiteman, M., Fanshel, D., & Grundy, J. F. (1987). Cognitive-behavioral interventions aimed at anger of parents at risk of child abuse. *Social Work, 32,* 469–74.

Williams, G., & Mattaini, M. A. (1996). *Constructing positive alternatives to coercive parenting.* Manuscript submitted for publication.

Widom, C. S. (1989). Child abuse, neglect, and adult behavior: Research design and findings on criminality, violence, and child abuse. *American Journal of Orthopsychiatry, 59,* 355–367.

Wolfe, D. A. (1987). *Child abuse: Implications for child development and psychopathology.* Newbury Park, CA: Sage.

Wolfe, D. A. (1991). *Preventing physical and emotional abuse of children.* New York: Guilford.

10

TEENAGE SEXUALITY

STEVEN P. SCHINKE, MARY ANN FORGEY, and MARIO ORLANDI

INTRODUCTION

Despite great public health advances, sexually transmitted diseases (STDs), acquired immune deficiency syndrome (AIDS), and unwanted pregnancies continue to pose risks for millions of Americans. Consistently and unacceptably high prevalence rates are particularly disquieting because STDs and unwanted pregnancy are almost completely preventable. Lingering technological and institutional impediments notwithstanding, many of the conditions necessary for widespread behavior change have significantly improved. Recent advances in barrier and other forms of birth control, increased public awareness of the need for protected sexual behavior, and the lowering of legal and institutional obstacles to the distribution of information and devices for protecting oneself sexually have all contributed to positive behavior change. Although early efforts were somewhat haphazard, American educational systems have begun to address sex education (including disease and pregnancy prevention) on a national level. Given these developments, the absence of concomitant sharp decreases in the rates of STDs and unwanted pregnancy is counterintuitive and worthy of

Research reported here was supported by a grant from the National Institute on Drug Abuse (DA05321).

267

closer analysis. This disparity—between the ready access to the information about and tools for "safe" (i.e., protected) sex, on the one hand, and the high incidence rates of unsafe sexual contacts, on the other—is most striking among young Americans.

Compared with their adult counterparts, adolescent women and men in this country experience the highest prevalence rates and the largest increases of STDs and pregnancy relative to their numbers and proportional representation in the U.S. population. They are less informed about and frequently more susceptible to these health hazards. Adolescents have the biological capability for—and inclination toward—sexual activity but not necessarily the social or psychological skills to avoid its untoward consequences. Moreover, because of their youth, adolescents have more to lose by contracting an incurable disease or becoming pregnant accidentally. Because of their inordinate risk for STDs (including HIV infection) and unwanted pregnancy, and their likelihood of falling victim to extraordinary problems from early, unprotected sexual behavior, adolescents are the population focus of this chapter.

Besides focusing on adolescents, in this chapter we will also catalogue and critique past efforts to prevent STDs (including HIV infection) and unwanted pregnancy, according to theoretical and empirical support. In so doing, we divide programs to prevent STDs and unwanted pregnancy into two groups: early approaches and emerging approaches. We conclude the chapter with the implications of current knowledge on STDs and pregnancy prevention for future programming to reduce the risks of unprotected sex among American youths.

BACKGROUND

As of September 1993, 1,415 of the 339,250 cases of AIDS in the United States were diagnosed among adolescents 13 to 19 years of age (Centers for Disease Control [CDC], 1993a). This figure is even more alarming given the increasing rates of adolescent AIDS. In 1981, one new adolescent case of AIDS was reported; by 1992, this figure had ballooned to 159 (CDC, 1993a). At current rates of infection, the number of reported AIDS cases among 13- to 21-year-olds doubles every 14 months (Hein, 1992). Further, the typical 8-to-10-year delay between infection and overt symptomatology would indicate that relatively few HIV-infected youths will present with full-blown AIDS during adolescence (CDC, 1993b). Indeed, although the prevalence of AIDS within this age group accounts for only 1% of all AIDS cases, 19% (or 63,718) of all AIDS cases have been diagnosed among adults in their twenties; the disease is currently the sixth leading cause of death among 15- to 24-year-olds (CDC, 1993a).

Nationally, teenagers make up one in four cases of HIV infection (Hingson, Strunin, Berlin & Heeren, 1990). Given both the delay in the disease's presentation and the absence of any population wide HIV testing program, the actual rate of HIV infection among the adolescent population may be much higher than the records indicate. Rates of pregnancy and sexually transmitted diseases in the teenage population must therefore be used to estimate rates of HIV infection (DiClemente, 1989).

High rates of STDs in a population are widely believed to be indicative of high levels of HIV infection (Stein, 1992). STD rates reflect high-risk sexual activity, and the genital ulcerations that are symptoms of many STDs are considered significant cofactors for heterosexual transmission of HIV (Rolfs, Goldber, & Sharrar, 1990). Higher rates of syphilis, gonorrhea, and pelvic inflammatory disease in the adolescent population place them at particular risk for HIV (Jemmett, Loretta, & Fong, 1992).

Three million teenagers contract an STD every year, a quarter of the total yearly cases; in other words, one in eight 13- to 19-year-olds contracts an STD every year. That figure is double—one in four—for 13- to 19-year-olds who have had intercourse (Alan Guttmacher Institute, 1993). Even more alarming, STD contraction rates are on the rise among many adolescent populations (O'Reilly & Aral, 1985).

Adolescent girls are at particular risk of contracting an STD. Teenage girls exhibit the highest rate of gonorrhea, cytomegalovirus, chlamydia, cervicitis, and pelvic inflammatory disease of any age group (Cates & Rauch, 1985; Mosher, 1985). STDs can, in turn, result in a secondary series of public health problems, including infertility, complications in pregnancy, maternal mortality, and cervical cancer (Alan Guttmacher Institute, 1993).

Teenage pregnancy is an issue of great national concern because of the severe social and economic consequences teenage mothers and their children face, as well as for its heightened risk of medical complications (Carrera & Dempsey, 1988). Births to girls aged 15 to 19 numbered more than half a million in 1991, or 62.1 per 1,000. Births to girls under age 15 numbered just over 12,000, or 1.4 per 1,000 (Alan Guttmacher Institute, 1993). Almost 1 million 15- to 19-year-olds became pregnant in 1988, or 110.8 per 1,000; among 10- to 14-year-olds, there were 27,000 pregnancies, or 3.3 per 1,000 (Alan Guttmacher Institute, 1993).

Minority communities, people of low socioeconomic station, and those living in urban areas have been disproportionately affected by HIV, STDs, and teenage pregnancy (Holmes, Karon, & Kreiss, 1990). African American and Hispanic AIDS cases make up almost half of the nation's total (CDC, 1993b). Heterosexual HIV infection is also more prevalent among these urban groups than in any other group (Rolfs et al., 1990). The same population also reports the highest incidence of STDs, at rates between 2 and 3 times as high as the national average. Finally, African

American teenagers become pregnant twice as frequently as White teenagers (Jemmett et al., 1992).

According to current epidemiological data, African American and Hispanic adolescents living in urban centers are the groups at highest risk for STDs and HIV infection. The disproportionate effect of AIDS on minority communities is reflected in AIDS incidence rates, which are 6 times and 3 times higher, respectively, among African Americans and Hispanics than among Whites (CDC, 1994). As for behavioral risk factors, rates of intravenous drug use, sexual intercourse, and sexually transmitted diseases are also higher for African American and Hispanic adolescents than for majority-culture adolescents (CDC, 1990, 1993b, 1994).

Theory

Although eliminating behavior associated with risk for infection or pregnancies (e.g., intercourse) is one option for self-protection, it seems safe to assume that such a choice will never be adopted by the majority of the population. Yet, preventing risk behaviors through interventions that emphasize education and behavior change is paramount given the rapid rate of STDs and unwanted pregnancies among adolescents.

Theories on the etiology of problem behavior during adolescence have value for directing risk-prevention strategies. Rather than defining problem behavior as pathological, early theorists viewed youthful deviance as the result of socially induced pressures and normal developmental needs to achieve socially desirable goals (Cloward & Ohlin, 1960). Later, theorists perceived problem behavior among youths as the result of weak ties with conventional norms (Hirschi, 1969). Building on these tenets, theorists saw a pattern of problem behavior occurring when youths' conventional social bonds were neutralized through attenuating experiences (Elliot, Ageton, & Canter, 1979). To date, four major theories have guided interventions to reduce problem behaviors in the public health arena. These theories are social cognitive theory, conceptual change theory, problem behavior theory, and peer cluster theory.

According to social cognitive theory, interpersonal factors play a significant role in individuals' learning. The influence of these factors is not unidirectional. Rather, social factors influence and are influenced by personal and behavioral determinants (Bandura, 1986). For example, youths' perceptions that deviant behaviors are normative among their peers may promote deviance through the establishment of maladaptive beliefs. Such perceptions may persuade adolescents that deviant acts are socially acceptable and that these acts are necessary to be popular, grown-up, and sophisticated. Perceived payoffs from deviance increase adolescents' susceptibility to peer pressure.

Other evidence indicates that susceptibility to social influence in general (Bandura, 1969; Rotter, 1972) and to social influences promoting deviance in particular (Demone, 1973; Jessor, Collins, & Jessor, 1972; Wechsler & Thum, 1973) is related to low levels of self-confidence and assertiveness and to high levels of the need for social approval and of impatience to assume adult roles. Social cognitive theory also suggests that behavior is determined by self-efficacy and cognition. That self-efficacy is linked to the adoption and maintenance of health practices (Bandura, 1977, 1993; Condiotti & Lichtenstein, 1981; Maiback, Flora, & Nass, 1991) further argues for the relevance of social cognitive theory to guide interventions. In particular, the inclusion of self-protective skills, problem-solving steps, interpersonal communication skills to enhance social proficiency and resiliency, and self-efficacy components in risk-reduction interventions for youths mirrors tenets of social cognitive theory. Not surprisingly, interventions grounded in social cognitive theory have rendered promising results in influencing youths' risk-reduction behavior (Bandura, 1990; Schinke, Moncher, & Holden, 1989; Schinke et al., 1990).

Conceptual change theory, contrary to earlier theory, posited that youths' capacity for learning is not constrained by developmental stages (Piaget, 1954). Rather, according to conceptual change theory, cognitive development results from acquiring knowledge in particular content domains (Carey, 1985, 1990). Conceptual change theorists believe that learning occurs through cause-and-effect processes (Wellman & Gelman, 1992). For example, a youth may erroneously surmise that smokers contract cancer because of a virus. Traditional theory interprets such errors as the result of domain-general cognitive principles (Krister & Patterson, 1980; Kuhn, 1989). Conceptual change theorists, however, would suggest that the error stems from a lack of health knowledge. Conceptual change theory thus predicts that youths' misconceptions about health practices can be revised through accurate and germane learning about human functioning and health (Carey, 1985, 1990).

Problem behavior theory also provides an explanation for why youth engage in deviant acts (Jessor & Jessor, 1977). According to this theory, risk-taking behavior results from an interaction of personal, physiological, and environmental factors. The theory further suggests that some adolescents find deviant acts functional because the acts help them achieve personal goals. For example, for adolescents who are not doing well academically or socially, deviancy may provide a way of achieving status. Also, according to problem behavior theory, youths are more vulnerable to peer pressure when they have few effective coping strategies, few skills to handle social situations, and anxiety about social situations. Although deviant behavior is difficult to prevent if it is functional for youths, that functionality is vitiated when youths have positive ways of achieving their goals. Thus, effective interventions would incorporate coping skills for high-risk youths to handle peer pressure situations adaptively (Epstein, 1992).

Peer cluster theory assumes that peer interactions, and the tacit norms which govern them, largely determine risk-taking behavior (Oetting & Beauvais, 1986, 1987). Peer clusters include interactions among friends, dating dyads, and family constellations, as well as those within neighborhood settings, sports teams, and clubs. According to theorists, peer clusters and the norms they observe not only account for the presence and type of risk-taking among adolescents, but also may help youths reduce pressures and influences toward deviance. The therapeutic use of peer clusters in an intervention context may enhance efforts to reduce adolescents' risk-associated life-style behaviors. By providing positive alternatives and by changing perceived social norms, therapeutic peer clusters can be a source of social development.

Peer cluster theory further emphasizes the role of anger as an important trait in predicting adolescent risk taking. Anger increases the chances of forming peer drug associations and probably increases chances of developing deviant norms (Oetting & Lynch, in press). Peer cluster theory would indicate that preventive interventions should include the use of peer leaders to deliver information, components that address social norms, strategies to build and sustain positive peer clusters, and anger-management skills.

INTERVENTION COMPONENTS

Many educational initiatives have joined these theoretical models, along with general lessons on human sexuality, into a broader health and sex education curricula. In response to the growing threat of AIDS to adolescents, the development and implementation of such curricula has become a particular priority of public health. By 1990, 83% of students were receiving AIDS education—up from 52% in 1986 (Hingson & Strunin, 1992). The evaluation of health curricula has similarly become a national priority.

Combining the distinct but related struggles against unwanted pregnancy, STDs, and AIDS, school-based health education programs have emphasized avoiding unprotected sex as their foremost goal. But success in this endeavor has been triply qualified: Programs have been blocked by local political initiatives; programs have done a better job of imparting facts than changing behavior; and programs have unevenly distributed information among the adolescent population.

In analyzing prevention efforts, researchers have learned an enormous amount about the necessary components for encouraging safe, protected sex. These identified components include: (a) *knowledge* about disease transmission or conception, methods of prevention, and severity; (b) *perceived risk* in terms of increasing adolescents' understanding of their vulnerability to the condition; (c) *skills* pertaining to communication in high-pressure situations that involve sex and drugs; (d) *perceived norms* of peers regarding high-risk behaviors; and (e) *substance abuse prevention* related to decreasing the use of alcohol and other drugs that may contribute to sexual risk taking and to IV drug use.

Early Educational Efforts

Kirby (1992) described the major phases of modern sex education as it evolved in the U.S. The earliest efforts emphasized risks and consequences of pregnancy. Through these programs—heavily weighted in the perceived risk module—it was reasoned that if youths had the information to make an informed decision about pregnancy (or cancer or dependency), they would make it in favor of safe behavior. The next generation of instruction moved on to values clarifications, decision making, and communications skills, with the intention of helping students articulate their own priorities, comprehend the risks and advantages of a number of value-positions, and negotiate for their preferences by discussion.

Although both such early approaches did increase students' knowledge about sexuality (Kirby, 1984) and STDs (Yarber, 1986), their effect on high-risk behavior was minimal (Whitley & Schofield, 1985–1986). A possible explanation for the lack of effectiveness of these early approaches was their neglect of behavioral components in analyzing and attempting to change youths' patterns of sexual activity. The consequences and situational contexts, as well as the antecedents, of sexual activity are complex and demand careful attention and behavioral analysis. By studying the nature of adolescent sexual activity within a behavioral context, program planners and clinicians might have better determined not only the locus of youths' maladaptive and risk-taking patterns, but also may have designed more responsive and effective approaches to modifying those patterns.

More recently, AIDS-prevention education has relied heavily on conceptual change theory through the health belief model. This model posits that if subjects are fully aware of the consequences of various possible actions, the subjects' choice will be safe. These programs were widely implemented. In many respects, AIDS prevention education has made considerable strides in disseminating important medical information. Taking HIV knowledge as a rough indicator, a 1985 study of adolescents living in a low AIDS-incidence area revealed very little knowledge about HIV (Price, Desmond, & Kukulka, 1985). The situation was somewhat improved in high-incidence urban areas. A survey of people of the same age living in San Francisco found a high rate of awareness about sexual transmission of HIV, but not about the risks posed by intravenous drug use.

Moreover, only 60% of those surveyed understood that condom use could make sex safer (DiClemente, Zorn, & Temoshok, 1986).

In addition to the problem of students who were uninformed, many students were seriously misinformed. Strunin and Hingson (1987) found that 60% of their respondents believed blood donation was a high-risk activity. Fortunately, more recent studies have indicated significant advances in young people's understanding about the virus, its related syndrome, and the basics of prevention (Anderson & Christenson, 1991; Brown, Fritz, & Barone, 1989; Dawson, Cynamon, & Fitti, 1987; Fisher & Moscovich 1991; Hingson, et al., 1990; Malavaud, Dumay, & Malamaud, 1990; Roscoe & Kruger, 1990).

Despite the dissemination of vital health information to adolescent populations, several shortfalls remain. Health education initiatives are neither of long enough duration (the typical AIDS-education program in an American school lasts only 4 hours; Kirby, 1992) nor of effective enough content to reach even the most specific and captive audiences. Chervin & Martinez (1987), for example, described a university's intensive, week-long AIDS-awareness program, which featured lectures, public discussions, and free condoms. The event received heavy press coverage. In a survey conducted a few weeks after the program, more than a quarter of the students on the campus remained unable to define *safer sex*. As Bandura (1992) pointed out, too often the language of these programs is so desexualized and euphemistic that few people can actually understand the messages with which they may be consistently bombarded. Other studies have revealed that those students who did retain information from their health courses simultaneously retained a number of misconceptions about the subject matter or continued to exhibit significant deficits in some key topics (Fisher & Fisher, 1991; Hingson et al., 1989; Miller & Downer, 1988).

Information-dissemination programs' biggest shortfall, however, may be that they have failed to reach those adolescents who have historically exhibited the highest rate of infection or pregnancy. Several studies (DiClemente, Lanier, Horan, & Lodico, 1991; Morris, Baker, Huscroft, Evans, & Zeljkovic, 1991; Nader, Wexler, Patterson, McKusick, & Coates, 1989) have shown that undereducation is a disproportionate problem among adolescents who are incarcerated or in detention centers—a population already prone to high-risk sexual and drug-related activity. The homeless population and hard-core intravenous drug users (IVDUs) are also more frequently exposed to high-risk behavior than are most adolescents (Deisher, Robinson, & Boyer, 1982; Fullilove, Fullilove, Bowser, & Gross, 1990; Rahdert, 1988; Rotheram-Borus, Koopman, & Erhardt, 1991; Stein, Jones, & Fisher, 1988; Stricof, Novick, Kennedy, & Weisfuse, 1988). But because members of both of these groups are also more likely to switch schools or to drop out altogether, they are typically excluded from education efforts (Sondheimer, 1992). Outside of the schools, there exist few social programs for these populations.

In addition, even when people who abuse IV drugs can be reached by educational outreach, they are frequently blocked from receiving explicit and necessary information about how to clean needles. The political undesirability of addressing IV drug use in any way other than condemnation obstructs the dissemination of vital information. Finally, recent immigrants, who may not speak English, are also likely to be excluded from health-outreach curricula (Hingson et al., 1991).

AIDS prevention campaigns have apparently also missed the majority of African American and Hispanic adolescents. In contrast to the steady increase in the larger population's knowledge about HIV transmission and methods of prevention (Petosa & Wessinger, 1990), and despite the existence of highest levels of perceived risk among these minority groups, African American and Hispanic adolescents consistently exhibit a knowledge level well below average (Bell, Feraios, & Bryan, 1990; DiClemente, Boyer, & Morales, 1988; DiClemente, Zorn, & Temoshok, 1987; Sonenstein, Pleck, & Ku, 1989) Their major areas of deficit include misconceptions regarding sexual transmission (failure to recognize that oral sex, vaginal sex, and asymptomatic partners may involve risk; DiClemente et al. 1988; Lesnick & Pace, 1990) and misconceptions regarding casual transmission (which can lead to prejudice and increased anxiety regarding perceived susceptibility (DiClemente et al., 1988).

The local political battles that the proponents of school-based AIDS and STD curricula face are usually waged by school boards and community organizations that invoke a strict moral code coupled with the belief that any discussion of adolescent sexual activity other than simple condemnation will serve merely to encourage it. However, 94% are in favor of HIV/AIDS education, with 80% in favor of safer sex instruction (Gallup, 1987). This pattern—in which unwarranted fear of opposition, rather than opposition itself, is the most important obstacle to the development and adoption of sex education programs—is a familiar one to health educators, and it is consistent with the earlier findings of Scales & Kirby (1983).

Thus, the success of AIDS education programs is dependent not only on the quality, relevance, and accuracy of the information, but also on the forums in which it is delivered (Bandura, 1992). To date, the effectiveness of these programs has been heavily skewed in favor of the mainstream, school-attending White adolescent population. Prevention programs that are targeted at high-risk ethnic and racial minority youth, for example, might improve their effectiveness by delivering content via music, video, and other media that have particular attractiveness for these groups and in collaboration with community-based organizations that reach these populations.

Early Curricula Effects on Behavior

Early sexual education curricula tried to foster adolescents' ability and willingness to protect themselves and their partners. Unfortunately, their success was limited. Between 1986 and 1990 (Hingson & Strunin, 1992), the percentage of adolescents who said they used condoms as a response to the AIDS threat rose from 2 to 14. In 1989, respondents indicated a 10-year increase of 37%—to 58%—in the proportion of male adolescents who reported using a condom during their last sexual encounter (Sonenstein et al., 1989). And between 1982 and 1988, according to data from the National Survey of Family Growth, teenage girls who reported using condoms rose 22% to 32%. Yet, in terms of consistent condom use, the numbers are lower: In 1990 the total number of respondents to one survey (Hingson et al., 1990) who reported using condoms consistently was only 37%. Patterns regarding the correlation of contraception and education were similar (Brooks-Gunn, Furstenberg, & Frank, 1990; Carrera & Dempsey, 1988). Moreover, all of these gains were at least partially offset by a simultaneous increase in the proportion of adolescents who were sexually active.

Analyzing early STD/AIDS and pregnancy prevention curricula from a behavior analytic perspective sheds light on the relative failures of these programs. Because early intervention efforts emphasized knowledge—rather than behavior-change components—they did not address essential variables that have particular relevance for unprotected sexual behaviors. Armed with information only, youths had no counterinfluence against such societal forces as peer modeling and the frequently delayed consequences of unprotected sex. Some persons engage routinely in unprotected sex without immediately contracting or, for that matter, ever contracting an STD or HIV infection, or becoming pregnant. Of course, the vast majority of persons who engage in regular or even irregular unprotected sex eventually do become infected with an STD or become pregnant, but the delay in infection or pregnancy contributes to a perception among youths (and adults) that such behaviors are not necessarily risky. Moreover, the long incubation period associated with HIV infection further reinforces the erroneous message that punishment (for unprotected sex) is not inevitable. Further compounding the link between sexual risk taking and its consequences are adolescents' perceived invulnerability and fatalism. Without addressing these factors, STD/AIDS and unwanted pregnancy prevention programs have little hope of reaching their audience.

INTERVENTION STRATEGIES AND SUCCESSES

Some interventions have included basic information regarding AIDS knowledge or reproduction as part of a larger effort to change attitudes and behavior. Interventions targeted at attitudes and behavior have met with more success than programs that primarily delivered knowledge (without attention to attitudes and behavior). One comprehensive pregnancy prevention program provided services at both a local high school and a local clinic (Hardy, 1987). The program taught participating students to set limits for themselves and to value personal responsibility. Formal instruction emphasized abstinence (with skills to avoid unprotected sex) and included segments on the risks of STDs and the consequences, both adverse and intended, of pregnancy.

In addition to information transmission (to both parents and teens), key elements in this program's success were physician interest, empathy, and confidentiality, which combined to provide counseling and contraceptive advice. By promoting the use of effective contraception, the program achieved a significant decrease in the incidence of teen pregnancy, an increase in the age of first-time intercourse, and relatively rapid, positive changes in general sexual knowledge, attitudes toward sexuality, and use of the clinic (Zabin, Hirsch, Smith, Streett, & Hardy, 1986).

Clearly, information alone cannot effect behavior change. The information must be adapted to the underlying social and psychological contexts within target populations. An effective sexual education curriculum needs to do more than merely deliver information about barrier birth control and the horrors of STDs, AIDS, and unwanted pregnancy. Such information must be joined with guidance for youths' personal and social growth, life skills to avoid risk behaviors (e.g., assertion skills, communication skills), and a redefining of social norms that are incompatible with sexual risk taking. It must also promote the practice of positive alternatives to unprotected sex and foster those characteristics that are associated with low susceptibility to negative health influences. As important, each curriculum component benefits from a heightened sensitivity to the culture of the target group. An understanding, appreciation, and integration of the target culture is essential not only to the content of the program, but also to its development, implementation, and evaluation.

Attitudes, beliefs, and practices have been significantly associated with risk-reduction behavior. Research (Hingson & Strunin, 1992) is currently investigating the relationship among these various factors—knowledge, attitudes, beliefs, and practices—often tapping into such social psychological models and theories as the health belief model, the theory of reasoned action, problem behavior theory, and social learning theory.

Some studies have found significant correlations between high levels of perceived risk and risk-reduction behavior (Goodman & Cohall, 1989; Hingson et al., 1990). More recent studies, however, have not found perceived risk to be significantly associated with the reduction of AIDS risk behaviors when other socioenvironmental constructs (i.e., norms, self-efficacy) are controlled for (Brooks-Gunn et al., 1990; Pendergrast, Du-Rant, & Gaillard, 1992; Weisman, C. S., Plicta, Nathanson, Ersminger, & Robinson, 1991; Walter et al., 1992). Consequently, perceived risk as a determinant for reducing AIDS risk behaviors is now being questioned in a fashion similar to knowledge. In short, perceived risk alone is not a sufficient motivator of the adoption and maintenance of behaviors that reduce AIDS risk.

Social Skills and Communication

The efficacy of certain social skills, particularly communication with sexual partners, is increasingly being identified as a significant factor in sexual risk-reduction behavior among adolescents (Allen-Meares, 1984; DiClemente, 1991; Goodman & Cohall, 1989; Walter et al., 1992; Weisman et al., 1991). In particular, a willingness to request condom use predicted subjects' consistency of condom use in a study of adolescent girls. In that study of high school girls, those willing to request condom use during a sexual encounter were 5 times more likely than unwilling subjects to be consistent condom users. Gender differences in levels of efficacy have also been identified, but with inconsistent results (Goodman & Cohall, 1989; Walter et al., 1992).

Studies of effective contraceptors (Campbell & Barnland, 1977) have revealed several consistent personality traits. These traits include an ability to defy convention and disregard rules, which in turn suggests an ability to apply personal values to important situations. Also, effective contraceptors demonstrate the ability to detach themselves from societal expectations in selecting contraceptives. Finally, adolescents who consistently use contraceptives demonstrate self-efficacy—the belief that one has the capability to alter one's health habits and that individual setbacks do not indicate a total failure. Self-efficacy is a useful index to how well information will withstand the often competing pressures, social and otherwise, toward risk behavior. Self-efficacy has also been shown to predict safer sex practices in adolescents (Bandura, 1992).

An example of an education and attitude intervention included social skills-building in its education component, along with AIDS and STD knowledge. Adolescents spent a day with a trained facilitator learning HIV/AIDS information, practicing interpersonal skills, and engaging in role plays. A control group received a similarly structured and equally informative intervention on career opportunities. Three months after the intervention, the adolescents who had received the AIDS intervention reported fewer occasions of coitus, fewer coital partners, greater use of condoms, and a lower incidence of heterosexual anal intercourse (Jemmett et al., 1992).

A series of reports by Schinke and associates demonstrates the advantages of a behavioral approach to analyzing and modifying adolescent sexual risk taking. An initial study by Schinke and colleagues found that unwanted and unprotected intercourse sometimes occurs because adolescents lack social and communication skills (Schinke, Gilchrist, & Blythe, 1980). Such a lack of interpersonal skills can interfere with contraceptive use, even when knowledge of birth control is adequate. Thus, Schinke and colleagues launched a group of studies designed to increase youths' interpersonal communication skills, decision-making skills, and problem-solving abilities. Participants who received the short-term prevention programs demonstrated greater perceived control over their lives, more persuasive interpersonal skills, better problem-solving skills, and greater assertiveness and reported more birth control use and fewer instances of unprotected sex at posttest and follow-up measurement occasions (Schinke, 1984).

Drug Use

Recent findings have shown that using alcohol and marijuana, particularly before to sexual activity, may reduce the likelihood that adolescents will use condoms (Fullilove et al., 1990; Hingson et al., 1990). Other studies have found strong correlations between African American youths who use crack and their incidence of STDs (Fullilove et al., 1990). Also in this study, stronger correlations between crack and STDs were found for those who combined crack use with sexual activity. Although not all of these studies focused on inner-city minority adolescents, the increased exposure of inner-city minority adolescents to substances like crack cocaine argues for its relevance in AIDS prevention curricula for this population.

Peer Norms

Peer norms regarding condom use, contraception, and other risk-reduction behaviors have emerged as an important new arena for tracking and influencing risk behaviors (DiClemente, 1991; Lowe & Radius, 1987; Stanton, Black, Keane, & Feigelman, 1990; Walter et al., 1992). The relative age of the participants is a likely factor in the relevance of this module; younger adolescents may be particularly susceptible to peer pressure (Brooks-Gunn et al., 1990). Both age at first intercourse and frequency of contraceptive use have been shown to be highly associated with perceptions of peer norms (Brooks-Gunn et al., 1990). One study of incarcerated youths, for example, found them 5 times more likely to use condoms when they believed that activity to be supported among their peers (DiClemente, 1991).

Similarly, an ethnically diverse sample of inner-city adolescents revealed perceived normative support to have a four-fold increase of likelihood of condom use (DiClemente & Fisher, 1991). Based on this and other data, several researchers have argued convincingly that effective interventions must include efforts to alter group norms (Miller, Turner, & Moses, 1990). Others argued that prevention efforts would also benefit from a community-based component (Coates & Greenblatt, 1989).

One successful community intervention incorporated peer norms and role models by using peer leaders and adult male community residents to recruit teenage boys. The intervention offered a comprehensive approach to teen services (including education), direct access to reproductive services, and holistic training and promotion of realistic life options (Carrera & Dempsey, 1988). Emphasizing behavior change through peer encouragement rather than authority figures was considered a key element of the program's potency.

A similar effort was applied to a gay population. Perceived leaders within the study's gay population participated in a series of seminars focusing on effective communication skills. Once trained, these peers and adults disseminated a risk-reduction intervention. Results showed that the men who successfully reported behavior change also reported greater peer support than did those who reported no change. In addition, participants were more likely to comply with the intervention if they believed that their friends would accept these changes.

Heterosexual groups are also highly sensitive to perceived social norms. In particular, boyfriends exert a critical influence on their girlfriends' contraceptive behavior. Significant correlation has been shown between women's dependence on boyfriends' advice and their own contraceptive effectiveness. In one study, girls who perceived partner support were 4 times as likely to use contraception than those who did not (Weisman et al., 1991). Yet, girls who used contraceptions both effectively and ineffectively stated that their birth control attitudes were influenced by peers. Girls who used contraceptives effectively reported that their best female friends had the most influence on their birth control attitudes. Those who used contraceptives ineffectively cited boyfriends', parents', and self-influenced attitudes (Allen-Meares, 1984).

Parents also have a significant social influence on their adolescent children. Predisposition to risky behaviors can be correlated to teens' experiences with parents during their adolescence (Abernathy, 1974). In addition, there is an association between daughters' responsible sexual behavior and frequency of parental communication during adolescence about sex (Fox & Inazu, 1980). Strong mother-daughter relationships have also been shown to help prevent adolescent pregnancy (Olson & Worobey, 1984). Attitudinal and behavioral norms regarding reproductive behavior are transmitted through teens' interactions with parents (Sussman, 1974).

Because the community and church can also play important roles in establishing social norms, some interventions have attempted to incorporate them.

CONCLUSION

Despite the disheartening record of educational interventions to influence adolescent sexual-risk behavior, there is significant reason for cheer. Although it is true that sexual behavior is resistant to change, adolescents are a highly educable population. Having arrived more recently at a stage of sexual activity, adolescents are less set in their sexual habits than most adults. Further, intervention efforts designed for specific populations have proven quite successful. The most illustrious example is that of the highly effective effort to curb unprotected sex among urban gay men. In accordance with the particular needs of the community to which they were directed, the effort sought to encourage sexuality while encouraging safety. The AIDS epidemic was not treated as a vague threat, but rather as a known quantity—the cause of death of many members of that community. Other similar successes include interventions among persons who use drugs, adults in methadone maintenance, runaways, and gay youth. The success of intervention efforts in these individual communities is a direct source of encouragement for similar efforts among young people. In addition, recent years have seen a nationwide increase in adolescent condom use that, while outpaced by the geometric increase of HIV infection, nevertheless suggests the possibility that better designed programs will yield even greater results.

The development of content, as we have seen by both the great number of psychosocial cofactors and the frequently qualified successes of efforts to date, is a difficult task. But educators and health workers can learn much from the close analyses that have been rendered on the record of early intervention efforts. The next generation of curricula and interventions will have to continue to explain the major modes of disease transmission and conception.

However, this content functions as an explicit means of helping adolescents modify their behaviors—not as an end in itself. Frank discussions of condom use (where to get them, how to use them), role playing and imaging to encourage confidence and skill in safe sex negotiation, and reinforcement of the social normalcy and desirability of condom use are all integral components of any intervention. Furthermore, these messages should be disseminated through as many channels as possible (classroom, health program, counseling, peer leaders, community groups, and mass media) and, as always, with as close an eye as possible to the distinct epistemological and cultural needs of the target population.

Clearly, a behavior analytic approach to untoward sexual activity among adolescents offers several advantages. These advantages include the analysis of youths' behavior within a situational context. By focusing on youths' sexual activities in the context of media influences, peer pressures, and risk-taking preferences, behavior analysts can better identify likely forces that shape and that are thereby amenable to changing exposure to unwanted pregnancy, HIV infection, and other sexually transmitted diseases. Most importantly, when prevention programs are designed to fully exploit behavioral principles, youths can reduce their sexual risk. Behavioral principles highly suitable for changing adolescent sexual activity include modeling, shaping, behavioral rehearsal, social reinforcement, and contingency management.

To conclude, adolescent sexual activity viewed and analyzed within a behavioral perspective will inform responsive prevention programs. In conducting such analyses and in planning and executing those programs, behaviorists and other clinicians will help America's young people avoid major, irreversible, sometimes life-threatening problems with their sexuality and, in so doing, enable youths to reach their full potential as appropriately sexual adults. To not address these needs of American youth is to relegate too many young women and young men to needlessly suffering the negative consequences of precocious and unprotected sexual activity.

REFERENCES

Abernathy, V. (1974). Illegitimate conception among teenagers. *American Journal of Public Health, 64*, 622–665.

Alan Guttmacher Institute. (1993). *Facts in brief: Sexually transmitted diseases (STDs) in the United States.* New York: Author.

Allen-Meares, P. (1984). Adolescent pregnancy and parenting: The forgotten adolescent father and his parents. *Journal of Social Work and Human Sexuality, 3*, 12–25.

Anderson, M. D., & Christenson, G. M. (1991). Ethnic breakdown of AIDS related knowledge and attitudes from the National Adolescent Student Health Survey. *Journal of Health Education, 22*, 30–34.

Bandura, A. (1969). *Principles of behavior modification.* New York: Holt, Reinhart and Winston.

Bandura, A. (1977). *Social learning theory.* Englewood Cliffs, NJ: Prentice-Hall.

Bandura, A. (1986). *Social foundations of thought and action: A social cognitive theory.* Englewood Cliffs, NJ: Prentice-Hall.

Bandura, A. (1990). Perceived self-efficacy in the exercise of control over AIDS infection. *Evaluation and Program Planning, 13*, 9–17.

Bandura, A. (1992). A social cognitive approach to the exercise of control over AIDS infection. In R. DiClemente (Ed.), *Adolescents and AIDS: A generation in jeopardy* (pp. 89–116). Newbury Park, CA: Sage.

Bandura, A. (1993). Social cognitive theory and exercise of control over HIV infection. In J. Peterson & R. DiClemente (Eds.), *Preventing AIDS: Theory and practice of behavioral interventions* (pp. 21–33). New York: Plenum Press.

Bell, D., Feraios, A., & Bryan, T. (1990). Adolescent males' knowledge and attitudes about HIV in the context of their social world. *Journal of Applied Social Psychology, 20,* 424–448.

Brooks-Gunn, J., Furstenberg, F., Jr., & Frank, F. (1990) Coming of age in the era of AIDS: Puberty, sexuality, and contraception. *The Millbank Quarterly 1* (Suppl.), 59–84.

Brown, L. K., Fritz, G. K., & Barone, V. J. (1989). The impact of HIV education on junior and senior high school students. *Journal of Adolescent Health Care, 10,* 386–392.

Campbell, B., & Barnland, D. (1977). Communication patterns and problems of pregnancy. *American Journal of Orthopsychiatry, 47,* 134–139.

Carey, S. (1985). Are children fundamentally different kinds of thinkers and learners than adults? In S. F. Chipman, J. W. Segal, & R. Glaser (Eds.), *Thinking and learning skills: Vol. 2. Research and open questions* (pp. 485–517). Hillsdale, NJ: L. Erlbaum Associates.

Carey, S. (1990). Cognitive development. In D. Osherson & E. Smith (Eds.), *An invitation to cognitive science: Vol. 3. Thinking* (pp. 147–172). Boston: MIT Press.

Carrera, M. A., & Dempsey, P. (1988). *Restructuring public policy priorities on teen pregnancy: A holistic approach to teen development and teen services* (pp. 6–9). New York: SIECUS.

Cates, W., Jr., & Rauch, J. L. (1985). Adolescents and sexually transmitted diseases: An expanding problem. *Journal of Adolescent Health Care, 6,* 1–5.

Centers for Disease Control. (1990). HIV related knowledge and behaviors among high school students: Selected U.S. sites in 1989. *Journal of the American Medical Association, 264,* 318-322.

Centers for Disease Control. (1993a). *Facts about adolescents and HIV and AIDS.* Atlanta, GA: Author.

Centers for Disease Control. (1993b). *HIV/AIDS Surveillance Report.* Atlanta, GA: Author.

Centers for Disease Control. (1994). *HIV/AIDS Surveillance Report.* Atlanta, GA: Author.

Chervin, D. D., & Martinez, A. (1987, February 19). *Survey of the health of Stanford students.* Report presented to the Board of Trustees of Stanford University, Stanford, CA.

Cloward, R. & Ohlin, L. (1960). *Delinquency and opportunity.* New York: Free Press.

Coates, T. J., & Greenblatt, R. M. (1989). Behavioral change using community level interventions. In K. Holmes (Ed.), *Sexually transmitted diseases* (pp. 1075–1080). New York: McGraw-Hill.

Condiotti, M., & Lichtenstein, E. (1981). Self-efficacy and relapse in smoking cessation programs. *Journal of Consulting and Clinical Psychology, 49,* 648–658.

Dawson, D. A., Cynamon, M., & Fitti, J. E. (1987). AIDS knowledge and attitudes. Provisional data from the National Health Interview Survey, August, 1987. *Advance Data, 146,* 1–11.

Deisher, R. W., Robinson, G., & Boyer, D. (1982). The adolescent female and male prostitute. *Pediatric Annals, 11,* 812–825.

Demone, H. W. (1973). The nonuse and abuse of alcohol by the male adolescent. In M. Chafetz (Ed.), *Proceedings of the second annual alcoholism conference* (pp. 24–32). Washington, DC: U.S. Government Printing Office.

DiClemente, R. J. (1989). Prevention of human immunodeficiency virus infection among adolescents: The interplay of health education and public policy in the development of school-based AIDS education programs. *AIDS Education and Prevention, 1,* 70–78.

DiClemente, R. J. (1991). Predictors of HIV-preventive sexual behavior in a high-risk adolescent population: The influence of perceived peer norms and sexual communication on incarcerated adolescents' consistent use of condoms. *Society for Adolescent Medicine, 12,* 385–390.

DiClemente, R. J., Boyer, C. B., & Morales, E. (1988). Minorities and AIDS: Knowledge, attitudes and misconceptions among Black and Latino adolescents. *American Journal of Public Health, 1,* 55–57.

DiClemente, R. J., & Fisher, J. D. (1991). *Predictors of HIV-preventive sexual behavior among adolescents in an HIV epicenter: The influence of communication and perceived referent group norms on frequency of condom use.* Unpublished manuscript, University of California, San Francisco.

DiClemente, R. J., Lanier, M. M., Horan, P. F., & Lodico, M. (1991). Comparison of AIDS knowledge, attitudes, and behaviors among incarcerated adolescents and a public school sample in San Francisco. *American Journal of Public Health, 81,* 628–630.

DiClemente, R. J., Zorn, J., & Temoshok, L. (1986). A survey of knowledge, attitudes, and beliefs about AIDS in San Francisco. *American Journal of Public Health, 76,* 1443–1445.

DiClemente, R. J., Zorn, J., & Temoshok, L. (1987). The association of gender, ethnicity, and length of residence in the Bay area to adolescents' knowledge and attitudes about acquired immune deficiency syndrome. *Journal of Applied Social Psychology, 17,* 216–230.

Elliot, D., Ageton, S., & Canter, R. (1979). An integrated theoretical perspective on delinquent behavior. *Journal of Research in Crime and Delinquency, 16,* 3–27.

Epstein, L. H. (1992). Role of behavior theory in behavioral medicine. *Journal of Consulting and Clinical Psychology, 60,* 493–498.

Fisher, J. D., & Fisher, W. A. (1991). *A general social psychological technology for changing HIV risk behavior.* Unpublished manuscript.

Fisher, J. D., & Moscovich, S. J. (1991). Evolution of college students' HIV-related behavioral responses, attitudes, knowledge, and fear. *HIV Education and Prevention, 2,* 322–337.

Fox, G. L., & Inazu, J. K. (1980). Patterns and outcomes of mother-daughter communication about sexuality. *Journal of Social Issues, 36,* 7–29.

Fullilove, R. E., Fullilove, M. T., Bowser, B. P., & Gross, S. A. (1990). Risk of sexually transmitted disease among black adolescent crack users in Oakland and San Francisco, CA. *Journal of the American Medical Association, 263,* 851–855.

Gallup, A. (1987). *The 19th Annual Gallup polls of the public's attitudes toward the public school.* Princeton, NJ: Author.

Goodman, E., & Cohall, A. T. (1989). Acquired immunodeficiency syndrome and adolescents: Knowledge, attitudes, beliefs, and behaviors in a New York City adolescent minority population. *Pediatrics, 84,* 36–42.

Hardy, J. B. (1987). Preventing adolescent pregnancy: Counseling teens and their parents. *Medical Aspects of Human Sexuality, 27*(3), 32–46.

Hein, K. (1992). Adolescents at risk for HIV infection. In R. J. DiClemente (Ed.), *Adolescents and AIDS: A generation in jeopardy* (pp. 3–16). Newbury Park, CA: Sage.

Hingson, R., & Strunin, L. (1992). Monitoring adolescents' response to the AIDS epidemic: Changes in knowledge, attitudes, beliefs, and behaviors. In R. DiClemente (Ed.), *Adolescents and AIDS: A generation in jeopardy* (pp. 17–33). Newbury Park, CA: Sage.

Hingson, R. W., Strunin, L., Berlin, B., & Heeren, T. (1990). Beliefs about AIDS, use of alcohol and drugs, and unprotected sex among Massachusetts adolescents. *American Journal of Public Health, 80,* 295–299.

Hingson, R., Strunin, L., Craven, D. E., Mofenson, L., Mangione, T., Berlin, B., Amaro, H., & Lamb, G. A. (1989). Survey of HIV knowledge and behavior changes among Massachusetts adults. *Preventive Medicine, 18,* 808–818.

Hingson, R., Strunin, L., Grady, M., Strunk, N., Carr, R., Berlin, B., & Craven, D. (1991). Knowledge about HIV and behavioral risks of foreign born Boston public school students. *Journal of American Public Health, 1,* 1638–1641.

Hirschi, T. (1969). *Causes of delinquency.* Berkeley, CA: University of California Press.

Holmes, K. K., Karon, J. M., & Kreiss, J. (1990). The increasing frequency of heterosexually acquired AIDS in the United States. *American Journal of Public Health, 80,* 858–862.

Jemmett, J. B., III, Jemmett, L. S., & Fong, G. T. (1992). Reduction in HIV risk-associated sexual behaviors among Black male adolescents: Effects of an AIDS prevention intervention. *American Journal of Public Health, 82,* 372–377.

Jessor, R., Collins, M. I., & Jessor, S. L. (1972). On becoming a drinker. *Annals of the New York Academy of Sciences, 197,* 199–213.

Jessor, R., & Jessor, S. L. (1977). *Problem behavior and psychosocial development: A longitudinal study of youth.* New York: Academic Press.

Kirby, D. (1984). *Sexuality education: An evaluation of programs and their effects.* Santa Cruz, CA: Network.

Kirby, D. (1992). School-based prevention programs: Design, evaluation, and effectiveness. In R. J. DiClemente (Ed.), *Adolescents and AIDS: A generation in jeopardy* (pp.159–180). Newbury Park, CA: Sage.

Krister, M. C., & Patterson, C. J. (1980). Children's conceptions of the causes of illness: Understanding of contagion and use of imminent justice. *Child Development, 51,* 839–849.

Kuhn, D. (1989). Children and adults as intuitive scientists. *Psychological Review, 96,* 674–689.

Lesnick, H., & Pace, B. (1990). Knowledge of AIDS risk factors in South Bronx Minority College students. *Journal of Acquired Immune Deficiency Syndromes, 3,* 173–176.

Lowe, C. S., & Radius, S. M. (1987). Young adults' contraceptive practices: An investigation of influences. *Adolescence, 22,* 291–304.

Maiback, E., Flora, J. A., & Nass, C. (1991). Changes in self-efficacy and health behavior in response to a minimal contact community campaign. *Health Communications, 3,* 1–5.

Malavaud, S., Dumay, F., & Malamaud, B. (1990). HIV infection: Assessment of sexual risk, knowledge, and attitudes towards prevention in 1,596 high school students in the Toulouse Education Authority Area. *American Journal of Health Promotion, 4,* 260–265.

Miller, H. G., Turner, C. F., & Moses, L. E. (Eds.). (1990). *HIV: The second decade.* Washington, DC: National Academy.

Miller, L., & Downer, A. (1988). AIDS: What you and your friends need to know—A lesson plan for adolescents. *Journal of School Health, 58,* 137–141.

Morris, R., Baker, C., Huscroft, S., Evans, C. A., & Zeljkovic, S. (1991). Two year variation in HIV risk behaviors in detained minors. *VII International Conference on AIDS, 2,* 51. (Abstract No. W.D. 109)

Mosher, W. D. (1985). Reproductive impairments in the United States, 1965–1982. *Demography, 22,* 415–430.

Nader, P. R., Wexler, D. B., Patterson, T. L., McKusick, L., & Coates, T. (1989). Comparison of beliefs about AIDS among urban, suburban, incarcerated, and gay adolescents. *Journal of Adolescent Health Care, 10,* 413–418.

Oetting, E. R., & Beauvais, F. (1986). Peer cluster theory: Drugs and the adolescent. *Journal of Counseling and Development, 65,* 17–22.

Oetting, E. R., & Beauvais, F. (1987). Peer cluster theory, socialization characteristics and adolescent drug use: A path analysis. *Journal of Counseling Psychology, 34,* 205–213.

Oetting, E. R., & Lynch, R. S. (in press). Peers and the prevention of adolescent drug use. In Z. Amsel & B. Bukowski (Eds.), *Drug abuse prevention: Sourcebook on strategies and research*. Westport, CT: Greenwood Publishing Group.

Olson, C. F., & Worobey, J. (1984). Perceived mother-daughter relations in a pregnant and non-pregnant adolescent sample. *Adolescence, 19*, 781–794.

O'Reilly, K., & Aral, S. (1985). Adolescents and sexual behavior: Trends and implications for STDs. *Journal of Adolescent Health Care, 6*, 262–270.

Pendergrast, R. A., DuRant, R. H., & Gaillard, G. L. (1992). Attitudinal and behavioral correlates of condom use in urban adolescent males. *Society for Adolescent Medicine, 13*, 133–139.

Petosa, R., & Wessinger, J. (1990). The HIV education needs of adolescents: A theory-based approach. *HIV Education and Prevention, 2*, 127–136.

Piaget, J. (1954). *The construction of reality in the child*. New York: Basic Books.

Price, J. H., Desmond, S., & Kukulka, G. (1985). High school students' perceptions and misperceptions of HIV. *Journal of School Health, 55*, 107–109.

Rahdert, E. R. (1988). Treatment services for adolescent drug abuse: Analysis of treatment research. In E.R. Rahdert & J. Grabowski (Eds.), *National Institute on Drug Abuse Monograph No. 77* (pp.1–3). Rockville, MD: National Institute on Drug Abuse.

Rolfs, R. T., Goldber, M., & Sharrar, R. G. (1990). Risk factors for syphilis: Cocaine use and prostitution. *American Journal of Public Health, 80*, 853–857.

Roscoe, B., & Kruger, T. L. (1990). HIV: Late adolescents' knowledge and its influence on sexual behavior. *Adolescence, 25*, 39–48.

Rotheram-Borus, M. J., Koopman, C., & Erhardt, A. A. (1991). Homeless youths and HIV infection. *American Psychologist, 46*, 1188–1197.

Rotter, J. B. (1972). Generalized expectancies for internal versus external control of reinforcement. In J.B. Rotter, J.E. Chance, & E.J. Phares (Eds.), *Application of a social learning theory of personality* (pp. 260–295). New York: Holt, Rienhart, and Winston.

Scales, P., & Kirby, D. (1983). Important barriers to sex education: A survey of professionals. *Journal of Sex Research, 30*, 229–237.

Schinke, S. P. (1984). Preventing teenage pregnancy. In M. Hersen, R. M. Eisler, & P. M. Miller (Eds.), *Progress in behavior modification* (Vol. 16, pp. 31–63). New York: Academic.

Schinke, S. P., Gilchrist, L. D., & Blythe, B. J. (1980). Role of communication in the prevention of teenage pregnancy. *Health and Social Work, 5(3)*, 54–59.

Schinke, S. P., Moncher, M. S., & Holden, G. W. (1989). Preventing HIV infection among black and Hispanic adolescents. *Journal of Consulting and Clinical Psychology, 58*, 432–436.

Schinke, S. P., Orlandi, M. A., Gordon, A. N., Weston, R. E., Moncher, M. S., & Parms, C. A. (1990). AIDS prevention via computer-based intervention. *Computers in Human Services, 5*, 147–156.

Sondheimer, D. L. (1992). HIV infection and disease among homeless adolescents. In R. DiClemente (Ed.), *Adolescents and AIDS: A generation in jeopardy* (pp. 71–85). Newbury Park, CA: Sage.

Sonenstein, F., Pleck, J., & Ku, L. (1989). Sexual activity, condom use, and AIDS awareness among adolescent males. *Family Planning Perspectives, 21*, 152–158.

Stanton, B., Black, M., Keane, V., & Feigelman, S. (1990). HIV risk behaviors in young people: Can we benefit from 30 years of social research? *HIV and Public Policy Journal, 5*, 17–23.

Stein, J. B., Jones, S. J., & Fisher, G. (1988). AIDS and IV drug use: Prevention strategies for youth. In M. Quackenbush, M. Nelson, & K. Clarck (Eds.), *The AIDS challenge* (pp. 273–295). Santa Cruz, CA: Network.

Stein, Z. A. (1992). The double bind in science policy and the protection of women from HIV infection. *American Journal of Public Health, 82*, 1471–1472.

Stricof, R. L., Novick, L. F., Kennedy, J. T., & Weisfuse, I. B. (1988, November). HIV seroprevalence of adolescents at Covenant House/under 21 in New York City. Paper presented at the American Public Health Association Conference, Boston.

Strunin, L., & Hingson, R. (1987). Acquired immunodeficiency syndrome and adolescents: Knowledge, beliefs, attitudes and behaviors. *Pediatrics, 79*, 825–832.

Sussman, M. (1974). The isolated nuclear family: Fact or fiction? In M. Sussman (Ed.), *Source book in marriage and the family* (pp. 25–30). Boston: Houghton Mifflin.

Walter, H. J., Vaughn, R. D., Gladis, M. M., Ragin, D. F., Kasen, S., & Cohall, A. T. (1992). Factors associated with AIDS-risk behaviors among high school students in an AIDS epicenter. *American Journal of Public Health, 82*, 528–532.

Wechsler, H. & Thum, D. (1973). Alcohol and drug use among teenagers. In M. Chafetz (Ed.), *Proceedings of the second annual alcoholism conference* (pp. 33–46). Washington, DC: U.S. Government Printing Office.

Weisman, C. S., Plichta, S., Nathanson, C. A., Ersminger, M., & Robinson, J. C. (1991). Consistency of condom use for disease prevention among adolescent users of oral contraceptives. *Family Planning Perspectives, 23*, 71–74.

Wellman, H. M., & Gelman, S. (1992). Cognitive development: Foundational theories of core domains. *Annual Review of Psychology, 43*, 337–375.

Whitley, B. E., Jr., & Schofield, J. W. (1985–1986). Meta-analysis of research on adolescent contraceptive use. *Population and Environment, 8*, 173–203.

Yarber, W. (1986). *Pilot testing and evaluation of the CDC-sponsored STD curriculum.* Bloomington: Indiana University, Center for Health and Safety Studies.

Zabin, L. S., Hirsch, M. B., Smith, E. A., Streett, R., & Hardy, J. B. (1986). Adolescent pregnancy-prevention program: A model for research and evaluation. *Journal of Adolescent Health Care, 7*, 77–87.

11

SEXUAL COERCION

ANTHONY BIGLAN

In this chapter, I discuss the problem of male sexual coercion in the United States. A high incidence of sexual coercion has been extensively documented (e.g., Craig, 1990), and its harmful consequences are well understood (e.g., Koss, 1990). Yet there has been little research on how we might reduce the incidence of such behavior. The factors that appear to contribute to the high incidence of male sexual coercion are analyzed in this chapter, and some specific interventions that might be evaluated as methods of reducing its incidence are proposed.

THE PROBLEM OF SEXUAL COERCION

The Incidence of Sexual Coercion

A significant proportion of women in the United States are subjected to rape at least once during their lives. In a review of studies of childhood sexual assault, Siegel, Sorenson, Golding, Burnam, and Stein (1987) found that 9.8% to 51% of White females reported having experienced

This chapter was supported by grants CA38273, National Cancer Institute; and DA07389, DA09678, and DA09306, National Institute on Drug Abuse.

sexual assault. The rates were lower among Hispanic and African American respondents. Siegel and colleagues also analyzed data from the Los Angeles Epidemiologic Catchment Area Project. They found that 15.2% of Non-Hispanic White females between the ages of 18 and 39 reported childhood sexual assault, whereas 4.6% of Hispanic women in this age range reported it. Burnam et al. (1988) analyzed the lifetime prevalence of sexual assault among the women in the Los Angeles study. The prevalence was 16.7%. In their study of the events influencing Post Traumatic Stress Disorder, Resnick, Kilpatrick, Dansky, Saunders, and Best (1993) studied a sample of adult U.S. women through random digit-dialing telephone calls. They found that 12.6% of the women had been raped, and 14.3% had experienced other forms of sexual assault.

Despite the epidemiological evidence to the contrary, it is widely believed that rape is a rare event perpetrated by a deviant male who is unknown to the victim. Crime statistics tend to support this view. However, crime statistics are biased by the underreporting of rape and by the fact that women are more likely to report a rape perpetrated by a stranger (Harney & Muehlenhard, 1991; Koss, 1992).

Yet even when conservative crime statistics are used, the rate of rape is higher in the United States than in other industrialized democracies. In the United States, the rate was 37.6 per 100,000 inhabitants in 1988 (Interpol, 1988). The next highest rate was 15.7 per 100,000 for Sweden; the rate was less than 10 per 100,000 for France, England, Germany, and Japan.

Men use other forms of coercion besides rape to obtain sexual gratification. For example, Koss & Oros (1982) reported that 21% of the university women whom they surveyed had had sexual intercourse with men when they did not want to because they felt pressured by the men's continual arguments. Of the men surveyed, 15% admitted to coercing women in this way. In addition, 20% of the women reported that men had lied to them about their feelings in order to have intercourse with them, saying things that they did not mean; 19.5% of men admitted that they had done this.

Sexual coercion also includes sexual abuse of children. Knudsen (1991) reported sexual abuse incidence of 20.89 per 10,000 children based on official reports. Knudsen went on to say, however, that data from survey studies indicate that 20% to 40% of females and 5% to 10% of men have had some form of sexual contact with an adult during their childhood or adolescence. The majority of perpetrators are men.

There are other ways in which men victimize women sexually. McKinney and Maroules' (1991) review of the literature reported that between 12% and 65% of female undergraduate or graduate students had experienced at least one incident of sexual harassment. In a large survey of federal employees, 42% of women reported that they had experienced sexual harassment within the previous 2 years (McKinney & Maroules, 1991).

The Consequences of Sexual Coercion

Women who are victims of rape are more likely to have problems with anxiety and depression, to report poorer social adjustment, and to experience more sexual dysfunction (Harney & Muehlenhard, 1991) than women who have not been victimized. It is not uncommon for these difficulties to continue for 2 years after the event (Nadelson, Notman, Jackson, & Gornick, 1982).

The long-term consequences of sexual abuse of children are substantial. They include earlier and greater sexual activity, failure to use contraceptives, alcohol and drug use, (Boyer & Fine, 1992) and prostitution (Simons & Whitbeck, 1991). Sexual abuse victims are more likely to experience depression, sexual problems, and other psychological difficulties (Gold, 1986).

In addition to the psychological consequences of sexual harassment, such experiences can force women to leave jobs that they would otherwise not leave (McKinney & Maroules, 1991).

In sum, despite many changes in the roles of men and women in the United States, male sexual coercion toward women is a significant problem. Reducing the incidence of such events is an appropriate goal for both public policy-making and behavioral science research. However, we must first have a way of thinking about the problem that will lead us to effective solutions.

A THEORETICAL FRAMEWORK FOR ANALYZING AND CHANGING THE CULTURAL PRACTICES INVOLVED IN SEXUAL COERCION

A theoretical analysis that would contribute to reducing the incidence of sexual coercion must proceed at two levels. We must first have an effective analysis of the behavior of individuals. Such an analysis would tell us how sexually coercive behavior gets established among certain males. It would also indicate what types of female behavior influence male coercive and noncoercive behavior, and how such female behavior is shaped and maintained.

The second level of analysis focuses on the factors that influence the incidence of sexually coercive behavior and the prevalence of young men who are prone to such behavior. It is this level of analysis that has often been lacking. Behavioral scientists have learned a great deal about the factors that influence the behavior of individuals, but they know far less about how to translate that knowledge into effects on the incidence or prevalence of behaviors.

In this section, I will briefly sketch a theoretical analysis relevant to each of these levels. The current discussion is derived from a recent book on a contextual approach to changing problematic cultural practices (Biglan, 1995).

The Behavior of Individuals

The fundamental concept of behavior analysis is the contingency. Behavior is understood to be function of its consequences and is analyzed in terms of the contingencies between behavior and consequences. McDowell (1988, 1989) summarized the evidence in terms of the matching law, which indicates that human behavior is a function of the positive and negative consequences for a given behavior, relative to the positive and negative consequences for all other behavior. If we want to increase the probability of a particular behavior, we can do any or all of the following: increase reinforcement for the behavior, decrease its aversive consequences, decrease the reinforcement for alternative behaviors, or increase the aversive consequences for alternative behaviors.

A traditional objection to analyzing human behavior in terms of its consequences has been that human beings are not affected simply by the consequences of their behavior; their cognitions also influence their behavior. The behavior-analytic rejoinder has been that cognitive concepts may be meaningful, but they do not help us identify manipulable environmental variables that are essential for changing behavior (Hayes & Brownstein, 1986). Until recently, however, behavior analysts have lacked a clear way of analyzing what have traditionally been seen as the effects of cognition or perception.

Relational frames theory (Hayes & Hayes, 1989) provides such an analysis. According to Hayes and Hayes, at least for verbally able human beings, the reinforcing or aversive effects of many stimuli are due to the way they are linked to other stimuli through relational framing. Framing involves an arbitrarily applicable *relational* response in which two or more stimuli are related in some way. For example, a child learning names is learning to treat the thing named and the name as the same within limits defined by the context of naming. Other arbitrarily applicable relations include similarity, difference, and opposites. Hayes and Hayes (1992) reviewed data supporting the notion that such relational responding is what underlies the functional effects of many stimuli. For example, it is because verbal humans can relate a dime to the things that a dime can buy that the dime itself is reinforcing.

This formulation has direct bearing on the issue of the role of cognition in behavior. A cognitivist might argue that behavior is not a function of consequences because it can be shown that people are not as influenced by the *actual* consequences as by the *perceived* consequences. The problem with this analysis from a pragmatic standpoint is that, if one is interested in influencing behavior, one still has to explain what a cognition is and how the environment affects it. The relational frames analysis does just that. It implies that a term like *perceived consequences* refers to the values that events have as a function of their participation in relational frames. If a person perceives a particular clothing style to be highly desirable, it is because he or she relates that style to other valued stimuli (such as to others' approval or to looking good).

Thus, to understand the behavior of humans, one must understand the consequences of their behavior. However, the functions of consequences have to be understood in terms of the verbal framing that link those consequences to other events. For example, to understand a young man's tendency to ignore a young woman's stated desire that he stop fondling her, one needs to understand how the young man relates such statements to other events. Has it been suggested to him, for example, that young women always say "No," even when they want the guy to go ahead? If so, the word *no* is less likely to function as a punisher than if it has been linked to a statement such as "To continue to make sexually advances toward a women who says no, is rape." Conversely, if a young man respects the wishes of a young woman regarding his sexual behavior, it is presumably because his social environment has taught him to relate the good opinion of the young woman to other things that he values, such as the approval of his friends and family.

McDowell's (1988, 1989) analysis showed that one can change behavior by changing its consequences. The relational frames analysis supplements that analysis in a critical way. It says that one way to change consequences is to change the way consequences are framed. For example, one can make a consequence punishing (such as a women saying no) by getting the young man's close male friends to label the ignoring of such statements as stupid or cowardly.

The Analysis of Cultural Practices

I have found it useful to think about cultural practices in terms of the behavior of individuals and the actions of groups and organizations. In the case of male sexual coercion, one can specify the incidence of sexually coercive behavior or the prevalence of young men who engage in such behavior. Given the particular setting for research or practical action, one can define these variables more precisely in terms of the population of males (e.g., all undergraduate males at a particular college or all teenage males in a city) and in terms of the specific behaviors involved in coercion (e.g., rape or unwanted sexual advances). The goal of a prevention effort can then be precisely stated. For example, one might set out to reduce the incidence of unwanted sexual advances among adolescent males in a small community.

An effective analysis of the factors influencing the incidence or prevalence of male sexual coercion must include an analysis of the actions of groups and organizations. This is because, in a complex social system, many of the contingencies for individual behavior are influenced by groups and formal organizations. For example, families, schools, churches, and social service agencies influence what young men learn about appropriate and inappropriate behavior toward young women.

The actions of groups and organizations can be conceptualized in terms of one or more of the following four variables: (a) the probability of an action (e.g., a school adopts a policy regarding sexual harassment among students); (b) the frequency of an action (e.g., the frequency with which a newspaper publishes articles favorable to policies that might reduce sexually coercive behavior); (c) the incidence of an action (e.g., the number of times churches in a community discuss inappropriate sexual advances with their parishioners); and (d) the prevalence of an action (e.g., the proportion of police forces in a state that have adopted appropriate procedures for investigating reports of rape).

As behavioral scientists identify institutional practices that affect individual behavior, they will need to analyze the costs and benefits to the organizations for these practices (Biglan, 1995). It will be necessary to increase the benefits to the organization for practices that would discourage sexual coercion and increase the costs of alternative practices. In analyzing costs and benefits for organizations, we must give special consideration to how any changes in practices will affect the reinforcing and punishing consequences for those with power to control the organizations' selection of practices (Biglan, 1995).

I have applied this general framework to the analysis of the context influencing the incidence of sexual coercion (Biglan, 1995). I will summarize that analysis here. Then I will sketch the kinds of interventions that might affect the incidence of male sexual coercion. In doing so, I will pay particular attention to how our society socializes young men to behave toward women. The analysis goes beyond the socialization of men who end up being convicted of rape. As the evidence already cited indicates, the incidence of sexual coercion is sufficiently high, that we must assume that we are socializing a much larger proportion of young men in ways that make them prone to be sexually coercive.

The Context for Male Sexual Coercion

Male Dominance

Sexual coercion can be seen as one facet of a more general tendency for men to dominate women. Male domination has been documented in most civilizations throughout history, although there is evidence suggesting that it was less common among prestate hunter-gatherer societies. Harris (1989) argued that male dominance developed when hunter-gatherer societies outstripped the carrying capacity of their environments. The population pressure that resulted gave an advantage to groups that developed fierce warriors. These groups could wrest control of hunting and gathering areas from other groups. The social system that came with warfare involved increased status and power for men because their generally larger musculature advantaged them in the warfare of those days. Harris argued that the practices of female infanticide and traumatic abortion also developed among these groups. By controlling the number of females, the number of births and thus the population could be controlled. It seems unlikely that groups could have adopted these practices without subordinating women because if women had equal power, they presumably would have prevented them from doing so.

Male dominance has by no means been uniform. It has varied as a function of the advantages it conferred to the group. For example, in areas where it was necessary to plow the fields with oxen, men clearly have been more dominant. In agricultural societies where male strength did not increase productivity—such as in parts of Africa—there has been less male dominance.

Harris (1989, 1974) suggested that, to a great extent, the continued dominance of men in recent centuries has resulted from their initial advantages. For example, men came to dominate trade simply because their use of horses and oxen in agriculture gave them the skills and equipment needed for transportation of goods.

In this context, sexual coercion can be seen as simply one of the ways that males have used their power over women. Women had relatively little power to resist male sexual coercion. Police officers and governmental authorities were all men, as were the heads of families and religious organizations. Effective opposition to sexual coercion required that at least some men take the side of the woman who was being coerced.

There have unquestionably been changes in women's status in recent years. Here, too, the consequences of given practices have influenced their prevalence. Harris (1989) suggested that women's status began to change with the advent of industrialization. It was advantageous for couples who lived on farms to have many children because the children could engage in productive labor by the age of 5 or 6. However, in urban, industrial settings the ratio of reinforcing to aversive consequences for having children is less favorable. Children cost more to raise in these settings and are less likely to contribute to the family's well-being. As the value of children diminished, the number of children per family also diminished. As families had fewer children, the possibilities for women working outside the home increased. More recently, as service sector jobs have increased and much work has come to be based on technology, the proportion of jobs that require physical brawn has diminished. Even in warfare, the decisive weapons rely more on technology than on strength.

As job opportunities for women have expanded, it has become less necessary economically for women to put up with men who are abusive or uncaring. The cost–benefit ratio for living with a man may not have gotten any worse for a woman, but the possibilities for a reinforcing life without one have gotten better. Thus, we have seen "the break up of the family." This seems due, in part, to the choices that women are making. A smaller proportion of women are getting married, and those that do are divorcing with greater frequency (Marshall, 1991).

From this perspective, it might appear that much of the remaining male dominance is vestigial, in the sense that it does not derive from any fundamental productive advantage for society. But much political and social power remains in men's hands. In particular, reform of the laws that disadvantage women is not yet complete in the United States.

As women's economic power grows, their political power will grow with it. However, there is no guarantee that laws and other practices that promote practices such as male sexual coercion will wither. Witness women such as Phyllis Schlafly, who has achieved fame through activities that have undermined women's well-being (Faludi, 1991). If we are going to end male sexual coercion, we shall have to bring about changes in the specific practices that maintain the high prevalence of such behavior.

The Socialization of Boys and Girls

Perhaps the key practices fostering male sexual coercion involve the socialization of boys and girls, particularly as it relates to what we teach children about interacting with persons of the opposite sex. Maccoby (1990) provided a comprehensive review of the evidence on this aspect of our socialization practices. According to Maccoby, boys and girls tend to be raised separately, and they develop strong preferences for playing with members of their own gender. Boys tend to play competitive, rough-and-tumble games, in which threatening, boasting, fighting, and giving commands are normative. Girls tend to play in small groups or dyads. Their games involve less conflict and more cooperation. They interrupt each other less frequently and are more likely to develop intimate friendships.

The different interactive styles persist in adolescence. However, by adolescence, boys and girls are beginning to interact with each other. Girls are more likely to listen and to show interest in another person, whereas boys are more likely to interrupt, to brag, and to compete. So when boy meets girl, the interactions are highly reinforcing for the boys, but less so for the girls.

Such interactive styles may contribute to the level of sexual coercion in our society. Some boys are not socialized to be sensitive to the feelings of others. Some of these boys will not care if their sexual advances are unwanted. Some girls are socialized to be highly motivated to please and are unlikely to be assertive. Some of these girls will not make their concerns about boys' behavior clear to the boys.

We also need to consider how boys and girls are taught to think about the concepts of gender. Bem (1993) reviewed how both boys and girls come to see the world through what she called the *lenses of gender*, that is, pervasive belief systems in which maleness seems to be the norm and in which distinctions are made between male and female when none are needed. These belief systems also make male–female differences seem biologically rather than culturally based.

With respect to sexual coercion, there are specific beliefs that appear to make coercion seem appropriate. For example, Muehlenhard & Falcon (1990) found that young men who subscribed to traditional beliefs, such as "a wife should never contradict her husband in public," were more likely to admit, on an anonymous questionnaire, that they had raped a woman. Similarly, men who subscribed to beliefs that legitimated sexual dominance such as "You don't ASK a girl to screw you, you TELL them to screw you," were more likely to report having obtained sex with women by lying, getting them drunk, or raping them than those who did not subscribe to such beliefs. There are numerous other studies that have shown that men who hold traditional views about the role of women or who view male–female relationships as adversarial are more likely to be sexually coercive (e.g., Craig, 1990).

Clearly, not all young men are socialized to hold these beliefs. However, this might be a good point to remind the reader that sexually coercive acts are not committed simply by a small group of extremely deviant men. Given the rates of such behavior that have been reported by college women (Koss, 1992), it appears that a significant minority of otherwise normal men are sufficiently insensitive to women's feelings (Hall, 1987) and sufficiently confident in their beliefs that they are willing to force or deceive women to obtain sex. Reducing the prevalence of men with such orientations would appear to be an appropriate goal for our society.

Alternative Socialization Practices

Are there alternative practices that might make the prospects for boy–girl relationships more favorable? It seems appropriate to try to teach young men to be less aggressive and young women to be more assertive. It appears appropriate to foster cross–gender interactions throughout childhood. And, it appears necessary to teach young men and young women what is appropriate and inappropriate social and sexual behavior.

It must be admitted, however, that empirical evidence on the effects of such alternative ways of socializing boys and girls is lacking.

Socializing Institutions

Male and female socialization occurs as a result of the actions of many groups and organizations. The most important would appear to be families, schools, the media, and sports. Families undoubtedly play a key role in gender role socialization, yet there is surprisingly little research that pinpoints how the just-described gender differences in social behavior arise or are maintained. Presumably, parents could influence boys and girls to play together more; they could also influence boys to be less aggressive and more considerate of others' feelings and girls to be more assertive. Yet, I am unaware of any studies that have investigated how parents might influence such behaviors. None of the evaluated parent-training programs that I am aware of attempt to inform parents about the possible value of changing gender role behavior. Apparently, our culture views parenting practices and even parent training through the lenses of gender (Bem, 1993); obvious gender differences in behavior are simply accepted as normal.

School is the primary place where boys' and girls' social behavior is shaped. The correlational research already cited has indicated that boys and girls are learning distinctly different social behaviors and that those behaviors contribute to difficulties between the sexes when boys and girls begin to interact in adolescence. Yet, little is known about how schools might change their socialization practices. If schools are the major training ground for gender role socialization, it would seem imperative that we learn how school practices might prevent deleterious outcomes of the sort already noted.

There is, as well, very little research on how media depictions of gender role behavior influence boys' and girls' social behavior. There is evidence indicating that the media influence sexually coercive behavior. Most of the research has focused on pornography. Depictions of both sexual and nonsexual aggressive behavior have been shown to increase men's aggressive behavior toward women (Donnerstein, 1984). Some findings have suggested that extensive exposure to nonaggressive pornography leads both men and women to be more accepting of rape (Zillman & Bryant, 1984).

Moreover, there is evidence both that increases in the availability of pornography are correlated with increasing rates of rape and that the rate of sales of pornography in specific localities is correlated with the rate of rape (Murrin & Laws, 1990).

Much less is known, however, about the degree to which the popular entertainment media influence young men's attitudes and behavior toward women. The evidence just cited would suggest that the high levels of aggression in popular movies and television help to maintain a high incidence of aggressive behavior toward women, but more precise study of this issue is needed. Depictions of "good" or "successful" women as subservient (e.g., Faludi, 1991) are commonplace. Research is needed on whether such depictions influence women to be less assertive and influence men to expect women to be subservient.

Finally, sports should be considered. Involvement in college athletics is a predictor of young men's sexual coercion (Koss & Gaines, 1993). Why would this be so? There are a number of interconnected possibilities. Sports support aggressive social behavior. They may increase young men's segregation from young women. And, they may provide a social setting in which sexually coercive beliefs, attitudes, and behaviors are reinforced.

Of course a relatively small proportion of young men participate in organized sports. It is the effect of sports on young men who are not athletes that needs to be examined. Consider the model that successful athletes provide for the young sports fan. The successful athlete is tough, often angry, and typically successful with women. To what extent do they influence young men to be aggressive toward women?

In considering the effect of institutions such as schools, media, and sports, we need to examine not only their direct effect on the behavior of young men and young women, but also their effects on the practices of other organizations in society. If the media depict male dominance and sexual coercion in positive ways, it is less likely that other organizations will take steps to reduce male sexual coercion. If, however, the popular entertainment media depicted male sexual coercion as (a) frequent, (b) problematic, and (c) something to be opposed, it seems likely that a public climate far more favorable to business organizations preventing sexual harassment would exist.

A Framework for Guiding Efforts to Change Cultural Practices

In my book, *Changing Cultural Practices: A Contextualist Framework for Intervention* (Biglan, 1995), I articulate a theoretical framework that might guide efforts to change cultural practices. Despite the many weaknesses in our current knowledge base, it is worthwhile to try to specify the generic features of organized efforts to change cultural practices. Such a framework might help to organize empirical research and to provide a plausible argument for societies to devote resources to conducting such research.

One chapter of my book addresses how the framework might be applied to changing the cultural practices involved in male dominance, one facet of which is sexual coercion. Here I will summarize what might be done about sexual coercion within such a framework.

Specification of the Targeted Practice

The first step in changing cultural practices is specifying the particular events to be changed. In the case of sexual coercion, one might seek to reduce the incidence of sexually coercive behavior. For example, one might specify the incidence of sexually coercive behavior per week or month on a college campus, among the students at a high school, or in an entire community.

Of course this raises issues about the precise definition of sexual coercion as well as about its measurement. The literature suggests that women are more likely to label an interaction as sexually coercive than are men, and the precise events leading to these labels are unclear. One approach would be to say that if a woman feels she was coerced, then she was coerced. This definition might be workable if the purpose were simply to measure—say, through repeated anonymous surveys—the incidence of coercion for the purpose of reducing it. However, such a definition would be highly problematic if it were used in the legal system, because it would leave men open to unfair charges.

Another approach might be to define specific types of coercion, as Koss and her colleagues did (Koss, Gidycz, & Wisniewski, 1987). The events to be classified as coercive might include (a) the use of force or threats of force to obtain sexual contact (including intercourse and fondling); (b) the use of emotional responding, such as anger or depression, to influence a woman to have sexual contact; and (c) the use of deceit to obtain sexual contact. The first of these is essentially the legal definition of rape. The other two categories involve behaviors that are not—and should not be—illegal. Imagine the problems that making them illegal would create. Yet, they are types of behavior that society would do well to discourage—at least that is what most women would presumably think. Discouraging the use of emotional coercion could also help to prevent some cases of rape.

How might sexual coercion be measured? The Sexual Experiences Scale (Koss et al., 1987) provides a useful measure suitable for obtaining reports from both men and women. If one were interested in reducing the incidence of sexual coercion, one could administer the instrument repeatedly to samples of women and men in a defined population. For example, suppose one was trying to evaluate the effects of a campaign to reduce sexual coercion on a college campus. One might assess representative samples of men and women each quarter to examine whether reported incidence changed with the introduction of the campaign. If comparable data from a campus that did not receive the intervention were available, that data would provide a control for possible changes in incidence as a function of time of year and other history or maturation effects.

A Contextual Analysis of Targeted, Supportive, and Opposing Practices

The next step in changing cultural practices is a contextual analysis of the targeted practice and of the practices that support or oppose the targeted practice. We seek to understand the reinforcing and aversive consequences of the practice for those who engage in it. Such an analysis would enable us to examine the ways in which practices of groups and organizations support or oppose a targeted practice by affecting its consequences. One must, in turn, understand how the practices of groups or organizations are influenced by the costs and benefits to the group or organization.

In the case of sexual coercion, much of this analysis already has been sketched out in this chapter. For the individual male, sexually coercive behavior is presumably reinforced by immediate sexual consequences. It may also be reinforced by social approval by other males and by feelings of conquest, success, and the like. Of course, men vary in the degree to which they find coerciveness in the context of sexual encounters reinforcing. Presumably this is a function of their history. If sexual coercion has been linked to other positive events—for example, depicted in the media in positive ways—it may be more reinforcing. If prior sexual behavior has involved sexual reinforcement associated with sexual coercion or fantasies of sexual coercion, it may be more reinforcing. Conversely, to the extent that such behavior has been linked to disapproval and has been punished or gone unreinforced, its reinforcing value should be diminished.

Sexual coercion might be punished by women's objections, rejection, or prosecution. However, in those situations in which women are unlikely to react aversively, these consequences are minimized. Thus, one practice for opposing sexual coercion would be a high prevalence of women who are skilled in punishing (or at least not reinforcing) men's coercive behavior.

Group and institutional practices that might oppose sexually coercive behavior could include increased parental socialization of boys and girls about these issues, law enforcement procedures that minimize the aversiveness of reporting sexually coercion and maximize the likelihood that illegal forms of coercion will be prosecuted, as well as effective programs in schools. The school programs might include validated curricula designed to discourage sexual coercion, discipline procedures that detect and punish instances of sexual harassment, and assertiveness training for young women.

The media might be induced to cover the problem of sexual coercion more extensively and in a way that encourages its prevention. Sports programs for men might be used as a credible channel through which to influence men's attitudes and behavior.

In short, reducing the incidence of sexually coercive behavior involves reducing its reinforcement, increasing its aversive consequences, or both by (a) linking it to aversive stimuli (e.g., calling it wrong), (b) ensuring that it is not reinforced (e.g., by increasing the prevalence of girls who see to it that it is not reinforced), and (c) ensuring that it is punished. Changing the distribution of these contingencies for the population of men will, in turn, require that we change the practices of women and of key institutions, including schools, families, law enforcement, workplaces, and the media.

Achieving these changes will require research at two levels. First, work is needed at the level of the individual to identify programs that affect the behavior of men and women. For example, curricular and discipline practices that might reduce the incidence of sexual harassment and coercion among middle school, high school, and college students have yet to be validated. We do not yet know precisely what parents might do to reduce the risk that their sons will be coercive or that their daughters will be susceptible to sexual coercion. Media campaigns that might affect male and female behavior relevant to this problem have yet to be developed and evaluated.

Second, research will be needed on how we can influence groups and organizations to adopt programs that are likely to contribute to lowering the incidence of sexual coercion. For example, Koss & Harvey (1991) described appropriate practices for assisting rape victims and investigating rapes. Research is needed on how law enforcement and judicial agencies can be influenced to adopt and maintain these practices.

In the following section, I concentrate on the second of these issues because research on the first is occurring (albeit at a lower rate than is needed). The question, then, is how to influence organizations to adopt programs and policies that might lower the incidence of sexual coercion.

A SKETCH OF THE COMMUNITY INTERVENTION RESEARCH THAT MIGHT BE DONE ON REDUCING THE INCIDENCE OF COERCIVE SEXUAL BEHAVIOR

It is not too early to begin experimental work on community interventions to reduce the incidence of sexually coercive behavior. Although more knowledge is needed about the contextual factors influencing such behavior and the organizational programs that might influence it, there is enough known that we can specify many ways in which communities could reduce the incidence of such behavior. Moreover, it may be that a comprehensive communitywide effort to address this problem would have effects that single programs in individual organizations would not have. For example, a school-based program to influence young men's and young women's behavior might be more effective if it occurred in the context of media activities to discourage such behavior. Finally, research is needed on community-level variables, including how to influence community organizations such as police and schools to adopt policies that would contribute to lowering the incidence of sexually coercive behavior.

An Experimental Design

One of the many obstacles to developing community interventions is the lack of efficient strategies for evaluating them. The "gold standard" in experimental research is, of course, the randomized control trial or group design experiment. An intervention is considered useful if it has been shown to be more effective than either no intervention or a comparison intervention when both have been administered to multiple cases. In the case of community interventions, this process requires multiple communities. The statistical power requirements for such a design are no less demanding than if the cases consisted of individual participants; many cases are required if an effect is to be detected. For example, in the case of the National Cancer Institute's evaluation of a community intervention to reduce the prevalence of adult smoking, 11 pairs of communities were believed to be required (Lichtenstein, Nettekoven, & Ockene, 1991).

The problem, of course, is that such experiments are costly. Given the paucity of our knowledge of sexual coercion, how can we justify the commitment of huge sums of money that would be needed to develop and test a community intervention in multiple communities?

This problem appears to have prompted two different types of practices among those who are concerned with solving important social problems. One has been for community interventionists to simply not apply the same standards to evaluating their interventions as do interventionists working with clinical interventions. Thus, interventions occur in communities, but they tend to be unique to the individual community; the issue of their replicability across communities is simply not raised. The other practice is to continue to do research with individual participants, even though the stated goal is to benefit whole communities.

Behavior analytic experimental methods offer a third way: repeated time-series experimentation (Barlow, Hayes, & Nelson, 1984; Sidman, 1960). In particular, this research group has found multiple baseline designs across communities to be helpful in developing and evaluating community interventions.

In the multiple baseline design, repeated measures are obtained from a number of cases, and an intervention is introduced or brought to bear on one case. Evidence that the intervention made a difference is indicated by changes in the level or slope of the time series in which the intervention is introduced. The belief that the intervention, and not some other factor, led to the effect is strengthened to the extent that the level and slope of the time series in the other cases remains unchanged.

Figure 1 illustrates the use of a multiple baseline design across to evaluate an intervention to reduce illegal sales of tobacco to young people in a pair of small Oregon communities (Biglan, Ary, Duncan, Black, & Smolkowski, 1995). Following three baseline assessments of illegal sales, the intervention was introduced in one community, while baseline assessments continued in the second community. Evidence of the effectiveness of the intervention came from the changes in the level of sales that occurred in each community when the intervention was introduced.

Such designs have several advantages for community intervention research. First, they are less costly than group designs. Second, they force the researcher to concentrate on achieving a big effect. This feature might seem problematic. However, if our interest is in preventing important problems in society, are we not looking for big effects? Ironically, sole reliance on group designs allows us to be satisfied with small effects—so long as there are enough cases to allow the result to be statistically significant.

The repeated measurements used in these designs provide a valuable management tool. When the process or event of interest is repeatedly assessed, it provides feedback about the success or failure of the efforts. This information motivates those working on the project to take every step possible to achieve an effect, and it guides the researcher to course corrections when the hoped-for results are not forthcoming.

Finally, these designs may be more appropriate than group designs for developing our understanding of the factors that influence practices in communities. As behavior analysts often have noted (e.g., Sidman, 1960), if one is seeking knowledge about the variables that influence a particular phenomenon, this information is best sought by manipulating the independent variable for an individual case and examining whether the expected influence on the dependent variable occurs. Group designs are useful for determining whether such effects are replicable, but they are an inefficient way for discovering what variables are influential.

An experimental design that might be used to evaluate a community intervention designed to reduce the incidence of coercive sexual behavior is illustrated in Figure 2. Imagine that three small communities (or three college campuses) are participating in the study. In each community, quarterly data could be obtained from young women regarding the frequency with which they had experienced various forms of sexual coercion in the prior 3 months. Following five baseline assessments in all communities, the

Sherwood

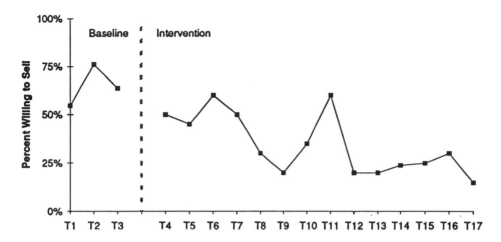

Hood River

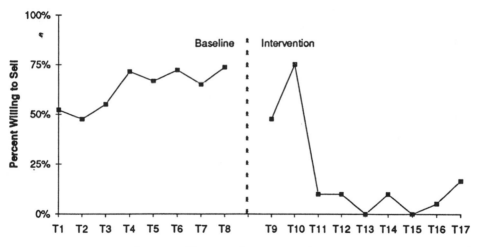

Figure 1. Proportion of stores willing to sell tobacco in Sherwood and Hood River. From A. Biglan, The experimental evaluation of anti-tobacco media campaigns, *Tobacco Control.* 1995 BMJ Publishing Group. Reprinted with permission.

intervention could be implemented in the first community, while baseline assessments continued in the other two communities.

A Modular Strategy for Intervention

The research group at Oregon Research Institute has developed a modular strategy for developing and implementing community interventions.

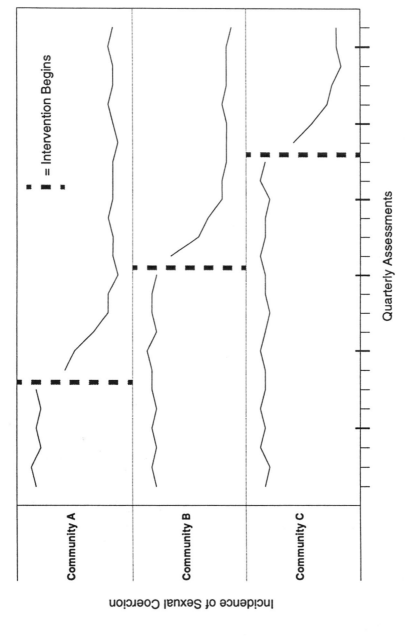

Figure 2. A multiple baseline design to evaluate the effects of a community intervention to reduce male sexual coercion (with fictitious data).

A module is a written description of a set of activities designed to influence one or more of the risk factors for a problematic cultural practice. For example, in a community intervention to prevent adolescent tobacco use (Biglan et al., 1995), my colleagues and I developed modules for (a) media advocacy about adolescent tobacco use, (b) youth antitobacco activities, (c) family communications about tobacco, (d) reducing illegal sales of tobacco to young people, and (e) policies regarding minors in possession of tobacco.

The modular strategy has two advantages in community intervention research. First, it provides a structured set of activities that are targeted at a known risk factor. Communities should not have to develop interventions from scratch, and the modules make it unnecessary for them to do so. At the same time, most modules have a menu of possible activities, thus allowing community members either to choose activities from among the menu choices or to develop additional activities. For example, our youth antitobacco module lists numerous activities that young people can engage in to influence other young people not to use tobacco. As the modules were implemented in different communities, young people and community coordinators added to the list.

The second advantage of using modules is that they permit the experimental evaluation of the effects of the specific intervention component on a particular risk factor. The experimental evaluation of our module on illegal tobacco sales is described above.

In the remainder of this section, I outline the kinds of modules that might be developed and evaluated for a community intervention on sexual coercion.

Community Organizing

Perhaps the pivotal issue in reducing the incidence of sexual coercion is to mobilize the leadership of communities. Men disproportionately represent the powerful and influential people in most communities. It is doubtful that many of them are currently engaging in sexual coercion. It is likely that few community leaders view sexual coercion as an important problem. The literature suggests that community leaders underestimate its incidence, are unaware of its consequences for women, and assume that it results from a few deviant males. The leaders of most communities probably do little to directly support sexually coercive behavior, but because they have not organized to combat it, the social practices that encourage it continue to survive. Thus, the goal of community organizing is to influence the influential people in the community to take steps to change the social practices that allow sexual coercion to occur.

The first step in community organizing is community analysis (Haglund, Weisbrod, & Bracht, 1990). The organizations in the community whose practices must be changed and the persons and organizations with the power to bring about these changes must be identified. Based on the contextual analysis already presented, it is clear that the organizations whose practices need to be targeted include: schools, local government, entertainment and advertising media, news media, sports teams and leagues, churches, and health care providers. I have enumerated elsewhere the practices of each type of organization that need to be increased or decreased if sexual coercion is going to be reduced (Biglan, 1995).

For each of these organizations, one must analyze the costs and benefits that would result if targeted changes in practices occurred. For example, if schools adopt programs to discourage sexual coercion, will parents object or be supportive? Will the adoption of such programs affect tax support for schools?

The consequences can be analyzed at both the level of the individuals involved in these decisions and at the level of the outcomes affecting the organizations (Glenn, 1988). For example, one might consider what the consequences would be for a clergyman to actively support anticoercion programs. One might also consider the effects on the church if it got involved. Would it lose or gain parishioners? Would it enhance its influence in the community?

In analyzing the contingencies for individuals, one is looking for consequences that might be mobilized to influence individuals to support a change effort. A city council member who is interested in running for mayor will calculate whether to get involved in terms of the change effort's impact on his or her electoral prospects. A male store owner may be influenced to join the effort if he is persuaded that his involvement will increase women's patronage at his store. Many individuals may be motivated to get involved because of personal experience with rape or other forms of sexual coercion.

A community analysis is based primarily on interviews with community leaders in each sector of the community (described previously). By interviewing a small sample (Haglund et al., 1990, recommended 50 to 100 interviews in small communities), one can get information about the likely consequences for both individuals and organizations. One can also identify those individuals who have the most power to influence the practices of particular organizations.

A community analysis consists of a breakdown of the organizational practices to be changed and the contingencies for organizations and community leaders that would be affected by these changes. It should specify the individuals who are most likely to be supportive of the hoped-for changes, and it should clarify kinds of consequences that might influence other community influentials to support the effort.

The second step of community organizing is to assemble a panel of influential individuals who represent or are linked to the key organizations of the community (Bracht & Gleason, 1990). The organizations to be involved would include not only those whose practices need to be influenced, but also the organizations that have the power to influence the targeted organizations. For example, one would want not only represented sports leagues but also business interests that help to fund the sport leagues.

The purpose of the panel would be to lead the change effort. The panel would review the analysis of the organizations whose practices need to be addressed and would revise the analysis in light of the members' own understanding of those practices. Experts would then suggest steps that might be taken to bring about targeted changes. Based on these suggestions and their own ideas, the panel would formulate a plan for working toward these changes.

In sum, if one can identify a group of influential community members who are willing to commit their time and their prestige to such a change effort, significant change may be possible. The composition of this group is critical. One would have little trouble getting social service and women's advocacy groups behind such an effort. If long-standing traditional practices of male and female socialization and interpersonal behavior are going to be changed, however, people must be brought into the effort who have never been involved with such issues. This requires an effective advocacy effort.

Advocacy

An effective advocacy effort requires that sexual coercion be articulated as a problem. It also requires an explanation of how a community can deal with the problem. The initial audience for these messages will be the community leaders themselves. Once leaders have been mobilized, advocacy can begin to focus on other groups that need to be influenced about the issue, such as law enforcement officials.

The messages designed to generate support for change must be evaluated. For many members of the target audiences, the case for doing something about sexual coercion probably can be made by informing them about its incidence and its costly consequences. However, one cannot simply assume that such a message will work for all audiences. Messages must be developed based on data about what themes are most persuasive with each target audience. There are a number of useful guides to the development of effective messages (e.g., McGuire, 1981, 1985; Worden et al., 1988), though none have been written specifically for advocating changes in sexual coercion.

Even the most compelling messages will do little good if they do not reach people. In small communities, the leading edge of advocacy will be personal contacts and group presentations to community leaders. However, to maintain the issue of sexual coercion as a priority in the community and to influence the views and behavior of a wider audience, it is necessary to get the issue covered by news media. Wallack, Dorfman, Jernigan, and Themba (1993) provided a very useful description of media advocacy activities, including those designed to ensure that an issue is covered in the media.

Changing the Consequences for Targeted Organizations

I have already sketched the kinds of organizational practices that would need to be influenced if male sexual coerciveness is going to be discouraged. Procedures are needed for bringing about changes in such organizational practices.

The general principles that might guide such effort are based on the theory that an organization's practices are a function of the costs and benefits of those. If we want an organization to adopt a new practice, we must increase the benefits to that organization for doing so and decrease the costs. Additionally, we will probably need to change the cost–benefit ratio for existing practices that compete with the practice we are trying to encourage.

We can increase the benefits for an advocated practice in several ways. First, we can mobilize social reinforcement for agency representatives who adopt or propose to adopt the new practice. The police chief who begins a review of how rape investigations are handled will be influenced by the extent to which social approval is forthcoming. The school board member who advocates reviewing the discipline procedures for detecting and dealing with sexually harassing behavior will be more likely to keep at the issue if others make their approval of his or her actions known.

How does one mobilize social reinforcement? If you have an organized group working for change, the members of it can be prompted to express their gratitude to people who bring about change in target organizations. Your group can seek publicity for those who bring about change. This will prompt others to approve of their actions.

We can also publicly recognize the efforts of organizations and agencies that take appropriate action. Most businesses, as well as governmental and civic organizations, benefit from public recognition. By seeking favorable news coverage for their efforts and commending them in public forums, we can help organizations receive such recognition. For example, if the police department adopts better rape victim assistance procedures, the community panel that has been established to work toward change can commend these efforts at city council meetings and at news conferences.

A third way to increase the benefit for improved practices is to provide funding for them. Agencies and organizations will be more likely to adopt new practices if they have the funds to do so. Schools' adoption of curricula and discipline procedures will be facilitated if there are funds available to train teachers, for example.

An attempt can be made to decrease the costs for organizations adopting practices that discourage sexually coercive behavior. One way to do this is through training. One of the costs of adopting a new practice is simply that those who might adopt it lack the necessary skills. For example, trying to encourage the news media to cover this issue more frequently and with a greater emphasis on the need for programs to prevent sexual coercion requires providing the media with information that can be used in their stories. Providing this information reduces the costs to news organizations of doing stories of this sort.

Another way to reduce costs to organizations is to help them reduce criticism. Most organizations are adverse to public criticism. Agency administrators who contemplate adopting programs or procedures to discourage sexually coercive behavior may be doing so because they have been criticized for past inactions. In this case, the community panel can readily assist the agency administrators by guiding them to adopt better practices and vouching for their efforts once they occur. On the other hand, many agency heads will hesitate to adopt such practices because they fear criticism for doing so. For example, school officials may worry that fundamentalist groups will criticize them if they adopt programs that challenge traditional conceptions of men's and women's roles. The community panel must help to minimize or overcome such criticism.

These suggestions are, of course, speculative. To my knowledge, there have been no experimental evaluations of the ways in which a group seeking changes in the practices of an organization might mobilize beneficial consequences or reduce costs for the practice to be adopted. Such research would be of great benefit in teaching us how to bring about changes in diverse practices in business, civic, and governmental organizations.

Modifying any of these contingencies requires that the group seeking change be successful in organizing community support for change among community leaders and in advocating for change among a large segment of the community.

Family Communications About Sexual Coercion

It may be possible to decrease the incidence of sexually coercive behavior among young people by teaching parents to communicate with their children about sexual coercion issues. Parental communication about sexual matters can influence children's sexual behavior (Newcomer & Udry, 1985). Unfortunately, parents seldom talk to their children about sex. Research is needed to evaluate whether parents can be prompted to talk to their children about sexual coercion. For example, it might be possible to encourage parents to talk to their daughters about what constitutes sexual coercion and how they should deal with it. And, it might be possible to prompt parents of boys to clearly define appropriate sexual behavior.

Obviously a good deal of research would be required for this. Messages would need to be designed for young men and young women that might be effective for parents to use. And, messages would need to be designed for parents that would persuade them to talk to their children.

There is also the question of how to reach significant numbers of parents. One method that my colleagues and I have found effective for prompting parent–child interactions about specific topics involves having students interview or quiz their parents about the topic. A quiz about tobacco use that middle school students gave to their parents led to significant increases in the proportion of parents who said that they had talked to their children about tobacco use (Biglan et al., in press). In a series of pilot studies, we found that the majority of families of middle school students could be influenced to talk about what students are doing in school and with their friends. These interactions constitute parental monitoring of the child's behavior—a parenting practice that has repeatedly been shown to be important in preventing the development of adolescent problem behavior (Ary et al., 1995).

Thus, it may be possible to craft a school-prompted interaction between parents and students that is designed to get parents to communicate their attitudes and expectations about their sons' and daughters' behavior relevant to sexual coercion.

Media By and For Youth

Given the importance of the peer group in influencing adolescent social behavior (e.g., Biglan, Metzler, & Ary, 1994), it could be useful if adolescents themselves communicated their opposition to such behavior.

In our work on adolescent tobacco use, we have been successful at prompting a good deal of antitobacco communication among young people. Our youth antitobacco module specifies a long list of activities that the young people in our intervention communities have developed and implemented. These activities include distributing T-shirts, doing radio spots and programs, quizzing young people about tobacco and rewarding them for correct answers, distributing posters throughout the community, and having older students perform skits for younger students (Biglan et al., in press).

It seems appropriate to develop and evaluate similar activities designed to influence how young men and women behave in their sexual encounters. Such efforts could be developed and experimentally evaluated in both high school and college settings.

INFLUENCING THE RESEARCH AGENDA

Most of the intervention components suggested here have not been evaluated. They are offered only as an outline of a research agenda that might bring about reductions in the incidence of sexually coercive behavior. If research along these lines is going to occur, however, it will be because those who favor such research have figured out how to influence relevant funding institutions to pay for it.

Research is, itself, a set of cultural practices. If we are going to influence the nation to allocate the money needed to develop effective deterrents to sexual coercion, we will have to influence specific funding agencies. This will require that we do the kind of advocacy with legislators and agencies that has been sketched in this chapter.

Such activities may not seem like the kinds of things that behavioral scientists have traditionally done. But, a thorough behavioral analysis of a culture examines all of the practices relevant to a problem, and allocating funds for research is a practice that is pivotal to bringing about changes in sexual coercion.

REFERENCES

Ary, D. V., Duncan, T. E., Biglan, A., Metzler, C. W., Noell, J. W., & Smolkowski, K. (1995). A social context model of adolescent problem behavior. Manuscript submitted for publication.

Barlow, D. H., Hayes, S. C., & Nelson, R. O. (1984). The scientist practitioner: Research and accountability in clinical and educational settings. New York: Pergamon Press.

Bem, S. L. (1993). The lenses of gender. New Haven: Yale University Press.

Biglan, A. (1995). Changing cultural practices: A contextualist framework for intervention research. Reno, NV: Context Press.

Biglan, A., Ary, D., Duncan, T., Black, C., & Smolkowski, K. (1995). A randomized control trial of a community intervention to prevent adolescent tobacco use. Manuscript submitted for publication.

Biglan, A., Ary, D., Henderson, J., Humphreys, D., Smolkowski, K., Black, C., Yudelson, H., James, L., Hood, D., Wright, Z., Koehn, V., & Levings, D. (in press). Experimental evaluation of a modular approach to mobilizing antitobacco influences of peers and parents. American Journal of Community Psychology.

Biglan, A., Metzler, C. W., & Ary, D. A. (1994). Increasing the prevalence of successful children: The case for community intervention research. The Behavior Analyst, 17, 331–335.

Boyer, D., & Fine, D. (1992). Sexual abuse as a factor in adolescent pregnancy and child maltreatment. *Family Planning Perspectives*, *24*, 4–12.

Bracht, N., & Gleason, J. (1990). Strategies and structures for citizen partnerships. In N. Bracht (Ed.), *Health promotion at the community level* (pp. 109–124). Newbury Park, CA: Sage.

Burnam, M. A., Stein, J. A., Golding, J. M., Siegel, J. M., Sorenson, S. B., Forsythe, A. B., & Telles, C. A. (1988). Sexual assault and mental disorders in a community population. *Journal of Consulting & Clinical Psychology 56*, 843–860.

Craig, M. E. (1990). Coercive sexuality in dating relationships: A situational model. *Clinical Psychology Review*, *10*, 395–423.

Donnerstein, E. (1984). Pornography: Its effect on violence against women. In N. M. Malamuth & E. Donnerstein (Eds.), *Pornography and sexual aggression* (pp. 53–82). Orlando, FL: Academic Press.

Faludi, S. (1991). *Backlash: The undeclared war against American women*. New York: Doubleday.

Glenn, S. S. (1988). Contingencies and metacontingencies: Toward a synthesis of behavior analysis and cultural materialism. *The Behavior Analyst*, *11*, 161–180.

Gold, E. R. (1986) Long-term effects of sexual victimization in childhood: An attributional approach. *Journal of Consulting and Clinical Psychology*, *54*, 471–475.

Haglund, B., Weisbrod, R. R., & Bracht, N. (1990). Assessing the community: Its services, needs, leadership, and readiness. In N. Bracht (Ed.), *Health promotion at the community level* (pp. 91–108). Newbury Park, CA: Sage.

Hall, J. A. (1987). On explaining gender differences: The case for nonverbal communication. In P. Shaver & C. Hendrick (Eds.), *Sex and gender* (pp. 177–200). Newbury Park, CA: Sage.

Harris, M. (1974). *Cows, pigs, wars, witches: The riddles of culture*. New York: Random House.

Harris, M. (1989). *Our kind*. New York: Harper & Row.

Harney, P. A., & Muehlenhard, C. L. (1991). Rape. In E. Grauerholz & M. A. Koralweski (Eds.), *Sexual Coercion: A sourcebook on its nature, causes, and prevention* (pp. 3–5). Lexington, MA: Lexington Books.

Hayes, S. C., & Brownstein, A. J. (1986). Mentalism, behavior-behavior relations, and a behavior-analytic view of the purposes of science. *The Behavior Analyst*, *9*, 175–190.

Hayes, S. C., & Hayes, L. J. (1989). The verbal action of the listener as a basis for rule-governance. In S. C. Hayes (Ed.), *Rule-governed behavior: Cognition, contingencies, and instructional control* (pp. 153–190). New York: Plenum.

Hayes, S. C., & Hayes, L. J. (1992). Verbal relations and the evolution of behavior analysis. *American Psychologist*, *47*, 1383–1395.

Interpol. (1988). *International Crime Statistics*. Report issued by the International Criminal Police Organization, Paris.

Knudsen, D. D. (1991). Child sexual coercion. In E. Grauerholz & M. A. Kora-lewski (Eds.), *Sexual coercion* (pp. 17–28). Lexington, MA: Lexington Books.

Koss, M. P. (1990). Violence against women. *American Psychologist, 45,* 374–380.

Koss, M. P. (1992). The underdetection of rape: Methodological choices influence incidence estimates. *Journal of Social Issues, 48,* 61–75.

Koss, M. P., & Gaines, J. A. (1993). The prediction of sexual aggression by alcohol use, athletic participation, and fraternity affiliation. *Journal of Interpersonal Violence, 8,* 94–108.

Koss, M. P., Gidycz, C. A., & Wisniewski, N. (1987). The scope of rape: Incidence and prevalence of sexual aggression and victimization in a national sample of higher education students. *Journal of Consulting and Clinical Psychology, 55,* 162–170.

Koss, M. P., & Harvey, M. R. (1991). *The rape victim: Clinical and community interventions.* Newbury Park, CA: Sage.

Koss, M. P., & Oros, C.J. (1982). Sexual experiences survey: A research instrument investigating sexual aggression and victimization. *Journal of Consulting & Clinical Psychology, 50,* 455–457.

Lichtenstein, E., Nettekoven, L., & Ockene, J. A. (1991). Community intervention trial for smoking cessation (COMMIT): Opportunities for community psychologists in chronic disease prevention. *American Journal of Community Psychology, 19,* 17–39.

Maccoby, E. E. (1990). Gender and relationships: A developmental account. *American Psychologist, 45,* 513–520.

Marshall, R. (1991). *The state of families, 3: Losing direction.* Milwaukee: Family Service America.

McDowell, J. J. (1988). Matching theory in natural human environments. *The Behavior Analyst, 11,* 95–109.

McDowell, J. J. (1989). Two modern developments in matching theory. *The Behavior Analyst, 12,* 153–166.

McGuire, W. J. (1981). Theoretical foundations of campaigns. In R. E. Rice & W. J. Paisley (Eds.), *Public communication campaigns* (pp. 41–70). Beverly Hills, CA: Sage.

McGuire, W. J. (1985). Attitudes and attitude change. In G. Lindzey & E. Aronson (Eds.), The handbook of social psychology: Vol. 2. (3rd ed., pp. 233–346). New York: Random House.

McKinney, K., & Maroules, N. (1991). Sexual harassment. In E. Grauerholz & M. A. Karalewski (Eds.), *Sexual coercion: A sourcebook on its nature, causes, and prevention* (pp. 29–44). Lexington, MA: Lexington Books.

Muehlenhard, C. L., & Falcon, P. L. (1990). Men's heterosocial skill and attitudes toward women as predictors of verbal sexual coercion and forceful rape. *Sex Roles, 23,* 241–259.

Murrin, M. R., & Laws, D. R. (1990). Influence of pornography on sex crimes. In W. L. Marshall, D. R. Laws, & H. E. Barbaree (Eds.), *Handbook of Sexual Assault* (pp. 73–91). New York: Plenum.

Nadelson, C., Notman, M., Jackson, H., & Gornick, J. (1982). A follow-up study of rape victims. *American Journal of Psychiatry, 139*, 1266–1270.

Newcomer, S. F., & Udry, J. R. (1985). Parent-child communication and adolescent sexual behavior. *Family Planning Perspectives, 17*, 169–174.

Resnick, H. S., Kilpatrick, D. G., Dansky, B. S., Saunders, B. E., & Best, C. L. (1993). Prevalence of civilian trauma and posttraumatic stress disorder in a representative national sample of women. *Journal of Consulting & Clinical Psychology, 61*, 984–991.

Sidman, M. (1960). *Tactics of scientific research.* New York: Basic Books.

Siegel, J. M., Sorenson, S. B., Golding, J. M., Burnam, M. A., and Stein, J. A. (1987). The prevalence of childhood sexual assault: The Los Angeles epidemiologic catchment area project. *American Journal of Epidemiology, 126*, 1141–1153.

Simons, R. L., & Whitbeck, L. B. (1991). Sexual abuse as a precursor to prostitution and victimization among adolescent and adult homeless women. *Journal of Family Issues, 12*, 361–379.

Wallack, L., Dorfman, L., Jernigan, D., & Themba, M. (1993). *Media Advocacy and public health.* Newbury Park, CA: Sage.

Worden, J. K., Flynn, B. S., Geller, B. A., Chen, M., Shelton, L. G., Secker-Walker, R. H., Solomon, D. S., Solomon, L., Cuchey, S., Constanza, M. C. (1988). Development of a smoking prevention mass media program using diagnostic and formative research. *Preventive Medicine, 17*, 531–558.

Zillman, D., & Bryant, J. (1984). Effects of massive exposure to pornography. In N. M. Malamuth & E. Donnerstein (Eds.), *Pornography and sexual aggression* (pp. 115–138). Orlando, FL: Academic Press, Inc.

IV

CHANGE FOR INDIVIDUALS

12

PSYCHOSIS

STEPHEN E. WONG

INTRODUCTION

Psychosis is a severe behavior disorder not directly attributable to central nervous system damage or mental retardation that disrupts social and occupational functioning. It is estimated that at least 1% of the world's population is affected by psychosis (Director-General of the World Health Organization, 1993). In the United States, the number of people diagnosed with schizophrenia—one form of psychotic disorder—exceeds 2 million (Bourdon, Rae, Narrow, Manderscheid, & Regier, 1994). Prevalence of psychosis is especially high within the ranks of homeless persons, one third of whom are believed to be "severely mentally ill" (Federal Task Force on Homelessness and Mental Illness, 1992)

Economic costs to the nation for the treatment and care of persons with psychosis are substantial. In 1985, U.S. expenditures for psychiatric hospitalization, residential treatment, and short-term hospital care for persons 15 to 65 years old with "mental illness" were approximately $17 billion (Rice, Kelman, Miller, & Dunmeyer, 1990). A little-known fact is that more than 60% of the admissions for inpatient psychiatric care are to general hospitals rather than psychiatric hospitals. Of these general hospital admissions, more than half result in diagnoses of psychosis (Kiesler & Simpkins, 1993). Given this information, it is reasonable to estimate the direct costs of psychotic disorders to be at least $8 billion annually. This figure excludes indirect costs to society including lost productivity, shortened life span, the time of family caregivers, and the expenses of the criminal justice system.

Behavior Analysis and Treatment of Psychotic Disorders

It is an enigma that behavior analysis has not had a greater influence on the treatment of psychosis. Experimental analyses of the behavior of persons which chronic mental disorders conducted in the 1950s and 1960s were among the first successful applications of operant psychology to human problems. Teodoro Ayllon's and Jack Michael's research at a large psychiatric hospital in Saskatchewan, Canada, led to their 1959 paper, "The Psychiatric Nurse as a Behavioral Engineer," which is among the earliest published articles on applied behavior analysis. Teodoro Ayllon, Nathan Azrin, and their associates went on to complete a remarkable series of studies that restored functional behavior in patients with chronic mental problems. These studies culminated in their 1968 book, *The Token Economy: A Motivational System for Therapy and Rehabilitation.* The token economy specified behaviors or tasks that clients should perform, gave immediate (token) reinforcement for task completions, and exchanged tokens for backup rewards (e.g., edibles, privileges). This comprehensive therapeutic program at Anna State Hospital in Illinois became the prototype for behavioral residential treatment (Kazdin, 1977).

Over the next 30 years, researchers carried out many controlled, within-subject experiments showing that behavioral interventions were effective in both reducing maladaptive response and increasing social, self-care, vocational, and recreational skills in persons with psychosis (for a partial review, see Wong, Woolsey, & Gallegos, 1987). Using a between-groups comparison with long-term follow up, Paul and Lentz (1977) found that intensive behavioral programming for patients with chronic mental disturbances was both more effective *and* more cost-efficient than structured milieu therapy.

Although a few states, most notably Florida, have implemented this technology on a wide scale (Jacobson et al., 1992; Jacobson, Hutchison, Coleman, & Harris, 1991), behavioral programs have not become standard treatment in public and private psychiatric hospitals across the country (Boudewyns, Fry, & Nightingale, 1986; Glynn, 1990; Moss, 1983). Furthermore, in the past 10 years, the number of behavioral studies conducted with patients with chronic mental disorders have dwindled (Scotti, McMorrow, & Trawitzki, 1993). The reasons for this regression are intriguing, but discussion of them will be deferred until later in the chapter. The main focus of this chapter is to examine psychosis from a behavioral perspective, looking at environmental conditions that contribute to or counteract aspects of this disorder. Although parts of this discussion are theoretical, its emphasis is practical and treatment-oriented, reflecting the perspective's roots in clinical research of psychotic behavior.

Usage of the Term "Psychosis"

In this chapter, I attempt to break free from the prevailing medical nomenclature and related concepts associated with mental disorders. The clients who are described in the following pages have been diagnosed as having schizophrenic, delusional, schizoaffective, organic mental, and mood disorders (American Psychiatric Association [APA], 1987). However, I do not adhere to these categories in this chapter. Instead, I refer to *psychosis*, a broader term with fewer unwanted connotations. Psychosis, as applied here, refers to the emergence of behavior problems and the concurrent breakdown in normal adaptive functioning. Persons with psychosis act bizarrely, in addition to displaying varying constellations of other problem behaviors that will be described in this chapter. Individuals with psychosis may retain useful capabilities; however, the clinical picture is that of persons who are severely impaired and who cannot fulfill normal role expectations. The stability of psychosis varies across individuals, appearing as a transitory state in some people and a lifelong disability in others. Numerous individuals who have psychosis reside in state psychiatric hospitals, private psychiatric hospitals, group homes for persons with mental disorders, or with family members. Many others are found in correctional facilities or are homeless (Bachrach, 1992).

There are good reasons not to be bound by the ubiquitous medical terminology. For one, use of a psychiatric diagnosis, such as schizophrenia, implies that this discussion deals with a homogeneous group of individuals with a disorder that has a uniform underlying cause (presumed to be biological). Neither of these assumptions is well substantiated, and both disregard other plausible accounts of the phenomena and the labeling process (Sarbin & Mancuso, 1980; Szasz, 1987). Researchers and clinicians know that individuals with schizophrenia differ greatly in their adaptive capabilities and behavior problems, so much so that the diagnosis is of little value in designing a client's rehabilitation plan (Anthony & Nemac, 1984). Predominant models of mental disorders also underrate powerful socioenvironmental conditions—such as undersocialization, aversive stimulation or deprivation, negative modeling, reinforcement for the sick role, and combinations of these factors—that can produce and support psychotic behavior. Modifying these conditions is essential for the successful treatment and reintegration of a person with psychotic behavior.

Another reason not to rely on the psychiatric diagnostic system is that its many ambiguous and arbitrary classifications (Kutchins & Kirk, 1993) are distracting. Although a vast amount of time and energy has been spent categorizing and recategorizing schizophrenia and other mental disorders, this work has been orthogonal to the development and application of effective psychosocial interventions. Unless you are a physician prescribing psychotropic medications to treat a person with psychosis, a psychiatric diagnosis is largely irrelevant to therapy and placement decisions. For clinicians who want to help clients by advising them, teaching them, motivating them, or assisting them with their finances, housing, work, recreation, social activities, and other personal matters, it is more useful to know the client's background (i.e., psychosocial history), current level of functioning, and behavioral disorders.

FUNCTIONAL ASSESSMENT AND TREATMENT OF PSYCHOSIS

From a behavioral and sociological perspective, psychotic behavior exists along a continuum with so-called normal behavior, but it differs in frequency, duration, intensity, and timing, or occurs in an inappropriate context (Ullmann & Krasner, 1969). For example, occasionally interrupting another person is acceptable in normal conversation, but frequent interrupting is rude or even aggressive. Similarly, thinking that other people are watching you and are about to harm you may or may not be reasonable, depending on who you are and what part of the city you are in at the moment. This model takes situational and cultural differences into account and seeks to alter the quantity and context of behavior. By using situational norms to gauge individual conduct, clinicians can first classify behavioral problems as excesses or deficits, and then subdivide these problems by their function or effect on the individual's surroundings.

Behavioral Excesses

In this treatise on psychosis, I will cover three behavioral excesses: bizarre behavior, oppositional behavior, and stereotypic behavior. Bizarre behavior will be discussed first and in greater depth because of its baffling and intricate nature.

Bizarre Behavior

Odd or strange behavior is probably the most striking feature of psychosis. Gordon Paul lists myriad bizarre responses of chronic psychiatric patients (e.g., unrealistic statements, laughing inappropriately, and peculiar mannerisms) in the *crazy behavior* category of his extensive observational scheme, the Time Sample Behavioral Checklist (Paul, 1987).

Bizarre behavior can be disorganized and seemingly nonsensical, or it can be coherent and dominated by religious, somatic, grandiose, persecutory, or other grotesque themes. The fourth edition of *Diagnostic and Statistical Manual of Mental Disorders* (APA, 1994) attaches much significance to psychotic verbal behavior and classifies patients based on both the structure and the semantic content of their speech (i.e., saying that one's thoughts are controlled by others would lead to a different diagnosis from saying that one is persecuted by others). Similarly, bizarre motoric behaviors of a specific typography (e.g., exhibiting rigid posture vs. ritualistic movements) lead to differential psychiatric diagnoses. Bizarre verbal and motoric behavior are viewed as manifestations of pathological internal processes or states (e.g., delusions, hallucinations, thought disorders), which are the focus of current research and theory. But preoccupation with the physical form of bizarre behavior and putative internal states has kept researchers from examining the strong relationship between bizarre behavior and environmental events. This focus ignores an immense body of empirical evidence showing that psychotic behavior, like other behavior, is controlled by environmental stimuli preceding and following the response.

Ironically, the most recent and compelling evidence that *antecedent stimuli* influence psychotic behavior comes from research of a cognitive-behavioral rather than a behavior-analytic orientation. These investigations (Alford, 1986; Chadwick & Lowe, 1990, 1994; Chadwick, Lowe, Horne, & Higson, 1994; Himadi & Kaiser, 1992; Lowe & Chadwick, 1990) showed that delusional beliefs of patients with schizophrenia could be altered with a combination of tactful suggestions and leading questions that negated delusional assertions while generating minimal client resistance. The general procedure, adapted from Watts, Powell, and Austin (1973), consists of: (a) beginning treatment by modifying the belief least strongly held, (b) asking clients to merely consider an alternative to their belief, (c) challenging evidence for the belief (rather than the belief itself), and (d) asking clients to present arguments contrary to their own beliefs. Although not described in these terms, the procedure seems to build appropriate responses (rational statements and explanations) through a process of progressive training that resembles shaping (Catania, 1984). Therapists shape appropriate verbalizations by positively reinforcing successive approximations or verbal responses that resemble or contain elements of rational speech. Social reinforcement is a critical component of the procedure because a sizable number of therapy sessions (6 to 12) are devoted to building therapeutic relationships before challenging clients' delusional beliefs (Chadwick & Lowe, 1994). By whatever mechanisms the just-described procedure operates, it has been used in the aforementioned studies to reverse long-standing delusional verbalizations in 12 out of 14 participants with schizophrenia.

Consequent stimuli can also give rise to and maintain psychotic behavior through the operation of *positive reinforcement*. Ayllon, Haughton, and Hughes (1965) vividly illustrated this process by experimentally creating and then eliminating bizarre behavior in a woman with chronic schizophrenia. The investigators arbitrarily selected holding a broom as the psychotic response to be fabricated. After baseline observations were conducted by the researchers, nursing staff prompted the patient to hold a broom and reinforced this peculiar and meaningless response with cigarettes and tokens. Nonexistent at the start of the study, the behavior increased until it occurred in 40% of daily observations. Two board-certified psychiatrists who examined the patient engaging in the broom-holding behavior pronounced that it was a symptom of infantile regression and magical thinking. Ayllon and his associates later completely eliminated this patient's contrived psychotic response by having nursing staff withhold reinforcement for it.

Humans live in societies; therefore, attention from others can be a source of positive reinforcement for conventional or eccentric behavior. I remember a patient diagnosed with schizophrenia who paraded in front of the psychiatric unit's nursing station with cigarettes sticking out of his nostrils and his underwear worn outside of his pants. These antics were not random behavior, but rather examples of low humor sustained by the laughter of other patients and the nursing staff. The comic demeanor of persons with psychosis was once formally acknowledged in the diagnosis of hebephrenic or silly schizophrenia listed in the *Diagnostic and Statistic Manual of Mental Disorders* (APA, 1968), but this diagnostic category disappeared from later versions of the manual.

The psychiatric nosology itself ensures that keen attention is paid to bizarre behavior. In their search for key symptoms, psychiatrists, psychologists, social workers, and nurses question clients in a way that evokes pathological verbalizations during informal conversations and clinical interviews (e.g., "Do you think other people are conspiring to hurt you?"). Mundane descriptions of life situations (e.g., disagreements with caretakers, shortage of funds) are quietly tolerated, but fantastic descriptions of life situations (e.g., staff tried to poison the client, the government stole the client's money) are carefully explored through further questioning. Bizarre verbalizations affect psychiatric decisions about the client's future treatment and living situation (e.g., medication, discharge, or continued hospitalization) in ways that ordinary statements could not. The social significance conferred on psychotic speech by the professional subculture probably helps to perpetuate this aberrant response.

Behavioral researchers have sought to redirect attention and other positive reinforcement as a therapeutic intervention for bizarre verbalizations. In their classic study, Ayllon and Haughton (1964) modified the speech of a 47-year-old female psychiatric patient diagnosed as having chronic schizophrenia. This woman had a 14-year history of delusional speech in which she frequently refered to herself as being Queen Elizabeth and a member of the royal family. After a brief baseline phase, the experimenters instructed nursing staff to reinforce delusional statements with cigarettes and social attention and to concurrently ignore appropriate speech. During this second phase, the rate of delusional statements increased to more than twice the initial baseline level while appropriate speech dropped close to zero. In the third phase, experimenters instructed staff to ignore delusional speech and to reinforce appropriate speech. During this third phase, the rate of delusional statements dropped to roughly one-quarter of the baseline level, and the frequency of appropriate speech quadrupled relative to the rates observed in the preceding phase. Thus, the amount of delusional and appropriate speech could be directly manipulated through the reinforcement contingency.

Since Ayllon and Haughton's study, researchers have modified psychotic speech by extinguishing inappropriate verbalizations and by positively reinforcing appropriate verbalizations with (a) therapist attention (Moss & Liberman, 1975); (b) staff attention, coffee, and snacks (Liberman, Teigen, Patterson, & Baker, 1973); (c) access to a preferred work assignment (Anderson & Alpert, 1974); (d) and tokens (Patterson & Teigen, 1973; Wincze, Leitenberg, & Agras, 1972). More recently, Himadi and associates (Himadi, Osteen, & Crawford, 1993; Himadi, Osteen, Kaiser, & Daniel, 1991) reduced delusional verbalizations in chronic psychiatric patients with a combination of subtle prompts for competing behavior and consumable and social reinforcement.

Through a different reinforcement process, consequent stimuli can operate as *negative reinforcement* when psychotic behavior prevents or terminates certain social stimuli. People are generally unprepared to deal with grotesque speech and actions. They might ask the individual to explain his behavior, stop interacting with him, or physically withdraw from him. Bizarre behavior will be negatively reinforced and occur more frequently if it interferes with or disrupts criticism, reprimands, demands, or other aversive social stimulation. My colleagues and I (Wong et al., 1987) reported the case of a woman with paranoia who effectively put off staff requests to get up in the morning and groom by making repetitive, delusional statements (e.g., by saying that she was being held in the hospital illegally). In a rare experimental analysis of psychotic speech, Mace, Webb, Sharkey, Mattson, and Rosen (1988) determined that the bizarre verbalizations of a woman with schizophrenia occurred at the highest rate when such behavior gained experimenter attention and a temporary escape from staff demands.

Bizarre behavior motivated by escape or avoidance must be treated differently from inappropriate behavior motivated by positive reinforcement. For example, consistently ignoring inappropriate verbalizations and attending to appropriate verbalizations is likely to be an effective intervention for a client who claims he is Satan, if attention from others is maintaining these statements. However, if the client makes psychotic statements to get other people to leave him alone, then ignoring him or withdrawing from him is likely to negatively reinforce this inappropriate behavior and increase the frequency of psychotic verbalizations. Unfortunately, the technology for treating inappropriate behavior that is negatively reinforced is a relatively recent development (Iwata, 1987; Iwata, Vollmer, Zarcone, & Rodgers, 1993) and has seldom been incorporated in clinical studies of individuals with psychosis.

Whether initially established by positive reinforcement, negative reinforcement, or a combination of both, bizarre behavior in adults with psychosis often evolves into a variform and durable response pattern. A person with psychosis can exhibit bizarre behavior that has a central theme (e.g., "The spirit of Mary Magdalene has entered my body . . .") and mold his or her actions to conform with his or her immediate surroundings (e.g., upon seeing a letter opener lying on a desk, asking, "Is this a spike you used to nail my beloved Jesus to the cross?"). Bizarre responses, most notably psychotic speech, will at times resist contingency management procedures (Wincze et al., 1972) or will spontaneously recover over time (Wallace et al., as cited in Wong & Liberman, 1981) or when training has ended (Himadi et al., 1991; Himadi et al., 1993). These results have been interpreted as showing that clients' underlying belief systems have remained intact despite behavioral training. However, multiform and persistent bizarre verbalizations can be parsimoniously viewed as generalized responses with a long history of intermittent reinforcement. After being positively and negatively reinforced by different people in various situations over many years, bizarre verbalizations could be overlearned responses that resist contingencies administered in circumscribed therapy sessions over mere weeks or months. Furthermore, it is difficult to prevent other patients, lay persons, and medical professionals from continuing to reinforce these verbalizations in the usual manner.

So far, I have discussed how bizarre behavior can be engendered and supported by social stimuli. Bizarre behavior can also stem from inadequate or insufficient social influence. In these cases, bizarre behaviors are poorly formed or undeveloped responses. The person with psychosis who walks up to a stranger and begins to stroke the stranger's tie while asking him what country he comes from might be exhibiting a lack of appropriate social skills. The professional literature is replete with reports on the interpersonal skill deficits of patients with chronic mental disorders. These deficiencies can be remediated through systematic social skills training, a topic which is covered later in this chapter.

Finally, a third category of bizarre behavior seems to operate independently of social interaction. Certain strange, repetitive responses endure for long periods without any identifiable external reinforcement. These responses are discussed in the section of this chapter that deals with stereotypic behavior.

Oppositional Behavior

If persons with psychosis would act in an acceptable manner whenever they were told to do so, this disorder would not be the serious problem that it is. In fact, the term *psychosis* implies a breakdown of responsiveness to instructions and social influence. Oppositional behavior among people with psychosis can vary in intensity, ranging from refusing to take a bath, to becoming loud and disruptive during a group meeting, to physically attacking a staff member after being told to complete a work assignment. Cloaked in strange mannerisms and accompanied by fantastic explanations, oppositional behavior may not be obvious even to the trained clinician. Nevertheless, this pattern can interfere with all forms of adult responsibility and productive activity.

Oppositional behavior usually emerges during the course of child development; disobedience is reported as a frequent problem among 50% of normal 4-year-old children (Kazdin, 1987). Noncompliance to instructions by adults is ordinarily not a clinical concern because society grants adults so much latitude in their day-to-day decisions. However, if adults are unable to care for their own basic needs *and* they are noncompliant with therapists or caretakers who attempt to change their behavior, serious conflicts will arise.

Persons with psychosis who exhibit oppositional and aggressive behavior have been treated in psychiatric hospitals with a variety of skills training and contingency management procedures (Wong, Slama, & Liberman, 1985; Wong, Woolsey, Innocent, & Liberman, 1988). Token economies have defined routine tasks in the hospital setting and provided tangible reinforcement for compliance or task performance (Atthowe & Krasner, 1968; Ayllon & Azrin, 1965). Therapists have conducted social skills training to impart appropriate, prosocial responses to replace disruptive and aggressive behavior (Frederiksen, Jenkins, Foy, & Eisler, 1976; Matson & Stephens, 1978). Individual programs, behavioral contracts, and differential reinforcement schedules exist that make praise, tangible items, and privileges contingent on prosocial behavior (or on the absence of inappropriate behavior). Concurrently, point fines, privilege loss, timeout from reinforcement, or some combination of these procedures have been applied as reductive consequences for noncompliant and aggressive behaviors (Wong, Woolsey et al., 1988).

Although studies have suggested that the aforementioned interventions have had favorable outcomes, this technology is becoming obsolete. Investigators in the previously mentioned studies imposed arbitrary reinforcers and reductive consequences to override inappropriate responses; however, they did so without first conducting a functional analysis that would have identified the preexisting reinforcement contingencies causing the problem behavior (Mace, Lalli, Lalli, & Shea, 1993; Mace & Roberts, 1993). Treatment that does not include such a functional analysis can result in presumed reinforcers and reductive consequences having unintended effects (e.g., a timeout procedure is counterproductive because the client misbehaves to escape demanding situations). And even if arbitrarily imposed consequences are potent, therapeutic gains may rapidly disappear as soon as the contrived reinforcers and consequences are withdrawn.

Another shortcoming of these early treatments is the absence of procedures designed to gradually shape compliant behavior or to make compliance more probable before the delivery of reinforcement. Current strategies for inducing compliance include giving clients a sequence of requests with which they typically comply immediately before giving them a request that they typically refuse (Mace & Belfiore, 1990; Mace et al., 1988) and presenting a graduated series of requests beginning with requests most likely to be followed and ending with those least likely to be followed (Ducharme & Popynick, 1993). The lack of specific shaping and compliance training procedures in previous clinical studies with clients who have psychosis reflects the age and scarcity of research with this population.

Stereotypic Behavior

Investigators employing divergent assessment methods have reported that individuals with psychosis who are being treated in psychiatric hospitals display repetitive behaviors such as strange rituals, pacing, posturing, and self-talk (Alevizos, DeRisi, Liberman, Eckman, & Callahan, 1978; Luchins, Goldman, Lieb, & Hanrahan, 1992; Paul, 1987). These behaviors occur for extended periods of time without any discernible social or external reinforcement.

Stereotypic behavior is not unique to individuals with psychosis; it is commonly seen in persons with mental retardation (O'Brien, 1981). Ferster (1973) noted that people of normal intelligence also engage in simple repetitive behavior (doodling, finger twiddling, and playing with one's hair) in situations in which more reinforcing activities are unavailable (such as when sitting through a boring lecture). Stereotypies are not inherently pathological. Repetitive movements are necessary for performing some productive activities (e.g., crocheting) and for learning certain skills (e.g., handwriting, playing musical instruments). Children without physical or mental disabilities display solitary and repetitive vocalizations, and this playful behavior may aid in language acquisition (Lovaas, Varni, Koegel, & Lorsch, 1977). Lovaas and his colleagues have suggested that stereotypic behavior is self-reinforcing because it provides stimulation necessary to sustain the nervous system (Lovaas, Newsom, & Hickman, 1987; Lovaas et al., 1977).

One treatment for maladaptive stereotypic behavior operates by restructuring the client's environment to promote alternative appropriate responses. This was done in early token economy programs by involving clients in an intensive daily schedule of self-care, work, and leisure activities. Ayllon and Azrin (1968) anecdotally reported that many bizarre behaviors of chronic psychiatric patients vanished when they were engaged in useful tasks. Paul and Lentz (1977) documented a sizable, long-term reduction of bizarre behavior in chronic psychiatric patients who participated in an enriched schedule of self-care, social, and educational activities.

A series of within-subject experiments that my colleagues and I conducted have demonstrated an inverse relationship between bizarre, repetitive behavior and involvement in productive activities. We found (Wong, Terranova et al., 1987) that psychotic self-talk and mumbling in two patients with schizophrenia decreased 60 to 70% when the patients were engaged in preferred recreational activities (reading, handicrafts, assembling models). Similar clinical improvements were obtained for the ruminating behavior (searching for dirt and feces) of a patient with obsessive-compulsive disorder and for the grotesque posturing behavior by a third patient with schizophrenia (Corrigan, Liberman, & Wong, 1993). Another study (Wong, Wright, Terranova, Bowen, & Zorate, 1988) showed a 70% reduction in a variety of bizarre behaviors in 10 chronic psychiatric patients when they were engaged in structured leisure and work activities (e.g., team sports, art projects, housework). These studies outlined a simple and efficient treatment for stereotypy and highlighted the need for ecological analyses of psychotic behavior.

Behavioral Deficits

The behavioral excesses of a person with psychosis can disrupt learning and performance of all forms of adaptive behavior, thereby causing a devastating array of disabilities. Impaired performance in critical formative contexts (e.g., school, workplace) impedes the accumulation of skills and achievements expected of an adult. As a result, the person with psychosis is prevented from meeting societal demands and is predisposed to assuming a dependent sick role (Ullman & Krasner, 1969) to satisfy his or her basic needs. In the material that follows, I briefly review four functional domains influenced by psychoses as well as behavioral interventions that have been applied to disturbances in these areas. The four domains are: social skills, personal hygiene, vocational skills, and recreational behavior.

Social Skills

Besides exhibiting bizarre behaviors, individuals with psychosis emit desired interpersonal behavior at lower rates than do those who do not have this problem. Because particular verbal and nonverbal responses weigh heavily in society's judgments about an individual's competence, behavioral researchers have taught these skills as a primary treatment for schizophrenia and other psychotic disorders (Bellack & Mueser, 1990; Donahoe & Driesenga, 1988; Halford & Hayes, 1991). Component skills that have been successfully trained include: eye contact and facial expression (Eisler, Blanchard, Fitts, & Williams, 1978; Hersen, Eisler, & Miller, 1974), simple greetings (Kale, Kaye, Whelan, & Hopkins, 1968; Wong & Woolsey, 1989), conversational skills (Holmes, Hansen, & St. Lawrence, 1984; Kelly, Urey, & Patterson, 1980; Wong et al., 1993), and assertive responses (Frederiksen et al., 1976; Hersen & Bellack, 1976; Hersen, Turner, Edelstein, & Pinkston, 1975).

Traditional social skills training is conducted under analogue conditions with the client and the therapist role playing interactions in a therapy room. Training typically consists of the therapist describing the desired behavior, modeling or demonstrating the behavior, having the client rehearse the skill during role plays, and either praising the client or giving him or her corrective feedback. Ample studies have confirmed the effectiveness of these procedures in teaching important interactive behaviors and have shown that trained skills will carry over to novel role plays and to role plays with novel conversants. However, data showing that these trained skills generalize to real-life encounters outside the therapy situation are scant (Donahoe & Driesenga, 1988; Halford & Hayes, 1991).

In one study that my colleagues and I conducted (Wong et al., 1993), we taught conversational skills to persons who were hospitalized for schizophrenia. We conducted the skill training in an office and covertly assessed generalization of trained responses to unit staff and strangers in the unit dayroom and courtyard. We found that spontaneous generalization to extratherapy settings and conversants was highly variable and inconsistent. However, it was possible to induce all participants to use target skills in the unit dayroom by introducing intermittent prompts and positive reinforcement for desired behavior in that setting. These results were replicated in a later study that taught social skills to adolescent psychiatric inpatients (Wong, Morgan, Crowley, & Baker, in press). Thus, techniques are currently available for reestablishing appropriate interactive behavior in psychotic (Kale et al., 1968; Wong & Woolsey, 1989) and postpsychotic clients; the more demanding feat is engineering the living environments of clients to motivate and sustain these preferred interaction patterns.

Personal Hygiene and Self-Care

Breakdown of adaptive functioning in individuals with psychosis can extend to the most basic of self-maintenance routines, including bathing, grooming, and dressing. Problems of this sort, at best, mar interpersonal relations and, at worst, cause social rejection and physical disease. Behavioral programs for self-care deficiencies have usually employed explicit instruction and positive reinforcement for desired self-care skills.

Token economies have been erected within hospitals (Ayllon & Azrin, 1968; Liberman, Wallace, Teigen, & Davis, 1974; Paul & Lentz, 1977) and community mental health centers (Liberman, King, & De Risi, 1976) to improve clients' grooming and housekeeping performances. Within these programs, staff awarded tokens or points (redeemable for consumable items or privileges) to patients for the completion of self-care tasks or gave tokens based on patients' appearances during periodic inspections. One early study (Lloyd & Garlington, 1968) showed that token reinforcement had a modest effect on overall grooming performance, whereas another study (Winkler, 1970) revealed strong effects when tokens were made contingent on a single self-care response (i.e., shoe cleaning).

Token reinforcement has produced significant improvements in multiple grooming skills patients in psychiatric hospitals when administered within a training program that included verbal instructions, modeling, and posters (Nelson & Cone, 1979). Using a step-by-step training procedure and tangible reinforcement, my colleagues and I (Wong, Flanagan, et al., 1988) taught hand and face washing, hair cleaning, toothbrushing, and proper dressing to patients hospitalized for chronic mental problems without a token economy program. Systematic training of 50 patients with chronic psychiatric problems was evaluated with a randomly selected sample of 9 individuals. After training, the average percentage of grooming tasks completed by this sample group rose from 57% to 88%. These two studies showed that regressed clients benefited from treatment packages that incorporated a task analysis of the required skills, instructions, and other prompts to perform component responses, as well as positive reinforcement for task completion.

The behavioral programs that I have just described overlap with the professional practice of occupational therapy. Occupational therapy, however, encompasses a wider spectrum of skills needed for independent living and community adjustment than was taught in the behavioral programs, including food preparation, money management, and mobility training (Dombrowski, 1990). Closer collaboration of behavioral clinicians with rehabilitation disciplines such as occupational therapy should advance the treatment of clients with psychosis. Whereas rehabilitation disciplines concentrate on specific content areas (e.g., occupational therapy on independent living skills, recreational therapy on leisure skills, vocational rehabilitation on work skills), behavior analysis focuses on fundamental psychological processes that underlie or hinder skill acquisition (e.g., motivational variables, instructional design, stimulus and response generalization, behavior disorders). For this reason, an infusion of behavioral technology into rehabilitation services is likely to enhance treatment outcome along multiple dimensions.

Vocational Skills

Work is another important area of human functioning in which persons with psychotic disorders need special assistance. Unemployment among persons with "severe mental illness" has been reported to be as high as 80% (Bond & McDonel, 1991). In contrast to psychiatric rehabilitation programs that offer comprehensive services for supported employment, socialization, case management, and supported living (Anthony & Nemec, 1984; Rodgers, Anthony, Toole, & Brown, 1991), behavioral programs addressing this problem have tended to focus on helping clients first to regain work skills and then to find jobs and keep them.

To curiously modest acclaim, behavioral programs have restored work behavior in severely regressed, hospitalized patients by prompting and reinforcing successive approximations to the terminal goal (Ayllon & Azrin, 1968). For example, such a client might have been initially rewarded for complying with the request, "Please pick up that piece of paper." The client was then awarded for picking up several pieces of paper and soda cans, then for picking up litter and sweeping the floor, and finally for picking up trash and sweeping the floor in several rooms. As compliance with instructions and work tolerance increased, the client would be assigned more demanding tasks. The first token economy had many well-defined hospital jobs, such as kitchen, personal care, clerical, and housekeeping aides, requiring from 10 min to 6 hr of work per day (Ayllon & Azrin, 1965). Using a reversal design in which token reinforcement was introduced, withdrawn, and then reintroduced, Ayllon and Azrin showed that clients consistently completed these job assignments only when they earned tokens for doing so.

Following the client's discharge from the hospital, vocational training can proceed to supported employment or participation in a community-based work program for disabled persons. Rise and Shine Industries (Ruiz, 1992), located in Stockton, California, and affiliated with the University of the Pacific, is one such program. It offers supervised employment for clients who are chronically mentally disturbed; they work during the week using high-pressure cleaning equipment to wash cars at local auto dealerships. The program is a commercially viable enterprise that gives clients 20 to 28 hours of work per week at or slightly above minimum wage. Rise and Shine Industries resembles a psychiatric rehabilitation program in that it is embedded within a community reentry program that furnishes congregate housing and teaches independent living skills (e.g., money management, cooking, shopping, apartment cleaning, recreation).

For clients who are able to join the regular workforce, securing employment is a prime concern. Focusing on the last critical step in the job search, investigators have used social skills training to improve how clients present themselves in job interviews (Furman, Geller, Simon, & Kelly, 1979; Kelly, Laughlin, Claiborne, & Patterson, 1979). Clients were taught to give positive information about previous work experiences and education, to ask questions, to use gestures, and to express enthusiasm during interviews. Training incorporated exposure to videotaped models, behavioral rehearsal during simulated interviews, praise for appropriate responses and corrective feedback for inappropriate responses, coaching to improve performance, and repetition of these steps. Data from these two studies showed that training increased the skills of all participants. It also boosted the performance ratings given by an actual personnel manager for most participants.

An example of a behavioral program that assists clients in all of the steps required to obtain employment is commonly known as a "job club" (Azrin & Besalel, 1980; Azrin, Flores, & Kaplan, 1975). A job club provides social support groups and guidance in preparing a resume, conducting a systematic job search, proper dressing and grooming, job interviewing, and following up on job leads. Jacobs, Kardashian, Kreinbring, Ponder, and Simpson (1984) adapted the job club for clients with chronic mental disorders by adding community survival skills to the curriculum. Survival skills addressed personal goal setting, problem solving, coping with daily problems, and maintaining one's employment. Job seeking and community survival skills were taught through lecture, programmed reading materials, role playing, and in vivo exercises. Evaluation of this expanded job club showed that 76% of the participants found jobs or started full-time vocational training by the end of the program and that 67% were still employed 6 months after the program's completion.

In summary, behavioral programs have proven valuable in reestablishing work behavior in persons with regressive psychotic disorders and in helping higher functioning clients obtain and hold jobs. These programs underscore the strengths of this technology in analyzing and teaching the complex skills needed for life in the community.

Recreational Behavior

The goals of recreation concern matters of personal choice and quality of life to a larger degree than areas previously discussed. Recreation can be a vehicle for pursuing objectives of social adjustment, physical conditioning, creative fulfillment, amusement, and relaxation (Nesbitt, 1970).

Individuals with psychosis rarely involve themselves in productive and socially acceptable leisure pasttimes, which is a deficiency also observed in some elderly populations (McClannahan & Risley, 1974) and in many persons with developmental disabilities (Matson & Marchetti, 1980). Lack of appropriate recreational behavior means that the individual has fewer rewarding activities available to him or her as well as a heightened probability that the individual will engaged in socially unacceptable diversions.

A few behavioral researchers have attempted to improve how individuals with psychosis occupy their leisure time. While setting up a token economy on a locked psychiatric unit, Nelson and Cone (1979) increased exercise behavior in a group of 16 inpatients through scheduled exercise sessions and token reinforcement. Working in a community group home, Thyer, Irvine, and Santa (1984) used consumable reinforcement to motivate two former mental patients to exercise longer and more frequently on an stationary bicycle. Both studies raised the amount of exercise that clients engaged in daily, thereby promoting their physical fitness and health.

Mentioned earlier in this chapter were two studies that reduced bizarre behavior by introducing sedentary recreational activities (Corrigan et al., 1993; Wong, Terranova, et al., 1987). An outcome not discussed in these articles was a large increase in appropriate on-task behavior during recreation sessions (rising from less than 15% in the baseline sessions to more than 80% in the recreation sessions). Patients' demeanor changed dramatically during recreational activities, and in these sessions they were indistinguishable from nonpatients. In another study, my colleagues and I (Wong, Wright, et al., 1988) quantified the effect of structured activities on positive behavior and showed that group activities increased socially appropriate and productive behavior 400% to 500% over that recorded during unstructured free time.

Although this research provided important data on the benefits of recreational interventions within this clinical population, they were only preliminary studies. Research is needed on how to restore former leisure interests, encourage self-initiated recreational behavior, and use recreational activities to teach other useful skills, as well as on other primary features of this therapeutic modality.

The Past and Future of Behavioral Treatment of Psychosis

The behavioral interventions described in this chapter were devised mainly for clients who are severely disturbed and who are being treated in psychiatric hospitals. This approach follows a tradition going back to the earliest applications of operant-learning principles to social problems and to the origins of applied behavior analysis (Ayllon & Michael, 1959). Behavioral treatment of chronic patients in psychiatric hospitals was initially a fruitful field of study that generated optimism about the development of this approach to rehabilitation. Experience over the past 30 years, however, has revealed daunting obstacles to the introduction and expansion of behavioral programs in psychiatric settings.

Behavioral clinicians interested in working with this population are confronted with the dual challenge of treating severe and complex behavior disorders while overcoming stiff sociopolitical resistance to their treatment methods. Psychiatric hospitals are, of course, medical institutions organized to administer biophysical therapies (i.e., drugs, nursing care). In these settings, rehabilitative and educative interventions are relegated to the status of ancillary treatments. Whenever behavioral clinicians attempt to adjust organizational priorities, they run up against the internal bureaucracy, laws, and quasi-legal regulations supporting the existing structure, as well as professional groups with vested interest in the status quo (Moss, 1983, 1993). Even when behavioral clinicians are allied with progressive administrators and receptive clinical staff, they must struggle against numerous opponents within their own and from other professional disciplines.

But there is a larger reason why behavioral technology has not been able to build on its early successes in state psychiatric hospitals. That is, for the past several decades, these facilities have been on the decline. The deinstitutionalization movement effectively reduced the census of state psychiatric hospitals throughout the country, and as a result, psychiatric units have closed, and entire facilities have been dismantled. This trend continues, albeit without adequate community-based services available to replace institutional care (Keisler & Sibulkin, 1987). I have worked in state psychiatric hospitals in three states, and I have seen facilities routinely threatened with fiscal cutbacks and possible closings. Such grim prospects eroded staff morale and undermined efforts to upgrade the institutions' operation and services.

The unfulfilled promise of behavior analysis in psychiatric settings may not be a tragic setback, however, if behavioral researchers can shift their attention to community adjustment programs for persons with psychotic disorders. Located in the community and aimed at helping clients to function independently, these programs pursue the same objectives and employ procedures analogous to those in model behavioral programs. Community adjustment programs provide graduated assistance and training in the skills needed for work, social relations, and activities of daily living. Moreover, emphasis is on in situ training in real-life situations that facilitate skill generalization. Community adjustment programs also give comprehensive support to clients in meeting their everyday material needs (i.e., food, housing, health care) and their social needs (relationships with staff, peers, and family) (Test, 1992).

CONCLUSION

Behavior analysis uses the principles of learning and motivation to analyze and modify psychotic behavior. Psychosis can be conceptualized as aberrant social and self-stimulatory responses combined with skill and performance deficits. Although psychotic disorders can be grossly debilitating, its components might only be primitive or extreme forms of normal behavior. Rather than speculating about the pathology of clients' mental or biophysiological states, the behavioral approach examines how environments can be designed to foster and maintain clients' adaptive behavior. Like other rehabilitation disciplines, this approach focuses on teaching clients skills that they need to live independently. Unlike other rehabilitation disciplines, behavior analysis has a methodology for understanding psychotic responses and treating both behavioral excesses and deficits.

Behavioral interventions have successfully reduced severe problem behaviors and restored skills in persons with otherwise untreatable psychosis; but, 30 years after their first unveiling, these procedures have barely penetrated the professions and institutions responsible for the treatment of this clinical population. Although the obstacles to developing and disseminating alternative therapies for individuals with psychosis are huge, they must be grappled with. The care and treatment of persons with psychosis continue to absorb tremendous financial resources of this society, while yielding dismal results. For those interested in this social problem, it is worth reexamining what behavior analysis offers to ameliorate this mystifying and crippling malady.

REFERENCES

Alevizos, P., DeRisi, W., Liberman, R., Eckman, T., & Callahan, E. (1978). The behavior observation instrument: A method of direct observation for program evaluation. *Journal of Applied Behavior Analysis, 11,* 243–257.

Alford, B. A. (1986). Behavioral treatment of schizophrenic delusions: A single-case experimental analysis. *Behavior Therapy, 17,* 637–644.

American Psychiatric Association. (1968). *Diagnostic and statistical manual of mental disorders* (2nd ed.). Washington, DC: Author.

American Psychiatric Association. (1994). *Diagnostic and statistical manual of mental disorders* (4th ed.). Washington, DC: Author.

Anderson, L. T., & Alpert, M. (1974). Operant analysis of hallucination frequency in a hospitalized schizophrenic. *Journal of Behavior Therapy and Experimental Psychiatry, 5,* 13–18.

Anthony, W. A., & Nemec, P. B. (1984). Psychiatric rehabilitation. In A. S. Bellack (Ed.), *Schizophrenia: Treatment, management, and rehabilitation* (pp. 375–413). Orlando, FL: Grune & Stratton.

Atthowe, J. M., & Krasner, L. (1968). Preliminary report on the application of contingent reinforcement procedures (token economy) on a "chronic" psychiatric ward. *Journal of Abnormal Psychology, 73*, 37–43.

Ayllon, T., & Azrin, N. H. (1965). The measurement and reinforcement of behavior of psychotics. *Journal of the Experimental Analysis of Behavior, 8,* 357–383.

Ayllon, T., & Azrin, N. H. (1968). *The token economy: A motivational system for therapy and rehabilitation.* Englewood Cliffs, NJ: Prentice-Hall.

Ayllon, T., & Haughton, E. (1964). Modification of symptomatic verbal behaviour of mental patients. *Behaviour Research and Therapy, 2,* 87–97.

Ayllon, T., Haughton, E., & Hughes, H. B. (1965). Interpretation of symptoms: Fact or fiction? *Behaviour Research and Therapy, 3,* 1–7.

Ayllon, T., & Michael, J. (1959). The psychiatric nurse as a behavioral engineer. *Journal of Experimental Analysis of Behavior, 2,* 323–334.

Azrin, N. H., & Besalel, V. A. (1980). *Job-club counselors manual: A behavioral approach to vocational counseling.* Baltimore, MD: University Park Press.

Azrin, N. H., Flores, T., & Kaplan, S. J. (1975). Job-finding club: A group-assisted program for obtaining employment. *Behaviour Research and Therapy, 13,* 17–27.

Bachrach, L. L. (1992). What we know about homelessness among mentally ill persons: An analytical review and commentary. *Hospital and Community Psychiatry, 43,* 453–464.

Bellack, A. S., & Mueser, K. T. (1990). Schizophrenia. In A.S. Bellack, M. Hersen, & A. E. Kazdin (Eds.), *International handbook of behavior modification and therapy* (2nd ed., pp. 353–369). New York: Plenum Press.

Bond, G. R., & McDonel, E. C. (1991). Vocational rehabilitation outcomes for persons with psychiatric disabilities: An update. *Journal of Vocational Rehabilitation, 1,* 9–20.

Boudewyns, P. A., Fry, T. J., & Nightingale, E. J. (1986).Token economy programs in VA medical centers: Where are they today? *The Behavior Therapist, 6,* 126–127.

Bourdon, K. H., Rae, D. S., Narrow, W. E., Manderscheid, R. W., & Regier, D. A. (1994). National prevalence and treatment of mental and addictive disorders. In R. W. Manderscheid & M. A. Sonnenschein (Eds.), *Mental health, United States, 1994* (pp. 22–51). Rockville, MD: U.S. Department of Health and Human Services.

Catania, A. C. (1984). *Learning.* Englewood Cliffs, NJ: Prentice-Hall, Inc.

Chadwick, P. D. J., & Lowe, C. F. (1990). Measurement and modification of delusional beliefs. *Journal of Consulting and Clinical Psychology, 58,* 225–232.

Chadwick, P. D. J., & Lowe, C. F. (1994). A cognitive approach to measuring and modifying delusions. *Behaviour Research and Therapy, 32,* 355–367.

Chadwick, P. D. J., Lowe, C. F., Horne, P. J., & Higson, P. J. (1994). Modifying delusions: The role of empirical testing. *Behavior Therapy, 25,* 35–49.

Corrigan, P. W., Liberman, R. P., & Wong, S. E. (1993). Recreational therapy and behavior management on inpatient units: Is recreational therapy therapeutic? *Journal of Nervous and Mental Disease, 181,* 644–646.

Director-General of the World Health Organization. (1993). Prevention of mental, neurological, and psychosocial disorders. In N. Sartorius, G. De Girolamo, G. Andrews, G. A. German, & L. Eisenberg (Eds.), Treatment of mental disorders (pp. 5–33). Washington, DC: American Psychiatric Press.

Dombrowski, L. B. (1990). *Functional needs assessment program for chronic psychiatric patients.* Tucson, AZ: Therapy Skill Builders.

Donahoe, C. P., & Driesenga, S. A. (1988). A review of social skills training with chronic mental patients. In M. Hersen, R. M. Eisler, & P. M. Miller (Eds.), *Progress in behavior modification* (Vol. 23, pp. 131–164). Newbury Park, CA: Sage.

Ducharme, J. M., & Popynick, M. (1993). Errorless compliance to parental request: Treatment effects and generalization. *Behavior Therapy, 24,* 209–226.

Eisler, R. M., Blanchard, E. B., Fitts, H., & Williams, J. G. (1978). Social skills training with and without modeling for schizophrenic and non-psychotic hospitalized psychiatric patients. *Behavior Modification, 2,* 147–172.

Federal Task Force on Homelessness and Severe Mental Illness. (1992). Outcasts on main street (DHHS Publication No. ADM 92–1904). Washington, DC: Interagency Council on the Homeless.

Ferster, C. B. (1973). A functional analysis of depression. *American Psychologist, 28,* 857–870.

Frederiksen, L. W., Jenkins, J. O., Foy, D. W., & Eisler, R. M. (1976). Social skills training to modify abusive verbal outbursts in adults. *Journal of Applied Behavior Analysis, 9,* 117–125.

Furman, W., Geller, M., Simon, S. J., & Kelly, J. A. (1979). The use of a behavioral rehearsal procedure for teaching job-interviewing skills to psychiatric patients. *Behavior Therapy, 10,* 157–167.

Glynn, S. M. (1990). Token economy approaches for psychiatric patients: Progress and pitfalls over 25 years. *Behavior Modification, 14,* 383–407.

Halford, W. K., & Hayes, R. (1991). Psychological rehabilitation of chronic schizophrenic patients: Recent findings on social skills training and family psychoeducation. *Clinical Psychology Review, 11,* 23–44.

Hersen, M., & Bellack, A. S. (1976). A multiple-baseline analysis of social-skills training in chronic schizophrenics. *Journal of Applied Behavior Analysis, 9,* 239–245.

Hersen, M., Eisler, R. M., & Miller, P. M. (1974). An experimental analysis of generalization in assertive training. *Behaviour Research and Therapy, 12,* 295–310.

Hersen, M., Turner, S. M., Edelstein, B. A., & Pinkston, S. G. (1975). Effects of phenothiazines and social skills training in a withdrawn schizophrenic. *Journal of Clinical Psychology, 34,* 588–594.

Himadi, B., & Kaiser, A. J. (1992). The modification of delusional beliefs: A single-subject evaluation. *Behavioral Residential Treatment, 7,* 1–14.

Himadi, B., Osteen, F., & Crawford, E. (1993). Delusional verbalizations and beliefs. *Behavioral Residential Treatment, 8,* 229–242.

Himadi, B., Osteen, F., Kaiser, A. J., & Daniel, K. (1991).Assessment of delusional beliefs during the modification of delusional verbalizations. *Behavioral Residential Treatment, 6,* 355–366.

Holmes, M. R., Hansen, D. J., & St. Lawrence, J. S. (1984). Conversational skills training with aftercare patients in the community: Social validation and generalization. *Behavior Therapy, 15,* 84–100.

Iwata, B. A. (1987). Negative reinforcement in applied behavior analysis: An emerging technology. *Journal of Applied Behavior Analysis, 20,* 361–378.

Iwata, B. A., Vollmer, T. R., Zarcone, J. R., & Rodgers, T. A. (1993). Treatment classification and selection based on behavioral function. In R. Van Houten & S. Axelrod (Eds.), *Behavior analysis and treatment* (pp. 101–125). New York: Plenum.

Jacobs, H. E., Kardashian, S., Kreinbring, R. K., Ponder, R., & Simpson, A. R. (1984). A skills-oriented model for facilitating employment among psychiatrically disabled persons. *Rehabilitation Counseling Bulletin, 28,* 87–96.

Jacobson, B., Baltzley, C., Harris, C., Barbee, S., Coleman, S., & Hutchison, M. (1992, September). *Current behaviorally related activities in state mental health facilities.* Panel discussion conducted at the 12th annual meeting of the Florida Association for Behavior Analysis, Orlando, FL.

Jacobson, B., Hutchison, M., Coleman, S., & Harris, C. (1991, September). *Behavior change in state mental health facilities: What's up?* Panel discussion conducted at the 11th annual meeting of the Florida Association for Behavior Analysis, Sarasota, FL.

Kale, R. J., Kaye, J. H., Whelan, P. A., & Hopkins, B. L. (1968). The effects of reinforcement on the modification, maintenance, and generalization of social responses of mental patients. *Journal of Applied Behavior Analysis, 1,* 307–314.

Kazdin, A. E. (1977). *The token economy: A review and evaluation.* New York: Plenum.

Kazdin, A. E. (1987). *Conduct disorders in childhood and adolescence.* Newbury Park, CA: Sage Publications.

Kelly, J. A., Laughlin, C., Claiborne, M., & Patterson, J. T. (1979). A group procedure for teaching job interviewing skills to formerly hospitalized psychiatric patients. *Behavior Therapy, 10,* 299–310.

Kelly, J. A., Urey, J. R., & Patterson, J. T. (1980). Improving heterosocial conversational skills of male psychiatric patients through a small group training procedure. *Behavior Therapy, 11,* 179–188.

Kiesler, C. A., & Sibulkin, A. E. (1987). *Mental hospitalization: Myths and facts about a national crisis.* Newbury Park, CA: Sage.

Kiesler, C. A., & Simpkins, C. G. (1993). *The unnoticed majority in psychiatric inpatient care.* New York, NY: Plenum Press.

Kutchins, H., & Kirk, S. A. (1993). DSM-IV and the hunt for gold: A review of the treasure map. *Research on Social Work Practice*, *3*, 219–235.

Liberman, R. P., King, L. W., & De Risi, W. J. (1976). Behavior analysis and therapy in community mental health. In H. Leitenberg (Ed.), *Handbook of behavior modification and behavior therapy* (pp. 566–603). Englewood Cliffs, NJ: Prentice Hall.

Liberman, R. P., Teigen, J., Patterson, R., & Baker, V. (1973). Reducing delusional speech in chronic paranoid schizophrenics. *Journal of Applied Behavior Analysis*, *6*, 57–64.

Liberman, R. P., Wallace, C., Teigen, J., & Davis, J. (1974). Interventions with psychotic behaviors. In K. S. Calhoun, H. E. Adams, & K. M. Mitchell (Eds.), *Innovative treatment methods in psychopathology* (pp. 323–412). New York: Wiley.

Lloyd, K. E., & Garlington, W. K. (1968). Weekly variations in performance on a token economy psychiatric ward. *Behaviour Research and Therapy*, *6*, 407–410.

Lowe, C. F., & Chadwick, P. D. J. (1990). Verbal control of delusions. *Behavior Therapy*, *21*, 461–479.

Lovaas, I., Newsom, C., & Hickman, C. (1987). Self-stimulatory behavior and perceptual reinforcement. *Journal of Applied Behavior Analysis*, *20*, 45–68.

Lovaas, O. I., Varni, J. W., Koegel, R. L., & Lorsch, N. (1977). Some observations on the nonextinguishability of children's speech. *Child Development*, *48*, 1121–1127.

Luchins, D. J., Goldman, M. B., Lieb, M., & Hanrahan, P. (1992). Repetitive behaviors in chronically institutionalized schizophrenic patients. *Schizophrenia Research*, *8*, 119–123.

Mace, F. C., & Belfiore, P. (1990). Behavioral momentum in the treatment of escape-motivated stereotypy. *Journal of Applied Behavior Analysis*, *23*, 507–514.

Mace, F. C., Hock, M. L., Lalli, J. S., West, B. J., Belfiore, P., Pinter, E., & Brown, D. K. (1988). Behavioral momentum in the treatment of noncompliance. *Journal of Applied Behavior Analysis*, *21*, 123–141.

Mace, F. C., Lalli, J. S., Lalli, E. P., & Shea, M. C. (1993). Functional analysis and treatment of aberrant behavior. In R. Van Houten & S. Axelrod (Eds.), *Behavior analysis and treatment* (pp. 75–99). New York: Plenum.

Mace, F. C., & Roberts, M. L. (1993). Factors affecting selection of behavioral interventions. In J. Reichle & D. P. Wacker (Eds.), *Communicative alternatives to challenging behavior: Integrating functional assessment and intervention strategies* (pp. 113–133). Baltimore, MD: Paul H. Brooks.

Mace, F. C., Webb, M. E., Sharkey, R. W., Mattson, D. M., & Rosen, H. S. (1988). Functional analysis and treatment of bizarre speech. *Journal of Behavior Therapy and Experimental Psychiatry*, *19*, 289–296.

Matson, J. L., & Marchetti, A. (1980). A comparison of leisure skills training procedures for the mentally retarded. *Applied Research in Mental Retardation*, *1*, 113–122.

Matson, J. L., & Stephens, R. M. (1978). Increasing appropriate behavior of explosive chronic psychiatric patients with a social-skills training package. *Behavior Modification, 2*, 61–76.

McClannahan, L. E., & Risley, T. R. (1974). Activities and materials for severely disabled geriatric patients. *Nursing Homes, 24*, 10–13.

Moss, G. R. (1983). Behavioral technology and hospital psychiatry: Considerations from the private sector. *Analysis and Intervention in Developmental Disabilities, 3*, 205–214.

Moss, G. R. (1993). A commentary on the status of the behavioral approach in the healthcare marketplace. *Journal of Behavior Therapy and Experimental Psychiatry, 24*, 311–319.

Moss, G. R., & Liberman, R. P. (1975). Empiricism in psychotherapy: Behavioural specification and measurement. *The British Journal of Psychiatry, 126*, 73–80.

Nelson, G. L., & Cone, J. D. (1979). Multiple-baseline analysis of a token economy for psychiatric inpatients. *Journal of Applied Behavior Analysis, 12*, 255–271.

Nesbitt, J. A. (1970). The mission of therapeutic recreation specialists: To help and to champion the handicapped. *Therapeutic Recreation Journal, 4*, 43.

O'Brien, F. (1981). Treating self-stimulatory behavior. In J. L. Matson & J. R. McCartney (Eds.), *Handbook of behavior modification with the mentally retarded* (pp. 117–150). New York: Plenum.

Patterson, R. L., & Teigen, J. R. (1973). Conditioning and post-hospital generalization of nondelusional responses in a chronic psychotic patient. *Journal of Applied Behavior Analysis, 6*, 65–70.

Paul, G. L. (1987). *The time-sample behavioral checklist: Observational assessment instrumentation for service and research.* Champaign, IL: Research Press.

Paul, G. L., & Lentz, R. J. (1977). *Psychosocial treatment of chronic mental patients.* Cambridge, MA: Harvard University Press.

Rice, D. P., Kelman, S., Miller, L. S., & Dunmeyer, S. (1990). *The economic costs of alcohol and drug abuse and mental illness: 1985.* San Francisco, CA: Institute for Health & Aging, University of California.

Rogers, E. S., Anthony, W. A., Toole, J., & Brown, M. A. (1991). Vocational outcomes following psychosocial rehabilitation: A longitudinal study of three programs. *Journal of Vocational Rehabilitation, 1*, 21–29.

Ruiz, A. (1992, May). *Rise and shine industries: A model of enclave employment for the mentally disabled.* Paper presented at the 18th annual convention of the Association for Behavior Analysis, San Francisco, CA.

Sarbin, T. R., & Mancuso, J. C. (1980). *Schizophrenia: Medical diagnosis or moral verdict?* New York, NY: Pergamon Press.

Scotti, J. R., McMorrow, M. J., & Trawitzki, A. L. (1993). Behavioral treatment of chronic psychiatric disorders: Publication trends and future directions. *Behavior Therapy, 24*, 527–550.

Szasz, T. (1987). *Insanity: The idea and its consequences.* New York: Wiley.

Test, M. A. (1992). Training in community living. In R. P. Liberman (Ed.), *Handbook of psychiatric rehabilitation*. New York: Macmillan.

Thyer, B. A., Irvine, S., Santa, C. A. (1984). Contingency management of exercise by chronic schizophrenics. *Perceptual and Motor Skills, 58*, 419–425.

Ullmann, L. P., & Krasner, L. (1969). *A psychological approach to abnormal behavior*. Englewood Cliffs, NJ: Prentice-Hall.

Watts, F. N., Powell, E. G., & Austin, S. V. (1973). The modification of abnormal beliefs. *British Journal of Medical Psychology, 46*, 359–363.

Wincze, J. P., Leitenberg, H., & Agras, W. S. (1972). The effects of token reinforcement and feedback on the delusional verbal behavior of chronic paranoid schizophrenics. *Journal of Applied Behavior Analysis, 5*, 247–262.

Winkler, R. C. (1970). Management of chronic psychiatric patients by a token reinforcement system. *Journal of Applied Behavior Analysis, 3*, 47–55.

Wong, S. E., Flanagan, S. G, Kuehnel, T. G., Liberman, R. P., Hunnicutt, R., & Adams-Badgett, J. (1988). Training chronic mental patients to independently practice personal grooming skills. *Hospital and Community Psychiatry, 39*, 874–879.

Wong, S. E., & Liberman, R. P. (1981). Mixed single-subject designs in clinical research: Variations of the multiple-baseline. *Behavioral Assessment, 3*, 297–306.

Wong, S. E., Martinez-Diaz, J. A., Massel, H. K., Edelstein, B. A., Wiegand, W., Bowen, L., & Liberman, R. P. (1993). Conversational skills training with schizophrenic inpatients: A study of generalization across settings and conversants. *Behavior Therapy, 24*, 285–304.

Wong, S. E., Morgan, C., Crowley, R., & Baker, J. N. (in press). Using a table game to teach adolescent psychiatric inpatients social skills: Do the skills generalize? *Child and Family Behavior Therapy*.

Wong, S. E., Slama, K. M., & Liberman, R. P. (1985). Behavioral analysis and therapy for aggressive psychiatric and developmentally disabled patients. In L. H. Roth (Ed.), *Clinical treatment of the violent person* (pp. 22–56). New York: Plenum.

Wong, S. E., Terranova, M. D., Bowen, L., Zarate, R., Massel, H. K., & Liberman, R. P. (1987). Providing independent recreational activities to reduce sterotypic vocalizations in chronic schizophrenics. *Journal of Applied Behavior Analysis, 20*, 77–81.

Wong, S. E., & Woolsey, J. E. (1989). Re-establishing conversational skills in overtly psychotic, chronic schizophrenic patients: Discrete trials training on the psychiatric ward. *Behavior Modification, 13*, 415–430.

Wong, S. E., Woolsey, J. E., & Gallegos, E. (1987). Behavioral treatment of chronic psychiatric patients. *Journal of Social Service Research, 10*, 7–35.

Wong, S. E., Woolsey, J. E., Innocent, A. J., & Liberman, R. P. (1988). Behavioral treatment of violent psychiatric patients. *Psychiatric Clinics of North America*, *11*, 569–580.

Wong, S. E., Wright, J., Terranova, M. D., Bowen, L., & Zarate, R. (1988). Effects of structured ward activities on appropriate and psychotic behavior of chronic psychiatric patients. *Behavioral Residential Treatment*, *3*, 41–50.

13

LONELINESS, SOCIAL ISOLATION, AND SOCIAL ANXIETY

EILEEN GAMBRILL

Loneliness, shyness, and social anxiety are common complaints. Extensive literature exists on the topics of loneliness, shyness, social anxiety, and social isolation and withdrawal, as well as the related causes, correlates, and consequences for each problem (for reviews of the literature, see Gambrill, 1995; Jones, Cheek, & Briggs, 1986; Leitenberg, 1990; Peplau & Perlman, 1982a). This chapter begins with a brief overview of this literature. Then, guidelines for behavioral assessment are offered, followed by an overview of intervention options. Barriers for success are noted in the last section of this chapter.

OVERVIEW OF TRADITIONAL LITERATURE

About 11% to 26% of individuals complain of loneliness (Peplau, Russell, & Heim, 1979). Loneliness and its possible causes have been of concern to poets and novelists as well as to psychologists, sociologists and commentators on the state of society (see, for example, Bellah, Madsen, Sullivan, Swidler, & Tipton, 1985; Lasch, 1977). It is generally agreed by scholars in the field that loneliness results from inadequacies in social relationships. In particular, loneliness is related to the quality of social contacts, rather than the sheer frequency of contacts. Being alone is not synonymous with loneliness, nor does being with other people prevent feelings of loneliness. Rook (1984) defined loneliness as

> an enduring condition of emotional distress that arises when a person feels estranged from, misunderstood, or rejected by others and/or lacks appropriate social partners for desired activities, particularly activities that provide a source of social integration and opportunities for emotional intimacy. (p. 1391)

Loneliness may be chronic, situational, or transient. Chronic loneliness occurs over many years, often as a result of an individual not forming satisfactory relationships. Situational loneliness may result from major life changes such as divorce or the death of a significant other. Transient loneliness refers to short periods of loneliness.

Loneliness has been linked with problems such as depression, substance abuse, delinquency, aggressiveness, physical illness, and suicide (see reviews referred to earlier). This connection is not surprising given the many provisions of social relationships. As described by Weiss (1974), these provisions include (a) attachment resulting in a sense of safety and security; (b) social integration (shared interests and concerns with others); (c) opportunities to nurture others; (d) reassurance of worth through acknowledgement of skills and abilities; (e) reliable alliance (can count on assistance); and (f) guidance (provision of advice and assistance).

Unwanted social isolation also refers to lack of positive social exchanges. Social isolation and withdrawal among children has been defined in terms of time spent with others as well as sociometric status (i.e., reported popularity among peers) (see, for example, Foster, Inderbitzen, & Nangle, 1993). Children who have low social acceptance by their peers are more likely to be poor achievers in school, to have learning difficulties, and to drop out of school than are their peers (see Asher & Coie, 1990). A lack of popularity has been found to predict delinquency in children as well as emotional and mental health problems in adulthood. Social isolation among adults is associated with psychopathology as well as with mortality from to suicide and alcoholism (see, for example, Sabin, 1993).

About 90% of Americans report that they experience feelings of shyness sometimes; 50% report that their shyness is at times a significant problem (Zimbardo, 1977). Among adults who consider themselves shy, 36% reported that they have been shy since early childhood (see Cheek & Melchior, 1990). Shyness is characterized by a reluctance to initiate social exchanges and a subjective experience of anxiety in social situations that results in awkward behavior. It is related to other kinds of social anxiety such as embarrassment, shame, and audience anxiety, often called stage fright (Crozier, 1990). Interpersonal problems reported by shy people include difficulty in meeting people and making friends as well as anxiety, depression, loneliness, and excessive self-consciousness. Shy individuals experience inhibition in the presence of others as well as discomfort related to an awareness of the self, especially the possibility of negative evaluation. Transitory shyness is common and is situationally related. More enduring shyness may affect behavior across a range of situations.

Social anxiety may result in the avoidance of related situations and distracts attention from performance, often hampering success. Anxiety related to initiating conversations or speaking in public may result in lost opportunities for positive exchanges and interfere with success in work situations. Gilbert and Trower (1990) viewed a fear of compassion, love, and vulnerable desire as forms of social anxiety. Experiencing anxiety when being observed while performing a task (e.g., talking in public) is a hallmark of social phobia. There is a fear of being evaluated and criticized by others. Estimates of the prevalence of social phobia in the general population run from 1% to 15% (Barlow, 1988). Thus, social phobias have a much lower prevalence compared with other forms of social anxiety such as shyness. Not all persons with social phobias avoid social situations; however, a person's social anxiety may result in subtle avoidance behaviors that diminish success such as not initiating conversations and leaving events early (Butler, 1989).

Interrelationships

Shyness, loneliness, social isolation, and social anxiety are interrelated. As Peplau and Perlman (1982b) pointed out "it is at times difficult to distinguish among behavior that accompanies loneliness, behavior that leads to loneliness in the first place and behavioral strategies for coping with loneliness" (p. 12). Shyness, social anxiety, social phobia, and unwanted social isolation may be precursors to loneliness. The negative affective state that characterizes loneliness may increase shyness and social anxiety and encourage social isolation; it is often difficult to be socially outgoing when feeling lonely and alone. Factors related to loneliness include (a) emotional threats to relationships, such as arguments; (b) social isolation (e.g., being left out); (c) social marginality (being with strangers); or (d) romantic difficulties (Jones, Cavert, Snider, & Bruce, 1985). Loneliness is positively correlated with sensitivity to rejection, measures of shyness, and social anxiety; it is negatively correlated with measures of extroversion and sociability, likability, confidence, and the skills involved in dating and conflict resolution (Jones, Rose, & Russell, 1990). The greater the interest in being with people (the greater the sociability), the more intense the conflict caused by shyness and social anxiety may be, and the greater the loneliness that results from ineffective behavior and less-than-satisfactory social outcomes.

EXPLORING CAUSES

Evolutionary, environmental, developmental, and individual factors are interlinked, and all contribute to loneliness, social withdrawal and isolation, and social anxiety.

The Evolutionary Roots of Social Anxiety

Some writers have emphasized the evolutionary roots of social anxiety. Social anxiety is viewed as arising "from the activation of evolved mechanisms for dealing with intra-species threat, which served a vital role in the evolution of social groups" (Trower & Gilbert, 1989, p. 19). In Trower and Gilbert's view, social anxiety may represent a failure of reassurance (e.g., absence of positive social contingencies). Related reactions may help to maintain ranking (status) differences that encourage order in society (Gilbert, 1989). The adoption of submissive styles of behavior (e.g., shyness) serves as a protection from negative consequences. Trower and Gilbert viewed the socially anxious or phobic individual as caught in a primitive defense system in which attention is focused on a particular form of social comparison. "The socially anxious are in effect monitoring their outputs (social signals) and checking out the potential for injury or put-down in the interaction. Hence appraisal is focused on the possibility that others can add to or subtract from one's status or prestige" (p. 21). Submissive gestures are offered to appease those perceived to be dominant. Ohman (1986) suggested that angry faces are evolutionary fear-relevant stimuli (i.e., that we are prepared to fear angry, rejecting, or critical faces). Conditioned responses of fear to angry faces have been shown to be more resistant to extinction than reactions to happy or neutral faces (Ohman & Dimberg, 1984). A certain degree of wariness to strangers and unfamiliar situations is adaptive.

Thus, it should not be surprising that social anxieties are common. Guerin (1994) suggested that

> phobias and avoidance are like a free form of motivation which can be used for group maintenance purposes . . . Once an avoidance or negative reinforcement contingency is set up, it needs little input to keep it going. Merely having nothing happen reinforces the behavior. Given the problems we have encountered of how groups are to maintain social compliance and cohesion when their benefits are often remote and not obvious, it is no wonder that this form of maintenance has been widely utilized. (p. 215)

Environmental and Cultural Factors

Environments differ in the number and variety of behavior settings and related contingencies as well as in the roles available and the number of people available to fill these roles. Opportunities to meet people differ in different situations. For example, it may be difficult for gay persons who live in rural environments to meet other gay individuals. Although some environments—such as college—provide rich opportunities for a variety of social contacts, others may offer only a limited and unsatisfactory range of behavior settings that encourage valued social contacts. Public spaces that permit informal social exchanges are decreasing (Schiller, 1989). Pollutants such as noise, high crime rates, and crowding may decrease opportunities for positive exchanges (see, for example, Krause, 1993). Lack of transportation or money also may limit a person's opportunities for social contacts. The emphasis on competition in American society rather than on cooperation and reassurance interferes with opportunities to develop and maintain nurturing, enjoyable social relationships. This is a source of competing contingencies. Living and working environments differ in the opportunities they provide for meeting people and maintaining relationships. Hectic work schedules, coupled with family responsibilities, provide little or no time for people to cultivate friendships and supportive social networks.

Certain social roles, such as that of caregiver, may leave persons in such roles prone to loneliness, social isolation, or both. Moving to a new area and leaving behind friends and relatives often results in loneliness. A happy marriage may not make up for the loss of friends when a couple moves to a new location (Weiss, 1973). Higher divorce rates, as well as increased lifespan, have contributed to an increase in the percentage of individuals living alone (about one third of the population). These factors may contribute to social isolation. Cutrona (1982) found that three quarters of college students experienced loneliness in their first year. Causes of loneliness identified included leaving family and friends to attend college (40%). Cultural factors influence how given kinds of social anxiety are viewed. Gilbert and Trower (1990) pointed out that someone who declares him- or herself a Type A personality—who neglects his or her emotional ties with others—may be positively viewed by others. They noted that "a serious difficulty [lack of intimately relating to others] can be provided as evidence of a positive self in a culture that is competitive . . ." (p. 171).

Developmental Experiences and Social Learning History

Developmental experiences such as exposure to social models influence both skill development and anxiety reactions. The parents of individuals with social phobia have been found to be more socially fearful and more preoccupied with what others think of them than are the parents of individuals with agoraphobia (Bruch, Heimberg, Berger, & Collins, as cited in Barlow, 1988). A person's social confidence may be compromised by parental discouragement of his or her childhood friendships. A past history of punishment, as well as a lack of positive consequences, may contribute to social anxiety (Gray, 1988). Thus, both conditioned cues for punishment and conditioned cues for lack of reinforcement may inhibit social behavior. Social goals may change over time as people age (see, for example, Carstensen, 1995).

Individual Characteristics

Individuals who are shy, lonely, and socially anxious differ from individuals who are not shy in their affect, behavior, and thoughts (see reviews referred to earlier). Behaviors that may interfere with the development of social skills or with their use include cognitive-verbal (e.g., negative thoughts, inadequate role-taking), overt (aggressive reactions, impulsive behavior), and physiological-emotional (e.g., anger, anxiety, depression or fear; Gresham, 1988). Fears of rejection, of being shy, and of not knowing how to start a conversation are frequently mentioned as causes of loneliness by chronically lonely students. As with lonely individuals, there is an absence of social responsiveness to others.

Coping strategies adopted to avoid criticism and rejection may contribute to loneliness. Shyness may serve a protective impression management function by protecting an individual from negative consequences. The reinforcer profile may be dysfunctionally balanced to avoid negative feedback rather than to seek positive social experiences. Shyness is often associated with physiological arousal, such as blushing, rapid heartbeat, and dry mouth, as well as with a variety of negative thoughts, such as worrying that one is doing poorly. Shy men do not interpret interpersonal cues as accurately as socially comfortable men, and they are more likely than are nonshy people to expect rejection from others. Shy men rate others more negatively (less friendly), expect to be rated negatively by others, and rate themselves as less friendly than do their nonshy counterparts. Shy people speak for less time, take longer to respond to others' comments, allow more uncomfortable silences to occur, and tend not to interrupt when compared with nonshy individuals. Both loneliness and social anxiety are related to disruptive self-focused attention (Jones, Hobbs, & Hockenbury, 1982).

Cognitive components of social phobia include extreme or misdirected standards for performance, overprediction of negative consequences, and misperception of negative evaluation (Heimberg, 1989). Behavioral correlates include avoidance of feared situations, escape or early exit from feared situations, behavioral disruption (fidgeting, stuttering, and pacing), disaffiliative behaviors (e.g., an averted gaze) and behavioral withdrawal (appearing shy, aloof, unnoticed). Physiological responses may include sweating, shaking, blushing, rapid heartbeat, rapid or shallow breathing, and difficulty concentrating. Barlow (1988) argued that to develop a social phobia, a person must be biologically and psychologically vulnerable to anxious apprehension. In such cases, relatively minor events or stress from negative life events may set off an "alarm." These alarms may result in further anxious apprehension. Another pathway to social phobia is through performance deficits; that is, a person who may not perform well in a situation will anticipate failure in future similar situations. This apprehension in turn triggers further alarms. Anxious apprehension concerning potential negative outcome will decrease risk taking and will increase the likelihood of alarm reactions that may further increase anxiety (Barlow, 1988). Personal characteristics are influenced by social-learning histories as well as current contingencies.

GUIDELINES FOR A BEHAVIORAL ASSESSMENT

Research concerning the role of environmental contingencies and obstacles, negative thoughts, excessive physiological arousal, and behavior surfeits such as aggressive reactions highlights the value of a careful assessment. Sources of information include the behavioral interview, standardized self-report measures, self-monitoring, sociometric ratings, and observation in role play and in real-life situations. Behavioral researchers and practitioners view social anxiety as a learned reaction that can be altered by learning new experiences and by acquiring cognitive, behavioral, and affect-regulation skills. Assessment involves discovering the unique meaning (e.g., behavioral indicators and related antecedents and consequences) of loneliness, shyness, social isolation or withdrawal for each individual. Feelings of loneliness may be related to the lack of certain kinds of relationships (e.g., friends). Weiss (1973) distinguished between emotional isolation loneliness (a lack of companionship with another person) and social isolation loneliness (a feeling of not belonging; of not being a member of a social network). The type of deprivation is important to identify. Assessment should clarify desired outcomes, the behaviors required to achieve those outcomes, and the situations in which they must occur. The required environmental changes and resources that can be drawn on and obstacles that may interfere with social success—such as behavior surfeits or deficits and related antecedents and consequences—must also be assessed. Assessment should include a review of the contingencies in settings that offer opportunities to gain valued outcomes and a description of significant others, such as peers, who could be usefully involved. Related self-management skills should be reviewed (e.g., setting goals, monitoring progress, prompting and reinforcing desired behaviors). Key questions for assessment include the following:

1. What specific social outcomes are sought?
2. What skills are required to attain them?

3. What social settings are involved, and how do contingencies in each influence the behaviors of concern (e.g., what behaviors of concern are reinforced, punished, or ignored in each)?
4. What skills are required to attain desired outcomes?
5. What skills in what situations must be increased, decreased, stabilized, or varied to attain outcomes?
6. What cognitive, emotional, or behavioral responses interfere with the acquisition, performance, or both of available skills? What functions do these serve?
7. What significant others (if any) should be involved, and if so, who, how, and when should they become involved?
8. What opportunities are available to use valued skills, and how can such opportunites be increased? Can social settings be modified or created to encourage valued behaviors?
9. What prompts and consequences (self-presented and environmental) can be arranged to encourage valued behaviors and discourage interfering ones?
10. What intervention formats are most likely to be effective at minimal cost in time, effort, and discomfort (e.g., self-help, skill training in a group, rearrangement of contingencies in real-life settings)?
11. What can be done to maximize generalization and maintenance of valuable skills?

Empirically based descriptions of behavioral, affective, and cognitive repertoires of value in attaining certain outcomes, as well as a description of cognitive, behavioral, and affective deficits and excesses that interfere with their acquisition and use, will aid in the selection of programs. Examples of skills of value can be seen in Table 1. As with all behaviors, the distinction between learning and performance is relevant. Many people who describe themselves as shy, socially anxious, and lonely have the social skills required to do well but, for a variety of reasons, do not use them. Clients may lack practice in using skills. Situations that should serve as cues for social behaviors may not. An overview of repertoires and contingencies to explore is given next.

Review of Environmental Contingencies, Constraints and Opportunities

A behavioral analysis requires the identification of contingencies (antecedents and consequences) that influence behaviors of concern. How complex the analysis should be depends on what is needed to attain valued

TABLE 1
Valuable Skills

Reviewing Skills and Knowledge	Social skills (verbal and nonverbal behaviors and behavior chains as well as established S^{Ds}).
	Cognitive skills (e.g., attending to positive consequences; social problem solving).
	Self-presentation skills (physical appearance).
	Affect management skills (e.g., anger, anxiety, attraction).
	Access competencies (locating promising settings to meet people, creating new settings).
	Self-management skills (e.g., setting goals, arranging establishing operations, planning graduated practice opportunities, prompting and reinforcing desired behaviors, monitoring progress).
	Accuracy and completeness of information about: 1) behavior and how it can be altered; 2) social relationships including norms; and 3) personal characteristics that influence social exchanges.
Reviewing Environmental Contingencies	What environments provide opportunities to attain valued social outcomes?
	To what extent are these sampled?
	How could they be made more accessible and promising (e.g., by rearranging social contingencies or the physical environment, for example, by increasing access to transportation)?
	What contingencies in what relevant social settings influence related behaviors (see, for example Odom, Peterson, McConnell, & Ostrosky, 1990)?
	What are sources of reinforcement for valued behaviors, and how could these be increased?
	What physical changes in relevant environments could be made that would increase valued behaviors and decrease competing ones?
	What prompts could be introduced that would increase desired behaviors?
	What prompts should be eliminated that increase unwanted competing behaviors?
	What are sources of punishment and lack of positive reinforcement for desired behaviors, and how could they be reduced?
	What competing behaviors are being reinforced and how could contingencies supporting them be changed?
	What models of desired behaviors are available and how could these be increased?
	What models of unwanted behavior are available and how could they be decreased?
	What new environments could be created (e.g., a social or support group)?
	How could technology be used to increase access to valued social reinforcers (e.g., via telephone support groups or electronic mail systems)?

outcomes (Goldiamond, 1984). A distinction between structure (form) and function (maintaining consequences) is key in applied behavior analysis. Relevant behaviors may be maintained by escape or avoidance of unwanted consequences, by gaining access to valued materials, feelings, or people, or by both (See Table 1).

Review of Social Skills

A review of each client's entering repertoire, including nonverbal and verbal behaviors, will indicate which skills are available and which ones will have to be increased, decreased, varied, or stabilized. Behavioral definitions of social skills include a clear description of behaviors as well as their antecedents and consequences. Accurate perception and translation of social cues is needed for effective social behavior. Ideally, a task analysis would be conducted (or already available) to determine what skills are required to attain valued outcomes in specific situations, and training should focus on these skills. Task analyses would also reveal the range of responses (the operant class) effective in attaining a certain outcome.

Review of Cognitive Repertoires

What people say to themselves may contribute to loneliness or social isolation. Clients may have incorrect beliefs that get in their way, such as the belief that they must please everyone. Incorrect beliefs may be encouraged by false information provided in the media, such as incorrect reports about the shortages of single men (Faludi, 1991). Shy and socially anxious individuals tend to blame their failures on personal characteristics and to attribute success to external factors. Attributions can be conceptualized as rules about contingencies, many of which are verbally mediated and which may not reflect real-life contingencies (see, for example, Poppen, 1989). The complexity of social behavior and the role of verbally governed behavior provide fertile ground for incorrect rules (those that do not accurately describe contingencies).

Review of Accuracy and Completeness of Information

Clients may lack knowledge of when and how to use valuable skills or rely on misleading or incorrect rules about social contingencies. Knowledge about how relationships are formed, deepened, and maintained has increased substantially over the past decade especially in the area of friendship (see, for example, Duck, 1983, 1986). Knowledge and beliefs about emotions and behavior, and how they can be altered, as well as about relationships and how they are formed and maintained, should be reviewed to identify rules in need of correction. Volunteering help in times of need, sharing views of success, and keeping confidences are examples of rules relate to maintaining friendships (Argyle & Henderson, 1984). Knowledge about promising social settings is also important.

Review of Self-Presentation Skills

The self-presentation of each client should be reviewed. Many physical characteristics, such as manner of dressing, are modifiable, and changes that would enhance success should be pursued.

Review of Affect Management Skills

Excessive attraction, anxiety, or anger may interfere with enjoyable social exchanges. Some individuals are very sensitive to physiological reactions—such as rapid heart rate—in social situations. Some people do not distinguish between negative and positive arousal; they react to both as unpleasant. Excessive self-attention may encourage a focus on physiological reactions that increases anxiety. The opposite problem may also occur; that is, clients may not identify emotional cues and therefore may not have access to this source of information. Shy individuals have less intense positive affect in response to favorable outcomes than do nonshy persons, but more intense negative affect in response to unfavorable outcomes (see literature reviews cited earlier).

Review of Access Skills

The importance of *access skills* has been suggested in a number of studies (Lipton & Nelson, 1980). Access skills or competencies refer to knowledge and behavior that increase the likelihood of gaining access to environments, situations, and interactions that provide reinforcement as well as opportunities for additional skill acquisition (Hawkins, 1986). Even if clients possess excellent social skills, if they do not seek out and take advantage of opportunities to use their skills, they will not achieve valued social goals. The importance of taking the initiative was shown in a study that investigated the effectiveness of direct requests and hints on the part of women who wanted to go out with men (Muehlenhard & McFall, 1981). If a man liked a woman, there was an 80% chance that he would accept a direct invitation from that woman.

Review of Self-Management Skills

The role of self-management skills is often overlooked. Examples of useful skills include (a) selecting specific goals and intermediate steps; (b) selecting clear, achievable, relevant practice assignments; (c) prompting and reinforcing valued behaviors (e.g., by use of rules); (d) monitoring progress; and (e) taking corrective action based on progress. Clients may set unrealistic goals (e.g., pleasing everyone or making a close friend within a week's time). Regulating affect (anger, anxiety, attraction) can be viewed as a self-management skill. Self-management skills are required to gain access to promising environments.

INTERVENTION OPTIONS

A variety of approaches have been used to prevent and decrease loneliness, social anxiety, and social isolation. A contextual approach calls for a spectrum of options, including enhancing opportunities for social reinforcement in current environments, searching for natural reinforcing communities, creating new social environments by rearranging physical and social characteristics, and using prosthetic devices to enhance access to social reinforcers (e.g., computer communication among people confined to their homes). Both indirect and direct approaches should be explored. With the latter approach, there is a direct focus on complaints (e.g., as in social skills training). In indirect approaches, outcomes such as network building are a beneficial side effect of other positive outcomes (e.g., having fun, helping to elect a politician). Indirect methods focus on enhancing opportunities for positive social exchanges in existing social settings and creating new settings (Favell & McGimsey, 1993).

The selection of intervention methods should be informed by a contextual assessment (see Table 2). This assessment will indicate the role of lack of social skills, interfering thoughts, social anxiety, environmental contingencies and obstacles, lack of self-management skills, and lack of social opportunities. Research suggests that programs tailored to the unique characteristics of each client are more effective than those that are not (Ost, Jerremalm, & Johansson, 1981; Trower, Yardley, Bryant, & Shaw, 1978). The likelihood of generalization and maintenance of valued behaviors can be enhanced by teaching relevant behaviors and recruiting natural communities of reinforcement (e.g., peers), by training diversely, and by using functional mediators of valued skills (e.g., rules; Stokes & Osnes, 1989).

Individual and Group Approaches

Individual and group approaches include social skills training, self-help programs, arranged practice, and cognitive-behavioral programs that focus on altering self-statements and arranging exposure to anxiety producing situations. Programs differ in the extent to which there is a strong educational component. Information can be used to correct misconceptions

TABLE 2
Linking Assessment and Intervention

What Assessment Reveals	Intervention
Few opportunities to use social skills.	Increase opportunities to use skills in current social settings and create additional ones.
Lack of reinforcement for desired behaviors (e.g., initiating conversations).	Rearrange contingencies so that desired behaviors are reinforced.
Reinforcement of behaviors that interfere with desired behaviors (e.g., aggressive reactions).	Rearrange contingencies so that these behaviors are no longer reinforced.
Few models of desired behaviors.	Increase models of desired behaviors.
Models of undesired reactions.	Decrease them if possible.
Behavior deficits.	Develop required skills through model presentation, coaching, instructions, practice and feedback.
Faulty discriminations.	Provide information about when to use skills; provide prompts and incentives to encourage use of skills in contexts in which they will be reinforced.
Inaccurate beliefs (e.g., rules) about the nature of social relationships.	Provide accurate information (e.g., regarding helpful rules) and increase constructive beliefs.
Not using social and self management skills.	Encourage use of skills by rehearsal, assignments; arranging prompts and incentives; and self-management training.
Behavior surfeits such as aggressive reactions.	Replace interfering responses with positive alternatives (e.g., via rearrangement of contingencies, anger management training, social problem-solving training).
Behavior surfeits such as high social anxiety; fear of negative evaluation.	Arrange exposure to feared situations; provide successful experiences in real-life, provide anxiety management training.
Unrealistic expectations such as excessively high performance standards.	Encourage realistic expectations (e.g., provide knowledge about social norms and rules).
Low sense of worth; hopelessness.	Offer positive social experiences; replace interfering behaviors (including thoughts and feelings) with positive alternatives.
Disinterest in other people.	Pair people with valued activities and consequences.

based on limited personal experiences. Topics of relevance include (a) relationships (how they develop, deepen, are maintained, and end), (b) social anxiety (its nature, etiology, and correlates), (c) skills of value, (d) social ecology (environmental opportunities for social contacts), and (e) cognitive ecology (influences of self-statements, rules).

Social Skills Training

There is an extensive literature both with adults and children describing the use of social skills training to enhance positive social exchanges (see for example Christoff et al., 1985; Gambrill, 1995; Valenti-Hein, Yarnold, & Heuser, 1994). Social skills training is designed to develop skills required to attain valued social goals. It is useful when needed skills are absent and when clients will participate in training. Components include clear descriptions of specific skills to be acquired, model presentation, rehearsal, coaching, feedback, programming of change, and homework assignments. Intervention may be offered individually or in a group setting. Outcomes of concern to the client, empirical data describing effective and ineffective behavior in situations of concern, as well as the client's entering repertoire (skills available and missing) should inform selection of the behaviors on which to focus.

Social skills training has been found to be more effective than relaxation training in enhancing dating skills of clients with developmental disabilities (Mueser, Valenti-Hein, & Yarnold, 1987). Some studies combined social skills training, exposure, and modification of self-statements. Some studies have found an enhanced effect when graduated exposure and social skills training are combined (Cappe & Alden, 1986). Applied behavior analysts have drawn on a generative model of social skills training in which attention is given to developing rules that encourage generalization (Park & Gaylord-Ross, 1989).

Programs Emphasizing Exposure to Feared Situations

Most programs designed to decrease shyness and social anxiety involve exposure to feared situations. There is considerable evidence that exposure to feared situations is a key ingredient in overcoming social anxiety (Barlow, 1988; Marks, 1987). Programs that emphasize exposure help clients maintain contact with feared cues until anxiety decreases (habituation occurs). Marks (1987) argued that most clients can successfully carry out live self-exposure without a counselor especially if the exposure is systematized with the aid of a manual and diary. When investigators compared self-exposure with the aid of a self-help book (*Living With Fear*, Marks, 1978) with treatment by both a psychiatrist and a computer, they found that all groups improved markedly and equally for up to 6 months after follow-up (Ghosh & Marks, 1987). Response-induction aids designed to help clients initiate and complete exposure programs included keeping a diary to record self-exposure homework and guidance by a manual. The acquired nature of social anxiety, as well as the rationale for exposure, is reviewed in this approach. Other aids included carrying out exposure in small, manageable bits, trying difficult tasks briefly at first, engaging in rather than dissociating from the task, varying tasks until fear decreased in response to all relevant cues, and fading out aids as confidence and competence was acquired. Problems that may arise with assignments in real-life settings include the unpredictability of most social situations, the brevity of some social exchanges, and the lack of clear feedback about other people's reactions (Butler, 1985).

Self-help programs involving minimal counselor contact are ideally suited for individuals who do not have extremely high levels of social anxiety, who have the skills required to do well in social situations, and who are motivated to carry out recommended procedures. A class format offers a normalizing context for instruction. Analysis of pre- and postquestionnaires completed by men and women who participated in a course called "Taking Charge of Your Social Life," which consisted of 6 weekly 2-hour evening sessions, suggested that this format is effective in decreasing loneliness and shyness (Gambrill, 1993; Gambrill & Richey, 1988). Weekly homework assignments provided an opportunity to identify and participate in activities of interest that also provided a context to meet people (e.g., volunteer work, a sport, or hobby). Although it is clear that many clients can benefit from a self-exposure program involving minimal therapist time, their failure to carry out recommended procedures is a key problem. The success of self-help programs suggests the role of self-management skills as well as the importance of exposure to feared situations.

Montgomery and Haemmerlie (1986) explored the effectiveness of positively biased interactions in decreasing anxiety among heterosexual persons. In two sessions given 1 day apart, each participant engaged in six, 10- to 12-minute positively biased exchanges with a confederate of the opposite sex. Conversational partners were coached to be pleasant and warm. This procedure was effective with both men and women on a variety of measures. Participants reported that the experience was enjoyable, and gains were maintained on a 6-month followup. Total treatment time was less than 3 hours. These talks provided success experiences. As Montgomery and Haemmerlie noted, it could be that social skills training programs succeed not because of reinforcement, modeling, or shaping of behavior and instructions, but rather because participants offered appropriate behavior. Positively biased interactions involve exposure to feared situations as well as vicarious modeling opportunities (i.e., watching how others act).

Simply arranging practice dates has been found to increase the dating behavior of college students (Christensen, Arkowitz, & Anderson, 1975). Offering clients practice in public speaking not only increased their comfort in this situation, but also increased social contacts initiated, even though no attention was given to increasing social contacts during intervention (Phillips & Sokoloff, 1979; Phillips, 1986). This finding suggests the generalization of effects from different kinds of practice opportunities.

In their review of the literature on dating anxiety, Hope and Heimberg (1990) concluded that practice dating, social skills training, systematic desensitization, and cognitive modification all appear to be effective.

Cognitive and Cognitive–Behavioral Methods

Cognitive methods focus on altering thoughts to alter feelings and behavior. In contrast, exposure procedures focus on decreasing avoidance with the assumption that cognitive and physiological changes will follow. Most cognitive methods involve exposure to feared events. Although the results of some studies have suggested that the addition of cognitive restructuring can increase the effectiveness of exposure, the results of other studies indicated that cognitive approaches add little to the value of exposure (Marks, 1987). Heimberg and his colleagues have developed a cognitive–behavioral program for clients with social phobia (Heimberg, 1989). Intervention takes place over 12 weekly 2-hour sessions with a group of 5 to 7 individuals. The primary goal of this intervention program is to expose the client to anxiety-provoking social situations and to provide practice in using cognitive-coping skills to alter interfering negative thoughts. The key role of avoidance in maintaining social anxiety is emphasized; clients are encouraged to stay in anxiety-arousing situations and to use their arousal-lowering cognitive-coping skills to stay in the situations until anxiety subsides. Comparison of this package with a credible placebo control showed that participants in the cognitive-behavioral program improved more at both posttest and followup than did participants in the lecture-discussion, group-support program (Heimberg et al., 1990).

Rearranging the Environment

Rearranging the contingencies in real-life settings that influence behaviors of concern is emphasized in applied behavior analysis. Such contextual intervention may be combined with skill-training approaches, as will be described in the case example given later in this section. Environmental changes such as arranging social hours, rearranging furniture, and serving food family style (rather than on individual trays), have been found to increase social interaction in residential settings for elderly clients (see, for example, McClannahan & Risley, 1975; Risley, Gottula, & Edwards, 1978). Many programs designed to enhance social integration have been located in schools. These include peer-mediated programs, such as those designed to enhance the social status of children with disabilities among peers who are not disabled. (Christopher, Hansen, & MacMillan, 1991; Mathur & Rutherford, 1991; Strain, 1991). Class-oriented, preventative, interpersonal problem-solving training (e.g., Weissberg et al., 1981) is another example of a school-based program. Peer-mediated programs have also been carried out with adults in residential settings (Dy, Strain, Fuller-ton, & Stowitschek, 1981). Significant others such as teachers may be involved, as described in the example given next.

Case Example

Lewis and Sugai (1993) examined the effectiveness of a contextual intervention strategy paired with an existing packaged intervention in increasing and maintaining social involvement among children who displayed socially withdrawn behavior and their peers. The packaged program, known as PEERS (procedures for establishing effective relationship skills), was designed by Hops, Walker and Greenwood (1988). PEERS consists of four components: (a) social skills training, (b) joint-task activities, (c) group contingencies, and (d) self-management. A contextual intervention program was added to this curriculum to explore whether it would maintain positive outcomes more effectively than PEERS alone. Three students identified as socially withdrawn participated in the study: Lisa, a 5-year, 6-month-old girl who attended a half-day kindergarten class with approximately 20 other students; Emily, a 7-year, 5-month-old girl who attended 2nd grade; and Chuck, a 9-year-old boy with a mild mental disability who attended 2nd grade in a self-contained special education classroom with approximately 12 students.

The communicative functions of involved behaviors were explored for these students, and an individualized, contextual plan was developed that would replace the withdrawn behavior with a prosocial response serving the same function. Observations of related behaviors and their antecedents and consequences were analyzed for predictable behavior chains. This analysis indicated that Lisa's socially withdrawn behavior was associated with contingent adult and peer attention. Following a teacher or peer question or an attempt at social interaction, Lisa typically looked at the floor and provided either a gesture or a no response. Teachers and peers typically re-asked or reprompted her. Following the second prompt, Lisa drew in her shoulders and continued to look at the ground. At this point, the teacher or a peer provided an answer for Lisa. This pattern of socially withdrawn behavior was observed in 70% of Lisa's opportunities for social interaction. An opportunity was defined as each teacher or peer question addressed to Lisa. Emily exhibited socially withdrawn behavior in 77% of opportunities presented to her for social interaction. "An opportunity was defined as Emily physically placing herself within 1 meter of peers or the teacher during activities or times when social interaction was appropriate (e.g., free time, working in small groups)" (p. 69). Chuck's withdrawn behavior was observed in 62% of the opportunities presented to him during class and in 100% of the opportunities presented during recess. "An opportunity during class was defined as each teacher or peer question addressed to Chuck. An opportunity during recess was defined as a negative peer interaction (e.g., peer calls Chuck a derogatory name, peer is physically aggressive toward Chuck)" (p. 70).

Teachers were trained to implement all intervention procedures. Intervention consisted of teaching, prompting, and positively reinforcing prosocial alternative behaviors:

> For example, if the child engages in socially withdrawn behaviors during academic tasks the child finds difficult (aversive) the child is taught to request assistance (i.e., ask for help, raise hand) and verbally praised if they use the skill. During the "aversive task," if the child engages in withdrawn behavior, teachers prompt the child to request assistance and maintain the original question or task until the child correctly responds or requests assistance. Once the child engages in the correct response or requests assistance, the child is verbally praised. (p. 67)

Teachers prompted the three target students to work with their peers if they were alone during periods of instruction; they also prompted socially competent peers to include the target child if he or she was noticed to be by themselves. Teacher praise was offered for cooperative work. Teachers were encouraged to continue to reinforce prosocial behavior and to ignore socially withdrawn behavior after the formal program ended.

Pre, post, continuous, and 1- and 2-month follow-up on dependent measures assessing each participant's level of social involvement were collected during the study. A multiple baseline design across all three participants indicated that the combination intervention increased social interactions (see Figure 1). The effects of the intervention were maintained 2 months after the intervention was terminated (see original study for further details).

Pilisuk and Minkler (1980) designed an innovative project to establish supportive social networks for isolated senior citizens who resided in an inner city, single-room occupancy hotel. A station was set up in the hotel lobby offering free blood pressure checkups. This program offered residents opportunities to meet and identify shared interests. Within a year, the residents had formed a Senior Activities Club that became an ongoing support group. This project made creative use of an indirect approach (provision of free blood pressure checkups) to encourage contacts among individuals who would otherwise have been isolated. Indirect approaches may be of special value in situations in which interacting with others is uncommon. Such methods may be required to enhance social opportunities for individuals who would not seek out or participate in support or treatment groups addressing loneliness or the other complaints discussed in this chapter.

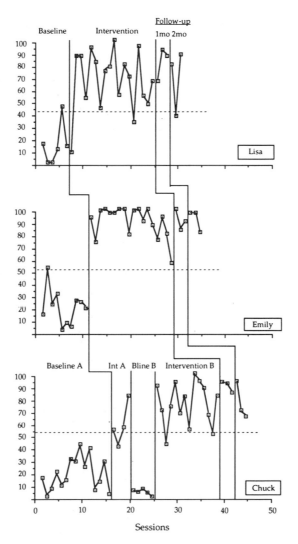

Figure 1. Percentage of intervals of social involvement across subjects. The dashed lines represent PEERS grade mean norms. *Note.* From "Teaching Communicative Alternatives to Socially Withdrawn Behavior: An Investigation in Maintaining Treatment Effects," by T. J. Lewis and G. Sugai, 1993, *Journal of Behavioral Education, 3,* 71. Copyright 1993 by Human Science Press. Reprinted with the permission.

PREVENTION OPTIONS

An emphasis on understanding how environmental characteristics influence behaviors of interest is a strength of a behavioral analysis. Restructuring social settings such as schools, churches, recreational centers, residential centers, and preschools provides opportunities both to prevent and address related problems. A contextual analysis will suggest options (see Table 3). The provision of interpersonal problem-solving programs in elementary and secondary schools, community awareness and educational programs, and the removal of obstacles that interfere with the use of valuable repertoires (Rook, 1984) are among the prevention options for loneliness and social anxiety. School-based programs designed to decrease behavior surfeits (e.g., bullying) should be valuable in decreasing the unwanted effects (e.g., social withdrawal) on persons who are the victims of such surfeits (Olweus, 1993). Contingency systems in residential settings should be examined to determine how they could be rearranged to enhance positive interactions. Future research could explore the value of helping people understand the evolutionary functions of social anxiety (e.g., to

TABLE 3
Describing the Ecology of Social Opportunities

A. Settings that provide opportunities for positive social exchanges	Their nature, variety, and availability. Kinds of individuals who participate including available models. Positive social consequences available and the probability of maximizing positive outcomes given needed skills. Negative social consequences likely and their schedule given high/moderate/low skill levels (e.g., lack of positive outcomes, aversive outcomes). Knowledge and skills required to obtain valued social outcomes in each setting. How often each can be sampled with positive effects and considering competing activities (e.g., work, sleep, child care). Current obstacles to taking advantage of opportunities: interfering responses such as social anxiety, aggression lack of social skills lack of self-management skills lack of transportation, money competing contingencies (work, child care) cultural norms/taboos competing cultural contingencies (to make money rather than provide social opportunities for citizens)
B. Settings that could be created	(Same questions as above.)
C. Obstacles to both A and B that could be removed and plan for doing so	e.g., lack of skills, social anxiety, lack of correct information.

maintain ranking hierarchies) and its resultant effects. This larger perspective may help people to not personalize related anxiety in a way that makes it easier to act in spite of anxiety. Common antecedents for loneliness, such as loss of a significant other, could be used as prompts to arrange support groups. Support groups for people experiencing recent losses of significant others may provide help in coping with loneliness as well as a source of new social contacts. A proactive stance to encouraging positive neighboring behaviors may be useful (Gambrill & Paquin, 1992).

OBSTACLES

Although some obstacles to successful intervention can be avoided by a careful behavioral assessment, this approach will not hold for all obstacles. Enhancing the skills of individuals who are lonely, shy, or socially anxious will not necessarily result in desired changes in the quality of interpersonal relationships. It is not surprising that achieving success with all clients is still an ideal to be hoped for rather than a *fait accompli*. The causative factors and selection of intervention methods for shyness, loneliness, social anxiety, and social isolation range from straightforward to highly complex. When the obstacles involved include patterns of behaviors and associated beliefs (e.g., rules) that do not change easily and environments that are difficult to modify, they are especially challenging. Social behavior is closely tied to verbal behavior. "It is partly because verbal mediators do not require direct contact with environmental contingencies that all sorts of 'irrational' beliefs can mediate the allocation of consequences" (Guerin, 1994, p. 215). Social situations are unpredictable, a characteristic that makes it impossible to fully control their outcome. Obstacles include work schedules that leave little room for social explorations.

Maintaining satisfying relationships is especially challenging given their voluntary nature and intimacy, which suggests expectations that should be fulfilled without special efforts (Rook, 1984; Wiseman, 1986). There is a limited pool of individuals who are open to forming new relationships in given environments. Given the uncertainty in arranging more rewarding social experiences for many people, Rook recommended that increased attention be given to enhancing competencies for coping with unwanted solitude (such as learning to enjoy solitary activities).

CONCLUSIONS

Identification of the skills required for success in specific situations is a research priority. Another is the integration of related literature with children and adults. For example, films and video modeling, as well as placing a child in a leadership role (pairing him or her with a younger child) have been found to decrease social isolation (Kendall & Morrison, 1984). Although some methods used successfully with children will not be relevant to adults, others will be. Rook (1990) argued that the development and maintenance of close relationships that provide companionship have been neglected by researchers. Characteristics of the helping relationship that may influence outcome should be identified, as should methods that encourage generalization across behavior, settings, and time. Further investigation of low-cost methods of enhancing quality of social life, such as arranged practice opportunities, should be investigated.

The consequences to individuals as well as to society of reticence and anxiety in social situations are great. Such anxiety results in unnecessary distress and lost opportunities and leads to dysfunctional ways of handling these outcomes, including substance abuse. There are losses for society as well. According to Gilbert and Trower (1990), the

> study of social anxiety provides more than an important insight into personal suffering. Social anxiety may also be apparent in the fear of acting morally, the fear of disobeying (shown in part by the preparedness to harm others), the fear of being shamed, and the avoidance of the truly social and compassionate life that is capable of seeking, finding, and giving reassurance. (p. 173)

These consequences call for greater attention to be paid to the prevention of shyness, loneliness, and social anxiety in the future (Rook, 1984), even though this public health model has not been popular in the past.

REFERENCES

Argyle, M., & Henderson, M. (1984). The rules of friendship. *Journal of Social and Personal Relationships, 1,* 211–237.

Asher, S. R., & Coie, J. D. (1990). *Peer rejection in childhood.* Cambridge, MA: Cambridge University Press.

Barlow, D. H. (1988). *Anxiety and its disorders: The nature and treatment of anxiety and panic.* New York: Guilford.

Bellah, R., Madsen, R., Sullivan, W., Swidler, A., & Tipton, S. (1985). *Habits of the heart: Individualism and commitment in American life.* New York: Harper.

Butler, G. (1985). Exposure as a treatment for social phobia: Some instructive difficulties. *Behavior Research and Therapy, 23,* 651–657.

Butler, G. (1989). Issues in the application of cognitive and behavioral strategies to the treatment of social phobia. *Clinical Psychology Review, 9,* 91–106.

Cappe, R. F., & Alden, L. E. (1986). A comparison of treatment strategies for clients functionally impaired by extreme shyness and social avoidance. *Journal of Consulting and Clinical Psychology, 54,* 796–801.

Carstensen, L. L. (1995). Evidence for a life-span theory of socioemotional selectivity. *Current Directions in Psychological Science, 4,* 151–156.

Cheek, J. M., & Melchoir, L. A. (1990). Shyness, self-esteem and self-consciousness. In H. Leitenberg (Ed.), *Handbook of social and evaluation anxiety* (pp. 47–82). New York: Plenum.

Christensen, A., Arkowitz, G. H., & Anderson, J. (1975). Practice dating as treatment for college dating inhibitions. *Behavior Research and Therapy, 6,* 510–521.

Christoff, K. A., Scott, O. W. N., Kelley, M. L., Schlundt, D., Baer, G., & Kelly, J. A. (1985). Social skills and social problem-solving training for shy young adolescents. *Behavior Therapy, 16,* 468–477.

Christopher, J. S., Hansen, D. J., & MacMillan, V. M. (1991). Effectiveness of a peer-helper intervention to increase children's social interactions. *Behavior Modification, 15,* 22–50.

Crozier, W. R. (1990). Social psychological perspectives on shyness, embarrassment, and shame. In W. R. Crozier (Ed.), *Shyness and embarrassment: Perspectives from social psychology* (pp. 19–58). New York: Cambridge University Press.

Cutrona, C. E. (1982). Transition to college: Loneliness and the process of social adjustment. In L. A. Peplau and D. Perlman (Eds.), *Loneliness: A sourcebook of current theory, research and therapy* (pp. 291–309). New York: John Wiley.

Duck, S. (1983). *Friends for life: The psychology of close relationships.* Sussex: Harvester Press.

Duck, S. (1986). *Human relationships.* London: Sage.

Dy, E. B., Strain, P. S., Fullerton, A., & Stowitschek, J. (1981). Training institutionalized, elderly mentally retarded persons as intervention agents for socially isolate peers. *Analysis and Intervention in Developmental Disabilities, 1,* 199–215.

Faludi, S. (1991). *Backlash: The undeclared war against American women.* New York: Crown.

Favell, J. E., & McGimsey, J. F. (1993). Defining an acceptable treatment environment. In R. Van Houten & S. Axelrod (Eds.), *Behavior analysis and treatment* (pp. 25–46). New York: Plenum.

Foster, S. L., Inderbitzen, H. M., & Nangle, D. W. (1993). Assessing acceptance and social skills with peers in childhood. *Behavior Modification, 17,* 255–286.

Gambrill, E. (1995). Helping shy, socially anxious, and lonely adults: A skill-based contextual approach. In W. O'Donohue & L. Krasner (Eds.), *Handbook of psychological skills training: Clinical techniques and application* (pp. 247–286). Boston: Allyn and Bacon.

Gambrill, E. D. (1993, September). *A class format for helping people to increase social contacts.* Paper presented at the European Congress of Cognitive and Behavior Therapies, London, England.

Gambrill, E. D., & Paquin, G. W. (1992). Neighbors: Their role and potential. *Children and Youth Services Review, 14,* 353–372.

Gambrill, E. D., & Richey, C. A. (1988). *Taking charge of your social life.* Berkeley, CA: Behavioral Options.

Ghosh, A., & Marks, I. M. (1987). Self-directed exposure for agoraphobia: A controlled trial. *Behavior Therapy, 18*, 3–16.

Gilbert, P. (1989). *Human nature and suffering.* New York: Plenum.

Gilbert, P., & Trower, P. (1990). The evolution and manifestation of social anxiety. In W. R. Crozier (Ed.), *Shyness and embarrassment: Perspectives from social psychology* (pp. 144–177). New York: Cambridge University Press.

Goldiamond, I. (1984). Training parent trainers and ethicists in nonlinear analysis of behavior. In R. F. Dangel & R. A. Polster (Eds.), *Parent training: Foundations of research and practice* (pp. 504–546). New York: Guilford.

Gray, J. (1988). *The psychology of fear and stress* (2nd ed.). Cambridge: Cambridge University Press.

Gresham, F. M. (1988). Social skills: Conceptual and applied aspects of assessment, training, and social validation. In J. C. Witt & S. N. Elliot (Eds.), *Handbook of behavior therapy in education* (pp. 523–546). New York: Plenum.

Guerin, B. (1994). *Analyzing social behavior: Behavior analysis in the social sciences.* Reno, NV: Context Press.

Hawkins, R. P. (1986). Selection of target behaviors. In R. O. Nelson & S. C. Hayes (Eds.), *Conceptual foundations of behavioral assessment* (pp. 331–385). New York: Guilford.

Heimberg, R. G. (1989). Cognitive and behavioral treatments for social phobia: A critical analysis. *Clinical Psychology Review, 9*, 107–128.

Heimberg, R. G., Dodge, C. S., Hope, D. A., Kennedy, C. R., Zollo, L. J., & Becker, R. E. (1990). Cognitive behavioral group treatment for social phobia: Comparison with a credible placebo control. *Cognitive Therapy and Research, 14*, 1–23.

Hope, D. A., & Heimberg, R. G. (1990). Dating anxiety. In H. Leitenberg (Ed.), *Handbook of social and evaluation anxiety* (pp. 217–246). New York: Plenum.

Hops, H., Walker, H. M., & Greenwood, C. R. (1988). *PEERS (procedures for establishing effective relationship skills).* Delray Beach, FL: Educational Achievement System.

Jones, W. H., Cavert, C. W., Snider, R. L., & Bruce, T. (1985). Relational stress: An analysis of situations and events associated with loneliness. In S. Duck & D. Perlman (Eds.), *Understanding personal relationships* (pp. 221–242). London: Sage.

Jones, W. H., Cheek, J. M., & Briggs, S. R. (1986). *Shyness: Perspectives on research and treatment.* New York: Plenum.

Jones, W. H., Hobbs, S. A., & Hockenbury, D. (1982). Loneliness and social skills deficits. *Journal of Personality and Social Psychology, 42*, 682–689.

Jones, W. H., Rose, J., & Russell, D. (1990). Loneliness and social anxiety. In H. Leitenberg (Ed.), *Handbook of social and evaluative anxiety* (pp. 247–266). New York: Plenum.

Kendall, P. C., & Morrison, P. (1984). Integrating cognitive and behavior procedures for the treatment of socially isolated children. In A. W. Myers & W. E.

Craighead (Eds.), *Cognitive behavior therapy with children* (pp. 261–288). New York: Plenum.

Krause, N. (1993). Neighborhood deterioration and social isolation in later life. *International Journal of Aging and Human Development, 36,* 9–38.

Lasch, C. (1977). *Haven in a heartless world.* New York: Basic Books.

Leitenberg, H. (1990). *Handbook of social and evaluative anxiety.* New York: Plenum.

Lewis, T. J., & Sugai, G. (1993). Teaching communicative alternatives to socially withdrawn behavior: An investigation in maintaining treatment effects. *Journal of Behavioral Education, 3,* 61–75.

Lipton, D. N., & Nelson, R. O. (1980). The contribution of initiation behaviors to dating frequency. *Behavior Therapy, 11,* 59–67.

Marks, I. M. (1978). *Living with fear.* New York: McGraw Hill.

Marks, I. M. (1987). *Fears, phobias and rituals: Panic, anxiety and their disorders.* New York: Oxford University Press.

Mathur, S. R., & Rutherford, R. B., Jr. (1991). Peer-mediated interventions promoting social skills of children and youth with behavioral disorders. *Education and Treatment of Children, 14,* 227–242.

McClannahan, L. E., & Risley, T. R. (1975). Design of living environment for nursing-home residents: Increasing participation and recreational activities. *Journal of Applied Behavior Analysis, 8,* 261–268.

Montgomery, R. L., & Haemmerlie, F. M. (1986). Self-perception theory and re-education of heterosocial anxiety. *Journal of Social and Clinical Psychology, 4,* 503–512.

Muehlenhard, C. L., & McFall, R. M. (1981). Dating initiation from a woman's perspective. *Behavior Therapy, 12,* 682–691.

Mueser, K. T., Valenti-Hein, D., & Yarnold, P. R. (1987). Dating-skills groups for the developmentally disabled. *Behavior Modification, 11,* 200–228.

Odom, S. L., Peterson, C., McConnell, S., & Ostrosky, M. (1990). Ecobehavioral analysis of early education/specialized classroom settings and peer social interaction. *Education and Treatment of Children, 13,* 316–330.

Ohman, A. (1986). Face the beast and fear the face: Animal and social fears as prototypes for evolutionary analysis of emotion. *Psychophysiology, 23,* 123–145.

Ohman, A., & Dimberg, U. (1984). An evolutionary perspective on human social behavior. In W. M. Waid (Ed.), *Sociophysiology* (pp. 47–86). New York: Springer-Verlag.

Olweus, D. (1993). *Bullying at school: What we know and what we can do.* Oxford: Blackwell Press.

Ost, L. G., Jerremalm, A., & Johansson, J. (1981). Individual response patterns and the effects of different behavioral methods in the treatment of social phobia. *Behavior Research and Therapy, 19,* 1–16.

Park, H-S., & Gaylord-Ross, R. (1989). A problem-solving approach tosocial skills training in employment settings with mentally retarded youth. *Journal of Applied Behavior Analysis, 22,* 373–380.

Peplau, L. A., & Perlman, P. (1982a). *Loneliness: A sourcebook of current theory, research and therapy*. New York: John Wiley.

Peplau, L. A., & Perlman, P. (1982b). Perspectives on loneliness. In L. A. Peplau & P. Perlman, *Loneliness: A sourcebook of current theory, research and therapy* (pp. 1–20). New York: John Wiley.

Peplau, L. A., Russell, D., & Heim, H. (1979). The experience of loneliness. In I. H. Frieze, D. Bar-Tal, & J. S. Caroll (Eds.), *New approaches to social problems: Applications of attribution theory* (pp. 53–78). San Francisco: Jossey-Bass.

Phillips, G. M. (1986). Rhetoritherapy: The principles of rhetoric in training shy people in speech effectiveness. In W. H. Jones, J. M. Cheek, & S. R. Briggs (Eds.), *Shyness: Perspectives in research and treatment* (pp. 357–374). New York: Plenum.

Phillips, G. M., & Sokoloff, K. A. (1979). An end to anxiety: Treating speech problems with rhetoritherapy. *Journal of Communication Disorder, 12*, 385–397.

Pilisuk, M., & Minkler, M. (1980). Supportive networks: Life ties for the elderly. *Journal of Social Issues, 36*, 95–116.

Poppen, R. L. (1989). Some clinical implications of rule-governed behavior. In S. C. Hayes (Ed.), *Rule governed behavior: Cognition, contingencies and instructional control* (pp. 325–357). New York: Plenum.

Risley, T. R., Gottula, P., & Edwards, K. (1978). *Social interaction during family and institutional style meal service in a nursing home dining room*. Paper presented at the Nova Behavioral Conference on Aging, Port St. Lucie, FL.

Rook, K. S. (1984). Promoting social bonding: Strategies for helping the lonely and socially isolated. *American Psychologist, 39*, 1389–1407.

Rook, K. S. (1990). Social relationships as a source of companionship: Implications for older adults' psychological well-being. In B. R. Sarason, I. G., Sarason, & G. R. Pierce (Eds.), *Social support: An interactional view* (pp. 219–250). New York: Wiley.

Sabin, E. P. (1993). Social relationships and mortality among the elderly. *The Journal of Applied Gerontology, 12*, 44–60.

Schiller, H. I. (1989). *Culture, Inc.: The corporate takeover of public expression*. New York: Oxford University Press.

Stokes, T. F., & Osnes, P. G. (1989). An operant pursuit of generalization. *Behavior Therapy, 28*, 327–356.

Strain, P. S. (1991). Modification of sociometric status and social interaction with mainstreamed mild developmentally disabled children. *Analysis and Intervention in Developmental Disabilities, 1*, 157–169.

Trower, P., & Gilbert, P., (1989). New theoretical conceptions of social anxiety and social phobia. *Clinical Psychology Review, 9*, 19–35.

Trower, P., Yardley, K., Bryant, B., & Shaw, P. (1978). The treatment of social failure: A comparison of anxiety-reduction and skills acquisition procedures on two social problems. *Behavior Modification, 2*, 41–60.

Valenti-Hein, D. C., Yarnold, P. R., & Mueser, K. T. (1994). Evaluation of the dating skills program for improving heterosocial interactions in people with mental retardation. *Behavior Modification, 18,* 32–46.

Weiss, R. S. (1973). *Loneliness: The experience of emotional and social isolation.* Cambridge, MA: MIT Press.

Weiss, R. S. (1974). The provisions of social relationships. In Z. Rubin (Ed.), *Doing unto others: Joining, molding, conforming, helping, loving* (pp. 17–26). Englewood Cliffs, NJ: Prentice Hall.

Weissberg, R. P., Gesten, E. L., Rapkin, B. D., Cohen, E. L., Davidson, E., Deapodaca, R. F., & McKim, B. J. (1981). The evaluation of a social-problem solving training program for suburban and inner city third grade children. *Journal of Consulting and Clinical Psychology, 49,* 251–261.

Wiseman, J. P. (1986). Friendship: Bonds and binds in a voluntary relationship. *Journal of Social and Personal Relationships, 3,* 191–211.

Zimbardo, P. G. (1977). *Shyness: What it is and what to do about it.* Reading, MA: Addison-Wesley.

14

DRUG ABUSE

CARL G. LEUKEFELD, THOMAS W. MILLER, and LON HAYS

This chapter focuses on drug abuse. In keeping with the overall purpose of this volume, the following areas are highlighted: (a) an overview of the severity and epidemiology of drug abuse, (b) a brief discussion of the biopsychosocial approach to addiction followed by a review of empirical data related to treatment and prevention, (c) a behavioral analysis of drug abuse, (d) a presentation of implications for intervention and prevention, (e) a case example related to cocaine use, and (f) a summary of conclusions and recommendations for cocaine interventions reached at a scientific meeting sponsored by the National Institute on Drug Abuse. It should be noted that the abuse of cocaine has been emphasized in this chapter's case example and for the recommendation section.

The authors wish to acknowledge the assistance of the Center for Prevention Research, University of Kentucky, funded by the National Institute on Drug Abuse, Grant Nos. DA-05312 and DA-081154A; the Department of Veterans Affairs Medical Center, Lexington, Kentucky; and the Substance Abuse Treatment Program and the Mental Health and Behavioral Science Service, Department of Veterans Affairs, Central Office, Washington, DC. Appreciation is extended to Deborah Kessler and Katrina Scott, Department of Veterans Affairs; Libby Van Hook, Center on Drug and Alcohol Research; and Tag Heister, Virginia Lynn Morehouse, Debbie Howard, and Robin Oakley, Department of Psychiatry, University of Kentucky, for their contributions to the completion of this manuscript.

SEVERITY AND EPIDEMIOLOGY

The following categories are commonly used to classify drugs that can be abused: (a) *narcotics* (includes opiates, heroin, and related analgesics); (b) *stimulants* (includes cocaine, amphetamines, and caffeine); (3) *sedative-hypnotics* (includes alcohol, barbiturates, nonbarbiturate sedatives, and minor tranquilizers); (d) *hallucinogens* (includes LSD); (e) *phencyclidine* (PCP); (f) *marijuana* (cannabis); and (g) *inhalants*.

Extent of the Problem

Estimates of drug use in the general population come primarily from two sources: the High School Senior Survey of the Monitoring the Future study carried out by the Institute for Social Research, University of Michigan, and from the National Household Survey.

Since 1975, The High School Senior Survey has collected data from approximately 16,000 seniors in a sample of about 130 public and private high schools across the country. This survey collects data on lifetime drug use (any drug use), drug use in the 12-month period prior to the survey, and current drug use (use in the 30-day period prior to the survey). The High School Senior Survey includes those students who remain in school (did not drop out) before their senior year and those attending school on the day of the survey. The survey has been criticized for underestimating drug-using behaviors. Because estimates suggest that about one third of 18-year-olds are generally absent or drop out of high school, drug use rates for those individuals are higher. The following provides an overview of drug use in the United States by senior high school students.

In 1991, marijuana was the illicit drug most used by high school seniors, with 44% of the survey's respondents reporting marijuana use. Lifetime use of marijuana peaked first in 1979 and again in 1980 at 60%. The annual use of marijuana was highest in 1979, at almost 51%, and the 30-day prevalence (use) peaked in 1978 at 37%. These rates began to decrease in subsequent years to 24% for annual use, 14% for 30-day, and 2% for daily use by high school seniors (National Institute on Drug Abuse [NIDA], 1991).

In 1991, the second most popular category of abused drugs was inhalants at 18%, followed by stimulants at 15%, hallucinogens at 10%, cocaine at 8%, tranquilizers at 7%, and steroids at 2%. Increases in lifetime illicit drug use for drugs other than marijuana were noted between 1976 and 1982, when the percentages rose from 35% to 45%. This level was sustained in the years 1983 and 1984 and then decreased to 36%. Annual and 30-day prevalence figures reflected similar trends.

The use of cocaine by high school seniors began to increase in the late 1970's. In 1975, 9% of seniors reported having tried cocaine. However, this level of use gradually increased to 17% in 1985–86 and decreased to 10% in 1989. Crack, a more potent and smokable derivative of cocaine, was not included in the High School Senior survey until 1986. In 1986, when seniors were asked specifically about the use of crack, 4% of the respondents admitted they had tried crack at least once; by 1991, this figure had decreased to 3%.

The National Household Survey presents a second view of drug use in the general population and includes respondents aged 12 and older, who are in or out of school. The National Household Survey was conducted biannually until 1979 when it became triennial; it is now conducted annually. Data for 1991 showed lifetime, annual, and past-month use rates for age groups 12 to 17, 18 to 25, 26 to 34, and 35 and older. Drug-use data for all age groups indicated that 33% of respondents reported marijuana and hashish use. Other drugs with high use (prevalence) levels in 1991 were inhalants at 6%, nonprescription analgesics at 6%, nonprescription stimulants at 7%, cocaine at 12%, hallucinogens at 8%, and nonprescription tranquilizers at 6%. Use of drugs in the year and month prior to the survey showed lower rates, with marijuana and hashish use at 5%, and inhalants at 4%. Use of cocaine and nonprescription analgesics, as well as inhalants, were about 1% each.

Before 1980, cocaine use was considered a minor, albeit serious, drug problem (NIDA, 1991). Cocaine was identified in admissions to federally funded treatment programs as a primary drug of abuse in only 5.8% of the cases reported by the Client-Oriented Data Acquisition Process for 1981 (NIDA, 1982). In 1990, the percentage of the National Household Survey population 18- to 25-years-old who reported thay they had "ever used" cocaine was 19.4%, but only 2.2% reported that they had used cocaine during the previous 30 days (NIDA, 1991), a decrease from 4.5% in 1988 (NIDA, 1990). Among those age 26 to 34 years, 25.6% reported ever having used cocaine, and 1.7% reported use in the past 30 days, down from 2.6% in 1988. The percentage of those age 16 to 17 reporting cocaine use in the past 30 days was just under 1% in 1990. It appears from this data that cocaine use has peaked.

According to Household Survey data, the estimated number of Americans using any illegal drug during the past 30 days decreased 37%, from 23 million in 1985 to 14.5 million in 1988 (National Drug Control Strategy, 1989). The 1988 Household Survey also reported that 72 million Americans age 12 and older (37% of the population) had tried marijuana, cocaine, or other illicit drugs at least once in their lifetime, and 28 million (15% of the U.S. population) had used some type of illicit drug in the past year. In addition, 24.5 million (7% of the population) had used at least one drug within the 30 days prior to the survey.

Data from both Household Survey and the student survey show similar peaks and declines in the use of marijuana, cocaine, cigarettes, and alcohol. Both show that, overall, the use of illicit drugs has moved downward for those persons who reside in households and for students who remain in school. However, other indicators show increases in illegal drug use. For example, the number of persons admitted to emergency rooms (N = 500 in 21 metropolitan areas) for cocaine and heroin use has increased. This trend began in the last quarter of 1990, when 10% of emergency room admissions involved cocaine. In the third quarter of that year, 13% of admissions were for heroin. In addition, the number of heroin and marijuana mentions (i.e., the number of times a drug is identified by emergency room staff) also increased for the same time period in emergency rooms (Adams, Blanker, Ferguson, & Kopstein, 1989).

Jails and lockups are a repository for large numbers of people who abuse drugs, most of whom are urban poor and minority group members. Data from the Drug Use Forecasting System (DUF) indicate that 40% to 60% of arrestees are using one or more drugs other than alcohol at the time of their arrest; this data was confirmed with drug testing (National Institute of Justice, 1993).

A related concern is the potential for transmission of human immunodeficiency virus (HIV) and acquired immune deficiency syndrome (AIDS). According to the Centers for Disease Control (CDC, 1993) about one third of the cases of AIDS in America are related to drug injection. Transmission of the virus through needle use is a major challenge that has been ignored by the medical community to some extent.

Studies (DesJarlais et al., 1988; Lang et al., 1988) have shown that between 70% and 100% of those who inject drugs share injection equipment. This behavior places themselves, their sex partners, and their children at high risk for contacting and transmitting AIDS. Of the AIDS cases that occurred through perinatal transmission (from mother to child during pregnancy or childbirth), about three-fourths occurred among children born to IV-drug-abusing women or women whose sex partners were IV drug abusers (Chamberland, White, Lifson, & Dondero, 1987).

Community outreach workers now educate drug abusers about HIV prevention and distribute bleach for needle cleaning as a method of controlling the spread of HIV. This prevention–education approach has been tried with some apparent success in large cities. However, this approach is not compatible with the no-drug-use goals of both drug treatment agencies and the justice system. Needle exchange and distribution programs designed to dampen the spread of HIV have also received media attention. These projects remain politically controversial, but appear to be of some use if well executed.

Effects on the Economy

Drug abuse is expensive for the United States. Harwood, Napolitano, Kristenson, and Collins (1984) estimated that drug abuse costs the United

States $47 billion each year. (This figure did not include alcohol-related costs.) These costs are distributed in billions as $25.7 in reduced work force productivity, $18.3 in crime-related costs, $1.2 in drug abuse treatment, $1.2 in drug-overdose deaths, and $0.6 in health support services and lost employment. These costs are likely much higher today, because crack cocaine, HIV/AIDs, and other costs were not factored into this estimate, which was based on 1980 data.

The economics of AIDS is a major concern for large urban hospitals. Treatment alone requires a major commitment of resources, and costs are being driven by injecting drug abusers who are infected with AIDS (Leukefeld, 1990; McGurk, Miller, & Eggerth, 1995). New York serves as an example: An estimated 57% of those in methadone treatment for substance abuse are infected with the AIDS virus (DesJarlais et al., 1989). These intravenous drug abusers are without health insurance (Andrulis, 1989), and many are homeless. In fact, the U.S. Conference of Mayors reported, based upon a survey of 27 cities, that 44% of the homeless population are drug abusers and that there is a direct relationship between the urban crisis of drug abuse and lack of shelter (Ifill, 1989).

EXISTING KNOWLEDGE AND CONCEPTUAL BASE

The overriding conceptual base that has been applied in the area of drug addiction intervention is biopsychosocial. This approach to addiction combines theoretical perspectives that were developed in three distinct areas of science and draws upon those perspectives for assessment, diagnosis, and treatment. The biological underpinnings of addiction are grounded in physiological factors and the genetic aspects of addiction; these factors have been more firmly established for alcohol than drug abuse, primarily through twin and adoption studies (Cadoret, 1992). There is a great deal still to be learned about genetic aspects of other drugs of abuse. Psychological factors have also been studied, and the associated comorbidity with anxiety and depression has been documented by such studies as the Epidemiological Catchment Area Study (ECA) (Regier et. al, 1990). Social and cultural variables have also been found to be important in the understanding of drug use, abuse, and dependency. Environmental factors incorporate family, schools, workplace, peer relationships and community institutions (Clayton & Leukefeld, 1993).

There is a substantial knowledge base related to treatment and prevention (Miller, Jefferson, Leukefeld, & Carmona, 1994; Tims & Leukefeld, 1993). Methadone maintenance treatment, therapeutic community treatment, and outpatient drug treatment represent the majority of treatment approaches used in the United States. There are about 1,600 drug abuse treatment programs and about 3,500 combined alcohol and drug treatment units of these type in the United States (Butynski, 1991). Two other treatment approaches are important. One is chemical dependency treatment programs, which typically involve a 10- to 30-day stay in residential treatment with self-help interventions. The other approach involves self-help groups such as Alcoholics Anonymous and Narcotics Anonymous. Research findings indicate that treatment is effective in reducing drug abuse (Hubbard et al., 1989; Simpson & Sells, 1990). Evidence for treatment effectiveness has been reported for methadone maintenance treatment (Ball, Lange, Myers, & Friedman, 1988; Blaine, Thomas, Barnett, Whysner, & Renault, 1981; McLellan, Luborsky, O'Brien, Woody, & Druley, 1982). Drug abuse treatment is also helpful in preventing the spread of HIV among injecting drug abusers (Battjes, Leukefeld, Pickens, & Haverkos, 1988; Hubbard, Marsden, Cavanaugh, Rachal, & Ginzburg, 1988; McGurk et al., 1995).

Medications to block brain pathways that are activated by drugs are now being developed. Medications that could possibly be used to treat cocaine addiction include: (a) a mixed opioid agonist-antagonist painkiller called buprenorphine, (b) an antidepressant called desipramine, (c) an antipsychotic called flupenthixol, (d) an antiseizure drug called carbamazapine, (e) an antianxiety drug called buspirone, (f) a dopamine antagonist called bromocriptine, and (g) a dopamine blocker called mazindol (Holden, 1989). These medications would produce pharmacological effects similar to what methadone does for heroin (Tims & Leukefeld, 1993).

The criminal justice system provides another perspective, including probation, parole, and prison services for the treatment of drug abuse. A high level of drug use was found not only in those entering jails and lockups, as previously noted by DUF, but also in a study of state prison inmates, in which 43% self-reported that they used drugs daily or almost daily in the month before their offense (Bureau of Justice Statistics, 1986). Drug abusers are often referred to treatment by the criminal justice system and are frequently on probation, parole, or mandatory release. In 1982, 27% of men and 15% of women in drug abuse treatment reported involvement with the criminal justice system (NIDA, 1982). Despite the overall decline in drug use, these data make clear that use among the population who comes in contact with the criminal justice system continues to increase.

Once a person is addicted, drug abuse tends to be a chronic and relapsing disorder (Leukefeld & Tims, 1990). Prevention and early intervention, therefore, are particularly important. These approaches show more promise now than ever before (Leukefeld & Clayton, 1994).

A particularly useful approach is framed in epidemiological terms. Drug abuse prevention has been described in a variety of ways. Drug prevention from this perspective refers to those activities that focused on decreasing the incidence (number of new cases) and prevalence (the actual number of cases) of alcohol and drug abuse. This approach makes it easier to assess the outcomes of prevention activities because strategies for the measurement of incidence and prevalence before and after a prevention intervention are available (Biglan, 1995; Leukefeld & Clayton, 1994).

The National Institute on Drug Abuse (1978) described four approaches in an early definition of drug prevention:

1. Distributing accurate and objective information about all types of drugs and the effects of those drugs on human systems;
2. Educating individuals through a well-defined and structured learning process to develop the affective skills they need to help themselves;
3. Providing challenging, growth-filled community experiences as alternatives to drug use; and
4. Providing intervention assistance and support to young people during critical periods of their life when person-to-person, experience-sharing, and empathetic listening would contribute to successful adjustment.

Early drug prevention activities involved disseminating information related to drug education and prevention (Leukefeld, 1991). Drug abuse prevention information included descriptions of drug users that were so detailed they (a) probably helped teach some persons how to use drugs, and (b) may have encouraged drug abuse by reinforcing curiosity. Studies by Evans and his colleagues at the University of Houston (Evans et al., 1981, 1978) demonstrated positive findings in reducing tobacco use among youth. This research highlighted two approaches, social inoculation/pressures training (Flay, 1985a) and social skills training (Botvin & Wills, 1985; Schinke, Gilchrist, & Snow, 1985), as promising approaches to drug prevention. Evans' findings were replicated by McAlister, Perry, and Maccoby (1979) and others (Perry, Killen, Slinkard, & McAlister, 1980; Perry, Maccoby, & McAlister, 1980; Perry, Telch, Killen, Dass, & Maccoby, 1983), who reported that "Just Say No" (psychological innoculation) combined with social skills training reduced tobacco use by school-age children (Leukefeld, 1991). Note that the combination was probably essential. Simply stating the rule, "Just say no," without providing skills training or attending to environmental contingencies constitutes a very weak intervention.

Psychological innoculation interventions were accepted as an approach to reducing tobacco use and perhaps other forms of drug use as well. "Just Say No" had developed and matured while data were still coming in (Leukefeld, 1991). Although there were analyses pointing out the weaknesses of these studies, the outcome data were generally positive (Biglan & Ary, 1985; Biglan et al., 1987; Flay, 1985b; McCaul & Glasgow, 1985). However, the results of studies were less clear with regard to school-only programs that focused on other drugs rather than on smoking (Gilchrist,

1990; Goodstadt, 1986; Moskowitz, 1983; Schaps, Dibartolo, Moskowitz, Palley, & Churgin, 1981; Tobler, 1986). Findings by Pentz et al. (1990) suggest the importance of multiple-component (i.e., peer, parents, and community) prevention interventions. These findings make sense from a behavioral perspective, given the powerful biological effects of psychoactive substances and the social matrices within which substance use is embedded.

BEHAVIORAL ANALYSIS OF THE PROBLEM

Focus on contemporary behavioral analysis with substance abuse (Mattaini, 1991a, 1991b) offers a methodology that has particular potential as a prevention–intervention tool. Behavior analytic theory addresses both contingency-shaped and rule-governed behavior. Glenn (1988) and Malott (1988) developed persuasive integrations of the principles of applied behavioral analysis with cultural anthropology that focus on four distinct but related response repertoires with important implications for understanding substance abusing behavior. These include (a) experimentation and initiation of substance use as contrasted with refusal, (b) regular use of substances as opposed to refusal and incompatible behavior, (c) continued problem usage as opposed to sobriety or moderation, and (d) relapse as opposed to sobriety or controlled drinking. An applied behavioral analytic perspective examining each of these related response repertoires has been summarized elsewhere (Mattaini, 1991b).

The last decade has witnessed the emergence of cocaine as a major drug of abuse. Because of the incidence of cocaine abuse and the need for more specific, cost-effective, and efficacious treatment methods, the role of behavior analysis has gained increased interest among research scientists and health care professionals.

A number of variables are associated with substance abuse, including level of self-esteem, attribution, dependency, education, family issues, and coping skills. Self-esteem appears to play a critical role as an antecedent to problem behavior in alcohol and drug abuse. Shame and guilt, coupled with the stigmatization related to the life-style associated with chemical dependency, are critical behavioral indicators and antecedents for substance-abusing behavior. Although self-esteem is a crucial issue for both men and women, the literature suggests that women suffer a greater negative impact on self-concept as a result of drug abuse (Babcock & Connor, 1981).[1]

---

[1] [From a behavior analytic perspective, the emotional and cognitive events associated with self-esteem are themselves behavioral phenomena, often involving equivalence relations and other verbal processes (see chapter 1). This is a hopeful view because it suggests that improved self-esteem can be shaped through a combination of verbal intervention and experience with new environmental contingencies.—Eds.]

Self-Attribution

There is limited evidence concerning the degree to which substance abusers generally accept responsibility for—and anticipate control over—the events in their lives. Various researchers have reported clinical evidence that suggests a relationship between locus of control and one's perception of chemically dependent behavior. Gutierres and Reich (1988) found that internal dispositional attributions for success—but not failure—predicted a positive outcome to rehabilitation with substance abusers. However, Birke, Edelmann, and Davis (1990) found no significant differences in attributional style between substance abusers, relapsers, and abstainers.

Marlatt and Gordon (1985) identified the importance of abstinence violation effect in understanding relapse. This effect is a reaction to breaking an absolute rule against any use of substances of abuse that increases the chance of lapse becoming a full-blown relapse. The effects of attribution are thought to be mediated through this abstinence violation effect. Marlatt and Gordon suggested that the intensity of the abstinence-violence effect is augmented by a personal attribution effect (blaming the self as the cause of the relapse). Furthermore, an increase in the abstinence violation effect is postulated to occur when the individual attributes the cause of the lapse to internal, global, and stable conditions that are perceived to be uncontrollable by the individual.

Janoff-Bulman (1979) argued that a distinction exists between behavioral and characterological self-blame. This suggested that blame directed at one's specific controllable actions is adaptive and leads to better future adjustment through enhanced perception of control. In contrast, blame directed at stable and uncontrollable aspects of one's character is maladaptive because it suggests the individual may well be in a state of hopelessness concerning the addictive behavior. Bradley et al. (1992) suggested that drug addicts who in general report having greater personal responsibility for negative outcomes in general have a better outcome for recovery. Thus, causal beliefs concerning relapse episodes strongly implicate perceived controllability, over and above other dimensions. Chemically dependent persons who perceive that they have more personal control over past or future relapses are more likely to remain abstinent and to contain the effects of brief lapses than those who do not have such perceptions, especially when their addictions involve opiate use. This finding is consistent with Marlatt and Gordon's (1985) relapse model.

Self-Esteem and Dependency

Dependency on others has been shown to be critically related to self-esteem. This may be particularly true for women. Women are often introduced to chemical abuse by men, which may establish a continuation of a pattern of dependence (Nichols, 1985). Women who experience feelings of low self-worth often develop and engage in relationships that are negative and further damaging to self-esteem (Reed, 1985). The commonly associated factors of physical and emotional abuse tend to perpetuate a cycle of violence and confirm low self-worth among these women. Dependence on men is often reinforced by being alienated from the social support of other women. This is coupled with feelings of low self-confidence, which often impede the development the coping skills necessary to break the cycle of violence and the abuse of drugs.

The longitudinal effects of dysfunctional families and their relationship with chemical dependence have been well-established (Rohsenow, Corbett, & Devine, 1988). The effects of physical, sexual, and emotional abuse in the family of origin have a profound implications for chemical dependence, and often precede its onset. The behavioral consequences of family abuse and drug abuse can include low self-esteem, sense of powerlessness, limited control over one's life, poor social skills, and difficulty in trusting others.

Coping Skills

To understand the behavior of chemically dependent drug abusers, it is essential to determine their level of coping skills. Individuals with stronger coping repertoires tend to present as well-motivated and realistic about themselves and their lives. Intellectual competencies in effective problem-solving and the ability to reason things through are important identifying characteristics of individuals who demonstrate effective coping skills. Chemically dependent individuals who show limited development in terms of life planning and decision making are at risks for *not* developing effective coping skills. As such, they tend only to perpetuate the cycle of low self-esteem, dependency, and substance abuse, in which low self-esteem and inadequate coping skills reinforce dependence. This dependence, in turn, further damages the individual's sense of self-worth.

Identifying antecedents associated with drug abuse and relapse is critically important. Relapse refers to a complex process that encompasses a number of stages or phases related to drug dependency. It is conjectured that the phases begin before the actual substance use is initiated and that they progress to maladaptive and dysfunctional states characteristic of chronic addictive behavior. In viewing relapse from this perspective, the initial phase of the relapse process is precipitated by an individual's experiencing difficulties in adapting to various stressful life experiences, or triggers, which can include both internal or external factors. Internal factors include the attitudes, values, beliefs, and emotions of the individual; external factors include interpersonal difficulties, job-related problems, marital discord, and financial concerns. If one or more of these internal or external stressors are not adequately addressed, drugging behavior is likely to emerge or reemerge. If, on the other hand, adequate coping repertoires are available, the individual is less likely to relapse.

In relapse prevention planning, specific focus must be placed on the key areas of social environment, coping skills, effective relationships, family functioning, and emotional and spiritual well-being. The consequences of problem behavior that appear to be involved in the acquisition and performance of drug abuse in a significant number of cases involve the social environment from which the chemically dependent individual emerges. A return to a drug-saturated environment is, unfortunately, unavoidable for many individuals. This environment negatively affects the behavioral patterns for coping with social needs, leisure time, and effective interpersonal relations. Skills to address boredom and difficult social situations, and to refuse substances in the face of peer pressure are essential for successful outcomes.

Poor family relationships and complexities of dysfunctional families present potential risk for relapse. Families may be disengaged, alienated, or significantly enmeshed, situations which result in poor communication, unresolved conflicts, guilt, dependency, and distrust. Interpersonal conflict and relapse are often the result. Both preventive and interventive programs, therefore, need to address these issues, either through restructuring family processes or by preparing patients to cope with them in new ways.

Ineffective relationships are built on low self-esteem and dependency, both of which are critical factors in recognizing relapse risk. Involvement in negative or destructive relationships frequently results in a person being resistant to change. Individuals in physically abusive relationships or in relationships with substance abusers are at high risk for relapse. Involvement in these kinds of relationships is often the result of issues related to trust, poor communication, and enabling behaviors, all of which may need to be addressed in treatment.

Littman, Stapleton, Oppenheim, Peleg, and Jackson (1984) recognized negative emotional states as critically important factors in precipitating relapse. Feelings of hopelessness, helplessness, guilt, shame, and loneliness, as well as difficulties in expressing anger, are all identified as high-risk relapse behaviors. Such emotional states are commonly related to both low self-esteem and dependency in sexual relationships. Often, such factors serve as relapse triggers and result in poor adaptation.

Intervention and prevention may assume several forms based both on clinical research results and the variety of orientations that address relapse treatment. It is not uncommon to find that chemically dependent individuals who seek treatment are ambivalent about drug use; therefore, relapse to drug use is not simply a positive or negative outcome. Certain forms of behavioral therapy provide promise within the context of treatment intervention. Conditioning is recognized as a critical ingredient in behavioral approaches. Conditioning is based on Hullian learning theory (Hull, 1952). Regrettably, however, various substance-abusing experiences reduce aversive tension, thereby acting as a reinforcer rather than as an inhibitor of the behavior.

Within the framework of operant conditioning, control involves staying away from environments in which adverse stimuli are likely to be present. For drug abusers, these adverse stimuli can include places where drugs were used as well as individuals with whom drugs were used. Such discriminative stimuli are important to address in treatment, through developing strategies to minimize exposure to them, desensitize the patient to them, or both. Further development of such behavioral models as systematic desensitization and covert sensitization may prove beneficial for relapse prevention.

Cognitive factors also are critically important in the selection of intervention strategies. The effects of substance abuse are often mediated by expectations rather than by a physiological marker, thus suggesting that treatment interventions should focus on attitudes, values, beliefs, and, perhaps, locus of control, as well as on changes in the complex networks of behavioral contingencies within which substance abusing behaviors are embedded.

Behavioral Analysis

Behavioral analytic approaches to the treatment of chemically dependent—and in particular cocaine-dependent individuals—have been the focus of recent research. Higgins, Budney, Bickel, Hughes, Foerg, & Badger (1993) compared the efficacy of a multicomponent behavioral treatment model for cocaine-dependent patients with a medical model approach. Intervention strategies using behavioral treatment were based on the community reinforcement approach (see chapter 1), whereas drug abuse counseling was grounded in a disease model of dependency and recovery. Patients in the behavioral approach, but not involved in the counseling treatment approach, received incentives contingent on submitting cocaine-free urine specimens. The results of this study suggested higher rates of compliance for the behavioral approach. In the behavioral treatment approach, more than two-thirds (68%) of the patients achieved at least 8 weeks of documented continuous cocaine abstinence, compared with fewer than 11% in the drug abuse counseling group. The authors of this study concluded that the multicomponent behavioral treatment was effective in intervening with and retaining outpatients in treatment and establishing abstinence from cocaine.

Other studies (Budney et al., 1993; Budney, Higgins, Delaney & Bickel, 1991; Mattiani, 1991a) have recognized the importance of behavioral approaches in the treatment of cocaine-dependent patients. The clinical findings in these studies suggested that injecting cocaine users can achieve in an outpatient setting a period of initial abstinence that is comparable to the duration of typical inpatient hospitalizations. The authors further noted that special types of outpatient treatment with a behavioral emphasis appear to have more positive outcomes than traditional approaches to drug counseling that do not include a behavioral component. These authors encouraged further examination of more structured and intense behavioral approaches because such approaches show promise for meeting the challenge of achieving initial cocaine abstinence with cocaine injectors. In addition, Higgins, Budney, Bickel, Hughes, & Foerg, (1993) noted that disulfiram therapy was associated with significant decreases in alcohol and cocaine use. Disulfiram—also called Antabuse—has been used as a pharmacological treatment for alcohol abusers. When Antabuse is taken according to its prescribed regimen, alcohol abusers become sick if they drink alcohol; thus, the desire to use alcohol is reduced or eliminated. However, compliance is a major issue for patients' use of Antabuse. This problem can also be addressed by the community reinforcement approach (see chapter 1).

EXTENDED CASE EXAMPLE

A single case study of an intervention and prevention plan addressing chemical dependency with specific emphasis on cocaine addiction will now be presented. The patient, a 26-year-old, unemployed, single, White woman with three children has a long history of multiple substance abuse. Drugs, including cocaine, have been a part of her life for more than 10 years. Snorting and smoking cocaine for up to 3 days a week and consuming several grams of cocaine per day have marked her most recent drugging activity. She has consistently shown poor motivation towards rehabilitation and continues a relationship with her physically abusing, drug-dealing significant other.

Social and Family History

The patient was raised in a single-parent home in a disadvantaged area. She is the youngest of six children and stepchildren. Her mother married at the age of 14. The mother's husband was addicted to alcohol and drugs and was physically and emotionally abusive during the course of their marriage. Throughout her childhood, the patient saw her mother receive both physical and emotional abuse. In addition, the children were abusive to one another. All of the patient's siblings were involved in substance abuse; two were involved in dealing drugs. These children received little positive direction from either of their parents.

The patient's school years were marked by a progressive pattern of behavior problems; she was disruptive in classes and by middle school had begun to use alcohol and marijuana. Her first exposure to cocaine and methamphetamine came in her sophomore year of high school. She became pregnant with her first child at the age of 17. She quit school to raise this child. The father of her child was already engaged in dealing drugs and other illegal activities. Although the patient recognized the negative aspects of these activities she continued her relationship with this man. Her poor self-image and low self-esteem resulted in her only goal of competence and skill being based on her ability to maintain the existing relationship with her significant other, regardless of the physical or emotional abuse she might receive. This case, therefore, exemplified many of the issues described in previous sections of this chapter.

Behavioral Analysis and Rehabilitation Plan

The Addiction Severity Index was used to identify that the patient had the following problems:

1. Cocaine addiction disorder.
2. Physically abusive relationship with significant other.
3. Poor environmental support system.
4. Low self-esteem.
5. Poor compliance with prior treatment.

Recognized within this case are critically important issues that have been addressed within the context of a behavioral analysis. Her current living relationship in a drug-saturated environment; the negative emotional states, feelings of hopelessness, helplessness, loneliness, guilt, and shame; a poor family history; and her continued involvement with a physically abusive and substance-abusing person are all conducive to the maintenance of chemical dependence and continued substance abuse. Therefore, a treatment plan needed to explore alternative living arrangements and a transitional living program while addressing the patient's ability to identify, label, experience, and process emotions. Improved communication skills and effective use of outpatient services, including family counseling, parenting skills, and support, were also important and warranted.

Obstacles to Rehabilitation

Perhaps the most significant obstacle to the patient's rehabilitation is her unwillingness (or inability) to terminate the relationship with her significant other. An alternative social environment that does not promote drugging and abuse is a critical element of the treatment plan. Without such a change in environmental contingencies, a positive outcome is unlikely. Given the patient's current resistance, intervention should focus on the development of new coping skills and cognitive repertoires that may result in a new perspective on life choices and their consequences. Efforts on the part of health care professionals to promote an aftercare plan to aid the patient in using the skills necessary for independent living and maintaining sobriety are essential.

Behavioral Intervention and Results

Poor skill development in terms of coping is seen as an obstacle to rehabilitation. Through the use of behavioral interventions—including coping skills training, anger management, assertiveness training, and psychoeducation—this patient may develop a better understanding of the disease of chemical dependency and become more aware of the risk factors involved in domestic violence. Furthermore, the recognition that she is the victim of the cycle of violence (which often results from dysfunctional relationships) may improve her self-image as well as her ability to seek more effective relationships with more socially effective persons. The psychological and physical effects of traumatic stress often lead to a stage of disorganization and denial, which may then be followed by a period of reevaluation. In this process, both the psychological and the physical components of the disorder are revisited. This then leads to an eventual acceptance of the trauma or a resolution to the psychopathological impact of the trauma. This process results in improved adaptation based, in part, on a cognitive-behavioral intervention that facilitates recognition of the stressor and may result in accommodation and acceptance of this stressful life event.

RECOMMENDATIONS FOR INTERVENTIONS AND RESEARCH

The following recommendations related to the treatment and prevention of cocaine use and HIV are summarized from a meeting held at the

National Institute on Drug Abuse in June 1990 (Tims & Leukefeld, 1993). Recommendations presented focus on interventions and future research.

Behavioral and Other Interventions

Given that our knowledge of cocaine treatment is not extensive, any recommendations for practice must also include cautions. Specific protocols for cocaine treatment have not been extensively validated; therefore, we must realize that cocaine treatment may have negative aspects. Nevertheless, treatment must begin where the client is (i.e., history, comorbidity, legal status, what the client has to lose). This is particularly important for cocaine treatment, given the high dropout rates and low motivation among those who seek treatment. Program flexibility, open attitudes, and attention to boundaries are important to increase the retention of cocaine users in treatment. Behavioral treatment contracts and contingencies should be clearly stated and agreed on at the outset of cocaine treatment. It is also important to remember that cocaine addicts are not just alcoholics who have selected a different drug. Based on initial data and anecdotal information, treatment programs for cocaine are most effective when they include (a) structure; (b) intense, planned interventions; (c) frequent attendance; (d) flexibility; (e) definition of treatment stages; (f) urine testing; and (g) targeted counseling.

Behavioral interventions to increase client motivation have been reported anecdotally to be effective for some cocaine addicts when frequent group meetings, urine testing, educational lectures, and individual counseling are incorporated. Cognitive behavioral approaches for cocaine treatment are seen as appropriate because treatment for this group needs to be structured. Specific pharmacotherapies for cocaine addicts are still undergoing testing, so recommendations are limited to approved uses, such as treatment of comorbidities. Practitioners are cautioned that some early medication trials thought to be promising have had disappointing results. To the extent that efficacious medications become available, programs should pay particular attention to medication dosage and compliance issues.

Diagnosis

The provision of treatment service must take into consideration the multiple problems associated with cocaine use, including route of administration (crack smoking, needle use), alcohol use, and compulsive sexual behavior. Psychiatric comorbidities are often present in cocaine users, including Axis I (especially depression and anxiety disorders) and Axis II diagnoses. While transient depression and some psychotic states associated with stimulant use may abate with entry into treatment, careful clinical evaluation of comorbidities on a continuing basis is needed. The implications of Axis II diagnoses, particularly antisocial personality disorder, must be considered in treatment planning. Frequent ongoing drug testing must be an integral part of treatment protocols for cocaine users. In addition, legal issues and legal involvement are important considerations when cocaine users receive treatment. Finally, relapse is an essential characteristic of cocaine addiction because cocaine addicts have high relapse rates as well as multiple relapses.

HIV and AIDS

HIV and AIDS are major risks associated with compulsive cocaine use, particularly for intravenous users and for women. Consequently, HIV risk reduction is an important aspect of cocaine treatment.

Training

Cocaine treatment training modules need to be developed. Counselors should be motivated to use research findings related to cocaine treatment as a means of increasing their effectiveness and improving their practice. In addition, counselors as well as outreach workers should receive training related to the specific characteristics of cocaine users and the implications for treatment.

Treatment Modalities and Therapy

Although cocaine treatment interventions have produced only limited results, the number of studies currently under way should lead to significant improvements in available treatment. Treatment studies should continue the emphasis on (a) identifying and systematically testing pharmacological agents that may be useful in achieving abstinence from cocaine and reducing the likelihood of relapse; (b) characterizing and understanding the processes and outcomes of existing treatment, using field studies with outcomes studied over a 1-year posttreatment period and longer; and (c) testing the efficacy of specific psychosocial interventions such as psychotherapies, behavioral treatments, and relapse prevention strategies that are theory based. Promising pharmacotherapies should be field tested in clinical programs to understand issues related to compliance with medication regimens.

The question of whether inpatient treatment has an inherent advantage over outpatient treatment must be addressed. Dropout rates from outpatient programs are relatively high, but it is not known whether inpatient programs are more effective. Studies should be designed and implemented to improve treatment retention for outpatient programs and to rigorously test inpatient compared with outpatient treatment for well-defined sub-groups of clients. Treatment approaches regarded as experimental or non-traditional should also be systematically investigated. For example, acupuncture is widely used in detoxification, yet its status as a somatic treatment for cocaine withdrawal remains to be scientifically established. Widely used approaches should be examined, including 12-step approaches, both as self-help programming and as formal treatment.

Studies should be undertaken to increase understanding of the factors and mechanisms related to client entry, engagement, retention, and compliance with treatment expectations. Research should also examine criteria for client-treatment matching, so that the most cost-effective treatments can be provided for cocaine-dependent clients. Research should focus on better understanding motivation as a factor for increasing the retention of cocaine users in treatment. In addition, the association between compulsive sexual behaviors and compulsive use of cocaine needs to be better understood to strengthen relapse prevention efforts. The initial high dropout rates from treatment during the first 60 days by cocaine users should receive specific attention when future studies are planned. Finally, treatment programs should not be content to reach those who present themselves for treatment, but should seek to increase treatment entry through outreach and to contact those reluctant to enter treatment.

Research Design

A variety of study types and designs are necessary to understand cocaine dependence, response to treatment, and the development of more effective treatments. Tightly controlled studies that use randomized designs will help define the relationship of targeted cocaine treatment and treatment outcome. It is important to document training and experience of treatment providers in cocaine-treatment outcome studies. Behavioral, intrapsychic, and survival rates as outcome measures should also be documented so that differences between study findings can be better reconciled.

SUMMARY AND CONCLUSIONS

We are beginning to understand more about the treatment of cocaine users and the relationship of cocaine with HIV. More promising behavioral interventions include the use of specific reinforcement contingencies combined with sanctions.

Behavioral analytic directions in drug abuse can include:

1. The use of contingency analysis in assessing substance use experimentation and refusal skills in the behavioral analysis of drug experimentation.
2. The use of prevention strategies, based on social learning theory, that include television public service announcements featuring highly visible leadership models discussing substance abuse problems and recovery.
3. The early identification of individuals at risk and the use of education and behavioral training models in building behavioral and other skills in these individuals.
4. The development of social support networks that reinforce refusal, a strategy that has been shown to be beneficial (Schinke, Gilchrist, & Snow 1985).
5. The recognition that aversive strategies alone are generally counterproductive. The use of mild aversives in conjunction with positive strategies to build alternatives may be essential for effective treatment.
6. The use of "life skills" as a model for intervention; this approach provides for self-instructions of competence through modeling as well as rehearsal of positive alternative strategies in problem solving and health management. (Schinke et al., 1985).
7. The establishment of community norms of abstinence, a process that would have significant effects on experimentation and may benefit those individuals at risk for substance use and abuse.
8. The development of specific social reinforcement for continuing sobriety. Such reinforcement has strong potential for management and maintenance of substance abuse.

Keeping in mind the relationship of drug abuse with HIV and AIDS, researchers should focus on cocaine-dependent clients who use cocaine alone or in combination with other drugs. The foci of such studies should include social and demographic characteristics, psychopathology, natural history, and treatment-seeking behavior. Studies should also focus on increasing the understanding of client needs and availability for treatment as well as of diagnostic subtypes. Given the differential access of various subgroups to treatment for cocaine, special attention should be given to the treatment needs of pregnant women and chemical abusers who have either mental impairments or who are HIV seropositive. The needs of cultural minorities should also be specifically addressed.

Attention should be given to clients with differing sets of natural contingencies, such as employed clients and those with different kinds of social networks. Finally, client population studies should focus on under-standing the natural-history context and dynamics of cocaine treatment. Little is known about how individuals recover from cocaine dependence over time, so long-term outcome studies are important both for cocaine abusers who receive treatment and those who do not.

REFERENCES

Adams, E. H., Blanker, A. J., Ferguson, L. D., & Kopstein, A. (1989). *Overview of Selected Drug Trends.* Rockville, MD: National Institute on Drug Abuse.

Andrulis, D. P. (1989). *Crisis at the Front Line.* New York: Priority Press.

Babcock, M., & Connor, B. (1981). Sexism and treatment of the female alcoholic: A review. *Social Work, 26,* 233–238.

Ball, J. C., Lange, W. R., Myers, C. P., & Friedman, S. R. (1988). Reducing the risk of AIDS through methadone maintenance. *Journal of Health and Social Behavior, 29,* 214–226.

Battjes, R. J., Leukefeld, C. G., Pickens, R. W., & Haverkos, H. W. (1988). The acquired immunodeficiency syndrome and intravenous drug abuse. *Bulletin on Narcotics, XL*(1), 21–34.

Biglan, A. (1995). *Changing cultural practices.* Reno, NV: Context Press.

Biglan, A., & Ary, D. V. (1985). Methodological issues in research on smoking prevention. In C. S. Bell & R. J. Battjes (Eds.), *Prevention research: Deterring drug abuse among children and adolescents* (pp. 180–195). Washington, DC: U.S. Government Printing Office.

Biglan, A., Severson, H., Ary D., Faller, C., Gallison, C., Thompson, R., Glasgow, R., & Lichtenstein, E. (1987). Do smoking prevention programs really work? Attrition and the internal and external validity of an evaluation of a refusal skills training program. *Journal of Behavioral Medicine, 10,* 159–171.

Birke, S. A., Edelmann, R. J., & Davis, P. E. (1990). An analysis of the abstinence violation effect in a sample of illicit drug users. *British Journal of Addiction, 85,* 1299–1307.

Blaine, J. D., Thomas, D. B., Barnett, G., Whysner, J. A., & Renault, P. F. (1981). Levo-acetylmethadol (LAAM): Clinical utility and pharmaceutical develop-ment. In Lowinson, J. H. & Ruiz, P. (Eds.), *Substance Abuse: Clinical Problems and Perspectives* (pp. 360–368). Baltimore: Williams and Wilkins.

Botvin, G. J., & Wills, T. A. (1985). Personal and social skills straining: Cognitive-behavioral approaches to substance abuse prevention. In C. S. Bell & R. J. Battjes (Eds.), *Prevention Research: Deterring Drug Abuse Among Children and Adolescents* (pp. 3–49). Washington, DC: U.S. Government Printing Office.

Bradley, B. P., Gossop, M., Brewin, C. P., & Phillips, E. (1992). Attributions and relapse in opiate addicts. *Journal of Consulting and Clinical Psychology, 60,* pp. 470–472.

Budney, A. J., Higgins, S. T., Bickel, W. K., and Kent, L. (1993). Relationship between intravenous use and achieving initial cocaine abstinence. *Drug and Alcohol Dependence, 32,* 133–142.

Budney, A. J., Higgins, S. T., Delaney, L. K. & Bickel, W. K. (1991). Contingent reinforcement of abstinence with individuals abusing cocaine and marijuana. *Journal of Applied Behavioral Analysis, 24,* 657–665.

Bureau of Justice Statistics. (1986). *State Prison Inmate Survey, 1986* (Special Report). Washington, DC: U.S. Department of Justice.

Butynski, W. (1991). Drug abuse treatment services: Funding and admissions. In R. W. Pickens, C. G. Leukefeld, & C. R. Schuster (Eds.), *Improving Drug Abuse Treatment* (pp. 20–52). Washington, DC: U.S. Government Printing Office.

Cadoret, Remi J. (1992). Genetic and environmental factors in initiation of drug use and the transition to abuse. In M. D. Glantz & R. W. Pickins (Eds.), *Vulnerability to Drug Abuse* (pp. 99–114). Washington, DC: American Psychological Association.

Clayton, R. R., & Leukefeld, C. G. (1993, December 2). *Basic etiology research: drug use and its progression to drug abuse and drug dependence.* Paper presented at the meeting of the Robert Wood Johnson Foundation, NJ.

Centers for Disease Control. (1993). MMWR.

Chamberland, M., White, C., Lifson, A., & Dondero, T. (1987, June). *AIDS in heterosexual contacts: A small but interesting group of cases.* Paper presented at the Third International Conference on AIDS, Washington, DC.

DesJarlais, D. S., Friedman, S. R., Novick, D. M., Sotheran, J. R., Thomas, P., Yancovitz, S. R., Mildvan, D., Weber, J., Kreath, M. J., & Maslausky, R. (1989). HIV-1 infection among intravenous drug users in Manhattan, New York City, from 1977 through 1987. *Journal of the American Medical Association, 261,* 1008–1012.

DesJarlais, D. D., Freidman, S. R., Southern, J. L., & Stoneburner, R. (1988). The sharing of drug injection equipment and the AIDS epidemic in New York City: The first decade. In R. J. Battjes & R. W. Pickens (Eds.), *Needle-sharing among intravenous drug abusers: National and international perspectives* (pp. 160–164). Washington, DC: U.S. Government Printing Office.

Evans, R. I., Rozelle, R. M., Maxwell, S. E., Raines, B. E., Dill, C. A., & Guthrie, T. J. (1981). Social modeling films to deter smoking in adolescents: Results of a three-year field investigation. *Journal of Applied Psychology, 66,* 399–414.

Evans, R. I., Rozelle, R. M., Mittelmark, M. B., Hanse, W. B., Bane, A. L., & Havis, J. (1978). Deterring the onset of smoking in children: Knowledge of immediate physiological peer pressure, media pressure, and parent modeling. *Journal of Applied Social Psychology, 8,* 126–135.

Flay, B. R. (1985a). Psychosocial approaches to smoking prevention: A review of findings. *Health Psychology, 4,* 449–488.

Flay, B. R. (1985b). What do we know about the social influences approach to smoking prevention: Review and recommendations. In C. S. Bell & R. Battjes

(Eds.), *Prevention research: Deterring drug abuse among children and adolescents* (pp. 67–112). Washington DC: U.S. Government Printing Office.

Gilchrist, L. D. (1990). Selected community groups: Schools. In C. G. Leukefeld, R. J. Battjes, & Z. Amsel (Eds.), *AIDS and intravenous drug use: Future directions for community-based prevention research* (pp. 150–166). Washington, DC: U.S. Government Printing Office.

Glenn, S. S. (1988). Contingencies and metacontingencies: Toward a synthesis of behavior analysis and cultural materialism. *Behavior Analyst, 11*, 161–179.

Goodstadt, M. S. (1986). School-based drug education in North America: What is wrong? What can be done? *Journal of School Health, 56*, 278–281.

Gutierre, S. E., & Reich, J. W. (1988). Attributional analysis of drug abuse and gender. *Journal of Social and Clinical Psychology, 7*, 176–191.

Harwood, H. J., Napolitano, D. M., Kristinson, P. L., & Collins, J. J. (1984). *Economic costs to society of alcohol and drugs and mental health; 1980.* Research Triangle Park, NC: Research Triangle Institute.

Higgins, S. T., Budney, S. T., Bickel, W. K., Hughes, J. R., & Foerg, F. (1993). Disulfiram therapy in patients abusing cocaine and alcohol. *American Journal of Psychiatry, 150*, 675–676.

Higgins, S. T., Budney, S. T., Bickel, W. K., Hughes, J. R., Foerg, F., & Badger, G. (1993). Achieving abstinence with a behavioral approach. *American Journal of Psychiatry, 150*, 763–769.

Holden C. (1989). Street-wise crack research. *Science, 246*, 1376–1381.

Hubbard, R. L., Marsden, M. E., Cavanaugh, E., Rachal, J. V., & Ginzburg, H. M. (1988). Role of drug abuse treatment in limiting the spread of AIDS. *Review of Infectious Diseases, 10*, 377–384.

Hubbard, R. L., Marsden, M. E., Rachal, J. V., Harwood, H. H., Cavanaugh, E. R., & Ginzburg, H. M. (1989). *Drug abuse treatment: A national study of effectiveness.* Chapel Hill, NC: The University of North Carolina Press.

Hull, C. L. (1952). *A behavior system.* New Haven, CT: Yale University Press.

Ifill, G. (1989, December 21). Drugs, homelessness increasingly linked. *Washington Post*, p. A6.

Janoff-Bulman, R. (1979). Characterological versus behavioral self-blame. *Journal of Personality and Social Psychology, 37*, 1798–1809.

Lang, R. W., et al. (1988). Geographic distribution of human immunodeficiency virus markers in parental drug abusers. *American Journal of Public Health, 78*, pp. 443–446.

Leukefeld, C. (1990). The nation's drug abuse strategy. *Health and Social Work, 15*, 87–90.

Leukefeld, C. (1991). The role of the National Institute on Drug Abuse in drug abuse prevention research. In L. Donohew, W. J. Bukoski, & H. Sypher (Eds.), *Persuasive communication and drug abuse prevention* (pp. 21–34). Hillsdale, NJ: Erlbaum.

Leukefeld, C. G., & Clayton, R. R. (1994). Drug prevention: The past as the future. *Journal of Primary Prevention, 15*, 59–71.

Leukefeld, C. G., & Tims, F. M. (1990). Relapse and recovery in drug abuse: Research and practice. *International Journal of the Addictions, 24*, 189–201.

Littman, G., Stapleton, J., Oppenheim, A., Peleg, M., & Jackson, P. (1984). The relationship between coping behaviors, their effectiveness and alcoholism relapse and survival. *British Journal of Addiction, 79*, 283–291.

Malott, R. W. (1988). Rule-governed behavior and behavioral anthropology. *Behavior Analyst, 11*, 181–203.

Marlatt, G. A., & Gordon, J. R. (Eds.). (1985). *Relapse Prevention.* New York: Guilford Press.

Mattaini, M. A. (1991a). Choosing weapons for the war on "crack": An operant analysis. *Research on Social Work Practice, 1*, 188–213.

Mattaini, M. A. (1991b). Substance abuse in rural Alaska: A behavioral analytic exploration. *Behavior and Social Issues, 1*, 3–26.

McAlister, A. L., Perry, C., & Maccoby, N. (1979). Adolescent smoking: Onset and prevention. *Pediatrics, 63*, 650–657.

McCaul, K. D., & Glasgow, R. E. (1985). Preventing adolescent smoking: What we learned about treatment construct validity? *Health Psychology, 4*, 361–397.

McGurk, D., Miller, T. W., & Eggerth, D. (1995). HIV status, substance dependency and psychiatric diagnosis. *AIDS Patient Care, 8*, 328–330.

McLellan, A. T., Luborsky, L., O'Brien, C. P., Woody, G. E., and Druley, K. A. (1982). Is treatment for substance abuse effective? *Journal of the American Medical Association, 247*, 1423–1428.

Miller, T. W., Jefferson, B., Leukefeld, C. G. & Carmona, J. J. (1994). Dual diagnosis: Clinical issues in substance treatment. *Journal of Contemporary Psychotherapy, 24*, 169–177.

Moskowitz, J. M. (1983). Preventing adolescent substance abuse through drug education. In T. J. Glynn, C. G. Leukefeld, & J. P. Ludford (Eds.), *Preventing adolescent drug abuse: Intervention strategies (pp. 233–249).* Washington, DC: U.S. Government Printing Office.

National Drug Control Strategy. (1989). Washington, DC: U.S. Government Printing Office.

National Institute on Drug Abuse. (1978). *It starts with people.* Washington, DC: DHEW.

National Institute on Drug Abuse. (1982). *Data from the Client Oriented Data Acquisition Process (CODAP).* Rockville, MD: Author.

National Institute on Drug Abuse. (1990). *National Household Survey on Drug Abuse: Main findings, 1986.* Rockville, MD: Author.

National Institute on Drug Abuse. (1991). *National Household Survey on Drug Abuse: Main findings, 1990.* Rockville, MD: Author.

National Institute of Justice. (1993). *Drug Use Forecasting.* (Special Report.) Washington, DC: Author.

Nichols, M. (1985). Theoretical concerns in the clinical treatment of substance abusing women: A feminist analysis. *Alcoholism Treatment Quarterly, 2,* 78–79.

Pentz, M. A., Dwyer, J. H., MacKinnon, D. P., Flay, B. R., Hansen, W. B., Wang, E. Y., & Johnson, C. A. (1990). A multi-community trial for primary prevention of adolescent drug abuse: Effects on drug abuse prevalence. *Journal of the American Medical Association, 261,* 3259–3266.

Perry, C. L., Killen, J., Slinkard, L. A., & McAlister, A. L. (1980). Peer training and smoking prevention among junior high students. *Adolescence, 15,* 277–281.

Perry, C. L., Maccoby, N., & McAlister, A. L. (1980). Adolescent smoking prevention: A third year follow-up. *World Smoking and Health, 5,* 40–45.

Perry, C. L., Telch, M. J., Killen, J., Dass, R., & Maccoby, N., (1983). High school smoking prevention: The relative efficacy of varied treatments and instructors. *Adolescence, 18,* 561–566.

Reed, B. G. (1985). Drug misuse and dependency in women: The meaning and implications of being considered a special population or minority group. *International Journal of the Addictions, 20,* 13–62.

Regier, D. A., Farmer, M., Rae, D. S., Locke, B. Z., Keith, S. J., Judd, L., & Goodwin, F. K. (1990) Comorbidity of mental disorders with alcohol and other drug abuse. *Journal of the American Medical Association, 64,* 19.

Rohsenow, D., Corbett, R., & Devine, D. (1988). Molested as children: A hidden contribution to substance abuse? *Journal of Substance Abuse Treatment, 5,* 13–18.

Schaps, E., DiBartolo, R. D., Moskowitz, J., Palley, C. S., & Churgin, S. (1981). A review of 127 drug abuse prevention program evaluations. *Journal of Drug Issues, 11,* 17–43.

Schinke, S. P., Gilchrist, L. D., & Snow, W. H. (1985). Skills intervention to prevent cigarette smoking among adolescents. *American Journal of Public Health, 75,* 655–667.

Simpson, D. D., & Sells, S. B. (Eds.). (1990). *Opioid addiction and treatment: A 12-year follow-up.* Malabar, Florida: Roger E. Krieger.

Tims, F. M., & Leukefeld, C. G. (1993). *Cocaine Treatment: Research and Clinical Perspectives* (National Institute on Drug Abuse Research Monograph No. 135). Washington, DC: U.S. Government Printing Office.

Tobler, N. S. (1986). Meta-analysis of 143 adolescent drug prevention programs: Quantitative outcome results of program participants compared to control or comparison group. *Journal of Drug Issues, 16,* 537–567.

15

"ACTING TO SAVE THE WORLD": THE ELEMENTS OF ACTION

MARK A. MATTAINI

When addressing the American Psychological Association more than a decade ago, B. F. Skinner elaborated on "why we are not acting to save the world" (Skinner, 1987, p. 1). The preceding chapters suggest that, at least in modest ways, recent advances may now permit us to apply the science of behavior to do so. Issues deeply embedded in the larger socio-cultural system (e.g., reforming the welfare system in a rational way; Opulente & Mattaini, 1993) require wide-ranging modifications to make a lasting difference, but in many problem areas, change can be initiated in one cultural entity at a time (e.g., a school or business). The challenges and obstacles are immense, but the overall situation is hopeful. In almost every chapter of this volume one can find data suggesting that the strategies presented can make a difference.

The preceding chapters have emphasized what can be done to address social issues. This final chapter examines who might take action, with particular focus on four areas:

1. Influencing decision makers (politicians, policymakers, and citizens) involved in shaping potentially effective social policy;
2. Clarifying classes of actors in positions to implement community-level interventions;

3. Examining obstacles that may interfere with taking these strategic directions and their resolution; and
4. Discussing the crucial importance of teaching behavior analysis, because a substantial cadre of well-trained professionals and an educated public will be required if effective intervention in social issues is to occur.

Over the long term, the authors contributing to this volume believe that the science presented, which captures the realities of the sociocultural world well and leads to effective intervention, will emerge as a powerful scientific and strategic paradigm. The question for us is not so much if, as when. Society—frustrated with the failure of traditional approaches—may be ready to move quickly into such an empirically rooted approach. For reasons noted later in this chapter, however, two or more generations may instead be required (as in the Darwinian battle—in which frequent skirmishes still occur).

INFLUENCING SOCIAL POLICY

This chapter was being written as a political pendulum swing is occurring, as has happened many times over recent decades. As noted by Thyer (chapter 2, this volume) decisions about social policy have commonly not been informed by empirical data, much less by our knowledge of how to change behavior. Yet changing (or maintaining) behavior is the goal of all social policy: As a society, for example, we wish to encourage saving, discourage overproduction of certain farm products, and provide medical care to the indigent. Decisions about what to change and how to make such changes are at the core of policy analysis, design, and implementation. Unfortunately, much political behavior (the matrix within which policymaking is embedded) is rule-governed and relatively insensitive to shifting consequences. One somewhat promising sign, however, is the recognition in some circles of the need to experiment, to design policy initiatives based on existing knowledge and theory, and then to *test* them before implementing them widely.

Given its strong commitment to empirical testing and to research methods that offer an ability to unpack the contingencies that differentially shape behavior under varying conditions, the science of behavior is well positioned to contribute to this movement. Although there may be disagreement about what outcomes are best for humanity (actually an empirical issue), once desired results are identified, behavior analysts have demonstrated that their science can provide substantial guidance for predicting and testing the outcomes of alternative policy arrangements (e.g., Lamal, 1984) and for selecting strategic directions (Zifferblatt & Hendricks, 1974), through the analysis of contingencies acting on relevant classes of actors.

A critical role for behavior analysts is that of the scientist–advocate who can not only empirically examine issues but also become part of the relevant contingency matrix for decision making. Recent work tracing effective ways that behavior analysts can present their research findings to influence political decisions is particularly valuable here (Seekins & Fawcett, 1986). Seekins and Fawcett go well beyond simply stating that scientist-advocates need to examine the contingencies that shape the acts of decisionmakers. They discuss practical approaches for doing so at multiple stages of the process, including agenda formation, policy adoption, policy implementation, and policy review. At many of these stages, a small number of persons are in positions to make crucial decisions, and the thoughtful analysis of the social antecedents and consequences that make it easier for them to respond in a data-based way can often guide action.

In the late 1980s, the Association for Behavior Analysis appointed a task force on public policy to examine ways that behavior analysts could function more effectively as citizen–scientists. The report issued by the task force (Fawcett et al., 1988) sketched approaches for effectively "creating policy-relevant conceptual analyses, generating research data, and communicating policy-relevant information" (p. 11). The emphasis on conceptual analysis is consistent with many of the chapters in this volume, which seek to organize and make coherent sense of data extracted from disparate sources. Recommendations regarding how—and when—to communicate policy-relevant information, both in Seekins and Fawcett and in the task force report are also very valuable because they are rooted in realistic analyses of the contingencies shaping the actions of decision makers. Both technical expertise and long-term commitment are clearly essential, as is recognition that timetables required for effective action may be quite different (shorter!) than those to which researchers and scholars may be accustomed.

Citizens, individually and as constituents of cultural entities, control many of the critical contingencies shaping the behavior of policymakers and public officials. Behavior analysts have made initial progress developing a methodology for expanding citizens' understanding of the potential consequences of policy decisions (*consequence analysis*) that may have significant promise, although it has not yet been broadly tested (Sanford & Fawcett, 1980). The heart of the approach is to ask citizens to consider multiple specific consequences of a policy decision in as many areas as are relevant and to rate the acceptability of those consequences. Preliminary work suggests that this approach leads to more careful consideration and to better-informed opinions. In theoretical terms, consequence analysis appears to result in persons more effectively extracting accurate rules about contingencies. An attractive aspect of this method is that it does not seek to persuade by manipulating or distorting information, but rather by facilitating more thoughtful participation. The potential applicability of consequence analysis may be quite extensive, and further research in this area is urgently needed.

Multiple stakeholders often control crucial contingencies, and an analysis of how each participates in interlocking networks of contingencies is often crucial for effective policy advocacy. Some years ago, for example, a group of parents of adults with mental illness persuaded an important state senator to commit to obtaining funding for enhanced services for the severely mentally ill. The tentative plan, however, was to build a large, centralized facility with residential, day-treatment, and outpatient services for both children and adults; the facility would serve a large area of the state. Although the principle of expanded funding was welcomed by everyone within the mental health network, the initial plan was neither state-of-the-art nor likely to be as effective as smaller, decentralized, carefully designed facilities and services closer to the patients' natural networks.

Key decisionmakers included this state senator and her staff, other legislators in the region, state and local officials who would ultimately control the expenditure of appropriated funds, advocates for the mentally ill, and a range of private service providers. This case of the senator and her staff can be used as an example of a process in which each group of stakeholders represented an important constituency. For the senator, contingencies were controlled by parent advocates for adult patients, by citizens' groups advocating for the interests of children, and by other legislators (with whom she needed to trade favors). Professionals who were part of the service system therefore developed targeted information for each group and also advocated to ensure that the interests of each were addressed in the final plan. This process required looking at the contingencies within which, say, rural legislators or parents were embedded. A satisfactory plan was ultimately established.

Advocating for effective policies requires, then, not only rational analysis of individual and aggregate outcomes of proposed policy alternatives but also identification of the persons in positions to establish and implement those alternatives and the contingencies affecting them. The reality is that more immediate contingencies (like reelection) often have a higher valence than those that are longer term. The evidence is very clear, for example, that further increases in the size of the prison population (which nearly tripled between 1975 and 1989) have not reduced the level of violent crime (Reiss & Roth, 1993). Nevertheless, appearing "tough on crime" currently results in votes, and legislation that tends to increase the prison population continues to be passed. Turning this around will probably require changing the behavior of voters, perhaps by clarifying the horrendous tax expenses involved. Increased registration of voters (particularly people of color) who are less likely to see increased incarceration as acceptable may also be required.

Although political realities viewed in this way may appear unpleasant and discouraging, in fact, they simply suggest that the actions of decision makers, too, can be understood using the science of behavior; their behaviour are neither random and unpredictable nor malicious. So, paradoxically, recognizing that political events also can be understood by analyzing the contingency webs associated with the behavior of political actors is actually grounds for hope. (The sort of diagram presented later in this chapter can be useful for such analyses.)

As this discussion suggests, addressing many social issues requires analyzing and influencing contingencies affecting multiple classes of actors concurrently. One approach for doing so, discussed in the following section, is to work within defined geographic communities where each important class of cultural entities can be incorporated into a comprehensive plan.

COMMUNITY INTERVENTION

In Biglan's chapter on male sexual coercion, he refers to work he and his colleagues have been conducting in several areas at a community level. Oversimplifying this elegant work, components of community intervention may include, for example, simultaneous and integrated work with parents, peers, schools, the broader neighborhood and community, the media, and policymakers (Biglan, 1995). This strategy involves more effort than interventions at a single systemic level, but provides a framework for designing interlocking contingencies that are more likely to stabilize and maintain desired patterns of behavior over the long term—that is, to be changes in cultural practices. Two examples of social issues where constructing such interlocks are expanding respect for diversity and increasing the prevalence of "successful" children. Similar analyses could be developed for many other community-level issues.

Encouraging Respect and Appreciation for Diversity

Racism, homophobia, sexism, ageism, classism, and other forms of bias are highly politicized; discussions of these issues are often viewed as exercises in political correctness, thus trivializing these oppressive sources of personal anguish and social strife. Unearned privilege and institutional biases survive, in part, because of the advantageous personal and aggregate outcomes of such practices for members of powerful groups, as noted by Briggs and Paulson (Chapter 4). Acts of prejudice and bias commonly occur among groups who look or live differently from each other. Despite possible short-term advantages for groups in power, practices associated with bias are now extremely costly at both the personal and the cultural levels. They are associated with physical, emotional, and economic violence perpetrated against members of more vulnerable groups and lead to expansions of undesirable coercive matrices at a sociocultural level (Sidman, 1989) and, potentially, to social disaster.

There is yet another reason, however, to build respect and appreciation for diversity. Each enduring cultural group, defined as an organized network of social reinforcement, has learned somewhat unique ways to obtain reinforcement and avoid aversives. Because these sets of practices have "worked" under somewhat different social and physical conditions, the diversity of repertoires represented among cultures is a source of potentially valuable variations. For reasons analogous to those for maintaining biological diversity, maintaining cultural diversity preserves banks of potentially useful possibilities for adapting to changing circumstances. Because not all of these are rule-governed, we may not be able to identify in advance which cultural components are potentially most valuable.

Contemporary anthropologists agree that even such defining characteristics as race are, at root, social and cultural constructions, not biologically meaningful units. As Marks (1994) noted

> Of course there are biological differences between people and between populations. The question is: How are those differences patterned? And the answer seems to be: Not racially. Populations are the only readily identifiable units of humans, and even they are fairly fluid, biologically similar to populations nearby, and biologically different from populations far away. (p. 35)

As might be expected, patterns observed in biological selection have analogues at the cultural level. Cultural practices vary along multiple continua; groups that have been more isolated, with more recursive and self-contained networks of interlocking contingencies, tend to evolve unique sets of practices. The resulting variations enrich the human repertoire, but are often seen by members of other groups as peculiar, or even as primitive and shameful. Admiration, fascination, and mutual regard appear to be distant goals, but the interconnected nature of the contemporary social world leads to ever-increasing contact, which must be managed somehow. This inevitable and accelerated contact may demand that more effective approaches be developed, and developed quickly.

In work to increase respect and appreciation for variations, multilevel community programming is likely to be crucial to minimize potential conflicting contingencies. How much difference is a media campaign likely to make if messages from family, friends, coworkers, teachers, and community and religious leaders conflict with those of the campaign? Interchange any single one of those other components with *media campaign* in the preceding sentence, and the same (minimal) outcome is likely to result.

As in other areas, a crucial first step in designing supports for practices and scenes that support respect and appreciation is a clear identification of what those required practices and scenes might be. At a minimum, these include the kinds of verbal, observational, and motor behaviors listed in Table 1, and scenes like the example provided in Figure 1. (Figure 1 traces contingency networks that might be relevant to an expansion of Hauserman, Walen, and Behling's [1973] study of "new friends," an approach to promoting positive interracial contact among 1st grade children. Note that most of the action occurs *outside the boundary* of the scene itself; it is these extrascene contingency interlocks, often neglected in planning for change, that are responsible for stabilizing and institutionalizing change.)

The contingencies that might support these practices and scenes then can be unpacked and clarified (as discussed in chapter 1). Strategic programming would then proceed with the design and construction of the specific networks of contingencies that have been identified, rather than relying on chance. Experimentation may often be required to test reasonable but uncertain hypotheses emerging from a first round of analysis.

Raising "Successful Children"

Beyond intervening when problems have already occurred, prevention of child maltreatment, substance abuse, violence and crime, and other serious problems has been identified in many of the preceding chapters as a priority. It may be possible to act to reduce the incidence of multiple interconnected problems on a community-wide basis, resulting in increased prevalence of successful children (Biglan, Metzler, & Ary, 1994). Building on their work decreasing tobacco use among youth, Biglan and his colleagues recently sketched the outlines of such a potential community intervention research strategy. Their program includes the components that are described next.

Parent Training and Social Support Arrangements for Parents

These are not new ideas. What is unique in the proposal is the offering of these supports in the context of each of the other suggested components within a targeted geographic area; linkages between parenting supports and community organizing and advocacy; and the attention paid to accessibility and marketing. These services should be accessible to all families, rather than exclusively to those seen as troubled.

TABLE 1
Examples of Practices That Characterize Respect
and Appreciation for Diversity

Verbal behaviors	Statements respecting what is not understood (e.g., parent says to child, "I am not sure why the X family does it that way, but it might be a good idea. Why don't you ask them about it?"). Respectful questions related to contingencies maintaining behavior (e.g., "Could you explain the meaning of that dance?" "What happens at those meetings?"). Self-talk (covert verbals), such as "That music is really different. I'd like to hear some more—if I can come to appreciate it, I could find a new source of pleasure." Statements of agreement or disagreement that communicate respect and clarify the contingencies involved (e.g., "In my religion, we think it is important to wait until marriage to have sex, because this can prevent a lot of pain and shows respect for the importance of marriage. But I know not everyone sees it that way; could you explain why you believe it can be a mistake to wait?"). Attempting to repeat and paraphrase what you hear from members of other cultural groups about their practices, thus ensuring understanding, and communicating authentic interest.
Observational Behaviors	Observing practices of other groups (listening to music, watching films, attending events) to broaden one's own experience (reinforcer sampling). Observing and identifying the relative consequences of one's own practices and those of other groups with a consciousness of avoiding seeing with one's own biases. Listening in a nonpunitive and nonjudgmental way to explanations and presentations of the practices of other groups.
Other Behaviors	Experimenting with practices observed in other cultural groups to experience the related contingencies (reinforcer sampling again). Includes sponsoring and attending multicultural events, taking "foreign trips" into a neighborhood with an ethnic base other than one's own, and similar activities. Inviting members of other groups to share in activities of your own. Reinforcing members of other groups for talking about their practices. Experimenting with innovations learned from other groups that may work better than some practices from one's own group (e.g., a largely European American organization might adopt Native American talking circles—in which each person who wishes to speaks in turn and uninterrupted—rather than a more typical debating style for meetings). Building close relationships with those from other groups in which discussion of differences is mutually reinforced.

404   *MARK A. MATTAINI*

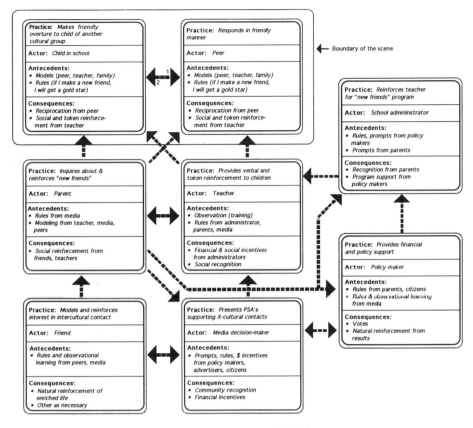

Figure 1. Interlocking contingencies present in a desirable scene.

Peer-Based Programming

This programming is crucial not only in schools, but in other settings as well. Given the extensive research support for the importance of peer influences and the energy often available among youth, this approach has probably been widely underemphasized. The explicit development of pro-social peer cultures should be viewed as a priority. (Note that although problems in adolescence often are embedded in deviant peer networks, earlier family influences shape this involvement; Patterson, Reid & Dishion, 1992.)

Effective School Disciplinary Approaches

Given the developmental importance of schools and education, and the time devoted to them, Biglan and colleagues remind us of the extensive evidence for the importance (and achievability) of effective school disciplinary approaches and the protective influences of academic success. At the same time, the record of adoption of these findings into community school systems has been discouraging; Biglan and colleagues' (1994) proposal includes ways to begin to address this issue, in part by linking such changes with other components.

Community Organizing

When focused on engaging community leaders, decision makers, and organizations of community members, community organizing may potentially lead to sets of consistent interlocking contingencies that can mutually support each other, leading to expanded and reverberating systemic effects. Despite the effort required to align multiple community constituencies around a common goal, when alignment can be achieved, the effects are likely to be strongly potentiated. Behavior analysis provides a good deal of guidance regarding effective community practice (Fawcett, 1991; Fawcett, Mathews, & Fletcher, 1980; Mattaini, 1993).

Supportive Media Campaigns

Members of contemporary communities are heavily influenced by the media. Media campaigns consistent with the other components identified are likely, once again, to buttress and support progress toward identified goals.

A coherent, integrated program that includes all of these components is likely to be far more powerful than a program focused on just one or two. In addition, an integrated program is likely to be more successful in reducing competing contingencies (say, between family and peers) and may, therefore, be the only strategy potent enough to have a significant effect on prevalence at a community level. Coherent analysis of the important interlocking contingencies (as outlined in chapter 1) is essential, to ensure both that the right behavioral networks are targeted and that crucial contingencies are not forgotten.

Establishing the multiple components of a project like this would require the concentrated and coordinated effort of many groups. Parents, for example, potentially provide important reinforcers for child peers (as members of parent groups), for political decision makers (as voters), for educators (as members of parent organizations), and for media decision makers (as consumers). Educators (as voters and union members) can influence political decision makers, as well as on parents and peer networks, through their educational role. Media, of course, can have a powerful effect on children and their peers as well as on parents. The core challenge, perhaps, is to build a small, enduring network of persons who can clarify the steps needed to achieve the goal of raising successful children using the science of behavior and who control sufficient reinforcers (often through personal relationships) to initiate a process that can systemically propagate through the multiple classes of actors and cultural entities required. As with social policy, community-level intervention requires the long-term commitment of behavior analysts.

OBSTACLES THAT MUST BE CONFRONTED

Despite the potential of the science of behavior to inform responses to serious social problems, there are a number of obstacles to its wider application. Some obstacles are practical; for instance, no effective work can be done without adequate resources. Although we know a good deal, there is much still to learn. Before dealing with these reality issues, however, it may be important to address certain philosophical barriers that, unacknowledged, may obstruct progress.

Philosophical Issues

Doubts About Empiricism and Science

In society, in intellectual circles, and even among some social scientists, recognition that people see reality through lenses shaped by their experiences (a recognition consistent with behavioral theory; see Ainslie, 1993) has, in some cases, resulted in a denial of the possibility of touching reality at all. Thus, the suggestion is that empiricism, science, and even the problems with which we are concerned about here have no objective validity. Empiricism and constructionism can be consistent, but only when the possibility of connecting with reality is acknowledged (Gould, 1993). If, however, one maintains that reality is essentially unknowable, that no attempt at developing knowledge corresponding to objective fact is possible, one also asserts that there is no hope for intervention. One can only design bridges—or cultures—in a planful way if one can actively contact reality. Radical constructionism and other antiempirical stances such as obscurantism, are inconsistent with understanding and actively engaging human problems (Harris, 1979; Searle, 1993).

In other circles, skepticism about science rooted in misunderstandings and bias reigns; antiempiricism and superstition can be explained by behavioral theory, but as long as social contingencies are shaped by them, progress is correspondingly more difficult. Action to expand alternative world views consistent with empiricism is therefore a priority.

Determinism

Determinism has perhaps caused more difficulty for behavior analysis than any other philosophical issue. *Beyond Freedom and Dignity* (1971) was Skinner's most controversial book because it clearly denied the possibility of human freedom. The philosophy of behaviorism is, in general, deterministic—but with the recognition that the effects of environmental conditions and events are probabilistic rather than mechanistic. As increasingly appears to be the case with regard to biological selection (Gould, 1993, 1994), the specifics of behavioral selection depend on probabilities and historical contingency; that is, the unpredictable but important effects of apparently minor and sometimes accidental events. (Acknowledging some indeterminancy, however, is, of course, different from confirming free will.) Determinism of strong and weak varieties continues to be debated in the philosophical literature (e.g., Baldwin, 1988; Rockwell, 1994). Most behavior analysts accept determinism as a working tenet (and many as a world view, interpreting their intuition of freedom itself as behavior shaped by social contingencies; e.g., Nevin, 1991). There is a certain austere elegance to this view of life, but one need not entirely embrace it to apply behavioral strategies.

Perhaps surprisingly, such debates are relatively unimportant for our current purposes, except as they interfere with the process of conducting science. Believing, or not believing, that behavior is shaped by biology and learning history does not make the proposition true or false. The crucial importance of environmental contingencies can be accepted as a useful working hypothesis without viewing this as capturing all of reality. Behavioral techniques can be used by those who do not accept the philosophical system from which they emerged. Either the approaches suggested (and usually supported by data) in this volume are effective to some extent, or they are not; these are empirical, not philosophical issues. If these strategies help in dealing with serious social problems, that is what matters.

The primary question is not whether people and events should be allowed to influence the behavior of others or not; they always do, whether by design or accident. The most important issues may be ethical; what forms of explicit behavioral intervention are consistent with accepted values? The most adequate response may be, those interventions that emphasize incentives for taking action consistent with the well-being of the actor and others. Such interventions are not rooted in coercion, and they do not encourage people to take actions inconsistent with their own and others' long-term good. Few would argue, for example, that salaries should not be given because they limit freedom by encouraging people to go to work instead of doing other things. Most would also agree that conditions like sexual coercion, violence, and child maltreatment are undesirable, and that social interventions to reduce them are ethically justified (assuming the interventive approaches selected are themselves ethically acceptable). These examples suggest that all forms of influence on others' behavior are not inherently unacceptable to most people.

Recognizing the power of their approach, behavior analysts have been among the most self-critical professionals in ensuring that the goals toward which they work are in the best interests of the client and, to the extent possible, are collaboratively chosen. Interventive strategy matters as well. Historically, professional behavior analysts have suggested that reinforcement is preferable to punishment for both humane and scientific reasons (Skinner, 1953), although this emphasis has not always been understood by the uninformed. Given all of these considerations, failure to at least consider use of approaches with strong empirical support in areas of serious human pain and suffering is, in itself, ethically questionable.

Blaming the Victim

People learn that some ways of behaving are wrong—are bad—very early in life. Given the human talent for linking objects and events that often occur together (see the technical literature related to equivalence relations; Hayes & Hayes, 1989), it is not surprising that when a person observes or hears about another acting in a way that he or she has learned is bad, he or she tends to view both the act and the actor as offensive. In contrast, if a person performs socially defined positive behavior, that person is seen as good. And, if a person acts in a way that hurts us or those we care about—it is natural (for reasons detailed by Sidman, 1989) for us to want to hurt back or to seek vengeance.

The preceding statements are only the sketchiest of treatments; however, they begin to suggest why people often act as if—and tell themselves and others that—those who perform undesirable actions are bad and deserve punishment, and those who do not are good and deserve credit. These responses may be in some sense natural (shaped by culture, in this case), but they are clearly inconsistent with viewing behavior as the result of biology, personal history, and current contingencies. The latter view (as asserted by the science of behavior) blames the contingencies for problems; the former blames the person behaving. The practical differences are profound.

If the person is viewed as responsible, it may be difficult to persuade those in a position to change the contingencies to reinforce alternative, more desirable behaviors. For example, teaching people who commit crimes new repertoires—and rewarding them for using these repertoires—may be viewed as rewarding criminals. Thus, the alternative would appear to be longer and more aversive punishment. The failure of this punishment strategy over the past two decades, however, suggests the lack of utility of that paradigm (Reiss & Roth, 1993). Blaming not only is philosophically questionable, it also does not work very well.

If the problem is seen as *lying in the contingencies*, very different approaches are likely to be viewed as acceptable, including many of those outlined in this volume that rely on teaching new behaviors by using incentives. Young offenders, for example, can either be sent to boot camps emphasizing aversive control, or they can be taught new social and vocational skills (Cohen & Filipczak, 1971/1989). Science suggests that the latter will work better, but it may not be easy to market politically.

Resource Limitations

Political considerations are likely to be significant in many of the areas considered in this volume. At the time of this writing, a new conservative political agenda was emerging; whether it will endure remains to be seen. Historically, neither liberals nor conservatives have consistently looked to science to make decisions; each side has relied instead on its understanding of how things work, ideas that are heavily rooted in the beliefs of the different groups (systems of rules that are often highly inaccurate statements of the actual contingencies). Few programs can be implemented with no resources, however; given deep governmental cuts, private sources of funding are likely to experience heavy pressure to simply maintain some parts of what is in place. New and expanded initiatives—including many of those outlined here—may therefore prove difficult to fund.

Ultimately, it is likely that the pressure of increasing problems and the lure of potentially more effective solutions will draw resources. In the meantime, many of those whose work is discussed here—and their colleagues named and unnamed—will do what they can to continue to experiment, to test, to develop, and to disseminate approaches rooted in the science of behavior. Resource limitations are likely to slow progress significantly, but will not block it entirely.

Limited Knowledge

As was suggested in most of the chapters in this volume, a wide range of areas exists in which our knowledge is too limited to be sure of the most effective and efficient approaches. The issues considered in this book, and others like them, are critical to the survival of our society and the cultures that constitute it. Serious social problems—violence, coercion, bias, economic and social vulnerability—may constitute the most important research agenda we currently face; they deserve support at a commensurate level. We need many more well-trained and adequately funded behavioral researchers if we are to learn rapidly how to have substantive impact in these areas. As in other areas of science, there is little doubt that the facts will eventually be discovered (assuming survival of the species); in this area, however, accelerating the process may significantly reduce human pain.

Limited Exposure to the Science of Behavior

The basic principles of behavior analysis are now well established, and progress in the field is rapid. Despite knowledge limitations, what we already know could enable us to dramatically improve the functioning of important social institutions (families, schools, workplaces). A crucial bottleneck, however, is the limited number of persons who are well trained in the application of what we know. Few teachers, fewer employers, and even fewer parents and peers know how to effectively use positive reinforcement and other behavioral strategies to "[bring] out the best in people" (Daniels, 1994). Those designing sociocultural systems often know nothing of the science that could underpin their work. When a new social problem emerges or an existing one is exacerbated, few human service professions know how to apply principles of the science to ameliorate the problem. Stakeholders at any of these levels (family, organizational, political) also know little or nothing of the science and therefore are unable to assist in leveraging change efforts.

This lack of knowledge is a serious problem. In a sense, it is a social metaproblem, because even if the basics of what current scholarship has learned were widely known, change could reverberate and be amplified throughout social systems. Therefore, teaching behavior analysis to professionals (teachers, psychologists, social workers), to policymakers and decision makers in the private and public sectors, and to parents and potential parents is a crucial priority.

Teaching science of any sort is difficult, requiring a cadre of dedicated, knowledgable educators; effective pedagogic methods and materials; and systems within which these can be integrated, which themselves must be designed with adequate contingency arrangements in mind. It is perhaps difficult to specify whether the most critical need at this point is for more research or for effectively disseminating what we already know, but the second may be at least as important as the first to contemporary society.

Human behavior is complex, especially at the level of cultural practices maintained by cultural entities; scientific understanding of these phenomena, therefore, is complex as well. Developing effective ways of communicating the core of the science to nonspecialists is a daunting task, but it is precisely what appears to be essential to move in a substantive way toward cultural design. (Doing so is the mission of the Education Board of the Association for Behavior Analysis: International.) Potent myths and superstitions must be challenged, and solid knowledge must be communicated in simultaneously accurate and engaging ways. There is, perhaps, no more important contemporary assignment and no more valuable vocational choice.

CONCLUSION

We may find some consolation in the fact that no true intervention is possible. We cannot step into the history of life on Earth as if we were not part of it. If people have ever changed the course of evolution, they have done so because evolved cultural practices made it possible. (Skinner, 1987, p. 12)

Perhaps paradoxically, from a radical behaviorist perspective, we are simply part of the ongoing stream of events; neither we nor anything else can intercede from an independent position outside the flow. This situation is by no means hopeless, however, because selection at all levels has taught us repertoires that work reasonably well—including how to affect the contingencies and interlocking contingencies that shape what we do, and thereby who we are. As the chapters in this volume attest, change directed toward increasing reinforcement and satisfaction for people as individuals and as members of groups is possible, and we have a good deal of data to guide us in shaping such variations.

We know a fair amount about changing individual behavior, both directly and indirectly (through changes in contextual factors that affect the contingencies that directly shape behavior; see Hayes, 1994). At the same time, stepping back and looking at the material in this book, we can see another message: the critical importance of cultural design. Changing the behavior of an individual often requires changes in environmental conditions and events that are themselves difficult to maintain; this difficulty is why achieving lasting change at a clinical level can be so troublesome. Systemic innovations in the interlocking contingencies maintained by cultural entities (what Minuchin, 1974, called *structure* in family work), being potentially self-perpetuating, are far more likely to result in enduring changes in behaviors, practices, and scenes.

We know more about cultural design than may be apparent at first glance; principles and strategies can be abstracted from effective work with cultural entities of many sizes and levels of complexity, including families, friendship networks, and organizations. Biglan's work (1995, this volume) with multilevel community interventions is an operationalized step toward work with larger and more complex interlocking behavioral systems. Addressing serious social problems in the near term will involve two interrelated streams of activity: the expansion of practical applications and applied research in the areas sketched in this volume and others like them and the conceptual and empirical clarification of the underlying principles of cultural design. Both are pressing strategic agendas.

REFERENCES

Baldwin, J. D. (1988). Mead and Skinner: Agency and determinism. *Behaviorism, 16*, 109–127.

Biglan, A. (1995). *Changing cultural practices.* Reno, NV: Context Press.

Biglan, A., Metzler, C. W., & Ary, D. V. (1994). Increasing the prevalence of successful children: The case for community intervention research. *The Behavior Analyst, 17,* 335–351.

Cohen, H. L., & Filipczak, J. (1989). *A new learning environment.* Boston: Authors Cooperative. (Original work published 1971)

Daniels, A. C. (1994). *Bringing out the best in people.* New York: McGraw-Hill.

Fawcett, S. B. (1991). Some values guiding community research and action. *Journal of Applied Behavior Analysis, 24,* 621–636.

Fawcett, S. B., Bernstein, G. S., Czywewski, M. J., Greene, B. F., Hannah, G. T., Iwata, B. A., Jason, L. A., Mathews, R. M., Morris, E. K., Otis-Wilborn, A., Seekins, T., & Winett, R. A. (1988). Behavior analysis and public policy. *The Behavior Analyst, 11,* 11–25.

Fawcett, S. B., Mathews, R. M., & Fletcher, R. K. (1980). Some promising dimensions of behavioral community technology. *Journal of Applied Behavior Analysis, 13,* 505–518.

Gould, S. J. (1993). *Eight little piggies: Reflections in natural history.* New York: W. W. Norton.

Gould, S. J. (1994). The evolution of life on the earth. *Scientific American, 271*(4), 85–91.

Harris, M. (1979). *Cultural materialism: The struggle for a science of culture.* New York: Vintage.

Hauserman, N., Walen, S. R., & Behling, M. (1973). Reinforced racial integration in the first grade: A study in generalization. *Journal of Applied Behavior Analysis, 6,* 193–200.

Hayes, S. C. (1994). Content, context. and the types of psychological acceptance. In S. C. Hayes, N. S. Jacobson, V. M. Follette, & M. J. Dougher (Eds.), *Acceptance and change: Content and context in psychotherapy* (pp. 13–32). Reno, NV: Context Press.

Hayes, S. C., & Hayes, L. J. (1989). The verbal action of the listener as a basis for rule-governance. In S. C. Hayes (Ed.), *Rule-governed behavior: Cognition, contingencies, and instructional control* (pp. 153–190). New York: Plenum.

Lamal, P. A. (1984). Contingency management in the People's Republic of China. *The Behavior Analyst, 7,* 121–130.

Marks, J. (1994) Black, white, other. *Natural History, 103*(12), 32–35.

Mattaini, M. A. (1993). Behavior analysis in community practice. *Research on Social Work Practice, 3,* 420–447.

Minuchin, S. (1974). *Families and family therapy.* Cambridge, MA: Harvard University Press.

Nevin, J. A. (1991). Beyond pride and humility. *The Behavior Analyst, 14,* 35–36.

Opulente, M., & Mattaini, M. A. (1993). Toward welfare that works. *Behavior and Social Issues, 3,* 17–34.

Patterson, G., Reid, J., & Dishion, T. J. (1992). *Antisocial boys: A social interactional approach* (Vol. 4). Eugene, OR: Castalia.

Reiss, A. J., Jr., & Roth, J. A. (Eds.). (1993). *Understanding and preventing violence* (Vol. 1). Washington, DC: National Academy Press.

Rockwell, W. T. (1994). Beyond determinism and indignity: A reinterpretation of operant conditioning. *Behavior and Philosophy, 22,* 53–66.

Sanford, F. L., & Fawcett, S. B. (1980). Consequence analysis: Its effects on verbal statements about an environmental project. *Journal of Applied Behavior Analysis, 13,* 57–64.

Searle, J. R. (1993). Rationality and realism, what is at stake? *Daedalus, 122*(4), 55–83.

Seekins, T., & Fawcett, S. B. (1986). Public policy-making and research information. *The Behavior Analyst, 9,* 35–45.

Sidman, M. (1989). *Coercion and its fallout.* Boston: Authors Cooperative.

Skinner, B. F. (1953). *Science and human behavior.* New York: Free Press.

Skinner, B. F. (1971). *Beyond freedom and dignity.* New York: Knopf.

Skinner, B. F. (1987). Why we are not acting to save the world. In B. F. Skinner, *Upon further reflection* (pp. 1–14). Englewood Cliffs, NJ: Prentice-Hall. (Originally delivered at the conference of the American Psychological Association, August, 1982)

Zifferblatt, S. M., & Hendricks, C. G. (1974). Applied behavior analysis of societal problems. *American Psychologist, 29,* 750–761.

INDEX

Abolishing operation, 22
Abstinence violation effect, 381–382
Abulia, 65, 67
Academic success, 405. *See also* Educational reform
Access skills, and shyness, 355
Acedia, 65, 67
Action focus, welfare policy, 43–44
Addiction Severity Index, 387
Adolescent sexuality. *See* Teenage sexuality
Adolescent violence. *See* Youth violence
Adventitious reinforcements, 64
Advocacy interventions, communities, 309–310
Affect management, shyness, 355
Affection, in child caretaking, 246–248, 258–259
Affirmative action, 150, 160–174
   economic contingencies, 166
   external contingencies, 163–166
   failure of, 160–161
   governmental enforcement, 165–166, 172
   implementation problems, 163–172
   informal organization dynamics, 170–171, 173
   minority group pressures for, 165
   minority group socialization in, 171
   official contingencies, 167–169
   organizational decision-making process, 171–172
   organizational resistance, 168–169
   unofficial contingencies, 170–171
African American adolescents
   AIDS prevention programs, 275
   sexually transmitted diseases, 269–270
Age at first intercourse, 277, 279
Aggression. *See* Oppositional behavior; Violence
Aid to Families with Dependent Children
   contingencies, 45
   empirical evaluation need, 47–48
AIDS-prevention programs

attitudes, beliefs, and practices focus, 276–277
   behavior analytic perspective, 276
   educational programs, limitations, 272–276
   Health Belief Model, 273–274
   peer norm alteration, 279–280
   social skill building, 278
Alcohol abuse
   child neglect factor, 245–246
   Community Reinforcement Approach, 35–38
   and condom use, 279
   and cultural design, 34–38
Anger management
   and adolescent risk-taking, 272
   child abusers, 230
   components, 96–97
   youth violence intervention, 96–97
Antecedents, 20–24
   basic principles, 20–24
   child maltreatment, 234–238, 242–246, 251
   design of, 32–34
   drug abuse, 381–384
   psychotic behavior, 323
Antabuse, 385–386
Apathy, 65, 67
APBC model, 182–183
Arousal, and rage, 95–97
Assertion training, 254
Athletes, and sexual coercion, 299
Attitudes, beliefs and practices, 276–277
   AIDS prevention, 276–277
   information program comparison, 277
   social policy focus, 43–44
Attributions
   and social anxiety, 354
   and substance abuse, 381–382
Aversives
   child maltreatment antecedent, 237, 239, 244–245
   youth violence, 86
Avoidance, and negative reinforcement, 17

"Baby-bonus," 50
Bakke case, 160
Behavior analysis, 3–5
    and determinism, 407–409
    domain of, 41–42
    ethics, 408–409
    focus of, 3–4, 43–44
    natural history methods in, 26–28
    philosophical issues, 407–410
    social learning theory difference, 23
    and social welfare policy, 41–57
    in strategic science, 2–3
    training needs, 411
Behavioral selection, 129–131
Biological theories, violence, 77–79
Birth control attitudes, adolescents, 280
Bizarre behavior, 322–327
    antecedents, 323
    consequent stimuli, 324–326
    and psychosis, 322–327
    social reinforcement contingencies,
        322–326
Blaming the victim, 409–410
Boys
    classroom differential treatment,
        202–203
    gender socialization, 296–298
    toy selection bias, 215
Breastfeeding, cultural practices, 210–211
Bullying, 364

CABAS educational model
    behavioral selection curriculum, 131
    community accountability, 124
    components, 116, 119, 144–146
    cost-effectiveness, 138–139
    criterion-referenced learning,
        133–135
    individualized instruction, 120,
        125–129
    interlocking contingencies, 29
    learn units, 120–122, 133–135
    measurement of, 120–122, 133–136
    objectives, 120–122
    parent curriculum, 123
    parents role in, 137–138
    research base, 115–118
    supervisor curriculum, 123
    teachers curricula, 122–123
Car sales, sexism, 216
Child abuse, 232–241. See also Child
    maltreatment

antecedents, 234–238
behavioral pattern, 232
coercive spiral, 233–234, 238
consequences, 238–241
intervention strategies, 239–241
    transfer enhancement, 240
natural history/course, 233–234
rule-governed behavior, 233–234
Child maltreatment, 223–266. See also
    Child abuse; Child neglect; Sex-
    ual abuse (children)
antecedents, 234–238, 242–246, 251
case example, 255–260
causal chain hypothesis, 253–254
community-level intervention,
    253–255
conceptual approaches, history,
    229–232
consequences, 238–241, 245–248,
    251
definitional issues, 225
epidemiology, 226–228
intervention strategies, 239–241,
    248–249, 251–255, 260
    case example, 255–260
    transfer enhancement, 240
legal and service framework,
    225–226
natural history/course, 233–234,
    241–242, 250
packaged interventions, 260
personal/social costs, 228–229
programmatic interventions,
    253–255
punishment approach, limitations,
    232
research needs, 262
risk variables, 228
rule-governed behavioral in,
    233–237
social interactional approach,
    231–232
social policy considerations, 260–262
survey data, 227
Child neglect, 232, 241–249
    behavioral analysis, 232, 242–248
    intervention strategies, 248–249
    natural history, 241–242
Child rearing
    cultural practices, 210–212
    women's role, rule changes, 213

Classical conditioning, and racism, 156–158
Cocaine abuse
    behavioral treatment, 385–386, 388–390
    case example, 386–388
    and condom use, 279
    diagnosis, 389
    drug treatment of, 378
    intervention recommendations, 388–390
    outpatient versus inpatient treatment, 390
    surveys, 374–376
Coercive spiral, child abuse, 233–234, 248
Coercive strategies. See Punishment
Cognitive–behavioral treatment
    child abuse, 230
    social anxiety, 360
Communication skills, adolescents, 278–279
Communidad Los Horcones, 216
Community analysis, 307–308
Community-level interventions
    advocacy efforts, 309–310
    children's programs, components, 403–407
    community analysis in, 307–308
    and media campaigns, 406–407
    multiple baseline designs, 303–306
    research design aspects, 303–305
    respect for diversity approach, 401–405
    sexually coercive behavior, 302–313, 401
Community Reinforcement Approach, 35–38
    alcohol abuse, 35–38
    components, 35
    as cultural design, 36–38
Community survival skills, 333
Compliance
    and contingencies, 210
    training in, psychotic clients, 327–328
Comprehensive Application of Behavior Analysis to Schooling. See CABAS educational model
Conceptual change theory, 271
Conditioned response, and racism, 156–157

Condom use
    drug use relationship, 279
    peer influences, 280–281
    sex education curricula effects, 276
    and social skills, 278
Conflict resolution training, 99–100
Conflict sequences, and violence, 97–99
Consequation, 238, 258
Consequence analysis, 399–400
Consequences, 14–20
    basic principles, 14–20
    and child maltreatment, 238–239, 245–248, 251, 258
    in policy decision analysis, 399–401
    psychotic behavior, 324–326
    in scene design, 32–34
    and selection of behavior, 14–20
    and youth violence, 82, 86–87, 93–94, 107
Constructionism, 407
Contextual factors. See Establishing operations
Contingencies, 24–25
    in affirmative action, 163–171
    compliance role, 210
    in cultural practices, 15–16, 209–219
    design of, 30–38
    direct-acting versus indirect-acting, 210, 212–214
    versus entitlements, ethics, 54–56
    interlocking networks, 32–33
    intervention principle, 409–410
    maintenance of, 28–29
    in organizations, 161–163
    psychotic behavior, 324–326
    and sexism, 207–208, 212–214
    in social welfare policy, 44–53
    young offender intervention, 409–410
Contingency management
    basic principles, 49–53
    in social welfare policy, 45–53
Contraceptive use, adolescents, 277–280
Controllability, and relapse, 382
Conversational skills training, 359
Coping skills, and drug abuse, 383–384
Cost-benefits, and organizational change, 310–311
Cost-effectiveness, CABAS program, 138–139
Crack cocaine abuse

and condom use, 279
surveys, 375
Cues. *See* Occasions
Cultural analysis, 26
Cultural design, 3–4, 13–40
    alcohol abuse application, 34–38
    critical importance of, 412
    definition, 3
    maintaining contingencies in, 28–29
    natural history methods in, 26–28
    "scene" analysis in, 32–34
    steps in, 30
Cultural determinism, 149–150
Cultural entities
    and cultural design, 28–30, 36
    definition, 15
Cultural materialism, 208–209
    and breastfeeding practices, 211
    fundamental principle, 209
Cultural practices
    definition, 208–210
    design of, 25, 27, 32–34
    and diversity, 402
    identification of, 403–404
    and intervention, communities, 302–313
    levels of, 208–209
    metacontingencies in, sexism, 209–214
    sexist behavior role, 210–217
    survival value changes, 212–214
    and sexual coercion, 293–313
    youth violence role, 103–106

Dating anxiety, 359–360
Delinquent behavior. *See* Youth violence
Delusions
    antecedent stimuli, 323
    behavioral interventions, 323–325
    consequent stimuli, 324–326
Dependent behavior
    noncontingent benefits effect, 54–55
    and social policy contingencies, 45–46
    substance abuse antecedent, 382
Deprivation, and youth violence, 92–93
Determinism, 407–409
Direct-acting contingencies
    behavioral effects, 210
    and sexism practices, 212–214
Direct Instruction, 115
Discriminative stimulus. *See* Occasions

"Disrespect" response, violence, 88–91
Disulfiram therapy, 385–386
Drug abuse, 373–396
    antecedents, 381
    and attribution style, 381–382
    behavioral analysis, 380–386
    behavioral treatment approach, 385–386, 388–390
    biopsychosocial approach, 377
    case example, 386–388
    child neglect factor, 245–246
    Community Reinforcement Approach, 36
    and condom use, 279
    and coping skills, 383–384
    diagnosis, 389
    economic effects, 377
    epidemiology, 374–377
    intervention recommendations, 388–390
    outpatient versus inpatient treatment, 390
    prevention knowledge base, 379–380
    treatment knowledge base, 378–380
Drug Use Forecasting System, 376

Ecobehavioral Analysis, 115
Ecological perspective, 27
Educational reform, 113–146. *See also* CABAS educational model
    add-on versus redesign approaches, 132–133
    behavioral selectionist curriculum, 129–131
    CABAS approach, 29, 116–140
        versus traditional approach, 125–126
    cost-effectiveness, 138–139
    criterion-referenced learning, 133–135
    individualized instruction, 125–129
    learn units, 120–122, 133–135
    personalized systems, 127–128
    portfolio assessment in, 127
    systems redesign in, 29, 129–131
Emotional abuse. *See* Child abuse
Empirical evaluations
    in educational reform, CABAS program, 133–136
    sexual coercion interventions, 303–306
    welfare policy need, 47–49

Empiricism, 407
Employment, psychotic clients, 332–333
Enrichment strategy, 90
Entitlements, ethics, 54–56
Environmental management
     behavior analysis strategy, 43–44
     youth violence prevention, 94
     Equivalence relations, 409
Establishing operations
     basic principles, 21–22
     child maltreatment, 237, 243–245,
          253–254
     and violence, 78, 105
Ethics, 61–72, 408–409
     and behavior modification, 61–72,
          408–409
     entitlements versus contingencies,
          54–56
Evaluation studies. See Empirical evalua-
     tions
Exercise, psychotic clients, 334
Existential Feminism, 205
Exposure techniques, social anxiety,
     358–360
Extinction
     basic principles, 18–19
     social welfare policy application,
          52–53
     youth violence prevention limita-
          tions, 89
Extinction burst, 19

Families
     cultural design principles, 29
     gender socialization role, 298
     sexism intervention, 214–215
     sexual coercion communication,
          311–312
"Family conference," 240
Feedback strategy, and performance,
     193–194
Feminism
     consciousness-raising function,
          213–214
     theoretical approaches, 204–207
Food Stamp program, 47–48
Free will, 408

Gender roles. See also Sexism
     and cultural practices, 210–212
     socialization of, 296–299
     survival value influences, 212–214

Generalization
     child abuse interventions, 240
     racism conditioned responses, 157
     social skills training, 330
Genetic selection, 14
Genetics, and violence, 77
Girls
     differential treatment, classrooms,
          202–203
     gender socialization, 296–298
     toy selection bias, 215
Group design experiments
     community-level interventions, 303
     limitations, 231, 304
     multiple baseline design comparison,
          304
Group instruction
     educational settings, 125–129
     versus individualized instruction,
          125–129
Guided self-change treatment, 35

Hallucinogen use, surveys, 374–375
Handgun violence, 81
Health Belief Model, 273
Health education
     outreach programs, 275
     and teenage sexuality, 272, 274–275
High School Senior Survey, 374–376
Hispanic adolescents
     AIDS prevention programs, 275
     sexually transmitted diseases,
          269–270
Home-based services, child abuse, 231
Homemaking, gender roles, 210–212
Homicide rates, 75
Howard University Violence Prevention
     Project, 81–82

"I-statements," 100
Imitation
     basic principles, 22–23
     child maltreatment, 234–237, 244
     violence role, 23, 89–90, 94
In-home services, child abuse, 231
Incentives, and performance, 194
Independent living skills, 331–333
Indirect-acting contingencies
     behavioral effects, 210
     and sexism practices, 212, 214
Individualized assessment, 231
Individualized instruction, 120–122

behavioral science view, 126–127
CABAS approach, 120, 125–129
in group classrooms, 127–129
versus group instruction, 125–129
Information-dissemination programs
adolescent sex education, 274–275
behavior analytic perspective,
276–277
drug abuse prevention, 379–380
Inheritance rules, cultural practices, 211
Inoculation interventions, 380
Institutional racism, 149–155
Insularity, and child abuse, 236
Intermittent reinforcement, 18
Intravenous drug users
economic effects, 377
HIV transmission, 376
information dissemination programs,
274–275
Issues, 201

"Job club," 333
"Just Say No" intervention, 380
Juvenile violence. See Youth violence

Law of Effect, 63
Learn unit, 120–122, 133–135, 139
"Learnfare" program, 52
Literacy, 130–131
Locus of control, and drug abuse, 381
Loneliness, 345–371
and access skills, 355
behavioral assessment guidelines,
351–356
causes, 348–351
definition, 346
environmental and cultural causes,
348–349
and individual characteristics,
350–351
intervention options, 356–363
obstacles, 365
prevention options, 363–365

Managed care, 29–30
Marijuana use, surveys, 374–376
Marxist Feminism, 205
Mastery, education goals, 126–127
Matching law
basic principle, 22, 90
equation, 93

sexual coercion application,
292–293
substance abuse, 246
and youth violence prevention, 90,
93
Maternal depression, 242
Media campaigns, 310, 406–407
Media influences
racism, 159
sexually coercion behavior, 298–299
Mediation skills, adolescents, 100
Medicaid reimbursement, contingencies,
45–46
Mental disorders. See Psychosis
Metacontingencies
behavioral effects of, 210
and cultural practices, 16, 209–210
sexism, 212–214
Methadone maintenance, 378
Miniaturization
in cultural design, 30
natural history method, 28
Modeling
basic principles, 22–23
child maltreatment, 234–237, 244
Morningside Generative Model, 115
Multiple baseline evaluations
advantages, 304
community-level interventions,
303–306
group designs comparison, 304
workplace interventions, 185–187

National Center for Child Abuse and
Neglect, 224, 227
National Child Abuse and Neglect Data
System, 227
National Committee to Prevent Child
Abuse, 227–228
National Household Survey, 375–376
National Organization for Women, 206
Natural history method
overview, 26–28
and youth violence, 83–85
Natural selection, 14
Negative punishment, 52
Negative reinforcement
basic principles, 17–18
psychotic behavior, 325–326
punishment distinction, 17
social welfare policy application, 51
youth violence factor, 87–91

Neglect. *See* Child neglect
News media, 310
Noncompliant behavior, 327–328
Noncontingent reinforcement, 54–56,
    63–64

Observational learning, racism, 159–160
Observational methods, 27–28
Occasions
    basic principles, 20–21
    and child abuse, 234–236
Occupational therapy, 331–332
On-task behavior, 334
Operant reinforcement
    basic principles, 14–15
    in drug abuse intervention, 384–385
    and mental patients' rights, 68
    racism role, 158–159
    social welfare policy application,
        49–57
    workplace performance management
        model, 181–183
Operant selection, 14–15
Oppositional behavior
    compliance training, 328
    functional analysis importance, 328
    psychotic clients, 327–328
Organizational behavior management, 29,
    180n1. *See also* Performance
    Management
Organizational-level interventions. *See
    also* Community-level interven-
    tions
    cost-benefit considerations, 310–311
    and sexually coercive behavior,
        302–313
Overlearning, 240

Paranoia, negative reinforcement, 325
Parent training
    child abuse, 239–240
    child neglect, 245
    in community-level programs, 403
    transfer enhancement, 240
Parental depression, 242
Parents
    child maltreatment antecedents,
        237–238, 242–245
    educational system role, 136–137
    gender socialization role, 298
    sexual coercion communication,
        311–312

Passivity, and noncontingent benefits,
    54–55
Pedagogy
    in educational reform, 114–115
    and individualized instruction,
        127–128
    selectionist curriculum development,
        129–131
Peer cluster theory, 272
Peer-mediated programs
    in community-level intervention,
        405
    and social behavior, 360–361
Peer norms
    sexually coercive behavior, 312
    teenage sexual behavior, 279–280
    violence prevention, 94
PEERS program, 361–363
Perceived consequences, 293
Perceived risk, 277–278
Performance Management, 180–195
    cash-based incentive plans, 194
    data-driven focus of, 183–185
    definition, 180–181
    feedback strategy, 184–185, 193–194
    four-term contingency model,
        181–183
    multiple baseline evaluations,
        185–187
    reversal design evaluations, 185–186
Personal control, 382
Personalized System of Instruction, 115,
    127–128
Physical abuse. *See* Child abuse
Pliance, 87
Policy decisions, 398–401
    consequence analysis, 399–400
    empirical testing, 398–399
    scientist-advocate role in, 399–400
Political contingencies, welfare policy,
    44–45
Pornography, 298–299
Portfolio assessment, 127, 134
Positive punishment, 51–52
Positive reinforcement
    basic principles, 17–18
    child maltreatment intervention,
        232
    psychotic behavior, 324–325
    social welfare policy application,
        50–51
    youth violence factor, 91–95

Postcedents. *See* Consequences
Postmodern Feminism, 206
Precision Teaching, 115, 128
Pregnancy in adolescence. *See* Teenage
    pregnancy
Prejudice, 149–150. *See also* Racism
Prisoners, operant reinforcement, 69
Problem behavior theory, 271–272
Productivity (workplace), 179–200
    data-based interventions, 183–185
    experimentation and evaluation in,
        185–187
    multiple baseline evaluations in,
        185–187
    measurement, 183
    performance feedback strategy,
        184–185, 192–194
    Performance Management approach,
        180–195
    problem solving flowchart, 188–194
    reversal design evaluations, 185–186
Programmed reinforcement, child abuse,
    240
Programmed Teaching, 115, 126–128
Project 12-Ways, 244
Prudential Health Care Plan, 50–51
Psychoanalytic Feminism, 205
Psychological inoculation, 380
Psychosis, 319–343
    antecedent stimuli, 323
    behavioral interventions, 320–336
        obstacles, 334–335
    bizarre behavior in, 322–327
    community adjustment programs,
        335
    compliance training, 327–328
    consequent stimuli, 324–326
    diagnostic aspects, 321–322
    economic costs, 319–320
    functional assessment and treatment,
        322–336
    personal hygiene, 331
    recreational behavior, 333–334
    reinforcement contingencies,
        322–327
    self-care deficiencies, 331–332
    social skills, 330
    vocational training, 332–333
Psychotic speech, 324–326
Public policy. *See* Social policy
Public speaking anxiety, 359
Punishment

basic principles, 19–20
child maltreatment strategy, limita-
    tions, 232
failure in crime prevention, 409
negative reinforcement distinction,
    17
seductive aspects, 19–20
social welfare policy application,
    51–52
youth violence control, 86, 89

Racism, 147–177. *See also* Affirmative ac-
    tion
    and affirmative action, 160–174
    classical conditioning, 156–158
    conceptual models, 149–150
    higher educational settings, 153–155
    incidence and prevalence, 148–149
    observational learning role, 159–160
    operant conditioning, 158–159
    society level factors, 153–155
    in urban settings, 151–153
Radical behaviorism, 412
Radical constructionism, 407
Radical Feminism, 205
Rage, and youth violence, 95–97
Random processes, 14
Rape. *See* Sexual coercion
Reciprocity Marriage Counseling, 36
Recreation, psychotic clients, 333–334
"Red-lining," 152
Rehabilitation, psychotic clients,
    331–332
Reinforcement, basic principles, 17–19
Reinforcer sampling, 22
Relapse prevention
    and coping skills, 383–384
    sexual abuse, 251
    substance abuse, 383–384
Relational frames theory, 292–293
Relaxation techniques, 96–97
Repeated measures. *See* Multiple baseline
    evaluations
Repertoire, 131
Repetitive behaviors, psychosis, 328–329
Respite care, 239
Respondent learning, and racism,
    156–158
Reversal design evaluations, 185–186
Reverse discrimination, 150
Rhode Island Children's Crusade, 50
Rights issues, 62, 67–68, 70–72

Rise and Shine Industries program,
332–333
Rogers, Carl, 63–64
Role plays, 330
Rule-governed behavior
basic principles, 23–24, 49, 210
child abuse, 233–237
child neglect, 242–244
in conflict sequences, 99–100
and cultural innovation, 26
and direct-acting contingencies, 210
policy applications, 49–53
youth violence, 86–87, 89–90, 92,
99–100, 105
Ruminating behavior, 329

Safe sex
education programs, limitations,
272–276
intervention successes, 276–279
and self-efficacy, 278
Satiation, 22
"Scene" concept, 32–34, 403, 405
Schedules of reinforcement, 18
Schizophrenia. See Psychosis
School-based programs
health education, 272, 275
social withdrawal prevention, 364
School disciplinary approaches, 405–406
School reform. See Educational reform
Science, attitudes toward, 407
Self-attributions, 381–382
Self-blame, 382
Self-efficacy
safe sex practices, adolescents, 278
and teenage problem behavior, 271
Self-esteem, and drug abuse, 382
Self-help programs, 358–360
Self-management
in school curriculum reform,
130–131
and social anxiety, 355–356, 359
Self-report methods, 44
Self-talk
child abuse antecedent, 236–237
youth violence prevention, 90
Sex education
adolescents, limitations, 272–276
behavior analytic perspective,
276–277
Sexism, 201–220
behavioral analysis, 207–208

cultural practices, 210–217
survival value changes, 212–214
definition, 202
family environment conditioning,
208
and feminist theory, 204–208
intervention/prevention, 214–217
prevalence, 202–204
in schools, 202–203
social costs, 204
verbal community contingencies,
207–208
workplace settings, 203–204
Sexual abuse (children), 250–252. See
also Child maltreatment
antecedents, 251
behavioral analysis, 232, 250–252
consequences, 251
intervention, 251–252
punishment strategy limitations, 251
Sexual coercion
community intervention research,
302–312
experimental design, 303–306
consequences of, 291
cultural practices relationship,
293–302
definition and measurement,
300–301
family communication factor,
311–312
and gender socialization, 296–298
incidence, 289–290
male dominance influence, 295–296
matching law application, 292
modular intervention strategy, 305
peer group influences, 312
relational frames theory, 292–293
Sexual Experiences Scale, 300
Sexual harassment, 290
Sexual risk behaviors
attitudes, beliefs, and practice
changes, 276–277
educational strategies, limitations,
272–276
peer norms, 279–280
perceived risk effects, 277–278
and social skills, 278
Sexually transmitted diseases
adolescent statistics, 269–270
educational preventive approaches,
272–276

intervention successes, 276–279
Shyness, 345–371
  access skills, 355
  causes, 348–351
  cognitive components, 350–351
  context-based intervention, 360–363
  definition, 346–347
  evolutionary roots, 348
  exposure programs, 358–360
  intervention options, 356–363
    obstacles, 365
  loneliness interrelationship, 347
  self-help programs, 358–360
  social skills training, 358
Single mothers, 45–46
Single-system experimental design, 27
Skinner, B. F., 4–5
Smoking 380
Social anxiety, 345–371
  and access skills, 355
  behavioral assessment guidelines,
    351–356
  causes, 348–351
  cognitive–behavioral treatment, 360
  cognitive components, 350–351
  definition, 346–347
  developmental experiences role,
    349–350
  evolutionary roots, 348
  exposure programs, 358–360
  intervention options, 356–363
    obstacles, 365
  loneliness interrelationship, 347
  prevention options, 363–365
  self-help programs, 358–360
Social cognitive theory, 270–271
Social interactional approach, 231–232
Social isolation, 345–371
  behavioral assessment, 351–356
  causes, 348–351
  and child maltreatment, 236, 242
  definition, 346
  environmental and cultural factors,
    348–349
  indirect interventions, 362
  intervention options, 356–363
    obstacles, 365
Social learning theory
  imitation explanation, 23
  and social phobia, 349–350

  substance abuse, 380
Social networks, 362, 391
Social phobia. See Social anxiety
Social policy. See also Social welfare pol-
    icy
  consequence analysis, 399–400
  empirical testing, 398–399
  resource limitations factor, 410
  scientist-advocate role in, 399–400
Social skills
  and adolescent sexual risk behavior,
    278–279
  psychotic clients, 330, 333
  shyness assessment, 354
Social skills training
  drug abuse prevention, 380
  generalization, 330
  mechanism of effectiveness, 359
  psychotic clients, 330, 333
  shyness, 358–359
Social welfare policy, 41–60
  and behavioral changes, 43–44
  contingency management principles,
    49–53
  definitions, 42
  empirical evaluation need, 47–49
  entitlements versus contingencies,
    54–56
  ethics, 54–56
  political contingencies, 44–45
  time-series analysis, 48
Social withdrawal, 361–363
Socialist Feminism, 206
Sociobiology, 14
Sports, sexual coercion influence, 299
STAR curriculum, 81–82
Stereotypic behavior, psychosis, 328–329
Stimulant use, surveys, 374–375
Stimulus delta, 21
Straight Talk About Risks program,
    81–82
Strategic science, 2–3
Street violence, 100–103
Structural antecedents
  basic principles, 21
  child abuse, 237–238
Student-teacher ratios, 120–121, 139
Substance abuse. See Drug abuse
"Successful children," 403–407
Support groups, 239, 241

Task analyses, 354
Teacher–student ratios, 120–121, 139
Teachers
    and educational reform, 134–135,
      137–138
    incentive system, 138
    performance measures, 134–135
    sexist behavior intervention, 215
    social withdrawal intervention, 362
Teenage pregnancy
    parental influences, 280
    peer norm influences, 279–280
    sex education curricula, 276
    statistics, 269
Teenage sexuality, 267–288
    intervention successes, 276–282
    parental influences, 280
    peer norms, 279–280
    sex education programs, limitations,
      272–276
    theoretical aspects, 270–272
Television
    racism influence, 159
    sexual coercion influence, 299
Textbooks, sex bias, 203
Theoretical constructs, 44
Time Sample Behavioral Checklist, 322
Time-series analysis
    community-level interventions,
      303–305
    social welfare programs, 48
Tobacco smoking, 380
Token economy
    mental patients, 320, 327, 331–332
    shortcomings, 328
Toys, sex bias, 215
Tracking, 87
Transfer-enhancing strategies, 240
Troubles, 201

Unprotected sex, prevention, 277–279

Verbal self-report methods, 44
Violence. See also Youth violence
    biobehavioral explanations, 77–79
    conceptual model, 83–84

    conflict sequences, 97–100
    definition, 86
    imitation role, 23
    natural history research method,
      83–85
    negative reinforcement, 87–91
    observational studies, 84
    positive reinforcement, 91–95
    prevention, 80–82, 89–91, 93–95,
      101–103, 106–108
    and rage, 95–97
    in youth, 75–111
Violence Prevention Curriculum for Adoles-
    cents, 80–82
Vocational skills, psychotic clients,
    332–333

Welfare mothers, 45–46
Welfare policy. See Social welfare policy
Women's issues. See Sexism
Work behavior, psychotic clients,
    332–333
Workfare programs, 46
Working women, 212–214, 296

Youth violence, 75–111
    antecedent strategies, 94
    behavioral framework, 85–95
    classification, 85–85
    conceptual model, 83–84
    conflict sequences in, 97–100
    consequences, 82, 86–87, 90, 93–94
    microcultural conflicts, 103–106
    natural history research methods,
      83–85
    negative reinforcement, 87–91
    observational studies, 84
    positive reinforcement, 91–95
    prevention, 80–82, 89–91, 93–95,
      101–103, 106–108
    rage motivation in, 95–97
    "respect" motivation, 89–91,
      100–103
    statistics, 75–76

ABOUT THE EDITORS

Mark A. Mattaini, DSW, ACSW, is associate professor, Columbia University School of Social Work; chair, Walden Fellowship, Inc.; and director, Musher Seminar Series on Science and Human Behavior. He has authored or edited five books and numerous articles and chapters dealing with applications of the science of behavior to serious social problems including youth violence and child maltreatment. His current research focuses on cultural design, the scientific construction of interlocking networks of reinforcement for positive community practices incompatable with violence and coercion.

Bruce A. Thyer, PhD, holds faculty appointments as a Professor of Social Work and Adjunct Professor of Psychology at the University of Georgia, and as an associate clinical professor of psychiatry and health behavior at the Medical College of Georgia. Dr. Thyer is a past Secretary-Treasurer of Division 25 (Experimental Analysis of Behavior) of the American Psychological Association and is a fellow of Divisions 12 (Clinical) and 25. He has written over 150 journal articles, 30 book chapters, and authored or edited 10 professional books. Dr. Thyer's major professional interest concerns the application of behavior analysis to the resolution of social and interpersonal problems.